EVALUATIONS OF US POETRY SINCE 1950, VOLUME 2

Recencies Series: Research and Recovery in Twentieth-Century American Poetics
Matthew Hofer, Series Editor

This series stands at the intersection of critical investigation, historical documentation, and the preservation of cultural heritage. The series exists to illuminate the innovative poetics achievements of the recent past that remain relevant to the present. In addition to publishing monographs and edited volumes, it is also a venue for previously unpublished manuscripts, expanded reprints, and collections of major essays, letters, and interviews.

Also available in the Recencies Series:

Evaluations of US Poetry since 1950, Volume 1: Language, Form, and Music edited by Robert von Hallberg and Robert Faggen
Expanding Authorship: Transformations in American Poetry since 1950 by Peter Middleton
Modernist Poetry and the Limitations of Materialist Theory: The Importance of Constructivist Values by Charles Altieri
Momentous Inconclusions: The Life and Work of Larry Eigner edited by Jennifer Bartlett and George Hart
Yours Presently: The Selected Letters of John Wieners edited by Michael Seth Stewart
LEGEND: The Complete Facsimile in Context by Bruce Andrews, Charles Bernstein, Ray DiPalma, Steve McCaffery and Ron Silliman
Bruce Andrews and Charles Bernstein's L=A=N=G=U=A=G=E: The Complete Facsimile edited by Matthew Hofer and Michael Golston
Circling the Canon, Volume II: The Selected Book Reviews of Marjorie Perloff, 1995–2017 by Marjorie Perloff
Circling the Canon, Volume I: The Selected Book Reviews of Marjorie Perloff, 1969–1994 by Marjorie Perloff
The Language Letters: Selected 1970s Correspondence of Bruce Andrews, Charles Bernstein, and Ron Silliman edited by Matthew Hofer and Michael Golston

For additional titles in the Recencies Series, please visit unmpress.com.

EVALUATIONS OF US POETRY SINCE 1950

Volume 2

Mind, Nation, and Power

Edited by Robert von Hallberg and Robert Faggen

University of New Mexico Press | Albuquerque

© 2021 by the University of New Mexico Press
All rights reserved. Published 2021
Printed in the United States of America

ISBN 978-0-8263-6315-2 (paper)
ISBN 978-0-8263-6316-9 (electronic)

Library of Congress Control Number: 2021948232

Founded in 1889, the University of New Mexico sits on the traditional homelands of the Pueblo of Sandia. The original peoples of New Mexico—Pueblo, Navajo, and Apache—since time immemorial have deep connections to the land and have made significant contributions to the broader community statewide. We honor the land itself and those who remain stewards of this land throughout the generations and also acknowledge our committed relationship to Indigenous peoples. We gratefully recognize our history.

Cover illustration: courtesy of DesignCuts.com
Designed by Felicia Cedillos
Composed in Minion Pro 10.25/14

CONTENTS

Introduction   1
    ROBERT VON HALLBERG AND ROBERT FAGGEN

INTELLECTUALITY

Chapter 1. Why the Poetry of Adrienne Rich Mattered and Still Matters   21
    CHARLES ALTIERI

Chapter 2. Michael Palmer and the Linguistic Turn   45
    V. JOSHUA ADAMS

Chapter 3. Susan Howe and Valuing   73
    OREN IZENBERG

Chapter 4. Fanny Howe's Power   95
    PETER O'LEARY

Chapter 5. A Field Guide to Robert Hass   119
    RICHARD STRIER

SUBJECT MATTER

Chapter 6. Anthony Hecht: Worth the Weight   147
    JONATHAN F. S. POST

Chapter 7. Ecovaluation   171
    JOHN SHOPTAW

Chapter 8. Sharon Olds and the Work of the Body   195
    SARAH NOOTER

Chapter 9. "A Kind of Life": On Lucille Clifton and Community   215
JONATHAN FARMER

Chapter 10. Ed Dorn's Vulgate   235
KEITH TUMA

NATION

Chapter 11. Strange American Heart: August Kleinzahler   261
PATRICK MORRISSEY

Chapter 12. Robert Pinsky's Affirmations   287
ROBERT VON HALLBERG

Chapter 13. On Michael O'Brien   307
AUGUST KLEINZAHLER

POWER

Chapter 14. Barbara Guest and Jorie Graham   323
CAL BEDIENT

Chapter 15. Ashbery's Power and the Phantom "I"   351
LAURA QUINNEY

Conclusion   365
ROBERT FAGGEN AND ROBERT VON HALLBERG

Contributors   369
Index   373

Introduction

ROBERT VON HALLBERG AND ROBERT FAGGEN

Subject Matter

In this second volume of *Evaluations of US Poetry since 1950*, a number of critics examine the subject matter of poems. "Subject matter" refers to an issue or series of events recognized by readers as consequential before a poet touches pen to paper. The Holocaust is subject matter because of commentary about what happened. Something similar can be said about race, the ecosphere, Christianity, America, immigration, city life, or even the body. Writers addressing these public subjects enter an already established discourse with a more or less identifiable audience whose positions can be plausibly imagined. A rhetorical bond, however alluring to poets, is in some measure constraining. The prospect of an established readership may reasonably mean a lot to poets who normally count on reaching only a few hundred readers. Allen Ginsberg's pocketbook *Howl* (1956) has sold an extraordinary number of copies. Beginning with *Leaflets* (1969), Adrienne Rich built up a large audience for her poems and prose. Gary Snyder, too, reached a large readership. He remarked that a poet who can't sell five thousand copies of a book should give up, though it took Wallace Stevens many decades to sell so many copies of *Harmonium* (1923). More recently, Claudia Rankine's *Citizen* (2014) has found a very large readership. Books of poetry with recognizable subject matter often have a path to relatively large audiences. Not all subjects are compelling to audiences, nor are all treatments of favored subjects. The essays herein by Richard Strier, Charles Altieri, V. Joshua Adams, Oren Izenberg, and Keith Tuma analyze the dynamic between subject matter and poetic value, the ways in which addressing an audience produces difficulties as well as advantages.

Poems do not stand or fall by virtue of subject matter, one says. Wonderful poems are often slight in terms of subject. What matters is the arrangement of words and sounds, or attention to memorable details. Some great poems seem improvisations, rich in surprise, whose literary value comes unforeseen. Poems often do not have a subject matter; they make their way regardless of extant discourses. Themes are not the same as subject matter. But consider Johnson's assessment of *Paradise Lost*. He claims that with regard to Milton's "design," *Paradise Lost* "may claim the first place . . . among the productions of the human mind."[1] He speaks (now controversially) of Milton's purpose as "the most useful and the most arduous; *to vindicate the ways of God to man*; to shew the reasonableness of religion, and the necessity of obedience to the Divine Law."[2] Readers now may consider this claim an imposition of doctrine on an audience. Johnson shared enough of Milton's faith to feel the grandeur of this subject matter, and he felt that it directly underlay the value of *Paradise Lost*.

Johnson explains his judgment with two other pertinent points: that this subject "is universally and perpetually interesting"; and that "the moral of other poems is incidental and consequent; in Milton's only it is essential and intrinsick."[3] The first point follows from the supposed fact that the book of Genesis explains the origin and purpose of all life. The second is that the value of this subject is present in all the poem's details; that it does not derive from instrumental causes. Allen Ginsberg declares in "Footnote to Howl" that "Everything is holy! everybody's holy!" Johnson's point is the contrary: that the story of creation and the fall is unlike most other subjects. Milton cannot add moral value to this subject. Some subjects still solicit a reader's consent to their relative importance. They entail a shared estimation, concern, and even deference; in taking them up, a poet more or less consents to a sense of propriety. When a poet shows too great deference to propriety, a critic complains of the performance as unremarkable, predictable, not for doubters. A poet thinking as Johnson does, that subject matter underwrites major poetry, is tempted to write steadily of the One Great Thing, and that is a stultifying career plan. The story Milton tells is of violation and ruin. Johnson deeply understood its force. The great subject takes one's breath away, makes it impossible to continue living as if it were untrue. Claudia Rankine is not Milton; *Citizen* is not *Paradise Lost*. Her story of a black citizen's interiority ultimately takes one's breath away, meaning it makes it difficult for social life to proceed. She tells of numerable social violations, even of particular ill-mannered people who are named. But the great truth of the book is that these events become metaphysical, something greater than their sum. One imagines that social wrongs may be corrected; we hear of the need for a racial dialogue or conversation. But the point comes when the wrongs so permeate life in America that one can no longer speak usefully about who did what to whom. This one great wrong obstructs analysis, speech, and understanding.

> What did he just say? Did she really just say that? Did I hear what I think I heard? Did that just come out of my mouth, his mouth, your mouth? The moment stinks. Still you want to stop looking at the trees. You want to walk out and stand among them. And as light as the rain seems, it still rains down on you.[4]

It is a large national subject that, so handled, stands in the way of lesser subjects. The allegation that poems are a form of private utterance, that lyric means personal address, is overstated. Poets rightly reach for general significance. The most traditional vehicle for this is to speak to the character of a nation, as Pinsky, Kleinzahler, Ginsberg, Ed Dorn, and C. D. Wright unhesitatingly do. "America" and "American" mean: "You, out there, listen up." *Howl* and now *Citizen*: this works. We are eager to stand together, at no cost, in poems. Johnson correctly saw that Milton had rendered moot the measurement of other poems.

Intellectuality

John Stuart Mill spoke of poetry—in particular, Wordsworth's—as addressed to the feelings. Wordsworth seemed to him an admirable model of a way of being. Allen Grossman argued that poems always exemplify ways of being. Some recent poets indicate by lexical, syntactic, or rhetorical means a connection less to the life of the mind than to that range of expression suited to ways of being in intellectual institutions. This is a very different matter from what Mill found in Wordsworth. What affirmation might such poems express? Insofar as poems are generally affirmative, one takes those turns of phrase to express confidence in the procedures of estimation, analysis, and resolution avowed by intellectual institutions: the citation of evidence, more than authority, to support a claim; the consideration of alternatives; the pursuit of fresh understanding, unconstrained by immediate self-interest. Intellectual institutions are in those ways admirable. Eliot, Pound, and Charles Olson, quibbles notwithstanding, admired those institutions. And one can see that such admiration has been more characteristic since 1945 of the experimentalist than of the centrist camp of poetry. The big collected editions of Olson, Robert Creeley, and Robert Duncan are handsomely published by a university press. Involvement with academic institutions has come with some unapparent complications that the chapters below on Olson, Michael Palmer, Fanny Howe, and Robert Hass examine.

Some major terms of academic discourse—"power" is one—generate variants for particular disciplines, such as "authority" for literary studies. This process proceeds effectively because academic discourse is a coherent minority dialect, and institutional incentives facilitate circulation. Critics often do not intend to formulate variants of the dominant discourse among intellectuals of their time, but when the institutional status of literary studies is insecure, as it has increasingly been for decades, scholars and poets feel some reassurance in a fit between esteemed terms and concepts and the literary forms and expressions they explicate. In 1937, poet-critic John Crowe Ransom argued that "criticism must become more scientific, or precise and systematic . . . which means that its proper seat is in the universities."[5] After World War II, poetry took a seat there, too. Professors of literature now connect even contemporary poetry to recondite terms in circulation in learned journals. Parents pay costly tuition for instruction in the history and forms of poetry. University presses publish new poetry every year. Ransom's moment was different. The poets discussed in volume 1 of *Evaluations* publish with trade presses that appeal to extracurricular readers seeking pleasure; the poets of volume 2 mean to please as well, but publish with presses oriented on, if not sponsored by, the accrediting institutions of higher education. Most of the poets in both volumes have drawn salaries from colleges and universities. The study of literature, even of poetry, is thought to contribute to the development of young minds. "The university has . . . become perhaps the most important patron of artistically ambitious literary practice in the United States," in Mark McGurl's view. "By far the largest number of serious readers in the postwar period . . . have been produced through the agency of the school."[6] In the late 1950s, McGurl reports, creative writing programs were advocated as correctives to the conformity of academia.[7] The institutional site of poetry is now well settled and extensive.

Universities are rightly considered engines of invention, but their daily activities encourage conformity, which is a problem for poetry. Many readers want something distinctive from a poem, a summons to an unfamiliar zone of mind, rather than the disciplined thought of the time. Eliot spoke of the terrifying honesty of William Blake; terrifying, because intellectual independence is costly. Yeats's fairies and gyres estranged him from his contemporaries.[8] We are speaking of prophetic poetry, a narrow range of the art, but we refer more inclusively to poems that press hard against the expectations of their readers. It was Eliot, who was not comfortable with the prophetic voice, who said memorably that old men should be explorers. They have little to lose by taking a false step. Academics on the contrary seek approval from one another; their institutions solicit the approval of benefactors, legislatures, and parents. Oren Izenberg says that "a professor-poet is charged with the reproduction . . . of the institution's values and protocols." This is one reason why sensitivity to impropriety has renewed currency on campus; one can be easily reproached for not conforming with one's words to the interests of the home institution. Mavericks are not legion in literary history, though Plato thought poets more like madmen than philosophers.

Four chapters in this volume explicitly assess intellectual independence. Peter O'Leary measures Fanny Howe's dissent not from late capitalism but from the secular liberalism settled in academia. Her Catholicism is a conspicuous indication of distance from colleagues at the University of California, San Diego, where she taught for more than two decades. She "seems to have thrived," O'Leary writes, "by making her intellectual life in the vicinity of those who are going other ways entirely. Her sister's career must have often seemed to her the very thing she meant to avoid." Ed Dorn was always pushing (from the populist left) against the enthusiasms of the literary left. Keith Tuma's recovery of Dorn's Christianity is surprising, but it shouldn't be: his real sympathies were with the working poor. "I never had to worry about being a success," Dorn observed. "Where I come from you were a success when you left town." Professions of Christian faith set poets in a dissenting relation to the convictions of an academically oriented literary audience.

Oren Izenberg and V. Joshua Adams come at intellectual independence from quite different cases. They remind one of poetry's affirmative function, in Marcuse's sense, though scholars more often speak of it as critical.[9] Izenberg wrote elsewhere that "[f]or both [Allen] Grossman and [Susan] Howe, traditional poetic questions of wisdom and freedom are experienced as a direct negotiation with the academic institution."[10] Izenberg claims in this volume that Susan Howe has been embraced by academics because she validates the concerns of their criticism and theory. Her work rests on the notion that one's intellectual formation is the story of one's life. And who among us disputes that? Her family life, she says, was an "intellectualized aesthetic domain." This estimation of the importance of skeptical inquiry is characteristic of academic culture. She demonstrates the aesthetic potential of literary theory. The discursive protocols of academic interpretation seem so rich that they have generated art itself. Her "method of assembling ... flatters our self-conception as interpreters," Izenberg says. This is nothing to hold against Howe, who does not count herself an academic, but it is to be alert to self-validation in academic criticism. Adams argues that Michael Palmer's "achievement ... is only fully intelligible against the backdrop of professional intellectual life." This is a sharp limitation, he finds, because the interests of professional intellectuals change: topics are exhausted, lines of inquiry reveal their limits. The linguistic turn to which Palmer tied his work is no longer so compelling as it was three decades ago. The center of philosophical debate has shifted away from the philosophical issues surrounding language. Palmer's work seems dated.

Contemporaneity

Our overall question here is which poems should survive their original audiences. "We cannot say with certainty what will live," William Gass observes, "and survival, by itself, is no guarantee of quality; but I think we can say something about what is deserving."[11] Yes, something, for curricula—and for our own conversations. Emerson thought that you should accept "the society of your contemporaries." "Great men have always ... confided themselves childlike to the genius of their age."[12] Matthew Arnold claimed that being in contact with the mainstream of "human life" is of greater consequence than any speculative thought.[13] That measure might not leave Blake, Gerard Manley Hopkins, or Emily Dickinson in the *Norton Anthology of Poetry*, but Arnold had a point, and not an eccentric one. As different a critic as Georges Bataille similarly held that poetry "seeks as far as possible to render palpable, and as intensely as possible, the content of the present moment."[14] W. C. Williams, not otherwise an Arnoldian, criticized Pound and Eliot for their failure to find wonder in the lives of those around them. The contemporaneity criterion assigns poets the task of representing the thoughts and experiences of others, a task dependent on a concept of a social group whose experience can be summed: as that of a nation, class, sect, race, gender, and so on. Many poets decline that dubious task, and others—Whitman, W. C. Williams, Langston Hughes, Amiri Baraka, and Robert Pinsky, say—take it on gladly.

Criticism of contemporary poetry faces one grand hazard: one easily overestimates poems that seem to express one's own experience. "The pleasure we derive from the representation of the present is due," Baudelaire said, "not only to the beauty it can be clothed in, but also to its essential quality of being the present."[15] Which is to say ephemeral; the resonance of familiar idioms and attitudes is bewitching, even for poets. Speaking of the transmission of poetic styles as if they were hallucinogens, Coleridge observed: "No models of past times, however perfect, can have the same vivid effect on the youthful mind, as the productions of contemporary genius."[16] Estrangement from one's moment is advantageous to critics who need to scrutinize representations skeptically. The prosodic forms of some few poets—think, for example, of James Merrill, Anthony Hecht, J. V. Cunningham, and Turner Cassity—summon memory of the long dead. Literary traditions, recognized in measures and conventions of phrasing, provide poets and critics with a critical distance on their own moment. The voices of the living ultimately need to be sounded in proximity to the illustrious and *surviving* dead. Pound thought that the "honest critic must be content to find a VERY LITTLE contemporary work worth serious attention; but he must also be ready to RECOGNIZE that little, and to demote work of the past when a new work surpasses it."[17] Echoes of the known past test the vigor of the present.

That some poet produces the art of the moment is often said, paradoxically, of a candidate for survival. Contemporaneity, like charisma in politics, generates an appeal in excess of achievements. A fit of poem to moment seems golden in the short term, leaden in the long. Lowell's "Inauguration Day: January 1953" and "For the Union Dead," Ginsberg's *Wichita Vortex Sutra*, Robert Bly's *The Teeth Mother Naked at Last*, Dorn's *Gunslinger*; the last half-century has been rich in poems that briefly commanded attention, but a case has later to be made, as Charles Altieri and Keith Tuma do here, that despite their timeliness, particular contemporary poets, Adrienne Rich and Ed Dorn, can be expected to endure. These critics have to overcome firmly entrenched skepticism concerning topical poetry. "For works of art, the rule reads: never enter Time," William Gass observes, "and you will never be required to exit."[18]

However clever, that can't be the whole of it: Dante, Milton, Pope, Blake all entered their moments and went on to enter many others. The *Norton Anthology* preserves for students and general readers a number of enduring topical poems. How have they survived? Samuel Johnson's countermeasure—that "nothing pleases many and pleases long but just representations of general nature"—appears irrelevant to these literary achievements. Several of these poems—Milton's "On the Late Massacre," Shelley's "England in 1819," Yeats's "No Second Troy"—are pitched in prophetic tones, severe, biblical, uncongenial. The poets present their moments as ruptures but repeats too, not entirely secular; time turns back on itself. The poems invoke a tradition that accrues power with its returns. These quite particular moments are presented as most general. Another line of canonical political poems—Milton's "To the Lord Cromwell," Marvell's "Horatian Ode," Blake's "London," Yeats's "Easter 1916," and Auden's "September 1, 1939"—are notably rational, displaying measured or even altered judgments. Both groups of poems explicitly concern retention, recovery, and literary survival. The prophetic voice is most familiar in paratactic forms: single lines, chant-like, in series. But the more apparently rational poems shift that voice toward hypotactic syntax in stanzaic verse, which is why the sonnet form is so amenable. Hypotactic sentences suit rational discourse: verbs that register distinctions of place, party, and manner, as in Milton's Cromwell poem; evidence cited, justifications proposed. The wonder is that prophetic assertions can be reconciled with the prosaic architecture of the sonnet; biblical rhetoric and native skepticism conjoined. Not only these intellectual qualities have made these poems indispensable to Milton's heirs, but they have helped. It is certain that later political poetry is measured, as Pound advocated, against these standards. Rationality does not require equanimity; prophecy alone, without support of prosaic discrimination, has difficulty pleasing readers who know from English literary tradition that outrage, vision, and analysis are not mutually exclusive. These will be the measures of Lowell, Ginsberg, and Rich.

Range

This book is an experiment in literary criticism. The particular qualities that critics admire in recent poetry are revealing, however attributable they may be to individual tastes and proclivities, or to the interests of social groups. A larger issue is what critics attribute to poetry in general: the qualities that seem to them not arguably but *inevitably* valuable. Or one might more modestly inquire of the qualities that seem especially likely to find consensus among readers. They would be values that seem not to owe their prestige to a social class or institution. Three great English critics have invoked the "sanity" of poetry, a value that might plausibly be said to have a claim on everyone's esteem. The first of these was Coleridge: "The . . . characteristic excellence of Mr. W[ordsworth]'s works is: a correspondent weight and sanity of the Thoughts and Sentiments,—won, not from books; but—from the poet's own meditative observation. They are *fresh* and have the dew upon them."[19] The normative claim is made on behalf of a quality of representation: Wordsworth writes in a manner that corresponds to thoughtful observation; he actually looked at what was before his eyes. Rather than fantasize, he observed life as it is. (This would later be pretty much August Kleinzahler's argument about Michael O'Brien, and Patrick Morrissey's about Kleinzahler.) Coleridge appreciates the absence of extremity in Wordsworth's poetry. The term "sane" is never far from its contrary. Praise of a poet's sanity implicitly acknowledges worry about what Plato spoke of as the madness of poets, their divine authority, or inspiration, which here Coleridge contests.

Poetry might rather be a medium of literally accurate (not just figurative) representation of observable events and verifiable claims. Sarah Nooter shows that just such an objective was Sharon Olds's. That is to say that poetry competes with other media of representation and explanation—exactly Plato's worry. Arnold, thirty-seven years after the *Biographia* appeared, was skeptical of Coleridge's claim: "Sanity,—that is the great virtue of the ancient literature; the want of that is the great defect of the modern, in spite of all its variety and power."[20] In the wake of Yeats, Pound, and surrealism, Arnold's dissent seems well taken. Eliot, though, was careful to express himself temperately when returning to Coleridge's suspicion of the relation between poetry and religion: "If I ask myself . . . why I prefer the poetry of Dante to that of Shakespeare, I should have to say, because it seems to me to illustrate a saner attitude towards the mystery of life."[21] The term "sane" indicates in particular *health* of mind. "Sensible, rational," according to the *OED*, "free from delusive prejudices or fancies." The absence of this quality forebodes mortality. Sanity facilitates survival, endurance. Eliot's point is that Shakespeare's secularity will seem to agnostics obviously saner than Dante's Catholicism. But Eliot registers the value of attention to life's mystery. This is a line of literary thought that now includes Ed Dorn and Fanny Howe, as Keith Tuma and Peter O'Leary explain.

However, no one any longer explicitly proposes sanity as an aesthetic category, though we have a substitute that conveys a comparable sense of being self-evidently attractive: *range*, which indicates a poet's access to differences of diction, syntax, tone, and subject. Like sanity, it is an antidote to an undesirable alternative. Poems that settle in the idioms of a dominant social group are put at risk. A critic does not want to advocate the claims of an art that overlooks or "silences," as we say, an unrepresented social group. The linkages of literary values and social practices are constructed and open to interpretation—anything but inevitable. In several essays here, poets are praised for their range of style and interest. One wants poets sufficiently free of social classes to see life steadily and whole, as Arnold urged. Not that recent critics mean to take instruction from Arnold, but they do so nonetheless. A rich diversity is the current version of disinterestedness and generality. "One of the most important attributes of humanity," the philosopher Christine M. Korsgaard observes, "is our nearly bottomless capacity for finding sources of delight and interest in nearly *anything*, and so for conferring value on almost anything. . . . That fact about human nature is part of what makes liberal democratic forms of the state the right ones."[22] She speaks plausibly of a connection between resourcefulness and liberal democracy.

All styles equal, all subjects, too. Poets who confirm that hope are praised for their range. Where Arnold treasured a synthetic vision, critics now approve of the mobility of a poet's investments of attention and honor. We press on the concept of range because more is meant by it than one may realize. From Korsgaard's point of view, though she does not speak of poetry at all, good citizens exemplify the advantages of flexibility. Range refers to the establishment of order among different things. Its primary sense indicates a "row, series, or line." Its tertiary sense refers to "an area, space, or stretch of ground" where one has liberty to move about freely. This sense includes "the area or extent which a particular concept or thing covers or includes"—its scope. One is reminded that a poet's range includes the extent of his or her efficacy. Heterogeneity of style or subject alone does not adequately reflect the ambitions of this criterion. A wide-ranging poet makes a distinctive sense of the differences that engage him or her. We might well consider a poet's success in reaching different audiences. The first quality of Shakespeare that Helen Vendler praises in her commentary on the Sonnets is not his universality (as Johnson had argued) but his "range of tones." Shakespeare has constant access to different rhetorical techniques because his mind is a "storehouse or bank"; that is what makes the speaker of the Sonnets a convincingly "real" and "existential" being. Vendler is a mightily cogent analyst of the poems partly because range is a rich notion of human being that many readers wish to adopt as an ideal. The "speaker's mind," she observes, "creates our own."[23] Range is a concept of betterment, not only for her. Many stand ready to extend their resources and sensibilities; that is what counts as good faith among democratic citizens.

The most radically pluralistic critic here is Stephanie Burt, who, in her chapter on C. D. Wright from volume 1 of *Evaluations*, begins with a practical account of the reception of poems:

> Poems, poets, books of poetry can get noticed when they do one thing exceptionally well: so well that readers with a few minutes to spare, and many other poems they could have chosen, pick *this* poem out of a magazine, or off the internet, or from a friend's notebook, and copy it over or read it aloud or forward it to the rest of their friends.

What that one thing done well may be is entirely open for her, and should remain so for others, because the future is unpredictable. She advocates no scale of various qualities of poems; all qualities are contenders. One cannot know which will draw readers in the future. The poets most likely to survive are those who do so many things well or distinctively that some number of those things have a chance of hitting.

> In general: poets who stick around do more than one thing, which means that they can also work on multiple readers, for multiple reasons. They are versatile: both of their time and not of it, interesting for reasons of diction or sound or line shape and, also, interesting for reasons of substance, for the claims they make about the world; interesting to readers who want to scrutinize one phrase forever, and to readers who take poetry in at great gulps. Poets who stick around are not . . . unitaskers.

C. D. Wright is likely to survive because she undertook diverse tasks: "More than any other American poet of her generation, Wright meant various things to various people, or to the same people in different poems: she was not only recognizable but at the same time versatile, variously emotionally engaging, both among her poems and between them." Burt does not mean that different subject matters alone may ensure a poet's survival. The virtues of styles, she says, determine survival. This raises a difficulty because one usually thinks of style as a unifying feature of a poet's work.[24] Burt's claim seems to be that those who write distinctively in diverse styles are most likely to survive. Think of Adrienne Rich or Robert Lowell more than Elizabeth Bishop.

Burt's pluralistic argument makes most sense if one imagines readers selecting this or that feature of this or that poet on the basis of established appetites. Burt draws on Allen Grossman's sense of a good poet as a "hermeneutic friend." Wright, she says, is the sort of person we would like as a friend, but concedes that some readers are attracted to uncongenial poets. Some great poets one would not want in close proximity. Think of Dante, Petrarch, Blake, Baudelaire, or Rimbaud as neighbors. We imagine companionable writers nearby because they are of our party, in terms of sensibility, manners, or politics. Burt's sense is that a poet meets readers as they are, not as they may become. How then do some poets turn one's head around? Do readers come inadvertently to antithetical reading? Burt's sense of reception best suits poets who are not off-putting. One needs another account of reception for the strangely mannered Whitman, Dickinson, Yeats, Pound, Hart Crane, and Lowell, too. We refer less to the authors themselves than to the persons implicit in the poems.

Attention

A few poets bend their idioms away from contemporary usage, as Milton and Hopkins did; their implicit dream is of those forms of attention triumphant, which is to say just and expository, in some future. Dryden instead advocated continuity (in terms of diction and syntax) between prose and poetry. Wordsworth made the case again in the preface to *Lyrical Ballads.* Many poets and critics now urge that poems serve the expository function of prose. Prose-envy has rendered Milton's dream an intermittent, minor phenomenon. Pound showed Ford Madox Ford his early poems in 1911 and Ford, Pound said, laughed so hard at the diction he fell from his chair and rolled on the floor. "That roll saved me at least two years, perhaps more," Pound later reflected. The upshot was a slogan: "Poetry should be at least as well written as prose."[25] Plain-style poetics have dominated poetry in English for two centuries. A number of the essays here speak of accuracy of representation: veracity, precision, actual, particular, ordinary are terms of praise that derive from the mission of the novel or essay. Very few focus on figuration, or the sonic contours of verse. Kleinzahler puts the poet Michael O'Brien in a line deriving from Baudelaire, Whitman, and Frank O'Hara, who all sought to capture in verse the distinctive features of an individual's experience in the great cities—"the confluence and interactions of the countless relationships" there, in Baudelaire's words.

But precision is an odd thing to praise in poetry. Poems traditionally concern that which is hard to name: qualities that are rendered figuratively because literal terms do not capture the relevant sense. Physical objects may be precisely described, particularly those that are numerable. But why this stretching toward physicality and demonstrable truth? The uncertainty of metaphysical discourse seems intimidating. What we ask of language that is relatively free of the constraints of literal truth and ordinary communication, as poems are, indicates where we want to go in some future, our hopes for language and mind. Dryden, Wordsworth, and Pound imagine a poetry that can take over some of the expository and analytical offices of prose. Plain-style poets want to adhere to all that is too solidly settled to be displaced. Or is this inclination toward the prosaic driven by a *wish* to speak from the material, secular lives that pass for inevitable?

The concept of attention is very attractive to critics, but why? This seems, on the face of it, an undemanding measure of poems. What are you thinking of? Penny for your thoughts. To attend to something is a basic activity, important if preliminary to some more decisive predicate. In French, *attendre* most commonly means to expect, to await. Poetry does traditionally identify people, places, and things worthy of attention. Cal Bedient measures poets partly by their relation to physicality. He holds not only that one should attend to the physical world, though that is true, but further that poets rightly attend to that which is neither grand nor obvious. August Kleinzahler and Ken Fields are in agreement on this. Everyone attends to mountains and storms. Kleinzahler praises O'Brien's restraint, austerity, and obliqueness, his ability to find in the noisy traffic of New York City unpredictable items that render the feel of experience. "O'Brien's poetry is, above all," he says, "about *attention*, attention to the smallest, most fleeting details . . . in the world at hand." We shouldn't say that attention is a small thing. Kleinzahler's implication is that not all poets give all that is due to the objects of their attention. Sianne Ngai has written well about the currency of "interesting" in our critical lexicon. "Attention" is a more definite term, but both indicate an awareness of further judgments deferred for the time being.

Richard Strier admires Hass's "Art and Life" as a "representation of someone paying full attention to a task." Strier appreciates Hass as a poet of close attention and lyrical description. But Hass is also ambitious in metaphysical analysis of his contemporaries' convictions concerning language and thought. This is to say that "full attention" is a matter not only of perception. Strier's Hass is an intellectual poet in dialogue with Lacan and Wittgenstein. One notices that Strier refers critically to passages where Hass is superficial or distracted by trivialities—where the poet is slipping. This critical angle is important because the criterion of attention can be too easily met. The best of Hass, Strier argues, moves toward a synthesis of practical observation and subtle reflection.

A poet's job is attentiveness more than judgment, Patrick Morrissey argues. Kleinzahler manages to record, he observes, the strangeness of

American public life. His layering of various historical moments, recondite terms, and unfamiliar voices is a technique of bearing witness to the life of the nation. Attention, on this account, expresses not only curiosity and alertness but warmth and affection, too. That is the crucial point about attention in lyric poetry. Kleinzahler appreciates it all, as Whitman, Williams, and Pinsky (all Jersey poets) do too. The advocacy of attention by recent critics is a restrained way of esteeming affirmation and generosity, even selflessness.

One makes a special claim for poets who direct attention to new topics. They may be limited in terms of craft, but they are nonetheless innovators because without their poems certain subjects would be less acknowledged and honored. This is Sarah Nooter's argument about Sharon Olds and physicality. Acknowledgment is a special concern in the wake of identity politics, but the matter goes further. The villagers of the victors in the ancient games had good reason to feel gratitude to a poet for recording their existence. Sarah Nooter feels the force of this one poetic office: esteem for service to a community is ancient. Since Pindar, the attention of lyric poets has conveyed admiration intended to preserve someone or some event in consciousness. Shakespeare's Sonnet 55 famously boasts this value rendered. Nooter's argument is that physicality is of concern to all. Any poet who directs attention to so pertinent and neglected a topic deserves wide acknowledgment, too. Shakespeare does not name his beloved: identity in that sense is irrelevant. His claim is that poetic attention defeats mortality. To be ignored because no one knows your name is one slight, but to be lost to oblivion because you are mortal is a bigger matter.

There is another dimension to this issue. One hears often of especially attentive language use by experimental poets. Distinctive manners of signifying are imitable at various levels. Jeremy Prynne's "underlying contention," John Wilkinson explains in his chapter from volume 1, "is that a poem apt to compel does so through a subtending linguistic structure that any native reader of its language already knows without knowing it—if a poem *feels* coherent in response to a reader's true attentiveness, however enigmatic and reluctant to yield its secrets it may seem, then it may indeed be trusted to support the reader in linguistically dwelling on earth." Those last words are amusing but serious, too. Pound and Eliot had stated repeatedly that poems are exemplary instances of language use; that poems help to keep a language in good working order, even for those who never read a poem. A poet's proper engagement, then, is with the words of a language community, for they facilitate commerce, social policy, legislation, litigation. Life is better for everyone when a clear word attains currency.

Experimental poets may be the last writers from whom one expects didacticism. Oren Izenberg remarks that "[o]ur present moment regards the pedagogical imperative ... suspiciously: as a dulling of our pleasures, as a descent from art's higher calling, or as laying bare its bullying or 'palpable design' upon us."[26] Allen Grossman admitted that "a successful poem seems to me a picture of a successful person."[27] A poem honors, in his sense, an imagined manner of existence. This is what Charles Altieri calls "exemplary value" in relation to Adrienne Rich. Experimental poetry is actually full of instruction, mostly indirect, not dependent on precepts. Think of Charles Olson, obviously, but Robert Creeley and Susan Howe, too: they were much imitated, and not only by writers. Wilkinson says that Olson's *The Maximus Poems* "is less a work that speaks for others than one creating a space for others' spoken and written records, as well as for others' furtherance." Louise Glück reads George Oppen as an exemplary character; the values of the poems and of the man, the same. She praises him as "model citizen and model poet." Katerina Stergiopoulou, in her chapter on Oppen in volume 1, rightly sees him as a figure of "deep skepticism, coupled with wonder." This is his "most lasting value." It makes sense that experimental poems and others too are esteemed less for the inculcation of propositions than for the exemplification of language use that renders some propositions plausible. What Izenberg nicely formulates concerning Susan Howe is conspicuous in Hopkins, too: "the force of feeling in perceptions of language in strange arrays." "Men are ... representative," Emerson argued, "first, of things, and, secondly, of ideas."[28] "Go and do likewise," these poets seem to urge, and this is a familiar didacticism.

In our moment, critics urge readers to sing of social needs. Even philosophers push intellectuals in this direction. Joseph Raz argues that "many values depend for their emergence on sustaining social practices, and that most others depend indirectly on social purposes for their existence."[29] This claim is discomfiting to literary critics who look to poetry for alternatives to social conformity. Poetry is the art least dependent on institutional order—and capital. Poets need only paper and pen. But Raz's claim is that virtually all values (not just aesthetic ones) have a social origin. One thinking person is not enough.[30] Lyric poets, philosophers, and those of faith are at a disadvantage in this intellectual regime. Consider the example of Czesław Miłosz in this regard. He reached a large English-language audience with an anticommunist prose volume, *The Captive Mind* (1955)—a portion of which appeared earlier in *Partisan Review* (1951). He established his US intellectual presence with prose and translations of Polish poets, especially Zbigniew Herbert. His own poems were another matter; they do without Cold War subject matter. Yet he retained the attention of American and British critics for years thereafter. His poems did not need topicality to hold an audience; true, the Nobel Prize (1980) fortified his reputation. We refer to him here to suggest that social engagement and advocacy help to establish an audience for poems, but that is not the *only* path to a large readership. We put the matter this way, it must be acknowledged, because of the exemplary impact of Rankine's *Citizen*. Bishop, Merrill, and others discussed here have established their authority without deferring to the narrow, dry notion that all values are social.

Notes

1. Samuel Johnson, *The Lives of the Poets*, ed. Roger Lonsdale (Oxford: Clarendon Press, 2006), 1:282.
2. Ibid., 283.
3. Ibid.
4. Claudia Rankine, *Citizen: An American Lyric* (Minneapolis: Graywolf Press, 2014), 9.
5. John Crowe Ransom, "Criticism, Inc.," in *The World's Body* (1938; Baton Rouge: Louisiana State University Press, 1968), 329.
6. Mark McGurl, *The Program Era: Postwar Fiction and the Rise of Creative Writing* (Cambridge, MA: Harvard University Press, 2009), 22, 64.
7. Ibid., 69–71.
8. Thomas Parkinson, "The Modernity of Yeats," *Southern Review* 5 (Summer 1969): 922–34.
9. Herbert Marcuse, "The Affirmative Character of Culture" (1937), in *Negations: Essays in Critical Theory*, trans. Jeremy J. Shapiro (London: Free Association, 1988), esp. 95, 122.
10. Oren Izenberg, "Poems in and out of School: Allen Grossman and Susan Howe," in *The Cambridge Companion to American Poetry since 1945*, ed. Jennifer Ashton (Cambridge: Cambridge University Press, 2013), 191.
11. William H. Gass, *Tests of Time* (Chicago: University of Chicago Press, 2003), 120.

12. *The Collected Works of Ralph Waldo Emerson*, ed. Joseph Slater, Alfred R. Ferguson, and Jean Ferguson Carr (Cambridge, MA: Harvard University Press, 1979), 2:28.
13. Matthew Arnold, preface to *Culture and Anarchy*, ed. J. Dover Wilson (Cambridge: Cambridge University Press, 1932), 30.
14. Georges Bataille, *The Absence of Myth: Writings on Surrealism*, ed. and trans. Michael Richardson (London: Verso, 1994).
15. Charles Baudelaire, "The Painter of Modern Life," in *Selected Writings on Art and Artists*, trans. P. E. Charvet (Harmondsworth, Middlesex, England: Penguin, 1972), 391.
16. Samuel Taylor Coleridge, *Biographia Literaria*, ed. James Engell and W. Jackson Bate (Princeton, NJ: Princeton University Press, 1983), 1:11–12.
17. Ezra Pound, *ABC of Reading* (New York: New Directions, 1934), 91.
18. Gass, *Tests of Time*, 126.
19. Coleridge, *Biographia Literaria*, 2:144–45.
20. Matthew Arnold, preface to *Poems*, 2nd ed. (1854), in *The Complete Prose Works of Matthew Arnold*, vol. 1: *On the Classical Tradition*, ed. R. H. Super (Ann Arbor: University of Michigan Press, 1960), 17.
21. T. S. Eliot, *The Sacred Wood: Essays on Poetry and Criticism* (London: Methuen, 1920), x.
22. Christine M. Korsgaard, "The Dependence of Value on Humanity," in *The Practice of Value*, by Joseph Raz, Christine M. Korsgaard, Robert Pippin, and Bernard Williams (Oxford: Clarendon Press, 2003), 73.
23. Helen Vendler, *The Art of Shakespeare's Sonnets* (Cambridge, MA: Harvard University Press, 1997), 47.
24. See Jeff Dolven, *Senses of Style: Poetry before Interpretation* (Chicago: University of Chicago Press, 2017), 99.
25. Noel Stock, *The Life of Ezra Pound* (New York: Pantheon Books, 1970), 103.
26. Izenberg, "Poems in and out of School," 187.
27. Allen Grossman with Mark Halliday, *The Sighted Singer: Two Works on Poetry for Readers and Writers* (Baltimore: Johns Hopkins University Press, 1992), 197.
28. Ralph Waldo Emerson, "Uses of Great Men," in *Collected Works of Ralph Waldo Emerson*, ed. Douglas Emory Wilson (Cambridge, MA: Harvard University Press, 1987), 4:6.
29. Joseph Raz, "More on Explaining Value: Replies and Comparisons," in *The Practice of Value*, by Joseph Raz, Christine M. Korsgaard, Robert Pippin, and Bernard Williams (Oxford: Clarendon, 2003), 138.
30. Raz acknowledges, though, that values may outlive their social origin, even when they do not originate in ideas of alternatives to social order. On this view, literary values may serve obsolete practices.

INTELLECTUALITY

CHAPTER 1

Why the Poetry of Adrienne Rich Mattered and Still Matters

CHARLES ALTIERI

VERY FEW CRITICS or readers would consider Adrienne Rich among the most gifted and imaginative poets of her generation (or generations, since her books date from 1951 to 2010). The laurels would undoubtedly go to Sylvia Plath and James Merrill and John Ashbery, with significant votes for Robert Creeley and Frank O'Hara—a pretty impressive list of entrants to my imaginary contest. Yet Rich is almost certainly a more important cultural figure than any of those poets, more important even than Allen Ginsberg, who did not produce a comparable level of significant prose. More importantly, she is probably at least as powerful a poet as any of those writers for how she makes poetry an instrument of both cultural and personal struggle.[1]

Contributors to this collection were posed this question: what poets who came to prominence after World War II have substantial claims to enduring value. I love this question because I idealize the critical task of providing languages of value that demonstrate how a poet's achievements can be best appreciated. But in Rich's case, that provides an especially challenging task because one has to ask poetry to pursue kinds of values from which it has for the most part become estranged in the twentieth century. Obviously we must address concerns for aesthetic value—deriving from the poet's capacity to engage our imaginations in worlds that require an appreciation of craft if we are to participate fully in them. But for the best poets there are also questions involving the capacity of a body of poetic work to take on what I will call "exemplary value." In this case, the poet's achievement is to define for others a linguistically dynamic way of engaging the imagination in issues of pressing historical importance. And Rich has chosen to define that historical importance primarily in cultural rather than in literary terms. So she seeks an exemplary value that depends on self-consciously asking lyric poetry to address and to alter pervasive public models of belief and of behavior.

I think that Rich is the poet of her generation who most radically altered the dominant intellectual culture's understanding of the work poetry could do, in large part because of how she performed that work. Rich's poetry mattered, and matters, primarily because of how she managed to correlate two strongly held commitments. First, poetry had to speak a common language with its intended audiences so that it could be felt as active and direct engagement in pressing social issues. This required recuperating for poetry the prose virtues of clarity, pointedness, directness, and the capacity of the speaker to appear to suppress private for public interests. Second, poetry had to resist what had become common coin in the aesthetic sphere—namely the loving and often epiphanic engagement in elaborate images that could anchor and resolve emotional intensities. Instead, Rich wanted a poetry that could provide life and passion to a woman's effort to present herself as directly speaking to matters of more than personal urgency. As we try to appreciate the power of these efforts to alter the domain of poetic ambition, we should also recognize the permissions Rich gave writers such as Claudia Rankine and Juliana Spahr to elaborate what can be done in poetry with the "intensity of language" developed by transforming the virtues of good prose.[2]

When I say that Rich changed the work ambitious poetry could do, I have to invoke two contexts. First is the obvious context of the poetry favored by the New Critics who dominated poetics when she started writing. They thought that poetry should emphasize impersonal stances in developing a structural complexity suited for the contemplative mind. Rich wrote her first volume in accord with these ideals, but in such a way that her Stoic pose revealed the agonies of making female identity conform to pictures of poetic labor completely inattentive to gender. Then she adapted a version of the personal modes of expression popular in the 1960s.[3] But hers was not the version of the person coming to dominance in confessional poetry, or at least not for long. Rich had to learn to inhabit a person who did not need the fantasy-prone, unstable, and theatrical ego of a Lowell or a Plath. As poet and as essayist,[4] Rich had to replace relying on lyrical images with an emphasis on prose virtues that could establish a persona capable of melding personal investment with discursive power. And then she could act as if the personal had the capacity to exemplify widely shared concerns.

Second, Rich had to carry out sustained warfare against a poetics of the epiphanic image that had dominated popular lyricism throughout the twentieth century. Rich would continue to rely on images for her love poetry, and often for the sense of nature that pervades her poetry from the 1980s to her death. But her insistently public poetry had to show by implication that the more poetry turned to lyrical images as modes of resolution, the more it exhibited modes of self-absorption and elitist idealizations of cultivated sensibility that blocked the work from any sustained commitment to social life. Her best public poems test what she can claim as truth by exploring how poetry could make present the satisfaction of passionate, lucid intelligence. This satisfaction involved a sense that a full adult life could be lived within the ways that this language could call attention to social evils and arouse sympathy for those oppressed by such evils. This model narrows our sense of the roles poetry can play in society. But Rich also establishes the necessity for her stripped-down lyrical presences by showing how elaborate or impersonal lyric expression finds its intensity primarily in self-absorption, rather than in recognition of pressing social demands on all citizens. By putting the self to work finding what can suffice as clear statement, Rich casts that lyric self as engaging history rather than evading it. Her critics are right that Rich can seem embarrassing in her less than capacious moral intensities and in the unevenness of a poetry not always able, or willing, to recognize differences between what passionate commitment pursues and what careful judgment might require. But when Rich succeeds—in her prose and in her poetry—she unites lyric with the best resources of analytic prose.

The best way of deflating my own rhetoric here is to turn to the charges leveled against Rich by Helen Vendler's influential essays in the *New York Review of Books*. These will directly set the challenges to which there must be a concrete and telling response if I am to make good on my claims. Vendler's writing on Rich changes some over the years, as Rich changes, but three substantial complaints persist: (1) Rich is too realistic, so she does not develop the space of imaginative possibility fundamental to the work of our major poets; (2) she does not sufficiently explore the imaginative resources of masks and personae; and (3) she writes oversimplified moral allegories instead of testing the imagination's powers to produce sympathy and understanding for all sides of significant issues.

Vendler's development of these charges is too sharp to be subjected to footnote status, so I will cite examples of all three charges. (1) "There is a pathos of self-mistrust in the belief that history, unlike autobiography, is 'objective,' and that the lyric poet should subordinate himself to this 'objectivity.' . . . The poet has no recourse other than to hope that both history and nature will become doubles of himself, while remaining themselves (as they did, for instance, for Lowell). 'Objectivity' is a trap for the lyric; all lyrics are fatally subjective, even when most objective in appearance—especially when most objective in appearance."[5] (2) Yet there are subjectivities and subjectivities. For Vendler, Rich suffers from a fatal "inflexibility of stance": "A poet who could conceive a topic other than autobiographically might have written the poem imagining herself as mother-in-law one day, when some daughter-in-law would find no easy way to address her inaccessible poet-mother-in-law, and vice versa" (ATR). Even Rich's poems about other people "strenuously pursue what it is to be Adrienne Rich in middle age—her investigations, her commitments, her memories, her outrage. I wish these poems were not so exclusively bound to that single realist vision" (ATR). (3) "In Rich, the moral will is given a dominating role that squeezes the lifeblood out of the imagination" (ATR). Rich is too much absorbed by social evils, where one can readily take sides, rather than focusing on "for instance, the kinds of sophisticated individual moral evil that interested Henry James or Proust" (ATR). Her poems usually become occasions for "realist oratory": "She presses points, she pursues an argument, she cites instances, and she pitches her voice above the conversational or narrative level—not always, but more often than not. Conscience, as she says, hurls questions at her; she hurls, in her turn, accusations at society" in a way that presents her as a "moral allegorist" (MA).

Vendler is crucially wrong and insightful at the same time. All three tendencies pervade Rich's poetry, although they take different shapes in different stages of her career. Yet, in my view, Vendler does not see the achievement that Rich's narrowness allows her, nor does she appreciate why and how Rich's construction of a distinctive lyric space for the immediately personal might matter for her time, and for ours. Therefore, I will argue that Rich offers a distinctive and valuable modification of the insistence on the personal established by confessional poets, the New York School, and Projective Verse, which was in turn a sharp break from the tenets of New Critical poetics. The confessional poets stage the lyric speaker as having a problematic inner life that produces a blend of intensity and pathos challenging any authority that might ground judgment or afford generalizations to which the individual might be bound. Deprived of judgment, the poet must rely on the power of the personal to provide an intricacy and vitality that can fascinate us with the presentation of differences from what is expected in bourgeois social life.

Generalization is intrinsically cruel when applied to such sensitive individuals. Rich, on the other hand, holds that strenuous attention and firm syntax can put poems in a public moral theater. That is the sort of personal poetry that satisfies her.

> The longer I live the more I distrust
> theatricality, the false glamour cast
> by performance, the more I know its poverty beside
> the truths we are salvaging from
> the splitting open of our lives.[6]

She tries to replace that theatricality with a personalism of will and intelligence capable of resisting a pursuit of the forces tormenting an inner life and requiring that the ego meet itself at its extremes of imagined personal anguish. For Rich, the theatrical plunges us into anxieties and pains that are a constructed mix of real pain and imaginary stagings that make it always difficult to know how to adapt in relation to the practical world.

My story begins with how the personal gets established, and misinterpreted, within the radically impersonal poetics governing Rich's first volume, *A Change of World*. Consider how "An Unsaid Word" completely satisfies New Critical criteria while allowing the personal to make its pressure felt as a measure of the difficulty involved in the Stoic vision the poem tries to celebrate:

> She who has the power to call her man
> From that estranged intensity
> Where his mind forages alone,

> Yet keeps her peace and leaves him free,
> And when his thoughts to her return
> Stands where he left her, still his own,
> Knows this the hardest thing to learn. (*FD* 5)[7]

This is terrific formalist poetry. The rhyme scheme provides a powerful containing force in its brilliant play of single and multisyllable linkages, all circling around "man," whose off rhyme is and is not part of the formal closure. After all, it is the man's "estranged intensity" whose freedom to travel where it must seems a given in the poem. Then there is the control of the poem's single sentence as it struggles to preserve the sense of impersonal containment on which the claim to knowledge must depend. In order to appreciate the pressure on the sentence, we have to recognize the complex double meanings within this single sentence that challenge and reward knowledge. "Hardest thing to learn" has to refer both to the simple difficulty of learning, and to the pain involved in that learning of what must be the case if the speaker is to be true to her task as wife.

It is tempting to read this poem in terms of Rich's later work as an attack on the husband's self-absorbed sense of privilege. But then there is no point to Rich insisting on discipline, and no sense of how her first volume seeks out the complex balances praised by the then dominant poetics articulated by the New Critics. I am pretty sure Rich wanted to provide a kind of nondiscursive knowledge of the copresence of opposites basic to married life. And this kind of knowledge in turn glorifies the Stoic role, since it offers the most comprehensive stance possible, and since it avoids unseemly acts of personal assertion that might rebel against the authority of that knowing.

Even the final "this" fits the picture of ambiguities contained within the imagination's efforts to present what might be capacious and disturbing in the poet's project. Yet there is something about this line that projects Rich's distinctive sense of what cannot be satisfied by the ideal of knowing by means of imaginative labor. The ambiguity in the rest of the line contributes to an idealization of the kind of knowing poems offer. But "this" is not quite a candidate for knowing because of the tension between its deictic multiplicity and the ways the resulting indefinite concreteness challenges any specific claim to know what "this" might involve. "This" clearly refers primarily to leaving the man free to establish the terms of relation with his spouse. But the way "this" resists articulation suggests significant, unacknowledged resentment. To be more accurate: "this" leaks resentment and covers it over or represses it at the same time, so the speaker can think what is being learned suffices for the roles she feels she must play.

If I am right, the demands for correlating the personal and the real that Vendler complains about take a good deal of their intensity from Rich's gradual understanding of how the heroics of the early poems were in fact aspects of the problems women faced rather than successful means of coping with limited options. A good deal of her later power stems from her ability both in poetry and in prose to confront the limitations of how these early poems seem exercises in a brilliance that is also a self-delusion. And when their limitations are exposed, there emerges the need to try out alternative accounts of how poetry might reveal what the prevailing poetics had a tendency to conceal. When Rich became aware of the problem of deliberate repression in the name of knowledge, she had to find ways of knowing that were compatible with her most basic personal commitments. Her poetry had to exemplify the capacity to trust those powers insofar as they could become articulate for a generation of women increasingly aware of the disjunct between their powers and the social pressures on their values.

But recognizing the need to correlate personal will with intelligence is a far cry from finding poetically engaging and satisfying means of staging the personal. I think most critics (including Vendler) have failed to see how thoroughly Rich, in the poetry between *Snapshots of a Daughter-in-Law* and *Diving into the Wreck*, tried to put to use, for different purposes, Lowell's theatrical, psychological version of the personal. Look at the first section of "Snapshots of a Daughter-in-Law" (and contrast this to Rich's later "Mother-in-Law"):

> You, once a belle in Shreveport,
> with henna-colored hair, skin like a peachbud,
> still have your dresses copied from that time,
> and play a Chopin prelude
> called by Cortot: "Delicious recollections
> float like perfume through the memory."
> Your mind now, moldering like wedding-cake,

> heavy with useless experience, rich
> with suspicion, rumor, fantasy,
> crumbling to pieces under the knife-edge
> of mere fact. In the prime of your life.
>
> Nervy, glowering, your daughter
> wipes the teaspoons, grows another way. (*FD* 35)

The description here is sheer Lowell. As in "Memories of West Street and Lepke" or the first half of "Skunk Hour," persons are reduced to fragmented features that evoke human lives without honoring anything human about them. All the feeling is left for the alienated figure of the poet.

Here, this distance between poet and her object is intensified because the second-person address generates only the heaping of descriptive detail rather than any promise of dialogue. And, more important, the ambiguous grammatical transition to the poet herself can only be presented in negative terms: whatever she is, that particularity can be defined only as growing another way.

The poem goes on like this for ten sections. At times the descriptions take on a historical pathos; at times repression comes brilliantly to the surface, as in section 8, where the repression solicits a moment of identification:

> ... Deliciously , all that we might have been,
> all that we were—fire, tears,
> wit, taste, martyred ambition—
> stirs like the memory of refused adultery
> the drained and flagging bosom of our middle years. (*FD* 37)

But how is the poet to develop that identification because its basis is so negative, so much a matter of suffering and impotence? This is how Rich ends the poem:

> ... poised , still coming
> Her fine blades making the air wince
> But her cargo
> No promise then

> Delivered
> Palpable
> Ours. (*FD* 39)

Notice two crucial features. The intensity here depends less on the situation than on the rather farfetched simile of the mother-in-law's arrival as the flight of a helicopter. And the identification can only repeat the sense of plight, but in a highly condensed fashion that eliminates all rhetorical posturing. The poet achieves a kind of resolution, but at best the recognitions involved remain ambiguously tied to a pathos that it is impossible to do anything with, except to name it as inescapable. There remains an intractable tension between the pull of lyric and the competing pull of a being left with only the fact of being abandoned, with nothing but the pain of historical being. The only trace of redemptive hope is this hovering "ours," which is potentially powerful only if it can be given significant attributes that are not reducible to distance, irony, or fantasy. Rich knows that she must own that identification and base on it her encounters with the women's frustrations. But all the grounding for her poetic intensity is contained in descriptions of a person whose situation she cannot identify with. She needs a public identity she can will privately, and she needs a language by which the power of that will might become manifest and capable of confronting the historical forces diminishing such power.

Rich's next volume, *Necessities of Life*, seems structured around precisely this effort to produce an "I" who can own her experiences and build community around the intensities by which she can establish a distinctive sense of "I" capable of choosing from history as well as suffering under it. But to my ear at least, this "I" remains a fantasy figure because it is established in metaphors that could be in Lowell or in Plath. And metaphoricity does not seem an adequate way of taking historical responsibility for the suffering the poems record:

> So much for those days. Soon
> practice may make me middling-perfect, I'll
>
> dare inhabit the world
> trenchant in motion as an eel, solid
> as a cabbage-head. I have invitations

> a curl of mist steams upward
>
> from a field, visible as my breath,
> houses along a road standing and waiting
>
> like old women, knitting, breathless
> to tell their tale. (*FD* 56)

All of the complexities of "breathless" and the force of the enjambment actually prove too much, too theatrical, so they displace the tales themselves into gestures about telling tales.[8]

Now we are ready to recognize the accomplishment in perhaps the first moment when Rich turns from metaphorically characterizing the "I" to syntactically embodying cadences as an effective power within history. The force of the poetry no longer depends on metaphors almost cancelled by their uneasy spacing:

>   I want this [leaflet] to be yours
> in the sense that if you find it and read it
>   it will be there in you already
> and the leaflet then merely something
>   to leave behind, a little leaf
> in the drawer of a sublet room.
>   What else does it come down to
> but handing on scraps of paper
>   little figurines or phials
> no stronger than the dried clay they are baked in
>   yet more than the dried clay or paper
> because the imagination crouches in them . . .
>   just as we almost miss each other
> in the ill cloud of mistrust, who might have touched
>   hands quickly, shared food or given blood
> for each other. I am thinking how we can use what we have
>   to invent what we need. (*FD* 103–4)

Here Rich in effect offers a powerful response to Vendler as she elaborates a poetry of the actual historical "I." It seems now that Rich does not so much renounce the theatrical as change its focus from being a condition of pathos to being an enticement to action: nothing less than the staging of committed and intelligent speech might allow women to face their oppression. Notice especially how three features of these lines work together to restore the emphasis on syntax that sustained the self-destructive Stoicism of Rich's early poems for what are now commitments to a new sensibility. First, there is a directness of speech, of good prose absorbed into lyric that replaces what we might call "the directed staging of traditional lyric modes of emplotment." Correlatively, there is a clear focus on objective conditions, at least in the sense that the passage establishes how few resources the women can share. That objectivity presents for Rich a demand that the poetry at least face the challenge of finding ways to transform those conditions without denying them—not by raising them into lyrical meditation but by testing how lyric intelligence might direct engagement in a future dictated by what it reveals about their condition in the present.

Finally there is a concrete matter of how the poet calls on the resources of language—not to produce images that engage the imagination but to manifest powers that might engage history. This poem faces the difficulty of having to construct from the intimate space of conversation about sending the leaflet something that approximates for the lovers the general force desired by the actual leaflet. At this point in her career, Rich has no vocabulary for facing such difficulties. But there is a metaphoric beginning of a response built simply on the way the issue of "use" is syntactically formulated. When Rich says, "its intent is clarity," she is speaking not just about a quality of the poetry but also about the satisfaction of an intention, and so a manifest condition of will. This will is realized in the passage we are reading by Rich's shift from the wanting that defines the rendered personal relationship to a "thinking" that seems an innocuous modification but carries the full challenge of the poem. Can there be a thinking that is not only a wanting, or only a complaining about the failure of those wantings?

Rich is too smart and too careful to propose a specific solution that thinking makes available, especially since the poem is concerned not with specific solutions but with extending an intimate relation into the public sphere. But the activity of thinking referred to by the poem, and demonstrated in the poem, can at least render its situation with a precision that generates confidence in the clarity of the poet's vision. Rich's poetry can make that clarity not just a condition of statement but an achievement by the language that constitutes the statement—in this case by the intricate balance of the closing assertion, "we can use what we have / to invent what we need." This balance seems to carry at least the notion of affirmation in the saying, so it nicely extends the intimacy. That intimacy is also addressed and extended by repeating "we" three times in the passage, as if all subject terms had to be willed to take on their full meaning. Rich complicates the passage by making the balance seem slightly awry, with six words in the first clause asked to balance only five in the second. But while the word count establishes contrast, the syllable count creates the equivalence on the level of poetic utterance. And it is that difference between the prose of the world and the lyric investment in that prose that suffices to carry intense personal investment not just in the future but in the linguistic resources by which we struggle to develop a new shape for that future.

Now I have to escape my own narrative and offer an analytic mode for responding to Rich and thereby fleshing out terms for appreciating what she accomplishes in the poems after the theatrics of *Diving into the Wreck*. My basic argument is that Rich rejects the idea that poems must appeal primarily to imaginative contemplation so that she can develop instead an exemplary mode of how poetry might think about the demands made on imagination by a practical world with seriously misplaced priorities. So I will show how Rich elaborates various ways that poems can transform the virtues of prose by means of the intensity, bite, and scope poetry brings to that practical world. Rich is distinctive and compelling in adapting a self-consciously charged syntax for exhibiting (and not merely using) the work a prose intelligence can do in making possible affective investments that challenge the regime of male power.

My favorite poems by Rich are "Transcendental Etude" and "Floating Love Poem"—the first exemplifying her interest in other women's lives, the second offering intense personal intimacy. But neither is quite fit for this essay—the first because it would take too much time to elaborate its intricate relations among natural process, love, politics, and compositional intensity, and the second because of a similar complexity in which sensuality also becomes a profound bond where intricate sound patterns constitute the background for a compelling event of past blending into a full present tense. So I will deal with comparable poems that address these two motifs, then turn to how she stages her commitments in the later phase of her work represented by *An Atlas of the Difficult World* (toward which Vendler seems more sympathetic but still misses much of the power in how Rich uses language).

In order to exhibit how Rich engages the lives of other women, I turn to "Paula Becker to Clara Westhoff," a rare use of explicit dramatic monologue even though that form often seems to hover in the background of her work as she sympathizes with women who have shown remarkable strength in the face of ideological oppression. Most memorable for me in the poem is the way the setting both establishes the themes and opens into the fundamental situation—how Paula Becker feels about giving birth to a child that will block her capacity to do the work she wants to do in resistance to the domination of male painters. We have to recognize in what I will quote that Rich probably fails to capture how people actually talk. But for Rich that demand issues from a silly realism. She wants to capture how they could talk if they were fully discursively aware of their interests and their feelings. The result is a dwelling on the ego that may prove uncomfortable for some readers but from Rich's perspective affords her only means of defining both need and the capacity to address that need:

> The autumn feels slowed down,
> summer still holds on here, even the light
> seems to last longer than it should
> or maybe I'm using it to the thin edge.
> The moon rolls in the air. I didn't want this child.
> You're the only one I've told.
> I want a child maybe, some day, but not now.
> Otto has a calm complacent way
> of following me with his eyes, as if to say
> Soon you will have your hands full!
> And yes I will; this child will be mine
> not his, the failures if I fail
> will be all mine. We're not good, Clara.
> at learning to prevent these things,
> and once we have a child, it is ours.

> But lately, I feel beyond Otto or anyone.
> I know now the kind of work I have to do. (*FD* 248)

The opening lines present a scene where time seems slightly out of joint, exemplifying the need to realize what the poem later will repeat twice as the condition in which "life and death take one another's hands." In the speaker's imaginary psychological world, time seems to produce a terrifying sense of change for the talented painter Paula (Modersohn) Becker. The imminent birth of a child threatens to change her life and block her capacity to work. Even the moon "rolls" because it feeds into her obsession with pregnancy, an emblem sufficiently powerful to produce a painful admission that she does not want the child. So the difficulty this monologue faces is finding out the sources and implications of this not wanting. In doing that, the monologue also establishes a substantial intimacy between two women whose pain becomes a window into a widely shared plight of an incomplete and so illusory freedom.

I admire most in this poem its capacity to embody the pain and loneliness that Paula refers to by placing that pain in the consequences of quite local details and the modes of speech those details elicit. Her loneliness is everywhere—in the estrangement from her husband caused by what she knows will be her responsibility for the baby; in her work, where she is estranged from tradition and from other painters because of her isolation and because of her quest for "new forms, old forms in new places"; and, ultimately, in her overall sense that she both knows and cannot know what she is searching for in every aspect of her life. It seems that almost all she has is the memory of the two women's intimacy in Paris before they found the men that they later married. Look at how the following passage emphasizes the pain both women face by presenting a strange blend of honest self-exposure and complete confusion about what she is doing in directly offering that self-exposure, perhaps as an expression of deep resentment of her friend:

> . . . Paris unnerved you,
> you found it too much, yet you went on
> with your work . . . and later we met there again,
> both married then, and I thought you and Rilke
> both seemed unnerved. I felt a kind of joylessness

between you. Of course he and I
have had our difficulties. Maybe I was jealous
of him, to begin with, taking you from me,
maybe I married Otto to fill up
my loneliness for you.
Rainer of course knows more than Otto knows,
he believes in women. But he feeds on us,
like all of them. His whole life, his art
is protected by women. Which of us could say that. (*FD* 249)

Paula's situation is intractable, perhaps made easier by reaching out to Clara but also made more definitive in its pain and in its inescapable wobbling among attitudes by the need to replay old memories. Perhaps all that the both of them can do is reconcile themselves to the inevitability of their situation. The poem is not without a problem of prosaic wordiness, but it may need all those words to make full sense of the ending: there, intelligence has to be manifested in recognizing its own limitations. And those limitations themselves make it clear why this has to be poetry, where the limitations can be inhabited rather than simply judged or employed as vehicles for complaint:

... Clara, our strength still lies
In the things we used to talk about:
how life and death take one another's hands,
the struggle for truth, our old pledge against guilt.
And now I feel the dawn and the coming day.
I love waking in my studio, seeing my pictures
come alive in the light. Sometimes I feel
it is myself that kicks inside me
myself I must give suck to, love ...
They say a pregnant woman
dreams of her own death. But life and death
take one another's hands. Clara, I feel so full
of work, the life I see ahead, and love
for you, who of all people,
however badly I say this
will hear all I say and cannot say. (*FD* 250)

By projecting various levels of enjambment in all but one of the final seven lines, Rich makes the poem visibly embody what Clara is asked to hear—in all the fullness of an incompleteness that can celebrate the virtues of prosaic directness now inseparable from complex feeling.

"Splittings" is also too long for extended treatment, but I think I can indicate Rich's skills as love poet, or the capacity of her style to offer a fresh perspective on love, by focusing simply on the modes of internal contrast that provide the visible structure of the argument. The poem begins with the poet registering the pain of waking in San Francisco without her lover. That pain, in turn, generates reflection on the trap of all emotional pain—that it embodies "the present of the past destructive / to living here and now" (*FD* 228). So there arises an extended set of conditional clauses staging fantasies in the subjunctive about how she might address her pain and call it to account.

The first section concludes with a risky and somewhat problematic speech on the pain of division, so that the poem can make articulate the challenge that this pain depends on. Rich's insistence on clarity about emotions can lead to moments of excess. But section 2 at least recognizes the danger because it shifts abruptly from identifying with imaginary states to present indicative efforts to treat the absence as a kind of presence:

> I will not be divided   from her or from myself
> by myths of separation
> while her mind and body in Manhattan are more with me
> than the smell of eucalyptus coolly burning   on these hills. (*FD* 229)

The literal use of separations within the line is a little heavy-handed. Yet that feature does make an important point: the speaker knows what she wills, but she is perhaps not yet sufficiently grounded in the love or in the world to satisfy these desires without relying on them as evasions of her actual needs.

The final section of the poem offers the necessary ground—first existentially and then syntactically. The previous choosings seem to be based on a fantasy of power, but the lovers have not suffered through a dialectical process sufficient to acknowledge all those forces that pull against their desires. So now we have to begin with the world rather than the self, then ground choosing on a very specific and definitive act of intelligent refusal:

> The world tells me I am its creature
> I am raked by eyes   brushed by hands
> I want to crawl into her for refuge   lay my head
> in the space   between her breast and shoulder
> abnegating power for love
> as women have done   or hiding
> from power in her love   like a man
> I refuse these givens   the splitting
> between love and action   I am choosing
> not to suffer uselessly   and not to use her
> I choose to love   this time   for once
> with all my intelligence. (*FD* 229)

The language has the logic and timing of good prose. But this message is by no means exhausted in the act of communication. Instead, an intelligence takes place that involves the text building on established interrelationships, so that it functions also as an exemplary object modeling possible attitudes that might prove useful in the real world.

What does it mean to love with all one's intelligence? First, it means trusting in the negative power to see one's illusions and draw out the general reasons why these illusions have force. So the poem moves from the temptation of an intimate image to a neatly balanced sense of how her weaknesses combine temptations that beset both women and men. Then there is the act of refusal. How can that not be melodramatic and narrowly self-centered? One answer is that Rich has set up the temptations that have to be refused in such a way that only a global statement will suffice. The refusal is not melodramatic to the extent that it is the only right gesture the poet can possibly make to deal with the scope and persistence of how conventional claims about love tie the self to an old and disabling order.

A better answer lies in how the language of the poem sustains the power gathered in this act of refusal. The refusal is justified in the poem by an initial brief summary of the only options seemingly available—to suffer uselessly like a woman or to use the woman like a man. Then "I choose" is repeated in a way that makes it much more than an empty or egocentric gesture. "All my intelligence" is called for, and is demonstrated by, how the combination of "this time" and "for once" insist on the specificity of her decision and, more important, on the limited nature of her power. One aspect of that intelligence is the demonstrated capacity for self-knowledge about what blocks her from what she thinks of as an authentic love, not based on weakness and desperation. The other main aspect is the poem's capacity to shape the refusal in such a way as to reinforce roles of these two temporal indicators. "This time" registers both the capacity of assertion to specify a deictic expression and the provisional awareness that there will be a constant challenge to repeat the terms of choosing. Then "for once" does not merely repeat the same idea. Instead it provides a balancing figure that parallels the reference to two kinds of temptation, female and male. "This time" binds the intelligence to the specific locale of choosing, but with a somewhat skeptical sense of wearying repetition. But "for once" is quite different in its assertion of difference that has the capacity to open into a possible future, provisional but also repeatable if the force of the refusals the poem realizes can hold up.

Finally, I want to show how Rich uses spacing in the poem to make "all my intelligence" a statement referring not only to the analytic mind but also to the mind that can build experiences of valuing by means of the control of formal elements. The additional spaces within the lines begin as markers of division—within herself and from her lover. But eventually the poem stylizes these gaps as something close to marked caesurae, in order to show how the dialectical intelligence can admit the separation and yet transform it into a creative force. The effect is especially strong for the double pause in the penultimate line, because it brings out the movement from negative aspects of the choice to the positive force of what intelligence can involve. The positive terms are seriously limited, but they have a potential to expand by including the entire process of spacing within their unfolding.

Rich's later poetry adapts its intelligence more to matters of nature and mortality, and it presents a more forgiving attitude toward human folly, as if understanding our vulnerability necessarily bonded all humans in possible sympathy for one another. But the clarity of her verse still poses stumbling blocks for critics, the most vocal of whom remains Vendler, who simply cannot register artifice that is not elaborately rooted in fictionality. She recognizes Rich's effort to expand her prosaic lines to take on a kind of Whitmanesque universal generosity toward the difficult world, but she cannot find any terms by which that comparison redounds to Rich's benefit. I cite first her basic description of the poems in *An Atlas of the Difficult World*:

> The value of Rich's poems, ethically speaking, is that they have continued to press against insoluble questions of suffering, evil, love, justice, and patriotism. For all their epic wish to generalize to the social whole, they are both limited by, and enhanced by, their essentially first-person lyric status. They hate what the person Adrienne Rich hates, love what she loves. Their sympathies are her self-sympathies, their victims the victims closest to her own heart. They are not dispassionately epic, and broadly socially curious, as Whitman's poems strove to be. Perhaps Whitman was more heterogeneously moved, emotionally speaking, than Rich; while his poems tend to arise from observations from without . . . , her poems are exfoliations from within. (MA)

Then Vendler focuses on the poem "Dedications" because it offers a Whitmanesque catalog "with its address to all readers of any poet" (MA). But she argues that "[w]hile Whitman's catalogs tend to summon together quite diverse species within the group (cf. 'The Sleepers'), Rich's tend to offer successive members of the same species" (MA), sorting the world still in terms of her moral categories rather than following Whitman's interest in plural modes of life.

Now look at "Dedications" with an eye for what Rich does with grammar as her primary means to bring self-conscious lyrical force to what otherwise seems sheer realist description. I must quote lengthy passages because the lyrical effect depends on how she correlates repetitions with differences. Here I cite the first four repetitions:

> I know you are reading this poem
> late, before leaving your office
> of the one intense yellow lamp spot and the darkening window
> in the lassitude of a building faded to quiet
> long after rush hour. I know you are reading this poem
> standing up in a bookstore far from the ocean
> on a grey day of early spring, faint flakes driven
> across the plains' enormous spaces around you.

> I know you are reading this poem
> in a room where too much has happened for you to bear
> where the bedclothes lie in stagnant coils on the bed
> and the open valise speaks of flight
> but you cannot leave yet. I know you are reading this poem
> as the underground train loses momentum and before running
> up the stairs
> toward a new kind of love
> your life has never allowed.[9]

Several things are going on here that are not at all present in Whitman. First, and most important, while Whitman's catalogs are primarily interested in the roles people play in life—nurse, farmer, builder—Rich is primarily interested in particular contexts of reading. In principle, the same "you" could be the referent in each of these contexts. Or anyone could enter all of the contexts. Second, we could imagine that "you" is utterly incomplete without context: it is our capacity to shift contexts that makes us persons and agents who can care about reading. Then her shifting contexts enables these "you"s to adapt to the poet's "I." The realization of being addressed invites response. At this point in her career, Rich wants to honor the loneliness that drives each of us to read, and to find potential gratification in recognizing the range of attitudes in which reading her work might matter. Again, readers are not pawns in games only the poet can play. The case is very different with Whitman. To be addressed as an exemplar of a social role is to confront a tremendous imbalance between the heroic poet, who can address all, and the addressee, for whom limited conditions are prescribed. It also matters that those addressed do not have their genders determined by the poem.

Finally, there may be a complex internal logic to the presentation of these various contexts of address. The first "I know you" is set in a specific room characterized as tranquil but lonely, so the reader in effect depends on the poem to have any social existence at all. There is pathos to reading. The second reader almost melds into his or her environment despite the fact that he or she is standing in a bookstore. The third reader, on the other hand, seems traumatized and incapable of relating to any environment beyond the room. None of them acts in any way that goes beyond their reading. Only the fourth reader has a sense of a future that may differentiate itself from the past because the reading is tied not only to need but also to possibility. As we read about these readers, I think we have to wonder in what contexts we would be placed, as well as what sympathy we might be able to muster for these other readers, these other *semblables*. Whitman asks his readers for direct sympathy and empathy; Rich asks first for a kind of understanding of the needs and hopes that may make the activity of reading a social phenomenon after all.

Now let us turn to the last three of the twelve envisioned readers:

I know you are reading this poem which is not in your language
guessing at some words while others keep you reading
and I want to know which words they are.
I know you are reading this poem listening for something, torn
between bitterness and hope
turning back once again to the task you cannot refuse.
I know you are reading this poem because there is nothing else left to read
there where you have landed, stripped as you are. (*ADW* 26)

Why does "I" appear only once as a desiring being, wanting "to know which words they are," as well as announcing its knowledge? And why introduce at the very end an "as" that may complicate all the knowing relationships? Perhaps "as" is the grammatical figure best attuned to how contexts affect our dispositions and our actions. Here, "stripped as you are" characterizes this "you" in terms of two basic contexts—a material condition and a temporal situation. The material condition is passive, a state of constant need. But the temporal condition suggests something quite different. It suggests a structure of possibility where the stripping is voluntary, indeed where the stripping away of all distraction and distinguishing existential markers may make this "you" the ideal reader because it can finally inhabit the "there" that all poetry seeks—a nakedness that can engage all of the contexts of knowledge that the poem stages. This "you" is capable of honoring the full ambitions and full needs of the speaking "I."

Or, in this instance, this "you" is capable of making us hear (and "here") again the first poem of the thirteen-poem sequence beginning the volume, of which "Dedications" is the final section. I quote the first three lines, then the final passage of that poem:

> A dark woman, head bent, listening for something
> —a woman's voice, a man's voice or
> voice of the freeway, night after night, metal streaming downcoast . . .
>
> . . . I drive inland over roads
> closed in wet weather, past shacks hunched in the canyons
> roads that crawl down into darkness and wind into light
> where trucks have crashed and riders of horses tangled
> to death with lowstruck boughs. These are not the roads
> you knew me by. But the woman, driving, walking, watching
> for life and death is the same. (*ADW* 3, 5)

This conclusion defines the quest basic to the entire sequence—for companionship and for something to care about intensely so as to enable the "driving, walking, watching" to take verbal form. And that verbal form invites a secondary reading of this last line that stresses its echoes of questing wanderers like the Ancient Mariner. In this reading, the particular poet is abstracted into the function of watching for how death and life can be treated as the same. For then all the wandering, all the experience of loss and of change, brings us closer to aligning with the one truth we have to recognize if we are to find any rest. From this perspective the two poems together stage a remarkable spirit of severe generosity in which abstraction strips off the contexts that both conceal and reveal the truth of second-person needs to find what might reconcile living and dying. This stripping in turn aligns "you" and "I" as themselves quite abstract and thus shareable roles, which at the same time take on an elemental concreteness as positions that have to be unified in the same way that life and death do.

I worry that I get pompous and mistake my own desire to stage myself as profound so that I miss what these poems are actually doing. Then I read again the final poem in *An Atlas of the Difficult World*, and I think I am on the track of how "I" and "you" become as complete and as elemental as the self-conscious relation between living and dying. This level of relation in this last poem is captured by the play of "it," because Rich can resist the appeal of elaborate dramatic images and rely on prose statements lyricized by the power of elements of grammar to indicate fundamental forces articulating social bonds shared by virtue of a common mortality:

it will not be simple, it will not be long
it will take little time, it will take all your thought
it will take all your heart, it will take all your breath
it will be short, it will not be simple

it will touch through your ribs, it will take all your heart
it will not be long, it will occupy your thought
as a city is occupied, as a bed is occupied
it will take all your flesh, it will not be simple

You are coming into us, who cannot withstand you
you are coming into us who never wanted to withstand you
you are taking parts of us into places never planned
you are going far away with pieces of our lives

it will be short, it will take all your breath
it will not be simple, it will become your will (*ADW* 57)

Walt Whitman, eat your heart out.

Notes

1. This chapter was written a year before the publication of Rich's *Collected Poems: 1950–2012*, ed. Claudia Rankine (New York: W. W. Norton, 2016). But I want to mention two notable, quite intelligent and sensitive reviews of the collected poems that nonetheless seem embarrassed by poetry trying to achieve the public significance that Rich sought. Both essays, by Marjorie Perloff ("The Will to Change," *Times Literary Supplement*, September 2, 2016) and Dan Chiasson ("Boundary Conditions: Adrienne Rich's *Collected Poems*," *New Yorker*, June 20, 2016, 78–81) clearly prefer the more private moments of self-conscious lyric in her work and ignore the struggle to test will by forcing it to take responsibility in public political efforts to speak a common language. Perloff does observe that Rich has turned out to be a crucial force in shaping the political turn in poetry, but in Perloff's essay this is not quite praise, perhaps because Perloff refuses Rich's challenge to imagine how such work might make demands on us to alter our models for judging the poetry.
2. I quote from Adrienne Rich, *Arts of the Possible: Essays and Conversations* (New York: W. W. Norton, 2001), 48. And I owe to Wendy Martin in

conversation this observation about contemporary poets interfusing poetry with prose forms of making sense.
3. Claire Keyes, in *The Aesthetics of Power: The Poetry of Adrienne Rich* (Athens: University of Georgia Press, 1986), makes this point forcefully in her second chapter. Keyes's book is also important as very intelligent testimony to what Rich's book meant for readers in an age characterized by efforts to think about gender in relation to issues of power. Keyes hears Rich's reliance on Lowell and Plath in her early efforts to develop a personal poetry (64–87), then stresses how Rich locates the power she seeks not in images of the self but in foregrounding how creativity becomes overtly present in the act of composition.
4. I will not address Rich the essayist here except to point out that her way of treating personal commitment as a measure of truth and opposition to the lie in poetry correlates closely with the emphases in her prose, and it is that relation which plays a large role in her achieving a distinctive and unreplaceable presence in the literary landscape.
5. There are two reviews from which I quote: Helen Vendler, "Mapping the Air," *New York Review of Books*, November 21, 1991; and "All Too Real," *New York Review of Books*, December 17, 1981. This quotation is from "All Too Real." I will cite in the text the first short essay as MA and the second as ATR.
6. I have taken all my citations of Rich's poems before *An Atlas of the Difficult World* from Adrienne Rich, *The Fact of a Doorframe: Poems Selected and New, 1950–1984* (New York: W. W. Norton, 1984). This citation is from page 266. I will put subsequent citations in the body of the text with the abbreviation *FD*.
7. Many other poems in the volume have this same aura of dissatisfaction with the very success of the control the poem aims at. See especially "Storm Warnings," "Aunt Jennifer's Tigers," and "Stepping Backward."
8. See the end of "Face to Face" for a more extreme version of assertions swallowed by the theatrics of metaphoric self-aggrandizement:

> How people used to meet!
> starved, intense, the old
> Christmas gifts saved up till spring
> and the old plain words.
>
> and each with his God-given secret,
> spelled out through months of snow and silence,
> burning under the bleached scalp; behind dry lips,
> a loaded gun. (*FD* 76)

I think the allusion to Dickinson only weakens any sense of a functioning independent subject. See also "The Demon Lover" and "Night-Pieces for a Child."
9. Adrienne Rich, *An Atlas of the Difficult World* (New York: W. W. Norton, 1991). Subsequent citations will be abbreviated *ADW* and placed in the main text.

CHAPTER 2

Michael Palmer and the Linguistic Turn

V. JOSHUA ADAMS

There is agreeable poetry.
There is poetry like a white cloth.
There's a poetry licking its tongue.

—"NOTES FOR ECHO LAKE 2"[1]

MORE THAN THIRTY years ago, Lee Bartlett introduced Language poetry to professional intellectuals in the pages of *Critical Inquiry*. The essay concluded with some recommendations for future work, including more thorough historical and sociological accounts of the group, and assessments of the political efficacy of their art, before asking the crucial question for literary critics: "Perhaps most important of all, are these writers, theory aside, producing poetry that matters?" Bartlett is initially circumspect—"Obviously this last question is the most difficult, and as usual we would be wise to let time sort it out"—eventually concluding that, even if Language poetry is "theoretically top-heavy" and "fails to hold a place in our imagination," the movement is nevertheless important as "an ongoing corrective to a prevailing workshop aesthetic" and, somewhat more grandly, "as an important irritant in its unwillingness to let us deny the myriad mysteries embedded in the very fabric of the poem." In between all of this academic judiciousness and its caveats, though, he comes clean: "I certainly suspect that Michael Palmer at least . . . is already emerging as an American poet of the first rank."[2] Even if it is not entirely accurate to group Palmer with the Language poets—he has distanced himself from what he has called the "myth of innovation" that underwrites a superficial avant-gardism[3] and has complained about the tendency of some of his friends among the Language poets toward "trashing the lyric"[4]—Bartlett's aesthetic judgment was borne out, and in a particularly notable way: Palmer is one of a small number of poets (among them Gwendolyn Brooks, Allen Ginsberg, Frank O'Hara, Sylvia Plath, Robert Creeley, John Ashbery, and Susan Howe) who are celebrated by peers and critics on both sides of the artistic divide in American poetry that has structured the literary landscape since (at least) the anthology wars of the late 1950s and early 1960s.

Apart from this recognition, though, what exactly makes Palmer a poet of "the first rank," someone whose work commands, or deserves, more attention than that given to other poets? Bartlett does not say. In his reticence, he stands in for academic literary critics in general: if we make evaluative judgments without defending them, it is not because we are supremely confident that they are true ("I certainly suspect that . . ."), but because our profession assumes (erroneously, I think) that such judgments cannot really be defended. There is another element to Bartlett's praise of Palmer, however, that also accounts for his reluctance to explain the grounds of his esteem: he praises Palmer's poetry in terms not only of its refusal to conform to a commodified poetry but of its commitment to mystery. Nonconformity and resistance to commodification are of course at the center of contemporary intellectual life; both assimilate easily to the critique of ideology. They fit into the modern, secular university. Mystery does not.

Certainly poets have allied themselves with mystery since time immemorial. They have sought the origins of poetry in divine inspiration and the effects of poetry in the charms of poetic language; and, more recently, they have located the value of poetry in the expression of an otherwise ineffable subjective experience. These alliances with mystery imbue poetry with authority, but they also make it intellectually dubious. The contributions that poetry (or the arts in general) might make to the Enlightenment task of demystification, and thus to the production of knowledge, are not clear. As Raymond Geuss has convincingly argued, poetry is not a form of knowledge in any of the traditional senses of that term.[5] How then are we to account for the fact that poetry is part of the university curriculum, both as an object of study and a practice? Flattening it into representation is not adequate, since poetry is not only a matter of representation. The centrality of Theodor Adorno to contemporary literary criticism rests, in large part, on the resistance he provides to such flattening. He argues that the artwork as such has cognitive significance—that it has a truth value—while also insisting that this cognitive significance of the artwork cannot be reproduced by, or translated into, propositions.[6] Justifying the artwork to an intellectual audience does not require giving up the category of art. Bartlett's judgment about Palmer's work (and about Language poetry) does not invoke Adorno explicitly, but it follows a similar path, resting on a deep investment in the authority of poetry and an equally deep investment in the claim that such authority has been undermined by modernity. Palmer's poetry matters because it embraces, but also defies, the intellectual life that would erase it. Theoretically sophisticated, it is also, in its fidelity to mystery, traditional. It serves the Enlightenment project by refusing to serve it fully. In doing so, it renews itself, ennobling or restoring something that had become debased. This is the ground on which Bartlett's judgment stands. Palmer's poetry renews the idea of poetic vocation.

If this sounds too idealistic or conservative for an experimental poet, consider the degree to which it resonates with Palmer's own description of his poetics:

> The commuter poem—you get on the 5:14 and you read a poem, and that's kind of nice. You recognize the experience and the people in it, and you have a little enclosed melodrama. I find that kind of work loathsome, although maybe I should just take it as part of the furniture of middle-class life and not worry about it. But I worry about it as something that represents itself as poetry. It's profoundly fraudulent, even when done in good faith. It's a kind of anti-poetry—*an erasure of the function of poetry in relation to the world*, a trivializing for which one is duly rewarded for making this thing manageable. Well, I think a poem has to be unmanageable. If western civilization is civilization, then it has to be uncivilized as well. Western civilization seems capable of the most extraordinary depravity, to which we are daily witness; perhaps it has forced upon the poem the acknowledgment of itself as something else in

regard to that, in its address to it. In that respect, it seems to me, an art has to maintain an oppositional character now.[7]

There is a lot in here, of course. Palmer, in interviews, is refreshingly full blooded, willing to acknowledge that his most sincere artistic commitments are, ultimately, part of his sensibility and thus contingent ("maybe I should just take it as part of the furniture of middle-class life and not worry about it"). But apart from giving us a sense of the man, the remark is important for the phrase: "an erasure of the function of poetry in relation to the world." This is what Bartlett picked up on, the degree to which Language poetry in general and Palmer's poetry in particular indicate that the function of poetry is in question. Talk of fraudulence, of witnessing and opposing the depravity within Western civilization, should be understood as subordinate to a larger crisis. If it is not, one could imagine that Palmer is suggesting that the measure of the art is its authenticity or its historical truth, and the relation of that authenticity to a vision of the good society. Yet Palmer's poetry is not well described as historical witness, nor is it written in service of a meliorist or utopian social vision, though it combines aspects of these sorts of poetry. It is just as frequently a weary, even bitter, critique of all of them. To have a poetry of authenticity or historical witness, of moral or social improvement, or even utopia, one has to imagine a potential connection between words and world. Palmer's poetry complicates that connection. "The world is all that is displaced" (*LB* 135) he writes in the poem "First Figure," intentionally misquoting Wittgenstein.

So just what *is* the function of poetry in relation to the world for Palmer? It is an amalgam of the ancient aspiration toward immortality and the Romantic commitment to subjectivity that we have come to expect from Western lyric poetry over the past two hundred years. But if the function of poetry is stable, the grounds on which it operates have changed. Palmer weds a traditional conception of lyric vocation to an idiom in which the authority of such vocation has been compromised by the formal study of language. This is what makes him a poet of "the first rank." He is the great lyric poet of the linguistic turn, a maker of musical artifacts that express subjectivity where the intellectual disciplines treat their objects as linguistic phenomena, to be elucidated by theories or therapies of language. The conflict between language as an art and as a means for producing knowledge is ancient. The contemporary version of the quarrel is more intimate, messy; rather than two separate discourses competing for authority, each discourse now seeks, plausibly, to absorb the other. In the wake of the linguistic turn, all the stuff of poetry—prosody, figuration, syntax, semantics, genre, rhetoric—becomes part of the project of knowledge production, and all of knowledge production becomes somehow figurative, poetic.

In saying that Palmer is the great lyric poet of the linguistic turn, then, I emphatically do *not* mean that he is a great poeticizer of twentieth-century intellectual history. Rather, the great lyric poet of the linguistic turn transformed that intellectual project into poetry, but also expressed subjectivity by means of that intellectual project in an exemplary way. (The poet's own term for this is "analytic lyric.") Palmer's poetry captures what it is like to think and feel with and through the linguistic turn. He maintains allegiance to the poetic fashioning of subjectivity while also acknowledging, and undermining, an intellectual project that constrains the freedom of poetic makers and the authority of subjects. This is a real and enduring achievement, even if it is only fully intelligible against the backdrop of professional intellectual life.

Let me begin with an early poem that shows his ability to make art out of, against, and within the linguistic turn:

A Reasoned Reply to Gilbert Ryle

(After Blake's Newton)

Sound becomes difficult
to dispose of

etc. You go to sit down
and hope for a chair.

One of a pair of
eyes

distends.
Redness begins

on the left side.
The car always starts

in the morning
and it takes me

where someone else
is supposed to be

going
twice each week.

Or else the problem
of light and air.

Upstairs a small leak.
Trouble through the other

eye
which stays open

unless the window itself
is broken. (*LB* 6)

Ryle, Blake, Newton. These giants of intellectual and literary history almost swallow the poem before it begins. Some context is necessary. Ryle rebuked our commonsense notion of the mind as something inner and hidden, the "ghost in the machine." Despite the fact that he would disavow the label of "behaviorist," he provided a compelling argument that many philosophical problems could be dissolved by paying closer attention to verbal behavior. Palmer casts Ryle in the role of Newton as depicted by Blake in his beautiful monotype. There the great scientist, naked and statuesque as a figure out of Michelangelo, sits hunched over his compasses and geometric figures at the bottom of a dark, mossy cave. The picture is a synecdoche for Blake's entire corpus and maybe for Romanticism in general: visionary critique of Enlightenment reason. Palmer's poem is "after" this painting chronologically but also analogically—Blake is to Newton as Palmer is to Ryle—albeit with the important difference that the later poetic reply is (supposedly) "reasoned," claiming philosophical technique for poetry.

I said that the poem's intellectually ambitious title almost swallows it. It wriggles free in a few ways: by keeping the proper nouns out of the stanzas, by resorting to chopped and enjambed couplets à la Creeley, which arrest the fluid prose we would expect in a "reasoned reply," and by engaging in the kind of counterintellectualism that Cleanth Brooks called "the language of paradox." "A Reasoned Reply to Gilbert Ryle" exploits an ambiguity in the word "reply" itself: is this a reply in the sense of a message, or a reply in the more adversarial, and customarily philosophical sense, of a rebuttal? Both, surely. The poem both describes and reports some problems with a behaviorist view of the mind that are also, plausibly, problems of poetic making. For example: "Sound becomes difficult / to dispose of / etc." For the behaviorist, sound is public, and thus potentially important for interpreting behavior. But sound is also underdetermined; it can signify, of course, but it need not be meaningful. The question of how we know if a sound is meaningful, what it means in particular (let alone how we recognize it as a sound) raises the specter of what W. V. O. Quine called the "indeterminacy of translation," a term that, like Wittgenstein's "form of life," places real limits on the empirical pretensions of the behaviorist. Of course sound is also difficult to dispose of for poets, and in both senses of the word "dispose": to order, and to get rid of. The lines can be read in a rueful (i.e., Yeatsian) or savvy (i.e., Adornian) commentary on the unruliness of meter, or they can be read as a more generally formalist prescription to maintain sound, lest one's work fall into prose. "Etc." recapitulates some of the indeterminacy of both meaning and sound: it gestures toward particulars without identifying them, and it sounds both playful and formal, maybe even pompous. How does one sound when reading Palmer's lines? Knowing, perhaps. "Etc." is shorthand for those who are already in the know. But are we knowing in a way that confirms the importance of Ryle's project? Or knowing in a way that makes fun of it? "You go to sit down / and hope for a chair" directs us toward parody. Who has not been so exhausted as to have done this at one time or another? On the other hand, who would do this, really do it, really only hope for the chair, on purpose? The lines describe the evacuation of cognition with a kind of exaggerated skepticism that dissolves in the face of experience. (It is the same exaggerated skepticism behind the old joke about two behaviorists after sex: "It was good for you. How was it for me?")

Palmer criticizes linguistic philosophy in a poem that also lets such philosophy trouble our sense of the art. In Blake's monotype, the naked Newton sits between the dark curves of the grotto and the pristine light and lines he draws with his compass; his body is a mediating figure, implicated in both structures. "One of a pair of / eyes // distends"—a clinical observation, it sounds as if it is made from the outside. Satisfying in its precision, it might have come from a doctor—William Carlos Williams, for example. "Redness begins / on the left side" maintains the clinical stance while also somehow internalizing it—this could be redness of the skin or redness in the visible field—while also picking up a rhyme on eyes that, along with the enjambments, remind us that we are not in a doctor's office but reading a poem. My point is just that Palmer connects the precision of scientific observation to that of a philosophy of language, and to that of one model for modernism. The connection is generative, but not necessarily all to the good. At a minimum, it alienates the human being who is the object of so much precision. Witness the middle of the poem, in which a longer narrative suddenly emerges in a series of song-like phrases: "The car always starts // in the morning / and it takes me // where someone else / is supposed to be // going / twice each week." Spread across stanzas, these lines surprise with their continuity. They describe a kind of captivity or mistaken identity, but they also capture the dissociation that is the logical culmination of behaviorism. For the behaviorist, who I think I am in the privacy of my mind is irrelevant to who I really am. Who I really am is what my body does. Consciousness is an illusion. So is poetry. Palmer's simultaneously plaintive and intellectual lines rebut the behaviorist in terms both poetic and reductive: the eyes are the windows to the soul, but these are broken.

Intellectually ambitious poetry like Palmer's easily comes off as pretentious. The poet manages to offset this charge with parodic repetitions and quotations, nonsense, snippets of overheard speech, vulgarities, stream-of-consciousness prose, jarring references to historical crisis. (The parallels to Eliot, more so than Pound or Zukofsky, even here, many years before the writing through of *The Waste Land* that occurs in *Sun*, are striking.) *The Brown Book* is named after Wittgenstein's early drafts for the *Philosophical Investigations* and includes an epigraph from it, but the language delights in the kind of idling that Wittgenstein thought was the source of philosophical difficulties. An awkwardly fragmented but nevertheless memorable prose poem called "Tomb of Baudelaire"—harkening back to Mallarmé's own awkward "Tombeaux de Baudelaire"—mentions "Plato's warning against telling stories, *mython tina diēgeisthai*," and repeats this a little later on, substituting "admonition" for "warning." Yet it also includes a mishearing of the phrase "poetry suicide" as "poultry recital," talk of Nixon's resignation, someone getting oral sex while discussing "the possibility of a job" on the telephone, Irving Berlin, and a bride and groom getting into a fistfight on the night before their marriage—among other things (*LB* 47–49). "On the Way to Language," after the Heidegger essay of the same name, starts out in a predictably portentous way—"The answer was / the sun"—before becoming the least Heideggerian of poems. There are rats in the Pentagon, dried bodies under floorboards, and a parody of upper-class confidence: "We're not ashamed / of our immense wealth // even somewhat proud / of the cleanliness of the servants' quarters // From the sound of their weeping / they seem happy enough // in their work, childlike / and contrite" (*LB* 53). This is not a poetry of high culture that looks askance at mass culture, but one that registers a conflict within high culture. The point is not only to understand the conflict but to feel it and hear it, and when Palmer is able to do this, he is at his best.

I find the poet best in verse or in versets. The early sequence "Notes for Echo Lake," which combines these forms with prose paragraphs, was influential in promoting serial compositions along the lines of those undertaken by Oppen, Duncan, and Creeley. The longer the paragraphs get, however, the less punch they have. Palmer is better stripped. Here is the opening of "Notes for Echo Lake 4":

Who did he talk to

Did she trust what she saw

Who does the talking

Whose words formed awkward curves

Did the lion finally talk

Did the sleeping lion talk

Did you trust a north window

What made the dog bark

What causes a grey dog to bark

What does the juggler tell us

What does the juggler's redness tell us

Is she standing in an image

Were they lost in the forest

Were they walking through a forest

Has anything been forgotten

Did you find it in the dark

Is that one of them new atomic-powered wristwatches (*LB* 77)

These questions without quotation marks are potential entries into dialogues that invoke a vast array of different tones and situations. The first three lines are doubtful, albeit in different ways. They could be the thoughts of a curious or even jealous lover, the inquiry of a critic or master manipulator, the beginnings of strategy. Yet just when we have become attuned to the rhetorical scenarios implicit in these opening lines, the poet surprises us with a line, "Whose words formed awkward curves," that would be less at home in conversation than in art criticism. "Did the lion finally talk," meanwhile, is an allusion to Wittgenstein's remark in the *Investigations*, "If a lion could talk, we could not understand him,"[8] a claim that underscores the degree to which languages depend on particular forms of life. Detached from its position in Wittgenstein, the phrase loses its critical significance and merges into mildly surprised leisure-class conversation; and then it takes a step further down the social ladder, since the "sleeping lion" evokes, for listeners of a certain age, anyway, the doo-wop smash hit "The Lion Sleeps Tonight." The recursiveness of these particular lines is bathetic, but the pattern they establish for the remainder of the poem is viable: the transition from what made the dog bark to what causes a grey dog to bark moves from generality to specificity, as does the transition from the juggler to the juggler's redness. We don't get answers to these questions, but answers are not the point, since the questions have not yet been asked. It is tempting to see a poem like this as a dance of the intellect, an attempt to take refuge in itself, a lingering in the conceptual-linguistic space that has not yet taken a final grammatical shape as a public utterance—even if that shape is only coming into view, conceptually. The poem suggests that, if interiority persists (and interiority has been under attack since the replies to Descartes's *Meditations*), it is here, in the porous but practical distinction between what is thought and what is said.

The suspicion, familiar from Mallarmé, that speech necessarily compromises poetry, generates some of Palmer's strongest poems in *First Figure*. But, at the level of rhetoric, Palmer doesn't give himself over to symbolist purity. The book possesses the sophistication, allusiveness, and pervasive frustration at the limitations of language that hover over all of the poet's work, but it also activates a form of direct address that helps his readers feel that there is something at stake. Witness the opening of "Lens": "I failed to draw a map and you followed it perfectly / because the word for 'cannot' inscribes itself here / to define an atmosphere of absolute trust / which both fastens and unfastens us" (*LB* 103). The phrase "First Figure" itself is likely an allusion to Roland Barthes, a writer who made the linguistic turn into a medium for prose as Palmer does for lyric poetry. Barthes's great genre-bending book, *A Lover's Discourse: Fragments*, begins with a discussion of figures: "The word is to be understood, not in its rhetorical sense, but rather in its gymnastic or choreographic acceptation."[9] There is no "first" figure in a strict sense, unless we mean the "amorous feeling" from which the figures arise. This is an implicit criticism of poetry, given the strong association of poetry with the origin of languages in Vico, Rousseau, Emerson, and others. By lifting and twisting the phrase, Palmer puts Barthes's "gymnastic or choreographic" approach to language back into service; Barthes himself, like most of the French poststructuralists (save Julia Kristeva), had little to say about poetry. To turn linguistic accusations against poetry into an affirmation of lyric poetry in particular, that is Palmer's project. Affirmation in and through negation.[10]

Such a stance—like that of Bartleby—depends on a position to be negated. The original (and still ultimately the strongest) negation of poetry in the West is the accusation of untruth. Palmer takes this up in "Lies of the Poem":

> We welcomed the breeze
> could not escape it
>
> The face is turned to an idea
> We will never be friends until it's done
>
> His words are over
> The false ceiling here
>
> emits a remarkable light
> The music is so-so
>
> Were you named for the painting
> of the moth of gold
>
> or the stain on the pillow
> The face is burned by an idea
>
> cannot escape it
> cannot escape or retain it
>
> The body tends to disappear
> beneath the wrapping
>
> The ink dries
> across a period of years
>
> in which fires occur
> at the midpoint between the eyebrows

> La-la-la is the germ of sadness
> said the speaker in sneakers
>
> Sound decays
> and then there is the story
>
> and then the features are erased
> The addition of one more chair
>
> and the arrangement is complete
> Here another festival
>
> to which no one is invited
> and where expectation plays no part (*LB* 99)

The language is completely general, frequently holding its nouns at the remove of the definite article. "Sound decays / and then there is the story / and then the features are erased" (which sound? what story? features of what? erased how?). Diction is flat, even monotonous. The poem lacks vivid imagery, lush sounds, variety. "Were you named for the painting / of the moth of gold // or the stain on the pillow" is funny in a deflationary way—but it does not bring the poem closer to any specific place or time, except perhaps through its invocation of a sardonic, vaguely surrealist sensibility. The poem avoids a definite scene, instead oscillating between an unnamed "we" and an unspecified "you." All sorts of conventional poetic desiderata are missing. The two formal features of the poem that are obviously pronounced are the couplets and the lack of punctuation, but, since some couplets are closed and others are open and some appear to be both, and since there is no punctuation to guide us in any case, the poem's form emphasizes a comprehensive ambiguity. And yet it is compelling and memorable for the way it integrates literary and philosophical concerns from antiquity and modernity into an expression of subjectivity. "Lies of the Poem" recalls the Platonic injunction against poetry to which Palmer repeatedly returns. Insofar as the poem is metapoetic, it recalls the great Romantic-modernist project of making poetry about poetry. The presentation of the poem as a lie recalls the paradox of the

Cretan Liar, which greatly vexed Bertrand Russell; and, insofar as the poem is such a paradox, it recalls Cleanth Brooks's stance that all poetry is the language of paradox. By making art out of all of these intellectual commonplaces, Palmer insists that poetry is equal to discourses that would dispel or domesticate it.

A closer look reveals more discourses: "We welcomed the breeze / could not escape it." While the lines are not, strictly speaking, a contradiction, they imply contradictory accounts of agency, glossing the supposed inescapability of the Romantic tradition. The breeze in question is no doubt the correspondent breeze of Wordsworth's *Prelude*—Palmer has a poem in *First Figure* entitled "Prelude"—a breeze that M. H. Abrams identified as a common metaphor for a change in the poet's mind. At the head of Palmer's "Lies of the Poem," this story of accommodating a force that one could not escape is criticized as a fiction that actually masks the poet's agency; the poem speaks of inevitability but points silently toward deliberate acts. The second stanza invokes a less specifically artistic context: a face turned to an idea is one that faces an idea and one that has been transformed into an idea. In each case, particularity is lost, resulting in an attenuated friendship that might also mask a bond that begins or persists in the task at hand. There is something forbidding about this turning. Later, "The face is burned by an idea // cannot escape it // cannot escape or retain it." Just when we are inclined to read these statements as forbidding, we remember that they might not be true—the poem might state that the face is burned by an idea, or that the body tends to disappear beneath the wrapping, or that the ink takes years to dry, but these might all be lies to see through. The point is to activate the reader's intelligence in a particular way: in service of distrust that will produce truth. That is the point of calling the poem "Lies of the Poem." By situating the poem within a paradox, however, one also needs to ask whether the activation of distrust is itself *based* on a lie. Palmer's poetry does not critique representation in the service of a discernible, or even a barely discernible truth. Truth is not, it turns out, its goal. Rather, it means to explore a situation that Nietzsche foresaw, in which truth is not only a mobile army of metaphors, but one whose compensatory Stevensian constructions are criticized as mere compensations. The supremacy of the poetic fiction is also a fiction. Such poetry has diminishing returns for some. Calvin Bedient, for example, accuses Palmer of nihilism, writing that the poet is "offended by language's pretensions to reason *and* to tracing over a world."¹¹ But by reducing the matter to one of personal offense, Bedient underestimates the problem to which Palmer responds; the language of reason does not merely trace over the world: it promises to obliterate it (remember the frightening image with which Max Horkheimer and Theodor Adorno begin *Dialectic of Enlightenment*: "The wholly enlightened earth is radiant with triumphant calamity"¹²). And there is no easy or honest way back, at least for the secular intellectuals who make up Palmer's audience, to the language of myth. So the poet produces a chastened poetry that flirts with nihilism, but one that also ironizes it: "Here another festival // to which no one is invited / and where expectation plays no part." The poet is not a nihilist—he opportunistically uses the idioms of nihilism to make art. At the very least, this means that art will survive.

Why not ask for more than just survival? However desirable such ends might seem to be, I take it that, for Palmer, they will inevitably compromise the art. At the end of "Music Rewritten," the poet writes:

Beneath the shadow of no and yes
nothing can be said

First there's sameness then difference
then the letter X across a face

then a line through a name
which is the wrong name in any case (*LB* 126)

Yes or no questions solicit the most basic answers we have. Nothing beneath them; they come in handy. On the other hand, since neither the public nor the private world can be reduced to a series of such questions, it might be only in the "shadow" cast by those questions that the "no-thing," the thing that is not a thing, i.e. the person, can emerge. Subsequent lines spell out this process. Sameness and difference are categories for dividing the world. These categories are superseded by the striking out of the image by the *X*—an act that carries threatening undertones—itself followed by the bureaucratic fulfillment of the negation of the person, the crossing out of that person's name. Such bureaucratic aggression is undercut, however, by the discrepancy between the person and name: it is "the wrong name in any case." First there is sameness then difference; the identity of a person with his or her face, then the difference of the person from his or her name. Where we might have taken refuge in the name as the proper designation, we come up against the fact that the name is mistaken. Thanks to Palmer's syntax, this unfolding seems inexorable: first, then, then. First sameness, then difference: no shortage of creation myths begin with this formula, including the myth of autonomous subject. Yes or no. Nothing can be said, but something can be shown. Binary thinking runs deep, but where it runs is beside the point.

Palmer's poetry is most alive when it can refuse a binary choice in the name of artistic integrity. One such choice is between engagement and disengagement from politics. His lively refusal is memorably displayed in "Sun":

Write this. We have burned all their villages

Write this. We have burned all the villages and the people in them

Write this. We have adopted their customs and their manner of dress

Write this. A word may be shaped like a bed, a basket of tears or an X

In the notebook it says, It is the time of mutations, laughter at jokes, secrets beyond the boundaries of speech

I now turn to my use of suffixes and punctuation, closing Mr. Circle with a single stroke, tearing the canvas from its wall, joined to her, experiencing the same thoughts at the same moment, inscribing them on a loquat leaf

Write this. We have begun to have bodies, a now here and a now gone, a past long ago and one still to come

Let go of me for I have died and am in a novel and was a lyric poet, certainly, who attracted crowds to mountaintops. For a nickel I will appear from this box. For a dollar I will have text with you and answer three questions (*LB* 191)

The opening refers to war crimes committed by the US military in Vietnam, and it evokes the central political problem for American poets of Palmer's generation who did not serve in the armed forces: how should one respond to atrocities committed in one's name? One way to respond is to criticize, hector, cajole those in power, to summon those outside of it to resist. Political engagement is by no means foolish, and might be ethical, if, for example, it did not serve to excuse one's receiving benefits from power. The problem with most antiwar poetry—and with the poetry of witness and testimony, which swept through the literary intellectual world in the 1980s, and to which *Sun* is a rejoinder—is that it reaches a moral high ground by leaving poetry behind. Sartre at least acknowledged this possibility when he set the terms of what it meant to be a committed writer. He did not think it possible to write politically engaged poetry. Poets disengaged—that was how they showed their commitment.[13] Carolyn Forché was rewarded for writing politically engaged poetry, but she initially believed that her experiences in El Salvador belonged in journalism.[14] Palmer's "Sun" is neither journalism nor a parody of the poetry of witness. Nor does it disengage from history. It responds to atrocity by revealing how even responsiveness is implicated in those atrocities. Language domesticates atrocity for readerly consumption. (One approves Walter Benjamin's remark, in the "Theses on the Philosophy of History," that "[t]here is no document of civilization which is not at the same time a document of barbarism,"[15] only to exempt our favored documents from this judgment—including the "Theses" themselves.)

"Write this." The terseness of the command, the quickness with which the poem reaches calamity, contrasts with the slow opening of Forché's famous poem, "The Colonel"—"What you have heard is true"[16]—which builds to a melodramatic flourish of human ears dumped onto the well-appointed table. As the phrase repeats, Palmer goes deeper into calamity: after the villages, the people in them, then their customs and manners of dress. Following this narrative of extermination and expropriation, a sudden transition to metacommentary: "A word may be shaped like a bed, a basket of tears, or an X." That rhyme of "dress" with "X" is outrageous, but it needs to be so, given the serious subject matter. It is an uncomfortable truth about "Sun" that its language shocks us more than the crimes to which it refers. That sudden shift is an avoidance, a move from realism to language play that prevents us from meaningful political intervention in the world. As Walter Benn Michaels has argued, foregrounding the "shape" of the signifier is an artistic practice compatible with, and maybe even indicative of, economic exploitation.[17] The line may be less an endorsement of attention to the shapes of words than an increase of self-consciousness about the limitations of those words, a warning against self-satisfaction. To write: "We have burned all their villages" is not to bear witness to the burning of actual villages. The person who writes this may have unattractive political motivations. He might be the masterly critic and interpreter who closes the circle, destroys the work of art, sexually dominates the woman, and, with a flourish, writes it all down on (i.e., destroys) the loquat leaf. He might be the egocentric who believes that he is a character in a novel, Zarathustra, a textual genie. The proximity of these intellectual fantasies to historical calamity is a reminder that the calamity itself is mediated by fantasy. Trying to get around this, even by means of some sophisticated theory, results in simplification: "Here is the poem called Theory of the Real, its name is Let's Call This, and its name is called A Wooden Stick. It goes yes-yes, no-no. It goes one and one" (*LB* 193).

The astonishing conclusion of "Sun" doubles down on the parity between writing and reality:

> Let me say this. Neak Luong is a blur. It is Tuesday in the hardwood
>   forest. I am a visitor here, with a notebook.
>
> The notebook lists My New Words and Flag above White. It claims to
>   have no inside
>   only characters like A-against-Herself, B, C, L, and
> N, Sam, Hans Magnus, T. Sphere, all speaking in the dark with their
> hands
>   G for Gramsci or Goebbels, blue hills, cities, cities with hills, modern
>   and at the edge of time
>   F for alphabet, Z for A, and H in an
> arbor, shadow, silent wreckage, W or M among stars
>
> What last. Lapwing Tesseract. X perhaps for X. The villages are known as
> These letters—humid, sunless. The writing occurs on their walls. (*LB* 193)

Amazingly dogged, these lines. Neak Luong is a village in Cambodia that was destroyed by an accidental bombing by a US B-52 in 1973; at least 137 people died, and several hundred more were wounded. (The event is mentioned in Roland Joffé's film *The Killing Fields*.) Such material begs for sensitive narrative reconstruction. But Palmer refuses this, and even finds space for linguistic play. He sticks with the tourist's notebook, overflowing with names that have nothing to do with Cambodia (and much to do with Western arts and culture), in an alphabet of floating signifiers.

The villages are known as "These Letters." But we have also burned all the villages, killed the people, adopted their customs and styles of dress. The writing "occurs" on walls that might as well be the pages we are reading. Or writing. Or burning. "Write this. We have burned all their villages"—in "Sun," the villages were always already our villages; the violence done to them is contained within the text we write. Something about this is discomfiting of course. Real people in Neak Luong died. Hundreds of thousands of others died due to US actions in Southeast Asia. Palmer wouldn't dispute those facts. He is not a linguistic idealist or relativist. But because he is a poet, and because poetry is an artistic form of language before it is a representation of reality, language comes first. His commitment to it paid off. Both poems entitled "Sun" in the book *Sun*, even though they resist the logic of representation that would allow for a traditional critique of the horrors of war, are a more compelling indictment of the whole Vietnam era than most antiwar poetry. This is not because they are *more antiwar* than other poems, but because they are *more poetic*. (There is a precedent for this: consider the relationship between *The Waste Land*, to which *Sun* is everywhere indebted, and the Great War.) Readers will turn the "Sun" poems (and the eponymous book) well into the future, and find there a terrible affirmation of artistic freedom and complicity both.

Poets with cerebral styles benefit from the palpable heat of emotionally charged subjects. Stevens, for example—how one feels about those late poems depends, in part, on the degree to which they are recognized as driven by feeling, not just philosophy. But they also benefit from subjects to which their cerebral styles can add something of substance. The moral imperative of confronting war and atrocity is serious enough to put a poetry of the linguistic turn in question, and "Sun" is bold enough to take this question up and answer it in the affirmative. If much of Palmer's later poetry feels less urgent than "Sun," it is not only because the poet is more confident about the place of poetry (these years coincide with vanguardist poetry finding a welcoming home in the academy) but also because the thinking that his poetry does and the position on which it insists are less risky. Here is "Autobiography 7," from *The Promises of Glass*:

> You go out for a walk in the rain.
> You make love in the rain.
>
> These are not the same
> acts. It might or might not
>
> be the same rain. The in
> might be two different ins,
>
> one an under, one a during.
> You sell fish of gold for a living,
>
> not goldfish, not living fish.
> You make a poor living.
>
> It rains day and night
> causing the river to rise
>
> and flood your knick-knack shop.
> You can step into this river twice
>
> unlike the river of life.
> Unlike the river of life
>
> this is a real river, brown and turbid,
> with many objects in it.
> Today I count: a drowned dog,
> short haired and of medium size;

an office chair, the kind that squeaks
when you lean back; the head of a stag

mounted on oak; endless mattresses
stained and striped like cheap ties;

a tongue-and-groove door lacking its knob;
a superannuated perambulator

such as I was paraded in as a child
by my mother in her cardigan, her blue

cotton skirt and sensible shoes;
the fractured limb of a buckeye

tree, whose fruit will paralyze
the nerves and lead to death;

an oar, a doll, an ice chest,
a camper shell and pesticide cans.

But what of these shadow-flowers with yellow stems?
What of panthers in the skins of men?[18]

Part of a series that runs through Palmer's late books, "Autobiography 7" confronts and parodies conventional wisdom about life writing (a challenge already issued in prose by Lyn Hejinian's *My Life*, and, more remotely, Gertrude Stein, in *Everybody's Autobiography*). This conventional wisdom is well-captured by Philippe Lejeune, who defined autobiography as "[r]etrospective prose narrative written by a real person concerning his own existence, where the focus is his individual life, in particular the story of his personality."[19] Palmer's poem does present a narrative, but it immediately departs from convention by its use of verse, its serial form (the title "Autobiography 7" invokes the prospect of multiple autobiographies, already a challenge to the idea that there is only *one* story of someone's personality), and by beginning not in the first but the second person: "You go out for a walk in the rain." From there, the poem plunges into the ambiguity of the preposition "in," which indicates either a space ("one an under") or a time ("one a during"). For the heirs of Saussure, close attention to language does not lead us to knowledge about the world but rather knowledge about language—signs lead us to other signs, each of which functions through its nonequivalence with the other signs in the language: "You sell fish of gold for a living, // not goldish, not living fish." When knowledge about the world seems to appear, we find more uncertainty: how could selling fish of gold make a poor living, unless the fish of gold were only valuable for their form (fish) and not their substance (gold)? Such a fixation on particular form provides a clue to the idea that the poem confronts, which is the reification of life via autobiography. It explains, too, the inversion of Heraclitus: "You can step into this river twice // unlike the river of life. Unlike the river of life // this is a real river, brown and turbid, / with many objects in it." You can only step into this river twice because it is *not* the river of life. The story of a personality is not the personality itself. Rather, this particular story is an artifact, just like the river and everything that comes floating down it—even artifacts that seem singular. "But what of these shadow flowers with yellow stems? / What of panthers in the skins of men?" These promise something unique but deliver something generic: a mashup of symbolist diction in the case of the flower, and, in the case of the panthers, a common forearm tattoo.

Now, I like this poem of Palmer's (and many of the other "Autobiography" poems). My criticism is not that it fails to deliver what it promises but that it delivers something we already know, and moreover something that we have not been tempted to forget. The conventional wisdom about autobiography is shot through with problems that are familiar to Palmer's readership: looking back, one reshapes the past to fit the present; the story of one's personality may actually be many stories, some of them contradictory, or it may not fit the shape of a story at all; the story of a life may be told with more insight by others, and so on. The reason these criticisms of conventional wisdom are so familiar is that they are regularly echoed by sensitive reading of the great literary autobiographies. The challenge to conventional wisdom is not wrong, but it is superfluous—except, and I think this qualification is important, if we are talking about a critique of "autobiography" as it appears in first-person autobiographical verse of the "commuter" variety. When set against that as a standard, "Autobiography 7" does succeed, in the way one succeeds at fishing in a stocked lake. The poem makes little use of the utopian, propulsive potential of verse, thematized in the unusual images of the closing couplet, a tendency that runs contrary to the retrospective, prosaic orientation of traditional life writing. Beginning with "I count," Palmer proceeds prosaically to his conclusion, frequently pausing at the ends of lines and dutifully deploying semicolons to retain grammaticality. Such fastidiousness kills the joy of parody.

It's not just the obviously literary poems in Palmer's late books that suffer in comparison with his earlier work. Even "I Do Not," which finds the poet returning to some of the ground covered in *Sun* (the war zone having shifted from Southeast Asia to the Middle East), is relaxed by comparison to its precursors:

I do not know English.

I do not know English, and therefore I can have nothing to
   say about this latest war, flowering through a night-
   scope in the evening sky.

I do not know English and therefore, when hungry, can do no
   more than point repeatedly to my mouth.

Yet such a gesture might be taken to mean any number of
   things.

I do not know English and therefore cannot seek the requisite
   permissions, as outlined in the recent protocol.

Such as: May I utter a term of endearment; may I now proceed
   to put my arm or arms around you and apply gentle
   pressure; may I now kiss you directly on the lips; now
   on the left tendon of the neck; now on the nipple of
   each breast? And so on.

Would not in any case be able to decipher her response.

> I do not know English. Therefore I have no way of
> communicating that I prefer this painting of nothing to
> that one of something.[20]

Timely and clever, the poem presents itself as a refusal that is really an acceptance: someone who says or writes "I do not know English" does know English, even if they don't know much. What are seemingly refused but secretly accepted are the moral implications of language use, including its use (and abuse) in wartime and its capacity to humanize those who do not speak our language. These issues are linked, of course: the more we humanize the enemy, so the story goes, the more difficult it will be to kill him. Modern warfare avoids this problem through technology, and technology turns war into a kind of poetry: "flowering through a night- / scope in the evening sky." The poet who would refuse war finds himself implicated in it. And as the poem proceeds, we find the project of humanizing the non-English speaker foundering on similar shoals, since what the poem ends up humanizing is not the non-English speaker but the poet himself. Humanitarianism becomes narcissism. This is a legitimate critique, particularly in the 1990s, when, "human rights" became a powerful justification for exercises of imperial power. The parody of consent ("may I now kiss you directly on the lips?") will offend some in the present moment, but it fits the critique the poem makes: the language of consent is a tool for domination. It is spoken only by the lover, not the beloved, and there is a strong indication that the lover might not be bound by it anyway (if he does not speak English, he would not understand the beloved if she spoke). Knowing English does not actually matter. It is an illusion to believe that it brings guarantees of mutual understanding, recognition, survival. These things are ultimately not effects of language but effects of power. One can speak the language of art criticism, one can tell jokes, one can describe cosmology or play with words—to mention just a few of the things that the non-English speaker does in "I Do Not." All this fluency, for what? "Still the games continue. A muscular man waves a stick at a / ball. A woman in white, arms outstretched, carves a true / circle in space. A village turns to dust in the chalk / hills."[21] As an expression of frustration and complicity in what then–*New York Times* correspondent Dexter Filkins called "the forever war," the poem succeeds. But aesthetically, it does lack something—friction, perhaps. The pervasive belief that language has the power to represent and thus deform a *given* world—the hard surface against which "Sun" strikes and ignites—is here abandoned in favor of the belief that language is *irrelevant* with respect to the world. The poem does criticize this stance, but readers of the poem are not tempted to take that stance in the first place. "I Do Not" is easier than the poems in *Sun*—easier to take up, easier to put away.

Should the difficulty of this body of work not be, in the long run, a liability? "[T]heir learning instructs and their subtlety surprises; but the reader commonly thinks his improvement dearly bought, and, though he sometimes admires, is seldom pleased." That is Dr. Johnson on the metaphysical poets. One might say something similar about Palmer. And critics have, frequently zeroing in on the ratio of ideas to pleasure in Palmer's poetry. They are not wrong to calculate this ratio, but their complaints (like Johnson's) say as much about them, and the pleasures they seek, as they do about the poetry and the pleasures it affords. If one looks to Palmer for the same sort of pleasure that one might find in, say, Allen Ginsberg, or Robert Hass, or Louise Glück (disparate though those pleasures might be), one won't find it. (One might, if one were reading Anne Carson or Jorie Graham). But just as Johnson's unnamed reader is not necessarily the best reader of Cowley, Donne, or Cleveland, neither would such readers be the best readers of Palmer. His best readers are going to have patience with the poetry of ideas because they will take pleasure in ideas as potential objects of art. Such readers will probably embrace Stein and Stevens, Olson and Oppen. They will be less impressed by the great stylists—Auden and Bishop and Merrill and the poets of the New York School, say—or poets whose achievements rest primarily in statement or pathos or both (for example: Adrienne Rich). Nevertheless, there are two serious limitations in Palmer's poetry that are important to note. Each of them is bound up with his strengths. The first has to do with the scope and durability of the linguistic turn as a theme. Obviously, by tying his work so closely to an intellectual project, the poet restricts his audience to a subset of the educated classes. But the move carries a greater risk, which is that intellectual projects wax and wane. The aftereffects of the linguistic turn are still with us, but on the whole fewer and fewer literary intellectuals (Lacanians excepted, of course) seem beholden to the idea that the formal study of language really can provide a method to solve otherwise intractable problems, or put our discipline on respectable footing once and for all. Ironically, it is Wittgenstein, a philosopher whose remarks crop up frequently in Palmer's work, whose later philosophy (and perhaps, indeed, his earlier philosophy) undoes the pretentions of the linguistic turn most completely. If we take seriously the claim that "to imagine a language is to imagine a form of life," then we need to revise our understanding of what attention to language gets us: not knowledge purified from, or everywhere opposed to, experience, but knowledge embedded in it. That said, the move toward thinking about language as a form of life also threatens the categorical distinctiveness of poetic language, which is why, I take it, Wittgenstein's appearances in Palmer's oeuvre are ambivalent: linguistic therapy would remove the conflict that underwrites Palmer's sense of vocation. As it stands, intellectual life may have left our poet behind. Lyric poetry that takes up the challenge of the linguistic turn might already be antiquarian.

The second limitation is Palmer's monotony. Tonally, he is a hedgehog, not a fox. "Ironic grimace after ironic grimace," writes Bedient, with a vengeance.[22] Apart from a few exceptions (the poems for Sarah, for example), he's right: Palmer's poems are a bitter tonic thematically, but they also sound bitter, as if lyric poetry of the linguistic turn disallowed emotional range beyond that found among the guests of the Grand Hotel Abyss. No doubt we have arrived at a point in history when it is very difficult to value the display of emotional range in art. "Emotional range" can seem worse than a pointless luxury item—it can seem obscene. But "very difficult" is not "impossible," and Palmer's work, in carving out a space for subjectivity between an art that would commodify it and an intellectual life that would dissolve it, fills that space with a tendentiously attenuated subject.

Given these limitations, I would probably not take the poet's complete works with me to a desert island. *First Figure* and *Sun* would suffice to cool the hottest, driest waste. In the meantime, however, the ambition and the self-critical skepticism of Palmer's poetic project are powerfully attractive. Eliot wrote in his defense of the metaphysical poets: "Our civilization comprehends great variety and complexity, and this variety and complexity, playing upon a refined sensibility, must produce various and complex results."[23] Palmer's poetry is complex but not various. If this means his sensibility is less refined than it might be, it also means that he possesses more commitment than we, the civilized, have come to expect from our poets, or ourselves.

Notes

1. Michael Palmer, *The Lion Bridge: Selected Poems, 1972–1995* (New York: New Directions, 1998), 69; subsequent references to this volume abbreviated as *LB*.
2. Lee Bartlett, "What Is 'Language Poetry'?," *Critical Inquiry* 12, no. 4 (Summer 1986): 750.
3. Keith Tuma, "An Interview with Michael Palmer," *Contemporary Literature* 30, no. 1 (Spring 1989): 10.
4. Thomas Gardner, *Regions of Unlikeness: Explaining Contemporary Poetry* (Lincoln: University of Nebraska Press, 1999), 289.
5. Raymond Geuss, "Poetry and Knowledge," in *Outside Ethics* (Princeton, NJ: Princeton University Press, 2005), 184–205.
6. Beyond Adorno, and the compelling interpretation of him put forth by Simon Jarvis, recent books by Brett Bourbon, Oren Izenberg, and Charles Altieri have attempted to theorize how poems (or poetry) might be compatible in some way with the larger project of knowledge production.
7. Gardner, *Regions of Unlikeness*, 279 (emphasis added).
8. Ludwig Wittgenstein, *Philosophical Investigations*, trans. G. E. M. Anscombe (London: Macmillan, 1953), 223e.
9. Roland Barthes, *A Lover's Discourse: Fragments*, trans. Richard Howard (New York: Farrar, Straus and Giroux, 1978), 3.
10. It explains his affinity for Paul Celan, whose work was even more radical and estranging than Palmer's in that it was not merely suspicious of poetry but of language as such. Celan supplies the epigraph for *First Figure*: "Niemandes Stimmer, wieder" (Nobody's voice, again).
11. Calvin Bedient, "Breath and Blister: The Word-Burns of Michael Palmer and Leslie Scalapino," *Parnassus: Poetry in Review* 24, no. 2 (2000): 171.
12. Max Horkheimer and Theodor Adorno, *Dialectic of Enlightenment: Philosophical Fragments*, trans. Edmund Jephcott (Stanford, CA: Stanford University Press, 2002), 1.
13. "For the word, which tears the writer of prose away from himself and throws him out into the world, sends the poet back to his own image, like a mirror." Jean-Paul Sartre, "What Is Writing," in *What Is Literature*, trans. Bernard Frechtman (London: Methuen, 1950), 32.
14. From the Poetry Foundation: "As reviewer Katha Pollitt observed in the *Nation*, Forché 'insists more than once on the transforming power of what she has seen, on the gulf it has created between herself and those who have seen less and dared less.' The poet herself admitted to the compelling nature of her Central American experience. 'I tried not to write about El Salvador in poetry, because I thought it might be better to do so in journalistic articles,' she told Jonathan Cott of *Rolling Stone*. 'But I couldn't—the poems just came.'" "Carolyn Forché (b. 1950)," Poetry Foundation, n.d., https://www.poetryfoundation.org/poets/carolyn-forche.

15. Walter Benjamin, "Theses on the Philosophy of History," in *Illuminations: Essays and Reflections*, trans. Harry Zohn (New York: Harcourt Brace Jovanovich, 1968).
16. Carolyn Forché, *The Country Between Us* (New York: Harper and Row, 1981), 16.
17. Walter Benn Michaels, *The Shape of the Signifier: 1967 to the End of History* (Princeton, NJ: Princeton University Press, 2005).
18. Michael Palmer, *The Promises of Glass* (New York: New Directions, 2000), 24.
19. Philippe Lejeune, *On Autobiography*, trans. Katherine Leary (Minneapolis: University of Minnesota Press, 1989), 4.
20. Palmer, *The Promises of Glass*, 97.
21. Ibid., 99.
22. Bedient, "Breath and Blister," 170.
23. T. S. Eliot, "The Metaphysical Poets," *Times Literary Supplement*, October 20, 1921.

CHAPTER 3

Susan Howe and Valuing

OREN IZENBERG

> The lyric poet reads a past that is a huge imagination of one form.
> —SUSAN HOWE

THE PREMISE OF this volume is that while the canon of poets in the period that we teach as "post-1945" has, to a large degree, been established by the combined hands of poets, critics, and anthologists, the same cannot be said of the poets we teach as "contemporary." Contributors have been charged to seize the reins of the sometimes haphazard process of literary evaluation; to go all-in for a poet, and to defend the claim that he or she *ought* to be one of the fortunate few used to characterize a period—just as Lowell, Bishop, Plath, Ginsberg, O'Hara, and Baraka are understood in their various ways to define the poetics of the mid-twentieth century.

One aspect of this charge is positive: we are to be explicit about the assessments that we propose, and to produce text in support of our judgments. The other is negative: "We don't want a lot of interpretation," contributors have been told; "we want what comes next." I have found this dual charge to be particularly challenging. Not so much the explicitness part; I am quite comfortable asserting that Susan Howe is an unassailably strong poet. I have been reading and learning from her work since I was seventeen years old, and she is a poet whom I am confident we will still be reading fifty years from now. Despite Howe's difficulty and idiosyncrasy, I don't think this is an idiosyncratic claim or even a particularly controversial one. The real difficulty lies in saying why we *ought* to value her in a way that deemphasizes the work of critical interpretation.

A plausible account of Howe's value will have to be able to address text like that found on the final page of "Fragment of the Wedding Dress of Sarah Pierpont Edwards" (see fig. 1), itself the final poem in the 2007 collection *Souls of the Labadie Tract*, and explain how such a narrow poem can give rise to the depth of feeling I experience in proximity to it.[1] Any account of Howe's persuasiveness as an artist will rise and fall on our ability to discover or grant the force of feeling in perceptions of language in strange arrays—the momentary shine of sense breaking through a cloud of letters or cutting through an aperture in space.

Figure 1

I'll confess in advance that it doesn't seem to me that I have *fully* honored the terms of our charge—the confident demonstration of what follows interpretation. I am more confident in my conviction that Howe is wrongly valued in ways that implicate interpretation—which is to say, not at all that she is unjustly esteemed, but that she has been esteemed for some wrong reasons. I hope that by saying something about why the wrong reasons are wrong, I will in the end be able make some preliminary claims about why the right reasons are right. What comes next will have to come next.

I

I will begin by producing some text: or some more, since text has already, though barely, begun to appear. Not quite—or not yet—in support of *my* value judgment; but first in order to see what aspects of the work seem to attract evaluation, or what there is in Howe's work for judgment to stick to. I want to say that there are three (or perhaps four) distinct modes of work standardly found in Howe's oeuvre. And to see that you only have to look.

First—and perhaps least (there is me, being explicit in my assessment)—there is the part of the work most recognizably "verse":

> A nightingale sings in
> secret language the bird
> is betrayed when her love
> song is made public in
> secret language a poet's
> public voice I bear the
> Mary Ellen name in ambiguity
> am a ghost you know
>
> Who was and was not
> What we come to know
> Who was and was not
> We sing side by side[2]

Divided into lines; plausibly, if not quite regularly, metrical (here, in the

1999 book *Pierce-Arrow*, they are dimeter lines—roughly anapestic); with diction that is recognizably, even stereotypically "poetic." Both its nouns (nightingale, voice, ghost, language) and its verbs (to sing, to bear, to know, and preeminently to be) are drawn from the not very deep well of nineteenth-century vocabulary that alerts us that poetry—perhaps even "lyric" (and here I note the proximity of the "secret" to "public")—is happening here. This mode is remarkably consistent across the long arc of Howe's work; while the poet's diction varies somewhat from project to project—incorporating proper names and terms of art from the compositional matrix of the archives that lie beneath so many of the poems—that variation makes less of a difference to the experience of the poems than one might imagine. Here are two examples—first from 1987, "Articulations of Sound Forms in Time":

> Occult ferocity of origin
> each winged ambition
> sand track wind scatter
>
> Inarticulate true meaning
>
> lives beyond thought
> linked from beginning[3]

and second from the 2010 elegiac volume *That This*:

> Is one mind put into another
> in us unknown to ourselves
> by going about among trees
> a garden to ease distance to
> fetch home spiritual things[4]

You certainly could not mistake one of these fragments or poems for the other; nor could you substitute one for another in the context of the sequences to which they belong; but the cumulative effect of these poems' insistent abstraction—abstraction of reference and from anything resembling a speech situation—is the emergence of something still more coherent and unifying than mere "style." We are put in possession of a distinctive sensibility: one that is announced by a uniform and unvarying tone, intense and impersonal and utterly without humor, as though spoken from a great distance by a machine or an angel.

Second, there is prose—a mode that oscillates between the voice of autobiographical narrative and the voice of scholarship in its historicist and high theoretical modes:

> I believed in an American aesthetic of uncertainty that could represent beauty in syllables so scarce and rushed they would appear to expand though they lay half smothered in local history.[5]

Even casual readers of Howe will be familiar with this mode from her best-known work, *My Emily Dickinson*, often misshelved as a work of literary criticism, largely on the merits of its prose argument.[6] But at a distance, and in the context of the work that follows, we can see that that volume's prosimetrical tendency is a consistent feature of all of Howe's poetic work for the past thirty years. The foundation of her commitment to scholarly excavation may be presented in more and less explicitly *psychological* terms (note the difference between the *aesthetic* justification of Howe's interest in history in *Souls of the Labadie Tract* and the sort of justification offered in *The Midnight*: "Maybe one reason I am so obsessed with spirits who inhabit these books is because my mother brought me up on Yeats as if he were Mother Goose"[7]), but it is always *autobiographical*. What the critical voice in Howe's work consistently tells is the story of its own development. *My Emily Dickinson* is in that sense paradigmatic—narrating, as it does, the emergence of a sensibility capable of laying claim to another writer as one's own, as though all the relevant aspects of what it is to be a person could be explained by a narrative of *intellectual* formation. It is as if the entirety of Wordsworth's *Prelude* consisted exclusively of the Cambridge books:

> During the 1980s I wanted to transplant words onto paper with soil sticking to their roots—to go to meet a narrative's fate by immediate access to its concrete totality of singular interjections, crucified spellings, abbreviations, irrational apprehensions, collective identities, palavers, kicks, cordials, comforts. I wanted jerky and tedious details

to oratorically bloom and bear fruit as if they had been set at liberty or ransomed by angels.

In 1862 Thoreau begins his retrospective essay called "Walking" by declaring: "I wish to speak a word for Nature, for absolute freedom and wildness." He tells us that when he walks or rather saunters out into nature from Concord, Massachusetts, "Hope and the future ... [is] not in lawns and cultivated fields, not in towns and cities, but in the impervious and shaking swamps." He enters each swamp as a sacred place, *a sanctum sanctorum*.[8]

Here, in *Souls of the Labadie Tract*, Thoreau's formative encounter with uncultivated nature is embedded within Howe's encounter with Thoreau's prose; the *sanctum sanctorum* of the "impervious" swamp has been transmuted into the bloom and fruit of language and narrative detail. In *The Midnight*, Howe's formative negotiation with maternal presence and absence, too, is narrated as an entry into an intellectualized aesthetic domain—into an encounter with poems, plays, painting, prose:

> Even before I could read, "Down by the Salley Gardens" was a lullaby, and a framed broadside. "He wishes for the cloths of Heaven" printed at the Cuala Press hung over my bed. . . . She hung Jack's illustrations and prints on the walls of any house or apartment we moved to as if they were windows. Broadsides were an escape route. Points of departure. They marked another sequestered "self" where she would go home to her thought. She clung to William's words by speaking them aloud. So there were always three dimensions, visual, textual, and auditory.[9]

Finally, and most distinctively, there is what we might call the visual mode of Howe's poetics, consisting sometimes of text that has been disoriented and layered to produce a page in need of navigation—as in a page from "Scattering as Behavior toward Risk" (1990) (see fig. 2)—and sometimes of images and objects that have been incorporated in whole or in part: Emily Dickinson's fascicle manuscripts; a fragment of lace from "Bed Hangings" in *The Midnight* (2003); a scrap of "Prussian Blue" fabric from Sarah Pierpont Edwards's wedding dress (reproduced several times: in *Souls of the Labadie*

Tract and again in *That This*); and most recently and strikingly of a hybrid between the two, as in the collaged textual materials of "Frolic Architecture" (2010). It may well be imprecise to conflate these different sorts of objects: Chelsea Jennings has recently and plausibly suggested that Howe's move from typographic experimentation to what Jennings calls a "facsimile aesthetic" represents a major transformation of the poet's work—thus my earlier uncertainty about whether there are three or four modes.[10] For the present discussion, however, I'd suggest simply that both of these modes occupy a similar *place* in Howe's work and the reception of it; they present similar hooks for attention, and give rise to similar acts of critical attention. I will treat them provisionally as belonging to the same category.

II

Howe herself has put us in mind of the multifarious and formative influence of Yeats in her coming to consciousness as an artist, and so it is to Yeats I

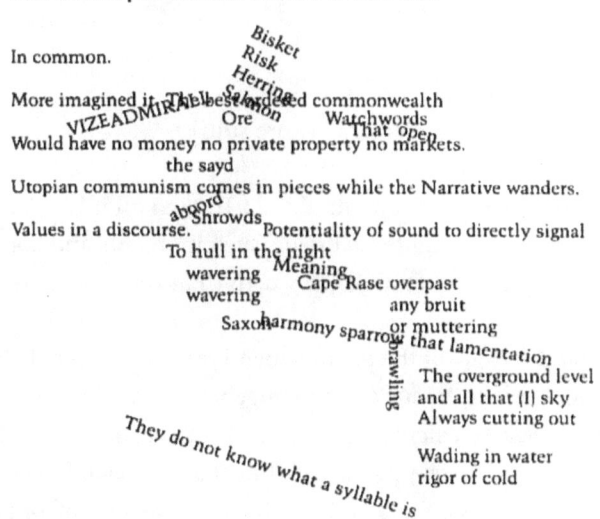

Figure 2

turn for some initial orientation in thinking through the problem of value in relation to such textual heterogeneity. Yeats's introduction to the aestheticized theory of history presented in "A Vision" begins with a meditation on Ezra Pound's Cantos, asking, in effect, where to locate the ground value in the face of such complex assemblage:

> For the last hour we have sat upon the roof which is also a garden, discussing that immense poem of which but seven and twenty cantos are already published. I have often found there brightly painted kings, queens, knaves, but have never discovered why all the suits could not be dealt out in some quite different order.... He has scribbled on the back of an envelope certain sets of letters that represent emotions or archetypal events—I cannot find any adequate definition—A B C D and then J K L M, and then each set of letters repeated, and then A B C D inverted and this repeated, and then a new element X Y Z, then certain letters that never recur, and then all sorts of combinations of X Y Z and J K L M and A B C D and D C B A, and all set whirling together.[11]

For Yeats, the poetic value of the Cantos—whatever it might be—would *not* depend on the considerable beauty of its component parts:

> Zeus lies in Ceres' bosom
> Taishan is attended of loves
>   under Cythera, before sunrise[12]

These are merely its A B C and its X Y Z. Though all might be, as the older poet acknowledged, "brightly painted," such moments and components are less kings and queens of established worth than they are knaves of dubious virtue.

Nor could the value of the poem depend merely on there being a statable compositional principle, such as the "algebraic" one Pound suggests in his back-of-the-envelope calculations; or in his tossed-off observation that the finished poem will "display a structure like that of a Bach Fugue"—a dubious proposition in any case. Yeats's mind rebelled at the idea of an order that did not comprehend everything. The very idea that Pound's poem might contain "letters that never recur" was anathema. An order must penetrate to the very bottom, or it is nothing. Indeed, as Yeats described it, even a total order is not enough, if it is not of the right kind:

> I may, now that I have recovered leisure, find that the mathematical structure, when taken up into the imagination, is more than mathematical, . . . that here is no botch of tone and colour, all Hodos Chameliontos, except for some odd corner where one discovers beautiful detail like that finely modelled foot in Porteous' disastrous picture.[13]

Order, as Yeats understood it, must be more than merely describable, like the rules of a game; and it cannot exist in a way that stands apart from human concern, like the rules of mathematics. Order must be *true*. Just as a beautiful foot cannot redeem a disastrous and chaotic picture, so too if the order of the poem does not meet the imperative of the unifying imagination, then that order is a "botch." What matters about a poem including history is that it tell you not what happened but what must happen, what always happens—again and again.

I'd like to keep these coordinates: the unorderable, the *merely* ordered, and the *significantly* ordered, in mind as companion to the three modes of text I have presented, in our effort to introduce some order to the whirling letterforms of Howe's oeuvre. Another way of describing the message of the concatenated forms of Howe's career is to observe that the recurrent theme of her work is precisely the *nonrecurrence of elements*: aesthetic AND historical—not infrequently of both at the same time.

In a brief essay on Howe and Allen Grossman for *The Cambridge Companion to American Poetry since 1945*, I described a change in what it means to think of a poet as an "academic poet," charting the transformation of that concept from a term of abuse aimed at rubbishing a poet's style as overelaborate and quiet to a poetry that engages seriously with the way knowledge is generated in the present.[14] In the contemporary moment, I argued, what counts as *knowledge* is so bound up with the institution of the university that it may plausibly seem that anyone who wishes to take seriously a critique of contemporary society must go through the university. The professor-poet is a knowledge worker of a particular sort, a salaried professional intellectual; she is charged with the reproduction not merely of her own subject but of the institution's values and protocols; with the conscious and deliberated reproduction of unconscious orientations.

And thus, although it seems to me that no poet has imitated her *style*—and perhaps having shown you her modes, we can see why: the tripartite structure is repetitive and distinctive enough that to do so would look slavish—she has been immensely influential in producing the *research project* as the sensible unit of composition. In this, of course, Pound is a predecessor—for what are the Cantos but the product of immense, if idiosyncratic research—and Olson an even more direct and acknowledged influence. But her own distinct institutionally inflected influence may be seen, both in those who were directly taught by her at Buffalo, in the documentary poetics of Jena Osman, who was her student (I am thinking here of a book like *Public Figures*, which creates a poem out of the narrative of the attempt to create a poem that would re-create the point of view of public statues by showing us pictures not just of them but of what they are looking at); and also in the work of Robin Schiff, whose style comes through Marianne Moore but whose orientation toward the richly textualized objects that allow for the construction of narratives of self, I want to say, derives in part from Howe. And so I proposed that in Susan Howe's poems, the forms and institutions of the contemporary condition of knowledge-work appears as the compositional matrix or "enabling condition" of the artistic work; and the social arrangements underwriting those forms and institutions emerge as a kind of antagonist.

Howe ties the narration of knowledge production as a whole to a specifically institutional critique: most obviously or vividly in *My Emily Dickinson*, where she was more or less singlehandedly responsible for opening a conversation about Dickinson's manuscripts: making the conditions of access to them, the normalizing alterations performed upon them, and the generic expectations with which we frame them into a subject with deep consequences for textual study. As she writes in "These Flames and Generosities of the Heart," her lyric essay most explicitly about the problem of value:

> I wonder at Ralph Franklin's conclusion that these facsimiles [she has just before reproduced an image of one of Dickinson's manuscripts] are not to be considered as artistic structures?
>
> How can this meticulous editor, whose acute attention to his subject matter has yet to be deciphered in the neutralized reading even her

fervent admirers give her, now repress the physical immediacy of these spiritual improvisations he has brought to light?[15]

Other, more unalloyed poetic texts, like "Thorow," nonetheless begin with prefatory mediations on the conditions that gave rise to the poem, which will be recognizable to the inhabitants of a slightly different stratum of university life, the professionalized creative writer:

> During the winter and spring of 1987 I had a writer in residency grant to teach a poetry workshop once a week at the Lake George Arts Project, in the town of Lake George New York. I rented a cabin off the road to Bolton Landing, at the edge of the lake. The town, or what is left of the town, is a travesty. Scores of two-star motels have been arbitrarily scrambled between gas stations and gift shops selling Indian trinkets, china jugs shaped like breasts with nipples for spouts, American flags in all shapes and sizes, and pornographic bumperstickers.[16]

While "Melville's Marginalia" launches its poetic flights from the abject depths of the hapless graduate student's labors:

> The extracts in *Melville's Marginalia* were collected, transcribed and collated by a dedicated sub-sub graduate student in a time before librarians, scholars and authors relied on computers or Xerox machines. Perhaps his leviathan dissertation exhausted him. The copyright page of the Garland edition lists Melville's dates, 1819–91 and the dates of Cowen, 1934–87.[17]

Here, the cumulative polemical effect of Howe's prose is an emergent global argument against all our learned attempts at putting things in order—both the methods of sense-making AND the social, economic, and institutional arrangements that support and are supported by them. The world as Howe's poetry finds it is a travesty; a travesty of a town in which the ostensibly creative labor of collecting and collating the world is enabled by grant grubbing, commodified into obscene and misogynist trinket making; "rewarded" only with exhaustion and immiseration.

There is a widespread critical consensus that this conjunction of description and critique lies at the center of Howe's contribution to contemporary poetry. Peter Nicholls affirms as much: "Howe clearly believes with Pound that the poetic medium offers a means by which to reactivate a 'history' long since atrophied under the dead hand of the academy.... The thrust of Howe's poetics is thus firmly against cognitive and narrative modes of historical understanding, against any secure position of knowledge from which we might view the past."[18] Ming-Quian Ma offers a similar argument in the form of a veritable collage of critical consensus:

> Howe's poems, on the contrary, subpoena history for an investigation of its violent crime against women. "Sometimes I think my poetry is only a search by an investigator for the point where the crime began," says the poet ("Difficulties"). That being so, poetry becomes for Howe counterdiscourse to history, a "rereading [of] the reading that a social status quo puts [her] through." ... When enacted in poetry "with the foregrounding of language" ..., Howe's rereading demonstrates itself through a complex and peculiar textual feminism that, "growing out of but rethinking the work of Stein," is characterized by its "rematerializing written expression."[19]

The consensus of the critics is justified, because they are right. They are right in that they are in line with Howe's accounts of her own intentions;[20] they are right in light of the threshold discourse framing her work, as in her oft-cited prefatory statement to the 1990 collection *The Europe of Trusts*: "I write to break out into perfect primeval Consent. I wish I could tenderly lift from the dark side of history, voices that are anonymous, slighted—inarticulate";[21] and they are also right in light of the prose statements that are inarguably *part* of the work.

Indeed, one effect of the prosimetrical erasure of distinctions between statements about the work, statements framing the work, and statements within the work is that we may feel defended in advance from the charge of failing to attend to the formal features of her poems as we produce our evaluation of them. In practice—which is to say, in practical criticism—this has meant that the account of the value of Howe's poems has emerged by placing what seems most idiosyncratic, distinctive, and resistant about her work—its working with text—in "productive" conversation with its own explanatory or internal interpretive discourse.

III

I have described the diverse and rebarbative elements of Howe's works, the critical celebration of (some) of them in terms of their resistance to "cognitive and narrative modes of historical understanding," AND the poet's apparent embrace of this celebratory account at some length. Now I want to state the insufficiency, not of the work, but of this account of the work: not because it is wrong as interpretation, but because it is inadequate to a defense of the value of the poems. It is inadequate on several grounds. The first is what I will call

A. OBVIOUSNESS

By obviousness, I mean a kind of attunement to audience, such that Howe's intentions, stated or implicit, flatter the theoretical tools that her interpreters bring to bear upon the work. Howe's work collaborates with our critical preconceptions and facilitates the kinds of analyses we are inclined to make. In essays and interviews describing her experience in the Poetics Program in Buffalo, for example, Howe may attest to her marginal relation to academia, to her autodidacticism, to her unsystematic reading of theory; but nonetheless, at the same time, she attests to the way that her integration into academic culture reinforced her intuitions and gave them a shape and a vocabulary. Another way of saying this is that critics have found Howe congenial and her difficulties worth pursuing because she presents recalcitrant mysteries to us embedded in themes that we recognize and analytical devices we trust:

> In the seventeenth century European adventurer-traders burst through the forest to discover this particular long clear body of fresh water. They brought our story to it. Pathfinding believers in God and grammar spelled the lake into *place*. They have renamed it several times since.
> In paternal colonial systems a positivist efficiency appropriates primal indeterminacy.[22]

The thrust of the argument here, in "Thorow," will be familiar: what we discover in the history of American settlement is that all forms of "normalization"—onomastic, syntactic, doctrinal, geographic—are of a piece; as are the "positivist," the "paternal," and the "colonial." The "method" of Howe's imaginings here and throughout the work may not be wholly forensic, or rational, or, for that matter, secular. Frequently they depend on the mystification of intuition, on reading chance as fate, or upon the magic of what she calls the "telepathy of the archives"; nevertheless, her method of assembly, too, flatters our self-conception as interpreters. What Howe affirms in her elaborate constructions is not just *what* our interpretations yield; it is that when we lean upon the texts, *they will yield*—turning the skein of surface into significance through the industry of our attention:

> Often by chance, via out-of-the-way card catalogues, or through previous web surfing, a particular "deep" text, or a simple object (bobbin, sampler, scrap of lace) reveals itself here at the surface of the visible, by mystic documentary telepathy. Quickly—precariously—coming as it does from an opposite direction.
>
> If you are lucky, you may experience a moment *before*.[23]

What is wrong with *obviousness*? What could be wrong with being right? We may recall here the grounds on which Yeats objected to Pound, for incorporating those "certain letters that never recur." Howe appears to be taking the other side. The truth of the work, she tells us, is not in the order that it imposes or discovers, but in "the moment before": in the particulars that order cannot assimilate. But I want to say that the form of the work—its prosimetrical oscillation between the particular in its "primal indeterminacy" and the discourse of value that would affirm it as particular—violates its own premises. Obviousness, that is, violates the textual condition of Howe's work by normalizing its strangeness under a discourse of antinormativity. The *argument* is that the unassimilable particular grounds a critique of the forms of order that seek to domesticate it: paternal, colonial, positivist. But such framed particularity is a *thematic*; and the production of the thematic premise of a puzzle assimilates the puzzle much more fully than any supposed "grammar" could ever do. The experience of reading on these grounds is not the experience of difficulty, opacity, or singularity, but of difficulty borne, opacity obviated, and singularity counted upon. And it contradicts its own thematics when the encounter with wildness is obviated—made into the obvious—its destination known in advance.

The second reason the critical consensus around Howe's work is inadequate—again, not in its evaluation but in its accounting for the grounds of value—is for what I will call

B. COMPREHENSIVENESS

Comprehensiveness, too, is a term of art for a particular analogical mode of theorizing. If there is a signature feature of Howe's many scholarly and poetic forays into the tradition she calls "antinomian," it is the way she unites all forms of dissent (theological, intellectual, political, gendered) with her own intellectual dissent, in a series of rhymes that echo across her work: her experience of being shut out of the stacks at Harvard's Widener Library as a teenager in the 1950s with Emily Dickinson, who "built a new poetic form from her fractured sense of being eternally on intellectual borders";[24] Howe's creative wandering through Melville's marginalia (themselves compiled by an obsessional graduate student) with the habits of mind afflicting the paradoxically central minor poet James Clarence Mangan; or here, in *Pierce-Arrow*'s elaborate description of Howe's discomfort in a frigid microform room in the basement of the Sterling Library at Yale with its account of logician Charles Sanders Peirce's own discomfort within the philosophical establishment he transformed with the anomalous force of his invention:

> Suppose a man is locked in a
> room and does not want to go
> out his staying is voluntary
> is he at liberty no necessity
> What shall we finally say if
> Members of the Department of
> Philosophy Harvard University
> undertake the task of sorting
> his papers now in the custody
> of Harvard's Houghton Library

> The Microform room at Sterling has several new microfilm readers with Xerox copiers attached. At the left of each viewing screen there is a thin slot for a copy card. Above each slot five singular electric letters spell H E L L O in red as if to confide affection
>
> in all their minute and terrible detail these five little icons could be teeth[25]

One could, without great difficulty, imagine trying to produce an analysis that might "complete" and justify the thrust of Howe's imaginative work here. It would connect the various forms of suffering entailed by the professionalization of intellectual life (whether Peirce's or Howe's) with the forms of thought that are reproduced by it (professional philosophy; the disciplinary orthodoxy that regards archival research as the province of particular modes of scholarship). One might further seek to connect both of these to the false welcome offered by a language that is "standardized" in both its material forms and its social decorum. One might aspire to connect *all* of these to the vague menace of technological reproduction and then to the largest material determinants of all of these disparate formations. If one were to succeed at such an explanation, we might find ourselves back on the terrain of obviousness. But as the accretive logic of this list begins to suggest, the more one seeks to imagine explaining, the more such an explanation begins to seem imaginary. Explanatory comprehensiveness is less a theme than a feeling; and it is a feeling purchased precisely by *not* offering an explanation, by locating the value of art in the feelingful assertion of one. If Howe is understood to stake the value of her poem on explanations that are not available by other means, then I want to suggest that the reduction of explanation to a feeling of explanation is the mark of an *absent* discourse for valuing art.

IV

So where do we find the distinctive power of Howe's work, if not in the statable ideas with which she has framed it, and not in the sentiment of comprehensiveness to which it gives rise?

Once again, I'll begin with some text: an "Existential Graph" from the

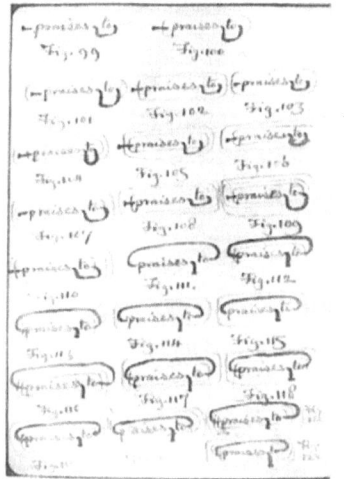

Figure 3

manuscripts of Charles Sanders Peirce (see fig. 3). It is also the beginning of Susan Howe's collection *Pierce-Arrow*, after the table of contents and acknowledgments and before the first section, entitled "Arisbe."[26] How shall we describe this text? It contains twenty-four iterations of the same phrase: "Praises to." The varying encirclements and loops that distinguish one from another and are decoded on the facing page are notations for forms of quantification that allow the mapping of natural language into logical space.

What shall we say about it? First: that Howe has made a poem out of Peirce's pioneering work in philosophical logic by means of recontextualization. The significance of this is, let us say, *obvious*—one would not have to work hard at all to produce the thematics in which this recontextualization will be seen as a trumping of arid rationality. Indeed, the poet has produced it for us: "Putting thought into motion to define art in a way that includes science, these graphs, charts, prayers, and tables are free to be drawings, even poems."[27] And critics have been quick to assent: as Will Montgomery tells us in his 2010 book devoted to the poet, "the visual threatens to supplant the symbolic. . . . Howe abstracts Peirce's symbolic logic and reads it against the grain, pursuing symbols at the expense of logic."[28]

This *obvious* account is also *comprehensive* in the way I have just described, because seeing logic and freedom as opposed—each undoing the other—is an intuitive or reflexive judgment that is sustainable only by refusing to engage in detail with the philosophical context in which Peirce was operating. That is, it is only by means of this *thematic* of oppositions that what looks like a conflict between institutions comes to look instead like a conflict with institutionality itself.

In contrast, I want to say instead that *Pierce-Arrow* gathers its considerable force not by pitting poetry against "logic"—the unassimilable opacity of the visual against the aspirational clarity and transparency of philosophical discourse, the unorderable particular against the misery of order—but precisely by inserting itself into an order whose entailments are *different* from those of philosophical logic, but not less clear, rigorous, or specific. Poetry, in other words, as mediated by its tradition, is itself an institution with an affirmative discourse of value.

The work of praise, or epideixis, is one of the traditional tasks of the poet. Tying the work of praise to the *rhythms* of praise is one of the fundamental methods of the poet. I want to say that the notation of praise in *Pierce-Arrow* is distinctly rhythmical, in a way that (pace Montgomery) is not constitutively visual (that is, its visuality is not of the essence) but constitutively *metrical*. Shall we not describe this page as a poem of praise in twenty-four stanzas? This description recontextualizes Peirce's existential graph, certainly, but not simply by "annexing" it to poetry understood as antagonist to philosophy; rather, Howe locates the graph (by formal means) in a poetic tradition that is already profoundly philosophical. The tradition includes the Akathistos, the sixth-century hymn of praise in which the Byzantine Church celebrates the mystery of the divine motherhood of the Virgin Mary and her role in the equally mysterious Incarnation in twenty-four stanzas:

> Seeking to know knowledge that cannot be known, the Virgin cried
> to the ministering one: Tell me, how can a son be born from a chaste
> womb? Then he spake to Her in fear, only crying aloud thus:
>
> Rejoice, initiate of God's ineffable will:
> Rejoice, assurance of those who pray in silence!
> Rejoice, beginning of Christ's miracles:
> Rejoice, crown of His dogmas!

> Rejoice, heavenly ladder by which God came down:
> Rejoice, bridge that conveyest us from earth to Heaven!

This tradition includes also Spenser's *Epithalamion*, a poem of praise in twenty-four stanzas in which the central problematic of an intricate calendrical organization is the problem of how to arrogate an act of praise traditionally belonging to God and his royal proxies on behalf of one's own ordinary life:

> Ye learned sisters which have oftentimes
> Beene to me ayding, others to adorne:
> Whom ye thought worthy of your gracefull rymes,
> That even the greatest did not greatly scorne
> To heare theyr names sung in your simple layes,
> But joyed in theyr prayse.
> ...
> Now lay those sorrowfull complaints aside,
> And having all your heads with girland crownd,
> Helpe me mine owne loves prayses to resound,
> Ne let the same of any be envide:
> So Orpheus did for his owne bride,
> So I unto my selfe alone will sing,
> The woods shall to me answer and my Eccho ring.

Within this context, we can "decipher" Howe's constellation of this page of apparently singular marking with Peirce's own "translation" of its abstractly praiseful meaning:

> Somebody praises somebody to his face
> Somebody does not praise everybody to his face
> Somebody is not praised to his face by anybody
> ...
> Nobody within himself praises all men
> There is nobody whom all men praise within themselves

The problem of the relation of quantification to the act of praise *is* a poetic problem. Let us say that the problem the Akathistos hymn is meant to address is given in 122: *There is nobody whom all men praise within themselves*—but there should be. Whereas the problem with which the *Epithalamion* must wrestle is at least twofold: "somebody is praised to his face by all men," whereas "somebody is not praised to his face by anybody"—a problem the poem aims to remedy. I might "translate" the problem of Howe's *Pierce-Arrow* by the following phrase: "Somebody who has praised *praising* to its face is not praised to his face by anybody—until now." This translation, because it contains a new object of praise (praise itself), and because it offers the possibility of changing the conditions it describes (what was dispraised is now acknowledged), cannot quite be rendered in Peirce's formal notation; it must take Peirce's formalization wholesale into itself, as its object of analysis. But the fact that praise is an unevenly distributed privilege is not an insight that challenges *all* available canons of value by focusing our attention on material that *cannot* be assimilated; it is precisely the grounds on which the poem inserts itself into an ongoing *poetic* conversation about value that must be entered if it is to be revised.

V

There are a variety of ways to assert the value of work that has not been recognized. There's an older way, now disfavored, that imagines the poetic tradition to be a single conversation, an order transformed by the appearance of the new poem. You will recognize it from T. S. Eliot's "Tradition and the Individual Talent":

> No poet, no artist of any art, has his complete meaning alone. His significance, his appreciation is the appreciation of his relation to the dead poets and artists. You cannot value him alone; you must set him, for contrast and comparison, among the dead. I mean this as a principle of æsthetic, not merely historical, criticism. . . .
>
> In a peculiar sense he will be aware also that he must inevitably be judged by the standards of the past. I say judged, not amputated, by them; . . . we do not quite say that the new is more valuable because it fits in; but its fitting in is a test of its value.[29]

Critics have taken Howe to be a poet of a more up-to-date sort; one who uses the systematically devalued particular as a lever for undoing the work of value altogether. At the beginning of this chapter, I suggested that the more obviously "poetic" parts of Howe's poems were the least distinctive—that they do not contain the hooks that attract the act of valuation. And indeed, we might note the striking absence of the "poetry part"—those lyrical bits that are squares and rectangles *not* because they are prose paragraphs, and *not* because they are archival material cut from some larger whole, because they are measured—from the dialectic between unassimilable particular and assimilating explanation.

I now wish to say something slightly different about them: that *whatever* we think of Howe's poems as *verse*, their presence is diagnostic of the kind of evaluation due to the whole—because metrically ongoing acts of valuation, the poetic intersection between particular and universal is the place where what is most distinctive about the poetry acquires its force. What Eliot gives us is not—or not only—a conservative's attempt to discipline poetic innovation by enjoining it to adopt a modest relation to traditional practice. He gives us also the insight that what it means to value poetry is (first) that we have taken it to be doing the kind of work that we take poetry to do. Such "insight" may have the structure of a tautology; but it is a tautology that is built into the structure of valuing itself. What Howe's text—in all of its variety—persistently shows us is that *not* just anything can be a poem; that what can be assimilated to the terrain of the poem illuminates *not* the arbitrariness of our purposes, but the purposiveness of poetry. The value of her poetry derives less from its forms than from its purposes: from its negotiations of praise; its navigations of the work of commemoration; and its ways of connecting these to the quantification of human actions. These are its moments of intense affective density, in which the rhymes of recurrence signal the presence of a persistent—and insoluble—problem.

Notes

1. Susan Howe, *Souls of the Labadie Tract* (New York: New Directions, 2007), 125.
2. Susan Howe, *Pierce-Arrow* (New York: New Directions, 1999), 101.
3. Susan Howe, *Singularities* (Middletown, CT: Wesleyan University Press, 1990), 30.

4. Susan Howe, *That This* (New York: New Directions, 2010), 104.
5. Howe, *Souls of the Labadie Tract*, 16.
6. Susan Howe, *My Emily Dickinson* (Berkeley, CA: North Atlantic Books, 1985).
7. Susan Howe, *The Midnight* (New York: New Directions, 2003), 74.
8. Howe, *Souls of the Labadie Tract*, 16. The bracketed insertion is Howe's.
9. Howe, *The Midnight*, 74–75.
10. Chelsea Jennings, "Susan Howe's Facsimile Aesthetic," *Contemporary Literature* 56, no. 4 (Winter 2015): 660–94.
11. William Butler Yeats, *The Collected Works of W. B. Yeats*, vol. 14: *A Vision*, ed. Margaret Mills Harper and Catherine Paul (New York: Scribner, 2015), 3–4.
12. Ezra Pound, *The Pisan Cantos*, ed. Richard Sieburth (New York: New Directions, 2003), 95.
13. Yeats, *A Vision*, 4.
14. Oren Izenberg, "Poems in and out of School: Allen Grossman and Susan Howe," in *The Cambridge Companion to American Poetry since 1945*, ed. Jennifer Ashton (Cambridge: Cambridge University Press, 2013), 187–201.
15. Susan Howe, *The Birth-Mark: Unsettling the Wilderness in American Literary History* (Middletown, CT: Wesleyan University Press, 1993), 146.
16. Howe, *Singularities*, 40.
17. Susan Howe, *The Nonconformist's Memorial* (New York: New Directions, 1993), 99.
18. Peter Nicholls, "Beyond *The Cantos*: Ezra Pound and Recent American Poetry," in *The Cambridge Companion to Ezra Pound*, ed. Ira B. Nadel (Cambridge: Cambridge University Press, 1999), 81–82.
19. Ming-Quian Ma, "Poetry as History Revised: Susan Howe's 'Scattering as Behavior toward Risk,'" *American Literary History* 6, no. 4 (Winter 1994): 718. Ma quotes from the work of Bruce Andrews, George Hartley, and Hank Lazer.
20. Maureen N. McLane, "Susan Howe, the Art of Poetry no. 97," interview, *Paris Review*, no. 203 (Winter 2012).
21. Susan Howe, *The Europe of Trusts* (Los Angeles: Sun & Moon Press, 1990), 14.
22. Howe, *Singularities*, 40.
23. Susan Howe, *Spontaneous Particulars: The Telepathy of Archives* (New York: New Directions, 2014), 18.
24. Howe, *My Emily Dickinson*, 21.
25. Howe, *Pierce-Arrow*, 5.
26. Howe, *Pierce-Arrow*, xii–xiii.
27. Howe, *Pierce-Arrow*, ix.
28. Will Montgomery, *The Poetry of Susan Howe: History, Theology, Authority* (New York: Palgrave Macmillan, 2010), 134.
29. T. S. Eliot, "Tradition and the Individual Talent," in *Selected Essays, 1917–1932* (New York: Harcourt, Brace and Company, 1932), 4–5.

CHAPTER 4

Fanny Howe's Power

PETER O'LEARY

TWO UNUSUAL FEATURES characterize the work of Fanny Howe. The first is its overt religious content, the Catholicism she converted to in the late 1970s. The second, which is sometimes the elephant in the room when talking about Howe's poetry, is the presence of her sister Susan Howe's work in any discussion about what makes Fanny Howe's work important. Both these elements, my frames here, deserve to be discussed in detail when making a claim about the value of Howe's poetry. In short, that value arises from an intellectual independence feeding her creativity. Both frames allow us to see this independence. From one view, despite significant but superficial similarity to her sister Susan's work, this is seen as a freedom from the intellectual context she shares with her sister, that of academically driven experimental poetry, Language poetry in particular. And from the other view, despite the implications of involvement with a vast institutional and doctrinal system, this is seen as a freedom won by way of her Catholic faith, which bluntly makes Howe quite different from nearly all of her peers, few others of whom readily profess such faith in their work, even fewer others of whom put that faith into action. It might seem counterintuitive, but the affirmation of a Catholic faith that Howe makes in her poetry is crucial evidence of her intellectual independence, from which her creative power clearly springs.

Religion

The first frame, her religious engagement, is unusual for a poet of Howe's generation (she was born in 1940). Until fairly recently, her work has been characterized as experimental, with much of her earlier work published by presses such as Littoral Books, Sun & Moon, and the Figures, which are associated with Language poetry. A sequence of her work was included in Ron Silliman's seminal anthology of Language poetry, *In the American Tree* (1986). As a group, Language poets are spiritually and religiously averse, committed instead to the tenets of cultural materialism. Howe's religious views are emphatic and prophetic; these modes of address saturate almost all aspects of her poetry. There can be no looking away from the religious element of her poetry, which makes her connection to Language poetry peculiar. She is an especially independent writer, something of a loner, a condition her conversion to Catholicism seems to have intensified. It was inspired by the circumstances of her marriage as a white woman to a Black man of mixed race, writer and activist Carl Senna, in the racially volatile climate of Boston in the 1960s, a situation dominated by Howe's conviction that "[o]nly white women in this country have historically been condemned to a lower status than black men, and that was when they crossed over and married black men."[1] It was also inspired by her respect and reverence for Senna's mother, a Black woman and devout Catholic, and then the unfortunate circumstances that befell her after her marriage to Senna dissolved and she found herself in racially divisive Boston with three mixed-race children trying to make ends meet.

The presence of Catholic thought and even doctrine in Howe's work is intense, magnifying crucial concerns about misfortune, poverty, disenfranchisement, and the promise of salvation into a curiously witty and anxious poetry of fable, aphorism, and rumination. A poem from *Second Childhood*, a collection published in 2014, has a characteristic combination of religious parable, private contemplation, and surrealistic, spiritual affirmation:

Mirror neurons experience the suffering that they see.
A forest thick with rust and gold that doesn't rust.

I saw a painting where the infant Jesus was lying on his back
on the floor at the feet of Mary
and his halo was still attached to his head.

And another painting where there were about forty
baby cherubs
all wearing golden halos. Gold represents the sun as
the sun represents God . . .

Figs, bread, pasta, wine and cheese.
These are not the subconscious, but necessities.
People want to be poets for reasons that have little to do with language.
It is the life of the poet that they want, I think.
Even the glow of loneliness and humiliation.
To walk in the gutter with a bottle of wine.
Some people's lives are more poetic than a poem
and Francis is certainly one of those.

I know, because he walked beside me for that short time
whether you believe it or not. He was thirteen.[2]

Francis of course refers to Saint Francis of Assisi, the mendicant friar and one of Catholicism's greatest saints (also the namesake of the current pope of the Church, for whom Howe has tremendous admiration and whose papacy had perhaps already begun when Howe was drafting this poem, first published in 2014[3]). Howe implies that Saint Francis is a kind of incarnated mirror neuron. Mirror neurons belong to a special class of brain cells that enable humans to imitate each other and, more crucially, to adopt other points of view and empathize. Neuroscientist V. S. Ramachandran has argued that mirror neurons lie at the root of culture, enabling what he calls our "two core mediums, language and imitation."[4] Francis's life is more poetic than a poem because the empathetic suffering he felt is a stigmatizing force of culture itself. Through Francis, a follower can feel Christ himself, like warmth from the sun. In Catholicism, the cult of the saints permits believers to access them as real, enduring, intervening personalities; as exemplary types, in the sense that Max Weber provides, but also as living, guiding forms, members of the communion of saints, who make up the faithful on earth, in purgatory, and in heaven. "Devotion to the saints is an expression of the doctrine of the communion of saints, a belief that even death does not break the bonds that tie Christians together."[5] What otherwise might read as fantasy or even delusion—especially among Language poets—elaborates powerful convictions, arising from the experience of uncertainty, humiliation, trouble.

Elsewhere, Howe writes of the "churn of creation," connecting this perception to feelings of loneliness and belonging: "For some persons, meditation, contemplation, prayer indicate that there is an emptiness already built into each body and it is that which (paradoxically) makes them feel at home in the cosmos."[6] Feeling at home, feeling the pressures of exile: these themes are repeatedly revisited in Howe's work, articulated as a critique of economic unfairness in the form of empathetic speculations. A poetry sequence entitled "In the Spirit There Are No Accidents" includes a page that runs:

> I feel the city grow wild with desire fertile
> as turned-over sod in the zoo at day's end.
> At the old Boston Lunatic Asylum
> the windows are smashed, packs of dogs live in the basement,
> elegant freezers unfold. Your heart you can hold in your hand
> and did, approaching from the side, my head bent with shame
> at having been in the world so long, and still feeling young.
> We should have walked on the esplanade twenty years ago.
> Now I know how to comfort a human like you;
> then I'd have held one.[7]

The lyric charge in these lines comes from the mystery of the identity of the "you" being addressed. Is "you" a lover, a friend in crisis, an invocation of an older self? The scene is fraught: a derelict asylum, packs of feral dogs, expressions of shame and regret. Each of these elements expands from the observation in the opening line, "I feel the city grow wild with desire." The expression of desire is lunatic, canine, shameful. What does she mean by, "your heart you can hold in your hand / and did"? It aligns somehow with the lines that follow, "my head bent with shame / at having been in the world so long, and still feeling young." Repeatedly, one encounters claims like this one, shame as an empathetic dowsing rod, alerting the poet to others' shame, reaching in imagination to embrace them.

In this same sequence, Howe demonstrates another characteristic of her work, which is an unusual attunement to forgiveness. She writes:

> Son the One who was also called Sun
> I crave your heat but fear the burning
> Domesticate your fire and send sufficiency
> Zero has gathered into a hole
> By the road where living gives
> An atavistic echo, the bank's
> A thief. And I am without
> Retinue. The feel of accidie
> Is a collar, metal and economic,
> When the world takes up no space but I[8]

Superficially, these lines enact self-deprecation, even a kind of self-flagellation. Where is the forgiveness? In the Catholic Church, forgiveness is sought in confession. These lines are richly confessional, admitting to the desire to be united with the burning power of God, but also admitting to finding in God only a hole of existential despair whose zero she cannot fill but feels instead as a collar of accidie. Accidie is acedia, which is spiritual sloth. It is torpid, tempting, and absorbing, like gazing into the black sun of melancholy (in which there is "no space but I"). In the Church, the sacrament of penance, which happens during confession, enacts both conversion and forgiveness. Only God can forgive sins; therefore, in seeking forgiveness, the faithful must turn back to God, to change their minds from sin and sinfulness; in short, to convert. Penance is called a sacrament of conversion because "it makes sacramentally present Jesus's call to conversion."[9] In light of Howe's conversion, the confession she makes in this poem seems all the more poignant. How can she be forgiven for such narcissism? The judgment implied by the absence of any punctuation after that final "I" is chilling. And yet, because of its confessional mode, the poem permits the reader of the poem to enact that forgiveness, to complete the penance it wants.

How else has Howe's conversion to Catholicism, and the doctrines of the Church, changed her outlook and thereby her poetry? Consider the opening poem in the sequence entitled "The Nursery," which situates an understanding of life recognizable to a believing Catholic but problematic to the typical liberal position on abortion. The poem begins:

> The baby
>   was made in a cell
> in the silver & rose underworld.
> Invisibly prisoned
>   in vessels & cords, no gold
> for a baby; instead
> eyes, and a sudden soul, twelve weeks
> old, which widened its will.[10]

"Twelve weeks old" is the telling phrase, the point when the baby (named as such rather than "fetus") suddenly gains its soul, along with its eyes, enmeshing it in an underworld of life, widening its will. ("Invisibly prisoned" is a nice lyric touch.) This is a bold poem for a poet who made her life in the corridors of liberal academia. She is claiming that a baby has a soul by the time the first trimester of a pregnancy ends. The shape of the life to come is "etched in this cell . . . / where no sun brushed its air."[11] She's denying the liberal position that an abortion is not the taking of a life. And yet, she is not completely reflecting the position of the Church, which states unequivocally, "Human life must be respected and protected absolutely from the moment of conception. From the first moment of his existence, a human being must be recognized as having the rights of a person."[12] You might argue that Howe is splitting the difference here—accepting that an unborn baby has a soul, which goes against the grain of secular liberal political beliefs, but placing the manifestation of that soul at twelve weeks, which goes against the grain of the catechism of the Church. I think this can be taken plainly as an example of Howe's independent streak. Another sequence, "Lines Out to Silence," concludes with a similarly striking statement. Unlike "The Nursery," "Lines Out to Silence" takes as its lyric subject the terms of a degraded relationship and the ruinous interiority they create in the poet. Here's the final poem in the sequence:

> I may never see the Vatican or Troy
> but only let me sit in a car somewhere

I recognize as home by the hand
of the one I love in mine—

just once—o universe—one more time[13]

The choice between the Vatican or Troy—between the solaces of faith or the mythical truths of war—seems altogether crucial in reckoning Howe's connection to the Church, which came into her life, after all, because of her fraught relationship with Carl Senna. The Church is a vexed source of meaning for her, but it is not a place of erotic vitality. In this light, the plaint of the last line of the poem is particularly affecting, a lyric gesture that would be as easily recognized by Sappho or Catullus as by a contemporary reader.

And yet Catholicism is a constantly informing source of her power. In her poem/essay "Catholic," Howe writes, "If you go into exile alone, without a companion or child the landscape remains hostile and nauseating. The hills and highways are emblematic of a purgatorial God-empty fate. What if we named certain places on earth after their metaphysical properties? For instance, what if a penitentiary was called Federal Exile or State Purgatory?"[14] *God-empty fate* is an especially wrenching prospect, and yet she suggests it as a default condition, including for herself and loved ones, to say nothing of most of the academics with whom she has spent her life. (She describes Carl Senna during the years of their marriage as "a Catholic without faith," for instance.[15]) And it's no coincidence that while she articulates her own despair, she turns her mind to those who suffer even more acutely, such as the imprisoned. But it is from this experience of God-emptiness that the welcoming aspects of her faith arise. In *The Winter Sun*, an autobiographical series of prose meditations, she writes, "I had been raised and continued to live among skeptics, scholars, atheists, and artists. What my conversion was meant to do was keep me safe from irony, to keep my childhood hope intact, to allow me to live with a certain schedule that occurred outside human time. Even if my faith was on a low burn," she confesses, "I still went to mass."[16] Skeptics, scholars, atheists, and artists: these are people who belong to academic culture. Howe, perhaps because of her long-standing residence among such people, regards her conversion as a talisman, protecting her from the allergy to the spirit that dominates academic culture, in the humanities especially, and also the Language poets, among whom irony and secular critique are the main salves against suffering and emptiness. Simone Weil, whose thought is vitally important to Howe's own, famously observed, "There are two atheisms of which one is the purification of the notion of God." This is a proverb people like to quote in various contexts. It occurs to me that Howe's work constitutes an effort to articulate the unmentioned, second atheism in Weil's quotation, which I might characterize, following a phrase in one of Howe's poems, as an atheism of disintegration: "The human is a thing / who walks around disintegrating."[17] "The avant garde," she insists in another poem, "worships history, the others / choose mystery. So far, God, this may be my last / book of unreconstructed poetry."[18] Though she belongs to the avant-garde, she has chosen mystery over history. The last observation in the poem, that this may be her last book of unreconstructed poetry, sweetly characterizes the wit that makes her poetry such a pleasure to read.

In a pastoral letter for Lent 2014, Pope Francis wrote about three kinds of destitution: material, moral, and spiritual. Francis defines destitution as "poverty without faith." It characterizes the experience of life for many people in the modern world, urged by circumstance to choose history over mystery. Material destitution is the state of those who lack basic rights and whose lives are thereby stripped of dignity. Moral destitution is slavery to sin and vice, especially the vices of greed and addiction arising from runaway capitalism. Spiritual destitution is turning away from God and rejecting his love.[19] Part of the thrill, the genius even, of Howe's poetry is the unusual force with which it engages states of material destitution—homeless tramps and seekers left by the wayside in various economies, material and spiritual—all the while making bold claims to rectify, improve, and heal the states of spiritual destitution that plague many of us, including (and perhaps especially) readers of contemporary poetry. And of how many contemporary poets is that true? It's not just that religion is her subject, but destitution and her own struggle with despair at ever rectifying it. Like Saint Francis himself, Howe's mission is to bring a message of compassion and salvation to her readers. Her poem/essay "Catholic" concludes with a claim, "I think you can know more if you do things that are fearful or unpleasant, as long as they do not include hospitals or jails," followed by what I take to be her evangelical credo: "This is why I keep moving and only stop for the Eucharist in a church where there are sick, vomiting, maimed, screaming, destroyed, violent, useless, happy, pious, fraudulent, hypocritical, lying, thieving, hating, drunk, rich, poverty-stricken people."[20] Her faith represents the prophetic strain of Catholicism, for me the most enduring and vibrant of its strains, which says, in essence, that the Church has problems and the world has problems, and both are on the road to perdition. So repent! An unreconstructed poetry will show you how.

Sisterhood

My second frame is the relationship between Howe and her older sister, poet Susan Howe, who was born in 1937. (There is also a third Howe sister.) Both poets have gained recognition, artistically and professionally: Fanny received the Ruth Lilly Poetry Award from the Poetry Foundation in 2009; Susan received the Bollingen Prize in American poetry in 2011 and the Robert Frost Medal from the Poetry Society of America in 2016. Both have held professorships at prestigious universities, Fanny at the University of California, San Diego, Susan in the Poetics Program at the State University of New York at Buffalo. Both are published by major independent poetry presses, Fanny by Graywolf Press and Susan by New Directions.[21] These recognitions are deserved: both are superb poets. Which is something quite rare in English-language letters, whose great sibling writers include the Jameses (Henry, William, and Alice), the Brontës (Charlotte, Emily, and Anne), and the Vaughan brothers (Henry the poet and Thomas the occultist). And not really any others.[22] This mutual achievement alone is a remarkable fact.

And perhaps it should be left at that. Is there actually any meaning that can be drawn forth from the achievements of the Howe sisters in poetry beyond accounts of sibling rivalry or cooperation, whatever the facts may be? I once heard the quip, "Henry James wrote novels as though they were philosophy; William James wrote philosophy as if it were a novel." Is there a plausible quip to be made about the Howe sisters? In some crucial respects, their work is remarkably similar: both emerged from associations with Language poetry before finding more widespread attention; both are unusually focused on religious themes, Susan on antinomian Christian themes and figures found in New England, Fanny on Catholic themes and figures more often of the twentieth and twenty-first centuries. In the likely event that their work endures, this second aspect will be a source of fascination (and potential confusion) to future readers and scholars. In fact, their very different work is mutually illuminating.

In an astute essay on the work of the Howe sisters, Albert Gelpi suggests that their divergent involvement with Emily Dickinson clarifies their own work. He claims that while Susan Howe has a historical imagination, Fanny Howe, like Dickinson herself, has a lyric imagination.[23] This claim is unusual because it is Susan Howe's work on Dickinson's poetry that has been epochal. In *My Emily Dickinson*, first published in 1985, and a subsequent essay, "These Flames and Generosities of the Heart," published in 1993, Susan completely transformed the way Dickinson's poetry is read. "In Howe's passionately argued reading," writes Gelpi, "Dickinson's feminism made her a radical experimentalist in poetic form. She withdrew not just from patriarchal culture but from the conformities of publication and print culture in order to be free to capitalize, to punctuate, and to lineate her poems on the page as consciously calculated spatial structures."[24] Gelpi goes on to describe Susan's perception of the male editorial control of Dickinson's printed poems, from Thomas Wentworth Higginson in the 1890s, to Thomas H. Johnson in the 1950s (who famously restored the dashes to the poems), to R. W. Franklin in the 1990s, to represent a distortion of the work so powerful, it has essentially eclipsed Dickinson's conception of and intention in her poems. "To Howe," writes Gelpi, "the printed versions are different poems, and such editorial intervention constitutes not just an aesthetic defamation but a hostile and repressive political act."[25] Gelpi argues that Howe sees Dickinson as a "crypto-Language poet," because of the materiality and implicit cultural critique in her poetry.[26]

Susan Howe's poetry typically derives from antecedent texts or even scholarly concerns.[27] This might explain her faddish popularity among academics in the early 1990s, when I was first encountering her work, which like many at the time I found intellectually exciting and thrilling in its diction. Susan was as likely then to give a lecture to a literature department as to give a poetry reading. Her books are made up of sequences of compressed, elliptical, and telegraphic poems swept along by a palpable, high-strung passion. A page from "The Nonconformist's Memorial," the title sequence of a book published in 1993, is characteristic of her work from this period and more generally:

> In the Evangelist's mind
> it is I absolutely I
> Word before name
> Resurrection and life are one
> it is I
> without any real subject
> all that I say is I
> A predicate nominative
> not subject the I is
> the bread the light the door
> the way the shepherd the vine[28]

The Evangelist refers to Saint John, the writer of the fourth Gospel. Though experimental in cast, Susan's language here (and typically elsewhere in her poetry) is traditionally poetic, if unpunctuated. The last two lines above could be a litany from a sermon or a list of keywords in a gospel concordance. Her poetry activates both of these valences: religious plaint and scholarly minutiae. Despite this traditional language, the scene of her poetry is in the vicinity of the antecedent texts or scholarly concerns that spark her imagination. Shelley, Melville, Charles Sanders Peirce, Jonathan Edwards, and Wallace Stevens: these figures are her sources.

Devin Johnston suggests, however, that Howe's penchant is less for these figures than for the "textual wilderness" their work invites her into, permitting her to equate wilderness and the literature they produce. "In a moment of terror or crisis," claims Johnston, "[Howe's] mind becomes other to itself, transcending the circumscribed palisades of order and rationality."[29] Lew Daly, in his spirited appraisal of the prophetic impulse in Howe's poetry, argues that "The Nonconformist's Memorial" relays "news of a power beyond the reach of mediators . . . , unmanipulatable [sic] at the level of language, like dictation in the Prophets is."[30] "Historical imagination gathers in the missing," writes Howe in "Frame Structures," the 1995 preface to her collected early poem sequences, published under the same title in 1996. What Johnston suggests is a penchant for the irrational, and what Daly claims as a kind of antinomian dictation, Howe herself says simply is the historical imagination itself. Gelpi believes that Howe's poetic imagination is essentially Protestant: "[Her] Protestant imagination assumes a fractured world, bereft of systems of certitude and structures of belief but haunted by the traces and intimation of ultimate meaning and truth, as the individual seeks, through and despite the ambiguous mediations and slippages of language, to piece out the possibilities of meaning and life." "What is left of God" for Howe, he continues, "is language,"[31] a truly modern dilemma she exacerbates, intensifies, and finally reifies through the use of a traditional poetic diction Shakespeare would recognize.

By contrast, according to Gelpi, Fanny Howe's poems seem much more like Emily Dickinson's than Susan Howe's. "It is not so much a matter, with Fanny," writes Gelpi, "of Dickinson's direct influence as a comparable focusing of verbal and structural means that determine word, image, and line and thereby center the psychological and emotional registration of the poem." Consider the following page, taken from Fanny's sequence *O'Clock*, initially published in 1995, in comparison with the selection from Susan's "The Nonconformist's Memorial" above. The themes are similar—both poems reflect the religious imagination, for instance—but the focus is quite different. Susan's poem enacts a public, impersonal hermeticism; Fanny's enacts something more cryptic, a private hermeticism tenderly exposed:

Into the forest I went walking—to get lost.

I saw faces in the knots
of trees, it was insane, and hands
in branches, and everywhere names.

Throughout the elms
small birds shivered and sang
in rhyme.

I wanted to be air, or wind—to be at ease
in outer space but in the world
this was the case:

Human was God's secret name.[32]

The human scale commands Fanny's attention: fears and anxieties especially, but also forests, small birds, milk and tea, rain, begging, what God might feel like to the human senses. The small birds shivering and singing in rhyme is the kind of note typically struck in Fanny's work: surreal but magical, like a fairy tale. (The names on the trees is familiar from *As You Like It*. Fanny invokes a Shakespearean fairyland, derived from the literary pastoral.) Scenes such as this one in her work have the effect of transforming obvious anxiety into a trait of a character in a classic work of children's literature. Anxiety begins to feel like a virtue. The opening line of the poem, however, alludes to the opening canto of Dante's *Inferno*, which serves as a prologue to the whole *Divine Comedy*. Who is the most famous poet to have gotten lost in a forest? Implied in these lines is a confrontation with the divine, one that leaves the poet, like Dante before her, uneasy. She claims to want to be "at ease," but the actuality of this forest is more forbidding, "insane," supersaturated with signs as in a manic episode. The human scale that absorbs her imagination is experiential at heart, which perhaps explains why, like Dante, she encounters the divine and the supernatural in her poems, rather than imagining in them suffusions by an immanent God.[33]

On another page in *O'Clock*, Fanny writes:

The dirt feels sweet
to the cheek of the sick.

When you're up against the grit
there's no more fear but fever
persists among fairy insects

and the smell of God is animal.
Cool grass is your nurse, and sandalwood.[34]

Here, the diction is lyrical and straightforward (no especially fancy or obscure words), but also echoing of fairy tales, whose elements it seems to compress. Fairies—even fairy insects—are frequent visitors to Fanny's poems. They focus human wishes, despite their supernatural provenance. Marie-Louise von Franz, a disciple of Jung's who one time lectured at Black Mountain College, studied fairy tales, which she suggested reveal unconscious truths otherwise hidden from view. For this reason, she argued, fairy tales infrequently involve the ethical concerns of a culture, which are often in plain view, but instead provide "guidelines of an *ethos* of the unconscious, that is, of *nature itself*."[35] In Fanny's poetry, children live in especially close proximity to the fairy world, as to nature itself. Adulthood brings with it forms of destitution. "[T]he smell of God is animal." Von Franz claims that all attempts to resolve fairy-tale morality result in paradox, with one exception: "*Anyone who earns the gratitude of animals, or whom they help for any reason, invariably wins out. This is the only unfailing rule*," which she interprets to mean that in the conflict between good and evil, "the decisive factor is our animal instinct, or perhaps better, our animal soul; whoever had it with him is victorious."[36] In Fanny's poetry, the presence of fairies—which are like manifestations of our animal souls—is a sign of victory.

Note as well her feeling for personal pronouns in the passage above, always in lyric poetry where the voltage comes from. "Her characteristically short, taut, sometimes witty poems are," writes Gelpi, "like Dickinson's, dense and centripetal, inscribing moments of a spiritual and psychological quest, word by packed word, image by edged image."[37] There is a subtle music to Fanny's poetry. Note the off-rhyme of "sweet" and "grit," the assonance that travels from "fear" to "fever," the mixture of assonance and alliteration that carries from "persists" to "fairy insects." "Grass" and "nurse" whisper to each other, and "sandalwood" merges sounds from "animal" and "cool."

While both Susan and Fanny are drawn to Dickinson, the most isolated of all American poets, only Susan has been able to explain her attraction in terms recognizable to academic readers. Fanny has not found so congenial a reception among such readers. Nor does it make much sense really that this intense, Catholic, lyric poet found publishers within the Language community. She is not drawing on the intellectual contexts of experimental writing and academic criticism in ways comparable to her sister. Fanny writes sequences of short and obsessive religious poems, as Dickinson often did herself. For over twenty years, she wrote and taught in a literature department at the University of California, San Diego, that has been especially committed to avant-garde writing, cultural studies, and literary theory. Somehow, she seems to have thrived by making her intellectual life in the vicinity of those who are going other ways entirely. Her sister's career must have often seemed to her the very thing she meant to avoid.

So how did Fanny manage to work in such an environment, and what comfort did she take in this academic world? In *The Winter Sun*, she describes the flimsy building in which she worked, which most other professors avoided, preferring to work at home, but where she "stayed locked in my office from 7 a.m. until 7 p.m. every day, reading, writing." She describes the corridors of the building as "cryptically empty," and which she seems to have haunted, finding nearby her office a photograph of Michel de Certeau, a Jesuit scholar and historian of mysticism, who worked for a time at San Diego. The photo "mysteriously impressed and comforted" her; she began to read de Certeau's book *The Mystic Fable*. She describes its effect on her as comparable to a communion wafer that is also a mind-altering drug. "No matter how exciting and recognizable his passages were," she writes, "I didn't dare speak of them to anyone. For one thing, no one talked about God there. For another, living imaginative writers were seen as bothersome in the Department of Literature and were not expected to have any ease with theory or cultural studies. It was a time of strange contradictions, when people who loved literature were considered reactionary and people who despised it were in the vanguard."[38] Amid these contradictions, Howe read de Certeau, and her curiosity about this writer and his thoughts intensified. "I was a convert after all," she writes. "I had decided to seek belief or die. That was my choice and part of my strange vocation."[39] In privacy, in solitude, de Certeau confirmed that choice to seek belief. Which also reaffirmed her status as an outsider, more like Dickinson and less like her sister.

What Makes Howe's Poetry Good

The basic elements of Fanny's poetry have not changed much over time: straightforward, often unadorned formal features and diction that suggest naïve, plainspoken convictions; a tendency toward aphoristic phrases that don't quite gel into aphorism, avoiding universal truth but suggesting something just as useful; and a pervasive fairy-tale quality. These elements belong to a rhetoric of sincerity, which hasn't been a feature of the experimental poetry traditions with which her work is most readily connected. Consider the opening of "Second Childhood," the title poem of a 2014 collection, which exhibits all of these features:

> I have a fairy rosary called Silver who answers questions when I dangle her in the sun at the window.
> So I've asked her if I have a big ego and she swings from side to side to say no.
> We have other children for friends.
> We don't understand why we are here in the world with horrible grown-ups or what the lessons are that we're supposed to learn.
> It's not helpful for us to hear ourselves described in religious, geriatric or psychological terms, because we don't remember what they mean.
> One cruel female said, "Don't laugh so much. You're not a child."
> My cheeks burned and my eyes grew hot.[40]

All the lines in this stanza are end-stopped, long and short sentences without any obvious prosody. How is this not prose? (It was first published in the "Comments," or prose, section of *Poetry* magazine as it happens.) Somehow, subtly, it isn't. Something about the naïve tone in the opening line especially propels these sentences into poetry. What is a fairy rosary? Lines later in the poem offer no help with this question, worrying instead about problems of the ego:

> One ego is like a spider clutched to a web of its own making.
> It turns to enamel and hardens on fulfillment.
> Many egos fill up the whole body, every part to the tiniest hair.
> Some egos are like fingernails that have been stifled by brittle paint.
> All egos have something impersonal about them. They live deep inside like viruses and unlike gods who play in outer air.[41]

All egos have something impersonal about them: that's her aphoristic style, but what does it mean? The statement that follows, "They live deep inside like viruses / and unlike gods who play in the outer air," demonstrates her poetic talents plainly: mildly surreal but more avidly visionary, the statement performs the kind of surprising comparison that characterizes her pleasing wit. A critic might speak of the charm of her poems. But *viruses* is the nasty, vivid word that flares out from this page.

In Fanny's poems, fairy tale verges into religious testimony: she conveys the urgency and excitement of both children's parable and spiritual confession. For Fanny, the divine is to be discovered like a monster in the forest springing out to frighten you. Like Dante encountering the leopard, the lion, and the she-wolf who stand in his way, driving him down into the Inferno in order to avoid their ferocity, Fanny confronts monstrous cruelties in her own poems, from her own acedia to the misfortune of the destitute. While she doesn't flinch from representing the horrors of the world in her poems, she also doesn't hide that fact that these horrors frighten her. Nevertheless, the proximity to horror as expressed in her poetry strengthens the resolve of her faith.

This, I believe, is where her lyric power originates: the desire, in the face of meaninglessness, misfortune, and all forms of human suffering, to express faith. "Nuns, monks and swamis / have fought this same anxiety. / (No meaning. No interiority.)"[42] "You find in Howe," writes Maureen McLane, "both an inward and an outward eye. Lyric may require solitude but most often you find in Howe's poems not the bliss but the agony of solitude. Before her solitudes, behind them, lies a sundering, an impasse. Howe the lyric surgeon is looking to suture these gaps with the threads of her lines."[43] The gaps McLane imagines the lines of Howe's verse stitching up are filled by her admirable and agitated gaze at the abyss, which she fortifies with a faith, often bewildered, in the redeeming grace of God. "There is nothing I hear as well as my name / Called when I am wild. The grace of God / Places a person in the truth / And is always expressed as a taste in the mouth / Walking with your arms wide open . . ."[44] The truth of God's grace is a taste in the poet's mouth, a desire to fling the arms wide open. The grace Fanny credits is incarnational, felt in the body, tasted on the tongue. In Catholicism, the doctrine of the Incarnation is "the assuming of a human nature by God, specifically by the Logos, the divine Word."[45] Unresolved questions arise from the statement of this doctrine, including whether the Incarnation would ever have occurred had Adam and Eve not committed original sin. Fanny, through her expressions of the misfortunes of others, is unusually attuned to good and evil:

The edge of the dome is slipping
like a fool's pudding
under silver. It's dawn, I'm up

aggressively begging: God

> give me a penitent haircut
> and a cell—not a hospital—
>
> to defend my errors in.
> And no answers, please, to any of my questions.[46]

"The theological stance of Fanny Howe's poetry," writes Gelpi, "strives to be incarnational rather than gnostic and 'antinomian.' That is to say, it assumes a world broken and fractured through human agency but also redeemable through human agency responsive to God's informing grace."[47] Like a desert father or mother, she contemplates the divine in matter, in its human form, focusing on mercy, magic, friendship, children, saints, scholars, sinners, and the oppressed. She couldn't be further from the skepticism of most contemporary literary intellectuals.

The connection to Dickinson's work that Gelpi establishes is helpful. But it doesn't quite explain the growing appeal of Howe's lyric poetry. "No meaning. No interiority," she insists. Her poetry is unusually attuned to the condition of the interior life from which lyric poetry arises; furthermore, she includes in her lyrics opportunities for her readers to join in a communion with her own inwardness, marked by desires and worries, thereby demonstrating the degree to which she respects her readers' own desires and worries. Consider this page from "Poem from a Single Pallet," which situates her desires in terms of the tenets of social justice that burn within her:

> But I, too, want to be a poet
> to erase from my days
> confusion & poverty
> fiction & a sharp tongue
>
> To sing again
> with the tones of adolescence
> demanding vengeance
> against my enemies, with words
> clear & austere
>
> To end this tumultuous quest

> for reasonable solutions
> to situations mysterious & sore
>
> To have the height to view
> myself as I view others
> with lenience & love[48]

The opening of the poem is sarcastic. Being a poet can't erase confusion and poverty from your life. (Often enough, being a poet increases these things.) After all, a poem describing the desire to become a poet is commonplace in lyric poetry, from Shakespeare's sonnets, to Wordsworth's meditative odes, to Williams's happy genius of his household. But it's not so common to connect that impulse to a gesture of self-improvement so that the poem aligns with many readers' hopes for themselves: *To have the height to view myself as I view others with lenience & love*. In the opening line of this lyric, there's a gentle echo and refutation of Marianne Moore's "I, too, dislike it."

Locating the tone of this wonderful poem is a challenge. Is the poem sincere? Almost all of Fanny's poetry is sincere. How then to account for the opening stanza, which suggests, contrary to what it says, that becoming a poet will in fact subject you to confusion and poverty, to abiding fictions and a sharp (presumably, vindictive) tongue? Will poetry really enable her to view herself and others with lenience and love? The poem concludes:

> To be free of the need
> to make a waste of money
> when my passion,
> first and last,
> is for the ecstatic lash
> of the poetic line
>
> and no visible recompense.[49]

The shift in tone in these concluding lines is striking, a rebuke of the more cynical opening. These lines suggest that becoming a poet in truth, and contrary to the implications of the first four stanzas, enables her to commit to the only economy that matters, "the ecstatic lash / of the poetic line," a richness whose invisible compensation is felt as freedom: freedom from money to express her great passion. What a poem!

In light of it, we can see that Howe's lyric inwardness, protected by an intellectual and literary independence that has appealed to a wide readership, bears some resemblance to Robert Creeley's, who likewise conveyed the vexed quality of his inner life, especially fraught in the famous earlier work, mellower and more contemplative in the impressive later work. Consider the poem "Consolatio" from *Windows*, published in 1990, which plays with the rhythms of nursery rhyme and aphorism:

What's gone is gone.
What's lost is lost.

What's felt as pulse—
what's mind, what's home.

Who's here, where's there—
what's patience now.

What thought of all,
why echo it.

Now to begin—
Why fear the end.[50]

The sing-song rhythms sway the poem from side to side to reveal an existential dread whose confusions, acknowledged and accepted, drift into the consolation indicated by the title of the poem. The Latin title alludes to the complex rhetorical moves of the genre of the consolatory oration, found in Plutarch, Cicero, and Boethius. And yet his poem couldn't be more plainspoken. Creeley here is availing himself of a classical tradition the way Howe invokes fairies and fairy tales.

Earlier, I invoked sociologist of religion Max Weber, attributing to his thought a focus on exemplary types, in reference to Saint Francis. Weber's focus was less on exemplarity than on charisma, a trait he judged essential to the "rise of religions" in the development of culture. By charisma, he meant the trait of having "extraordinary powers," which come from "a gift that inheres in an object or person simply by virtue of natural endowment" or "produced artificially in an object or person through some extraordinary means."[51] Whether inherent or extraordinary endowment, charisma in this definition operates precisely like grace, which in Catholicism is understood as "God's free and forgiving self-communication that enables humans to share in the trinitarian relationship of love."[52] For a Christian, Christ is the ultimate charismatic core from which all exemplarity and grace body forth. Even the materially, morally, and spiritually destitute person can be touched by this grace. In *Gravity and Grace*, Simone Weil wrote, "This irreducible 'I' which is the irreducible basis of my suffering—I have to make this 'I' universal."[53] Howe's poetry is an ongoing effort to transform through charismatic grace the irreducible lyric "I" of her poetry into a universal voice. For her, whatever the universal might consist of functions in her poetry as a set of moving, charming examples. ("I have a fairy rosary named Silver . . .") "Several times," writes Devin Johnston, "I have heard [Howe] say that she regrets titling poems, or numbering sections, or defining the relationship between parts. I think her ideal involves small poem/sections, one per page, that might be independent or part of a larger unit, ambiguously."[54] Each of these independent parts provides an example, not of fulfillment of some progressively realized goal but, instead, of itself, both its inward and outward aspects, reflected for a moment. Toward the end of her poem "A Vision," which includes the passage about Saint Francis quoted earlier, she writes:

> You may be called to a place of banality or genius,
> but as long as it is your own happiness that responds to it,
> you are available to something inhuman.
> Mozart sat at the piano for the better part of every day.
>
> All over the world monks have lived in desert hovels
> as scribes, prophets, mendicants.
> They are the extreme realization of one aspect of human personality
> that tends toward lack of possession and solitude.[55]

Monks, scribes, mendicants, Mozart, Saint Francis, prisoners, the ailing, fools, cruel females, people in prayer, the mistreated: each is treated in her compelling poetry as an example, an irreducible "I," a vessel into which some grace might be poured, because, as she says, human is God's secret name.

Finally, let me be clear about the meaning of Fanny Howe's work for young poets. What she rejects is a temptation that is readily available in the institutions that help poets produce their work nowadays. I'm speaking about practical choices that derive from a familiar state of mind that can be called incrementalist. Because the stakes for creating poetry are utterly professionalized, I think we've moved into a time of incrementalism, in which young poets make work that looks like the work the successful poets in the academy are making, which is work they admire but don't necessarily feel passionate about. As a result, they incrementally move through the system, taking a poetry workshop in which their work is praised but where the stakes are low, advancing to a creative writing degree, where it's mostly a project of conforming to expectations in the discipline (as in academia more broadly), and then on to publication and a position teaching workshops. Where the low stakes, occasionally interfered with by some kind of experiment, continue to guide the work. It's possible to imagine that as a result of positive reinforcement, many of these poets have arrived in their professional positions teaching poetry writing workshops to new batches of undergraduates without ever having actually chosen to be a poet, but only having chosen not to quit.[56] Fanny Howe's work as a poet is so striking in relation to this actuality because its stakes are so high (the salvation of her soul) and because she did it somewhat covertly (as a fiction writer at a university), hidden in plain view in their midst.

Notes

1. Fanny Howe, introduction to *The Wedding Dress: Meditations on Word and Life* (Berkeley: University of California Press, 2003), xix.
2. Fanny Howe, *Second Childhood* (Minneapolis: Graywolf Press, 2014), 68, 69.
3. The papacy of Pope Francis began on March 13, 2013.
4. V. S. Ramachandran, *The Tell-Tale Brain: A Neuroscientist's Quest for What Makes Us Human* (New York: W. W. Norton, 2011), 117.
5. Richard P. McBrien, ed., *The HarperCollins Encyclopedia of Catholicism* (San Francisco: HarperSanFrancisco, 1995), 1155.

6. Howe, *The Wedding Dress*, 109.
7. Fanny Howe, *Selected Poems* (Berkeley: University of California Press, 2000), 116.
8. Ibid., 124.
9. *The Catechism of the Catholic Church*, para. 1423 (Liguori, MO: Liguori Publications, 1994), 357.
10. Howe, *Selected Poems*, 33.
11. Ibid.
12. *The Catechism of the Catholic Church*, "Abortion," para. 2270, 547.
13. Howe, *Selected Poems*, 86.
14. Ibid., 103.
15. Fanny Howe, *The Winter Sun: Notes on a Vocation* (Minneapolis: Graywolf Press, 2009), 79.
16. Ibid., 122.
17. Howe, *Selected Poems*, 128.
18. Ibid., 203.
19. See Pope Francis, "Lenten Message of Our Holy Father Francis 2014," Libreria Editrice Vaticana, December 26, 2013, http://w2.vatican.va/content/francesco/en/messages/lent/documents/papa-francesco_20131226_messaggio-quaresima2014.html.
20. Howe, *The Wedding Dress*, 122.
21. Not to mention that a chapter on Susan by Oren Izenberg directly precedes this chapter on Fanny in the present volume.
22. Depending on your taste, you might also add the Sitwell siblings, Edith, Osbert, and Sacheverell.
23. Albert Gelpi, "Emily Dickinson's Long Shadow: Susan Howe and Fanny Howe," *Emily Dickinson Journal* 17, no. 2 (2008): 102.
24. Ibid., 101.
25. Ibid.
26. Ibid., 102.
27. Ibid., 103.
28. Susan Howe, *The Nonconformist's Memorial* (New York: New Directions, 1993), 10.
29. Devin Johnston, *Precipitations: Contemporary American Poetry as Occult Practice* (Middletown, CT: Wesleyan University Press, 2002), 146.
30. Lew Daly, *Swallowing the Scroll: Late in a Prophetic Tradition with the Poetry of Susan Howe and John Taggart* (Buffalo: M Press, 1994), 37.
31. Gelpi, "Emily Dickinson's Long Shadow," 109.
32. Howe, *Selected Poems*, 165.
33. Susan's poem "Articulation of Sound Forms in Time," published originally in 1987, tracks the story of Hope Atherton, a colonial minister who, as part of a military campaign against the Indians in Deerfield, Massachusetts, in 1676 "was unhorsed," went missing, wandered in the woods, perhaps went insane,

and reappeared mysteriously in the town of Hadley, on the other side of the river, several days later. Susan's poem suggests Atherton's wanderings as a kind of lunacy of language. The connections with Fanny's poem of her own personal wanderings to get lost in the forest are likely not oblique, especially since Fanny's poem appears to have been written after Susan's. See Susan Howe, *Singularities* (Middletown, CT: Wesleyan University Press, 1990).

34. Howe, *Selected Poems*, 156.
35. Marie-Louise von Franz, *Archetypal Dimensions of the Psyche* (Boston: Shambhala, 1999), 76.
36. Ibid., 89 (italics in the original).
37. Gelpi, "Emily Dickinson's Long Shadow," 103.
38. Howe, *The Winter Sun*, 120–21.
39. Ibid., 122.
40. Fanny Howe, *Second Childhood* (Minneapolis: Graywolf Press, 2014), 29.
41. Ibid., 32.
42. Howe, *Selected Poems*, 198.
43. Maureen N. McLane, *My Poets* (New York: Farrar, Straus and Giroux, 2012), 180–81.
44. Howe, *Selected Poems*, 10.
45. McBrien, *The HarperCollins Encyclopedia of Catholicism*, 659.
46. Howe, *Selected Poems*, 174.
47. Gelpi, "Emily Dickinson's Long Shadow," 110.
48. Howe, *Selected Poems*, 91.
49. Ibid., 92.
50. Robert Creeley, *The Collected Poems of Robert Creeley, 1975–2005* (Berkeley: University of California Press, 2006), 349.
51. Max Weber, *The Sociology of Religion*, trans. Ephraim Fischoff (Boston: Beacon Press, 1993), 2.
52. Mary Hilkert, "Grace," in McBrien, *The HarperCollins Encyclopedia of Catholicism*, 577.
53. Simone Weil, *Gravity and Grace* (London: Routledge, 1987), 129.
54. Devin Johnston, e-mail to the author, October 19, 2015.
55. Howe, *Second Childhood*, 72.
56. I am indebted to Stephen Williams for the notion of incrementalism.

CHAPTER 5

A Field Guide to Robert Hass

RICHARD STRIER

THE FIRST THING I should say is that the importance of Robert Hass (b. 1941) for the contemporary American poetry scene does not rely solely on his poetry. He has written important criticism; been a tireless translator of Czeslaw Milosz; been a proponent of a number of other poets, European and American; and he made a great effort, as poet laureate and ex–poet laureate, to make poetry a part of the daily lives of ordinary Americans.[1] But this chapter will deal with Robert Hass as poet—his primary identity, after all—and will try to identify what his best poems are, and what special qualities they share and exhibit. It will make a claim for the high quality of a number of his poems, from his first volume on, and for his extraordinary gift for formulations that are both lyrical and intellectually intriguing. I will not absolutely make the claim that he is—assuming the phrase still carries a meaning—a "major poet." In my thinking about this, I am influenced by T. S. Eliot's definition of a major poet as one whose oeuvre cannot be adequately represented in anthologies.[2] Hass can—perhaps—be adequately represented in anthologies. But—and this is a crucial point—one would need a healthy number of pages to do so. Some of his poems really are indispensable. One of the strange features of Hass in relation to anthologies is that everyone seems to agree, already (and, oddly, this has been true for a while) what his greatest poem is. "Meditation at Lagunitas," from his second collection, *Praise* (1979), occupies this position, and, as Dr. Johnson would say, I "rejoice to concur" in this judgment.[3] I will try to explain why this should be the case in the course of the chapter; I will treat that poem at length only at the end.

Hass's first volume, *Field Guide* (1973), won the Yale Younger Poets prize and begins with an introduction by Stanley Kunitz, who judged the contest that year.[4] Kunitz makes it seem as if Hass is an easy poet, one whose gift is primarily for lyric description. But Kunitz has to acknowledge that the volume also aspires, at times, to the public and the political. He does not explain how the lyrical and the political are to go together, and this is a real problem in this volume and throughout Hass's corpus.[5]

There is no doubt as to Hass's lyrical gifts, especially his gift for describing natural phenomena—vegetation, the sky, landscapes, and, to some extent, animals. His love for the scenery of the coast of northern California is unmistakable. A northeastern city boy like me has to look up many words referring to plants and plant life in reading the poems. But to stress this is to miss the sharp intelligence that permeates these descriptions.[6] Take the opening poem in *Field Guide*, "On the Coast near Sausalito." The title suggests a rather conventional nature poem. But the poem begins, strikingly, "I won't say much for the sea"—as if the poet were unimpressed by it, and is going to reject nature poetry. Instead, the poet does go on to say something "for" it—"it was, almost, / the color of sour milk." This is indeed not saying "much" for it. The poet is not committed to prettifying; he is trying to get things right, to be careful and precise; the very marked "almost" (at a line ending, surrounded with commas) is a signal for this. We are then told that "the sun in that clear / unmenacing sky was low." But why were we expecting the sky to be "menacing"? There is a human sensibility here that is registering the effect on it of nature, not simply "the look of things." But the stanza does end with straightforward, picturesque description: "hills dark green with manzanita." This is lyricism, but with a difference.

The second section describes "slimed rocks," but the point here is not the description but the line to which the section builds: "The old story: here filthy life begins." The author of that line wants to say something, not simply to describe. Whether what he says here is interesting or profound is a question, but there is no doubt that the poet is standing behind this very general assertion. The next numbered section jumps to thinking about fishing, and baiting a hook with peeled shrimp. But the author calls attention to his "clumsy hands" and says that they "bruise by"—and here, after the line break, is the surprise: "not touching." This is puzzling and not part of the fishing story, though the human story that it must be part of is left untold. In the third section, we learn what the speaker is fishing for—cabezone. After being given some detail on how this "not highly regarded" fish can be a delicacy (through proper Italian preparation), we get to the real point: it's an old and "atavistic" fish. The end of the section brilliantly evokes the moment of catching a fish. But it does more than evoke "the fierce quiver of surprise"—a very fine description—and tells us that the experience is "a recognition." Again, intelligence and something like philosophical weight enter here. But it seems reasonable, if not especially reverent, to ask, "a recognition" of what? The next numbered section gives us the answer: "It's strange to kill / for the sudden feel of life." The sudden feel of life is the recognition. And at this point, the poet is aware of the pressing possibility of commentary, especially of antifishing commentary. He wants to resist this, and to mark his resistance to it: "The danger is / to moralize / that strangeness." So the poem has to end some other way. Hass comes back to the idea of the "atavistic" that he developed in the second section. He ends by doing something like making the "recognition" mutual: "Creature and creature, / we stared down centuries." I am not sure this works. It seems too pat, perhaps almost overly prepared for. But it is where the poem was going, and it is not a matter of physical description. One could fairly call the intended effect "metaphysical."

At times, the poems are explicitly philosophical—or antiphilosophical (which of course, is the same thing). One poem disarmingly entitled "Spring" (*FG* 16) narrates an experience in a bookstore, where the poet and his lady friend are lectured to "interminably" by a "bearded bird-like man" on the topic of who Ugo Betti was (the woman had innocently asked).[7] The description of this encounter is vivid, if rather trivial, but the point (after a strained hyperbole—"Dusk was / a huge weird phosphorescent beast") is to capture the woman in question charmingly and nonsensically chanting "Ugo Betti has no bones," and the speaker pompously asserting, after he has been reading something, "The limits of my language / are the limits of my world." That claim is the basis of a great deal of analytic philosophy, and is a point on which analytic and continental philosophy converge. The poem ends with a "refutation" of it: "We spoke all night in tongues"—a wonderfully ambiguous assertion that does seem to push to the "limits of my language," since "speaking in tongues" involves (supposedly and mystically) speaking a language one does not know. But it turns out that the phrase is meant literally when, after the line break, the poem continues, "in fingertips, in teeth." This is the kind of speaking in tongues that forms Hass's credo. The whole thing is both lighthearted and serious, though the poem still seems a bit of a trifle.

Another attempt at antimetaphysical philosophical reflection immediately follows, in a poem about a "Graveyard at Bolinas" (*FG* 17). The poem begins with a solemn invocation of yew trees and herons but turns on a mordant joke when it states that the "transplanted Yankees" named on the markers "put down roots at last"—and produced flowers out of their graves. The speaker "picked a bunch / thinking to make / a salad of Eliza Binns." The speaker reflects on the graveyard later in the day while walking on a beach and states: "Some days it's not so hard to say / the quick pulse of blood / through living flesh / is all there is." This is again, as with the cabezone, a striking "recognition," whether it is fully earned or not. Again, it is where the poem was going. The assertion might well be saved by the qualification in its first line ("Some days it's not so hard")—on other days, it might in fact turn out to be "hard" to make the claim in question.[8]

The attempt to bring politics and history into *Field Guide* works better with past history and politics than with the history and politics of the period in which Hass was writing the poems. He is good at evoking what he calls "the other California," the California of nineteenth-century settlers and of displaced and destroyed Indian tribes. The poem from which that phrase comes, "Palo Alto: the Marshes" (*FG* 24), is successful in evoking various nineteenth-century situations, especially the figure of the dedicatee of the poem, a woman whose father owned the land where Hass grew up, who saw many of the same natural features that the poet sees, and who was victimized by the powers of the United States. The poem even more effectively dramatizes the depredations visited by Kit Carson on an Indian tribe that had, memorably and (as it turned out) uselessly, provided for itself "ten wagonloads / of fresh-caught salmon." A continuity seems to be established in a sentence that begins "A tanker lugs silver," but the enjambed next line continues "bomb-shaped napalm tins." This is a surprising and effective interjection of contemporary (late 1960s, early 1970s) politics. The poem ends with an evocation of the neutrality of nature ("the unembittered sun") followed by an assertion: "Citizens are rising / to murder in their moral dreams." The sentiment here is clear and admirable, but the question is whether the expression is distinguished. Does "Their *moral* dreams" provide enough of a verbal and conceptual surprise to redeem the moralism? I am not sure. Bob Dylan might do this better.

"Lament for the Poles of Buffalo" (*FG* 67) is heavy handed, but Hass succeeds when he evokes the world of an earlier California poet, Robinson Jeffers (1887–1962), whose "descriptive and meditative lyrics" sought, according to Hass as critic, "to claim for poetry the clarity and largeness of mind needed to compass the madness" of the twentieth century.[9] In "The Return of Robinson Jeffers" (*FG* 41), Hass produces a Jeffers-like poetic narrative in long lines about a dead man coming back to make love to a needy woman, who in her "after-tenderness"—a wonderful, very typical Hass phrase—finds her lover a living corpse who "had not thought afterwards" because "human anguish made him cold." This is very strong writing; one might call it Yeatsian. In the even stranger second part of the poem, "Jeffers" is transformed. He feels "an awkward brotherhood with the world's numb poor / His poems had despised," and he is transformed into a mourning woman. The poem ends with Hass imagining the Jeffers-woman being lifted into the sky as a kind of insatiable seabird. This poem is very different from those describing lovely, simple meals with a nice Chardonnay, but it is important to see both kinds of poem as produced by the same poet. Hass's historical awareness, domestic tenderness (and acuity), and (surprising?) bookishness come together beautifully in a medium-length lyric entitled, with consciously comic ponderousness, "Concerning the Afterlife, the Indians of Central California Had Only the Dimmest Notions" (*FG* 28). The speaker immediately identifies himself as a "natural man"; no clocks or radios for him: "It is morning because the sun has risen." He describes in some detail his morning activity of picking berries, and explains that in the afternoon, his (female) companion will swim and he will go to read a book by the author he wonderfully calls "that hard man Thomas Hobbes." Hass brilliantly notes that "there are no women in [Hobbes's] world," only "brothers fighting brothers." Hass's own world forms a contrast. Domesticity is regularly evoked, yet he also states that "[w]e may or may not / feel some irritation at the dinner hour"—a surprising touch right out of a realistic novel. Night is evoked, but then Hass returns to Hobbes (who also had only the dimmest notions of an afterlife). Hass sees Hobbes in exile in Europe during the English civil wars as, in another brilliant phrase, "haunted by motion"—"suddenly aware that all things move." This terror at evanescence is then assimilated into the domestic present where the couple "touch and drift toward morning," where the easeful "drift" does not entirely occlude the terror that haunted Thomas Hobbes.

Dr. Johnson (supposedly) said of Swift that the rogue never hazards a metaphor.[10] This is also almost true of Hass. The first poem in *Praise* (1979) is called "Heroic Simile" and begins by stating that a warrior in the film *Seven Samurai* "fell straight as a pine . . . as Ajax fell in Homer," but then goes on (characteristically) to describe or imagine woodsmen cutting down an actual tall pine.[11] The simile turns into a story—even more than in a heroic simile. The labor of the woodsman is described in detail, but in the middle of it, we are reminded that this is all just an imagined situation provoked by an episode in a film that provoked a simile. The laborers are stymied because, Hass says, "I have imagined no pack animal." They are waiting either for Hass to do something or for something to happen within the story. He then humorously goes back into the story—"How patient they are!" Their thoughts and feelings are described. But then Hass says, oddly, "I don't know / whether they're Japanese or Mycenaean." How can he, as the author of the story, not know this? But he is recognizing the scene as a general one, and remembering Homer as well as Kurosawa. He pleads inability ("there's nothing I can do") as if the story exists without him. But he then reminds us of the literariness of it: "The path from here to that village / is not translated." This is all very dazzling. He comes back to the opening image of the dying swordsman with a striking generalization—"A hero, dying, / gives off stillness to the air"—but one that requires some pondering, some real effort to grasp its meaning. The language could not be more lucid but the thought is intriguingly nonobvious. The poem ends by returning to the actual present: "A man and a woman walk from the movies." We have returned from the imagined, the heroic, and the ancient to the ordinary, even the banal. They walk "to the house."

But then we are told that they do so "in the silence of separate fidelities." Suddenly the "ordinary" is itself an object of intrigued lucubration. "Separate fidelities" is a completely unusual phrase; it forces one to think—not because of its slight semantic strangeness but because of its conceptual content. "Separate infidelities" would be immediately intelligible in a way that "separate fidelities" is not. There is a possible connection to the heroic here, and a sense of a mystery deeper than fantasy. The poem ends by acknowledging not just that storytellers can forget details, and so "strand" their creations, but that the problem of human relations is deeper: "There are limits to imagination." The poem, for all its detail and for all its commentary, is fully coherent.

The second poem in *Praise* is "Meditation at Lagunitas," which I will treat later. The volume includes longish poems that are easy to piece together ("Against Botticelli" for instance [10]), and others that are more difficult to see as wholes. "The Origin of Cities" (26) attempts to envision the economic and artistic life of a rich, Hellenistic polis. No commentary is provided. Slaves are part of the picture as are farmers, merchants, and "maimed soldiers." This last item threatens to destabilize the poem, almost breaking its detached tone (the maimed soldiers "ape monkeys for coins outside the wineshops"), but—probably because of the wineshops—the tone holds. Another poem about a place, this time a nonimagined one ("Old Dominion" [*P* 29]) is almost ruined by its political turn. The poem beautifully evokes ease and sadness through the connection between wearing tennis whites and the sad life, death, and writing of Randall Jarrell (who coached tennis while teaching at Kenyon College and also translated Chekhov). The thwack of tennis balls being hit reminds Hass of "an ax / in the cherry orchard," which picks up nicely on Chekhov. But the sound also recalls to Hass "machine guns / where the young terrorists are exploding / among poor people in the streets of Los Angeles." This is sudden and deflationary. The poem recovers with the speaker making resolutions, which include "to somehow do honor to Randall Jarrell" and also "never to kill myself" (which Jarrell almost certainly did). It ends by returning to the opening, when the speaker sees the tennis courts "and the people in tennis / whites who look so graceful from this distance." The effect is like that of the ending of William Carlos Williams's "The Yachts," where, after social hierarchy and economic inequality are fully recognized, "the skillful yachts pass over."

The last poem that I would praise in *Praise* (other than the one I am postponing) is another that thinks about a place. "Not Going to New York" (43) is an epistolary poem in long lines. We would not have expected it to be in rhymed couplets, but it connects its status as unrhymed to its lack of finality, of "the dazzling couplets of arrival." It recalls the messiness of February in upstate New York (Hass taught for a few years at the University of Buffalo), noting memorably and surprisingly that "thaws hardened the heart / against the wish for spring" since they ruined the snow. This "mottled" snow then reminds Hass of his grandmother's flesh, which is evoked in its physicality, its oversweetness and envelopingness, which suggests to the speaker "how death would come." Childhood terror reminds Hass of "the terrified figure dwarf-like" at the edge of Pierre Bonnard's painting *The Breakfast Room*. This is all perfectly coherent. The poem then moves to Hass's adult life in the present—not in upstate New York but in northern California with his children. A striking childish misdefinition is recorded (a "shepherd" is "Somebody who hurts sheep"), and the mention of hurt returns Hass's thoughts to the grandmother. A small child's "religious dread" of an old person is evoked, and we get another lovely piece of dialogue (presumably actual), when the grandmother winks at the child and says to Hass, "Old age ain't for sissies." He comes back to "the odd terror," which, he says, predates that remark and is brought on, in his memory, by the wintry season—either in California or New York. He says of the season, "It is not poetry where decay and a created / radiance lie hidden inside words the way that memory / folds them into living"—an astonishing formulation that links the residing power of words in poetry to the residing power of words in memory. Hass thinks of a metaphor in *Henry IV, Part 2*, which imagines a summer bird singing "in the haunch of winter." This leads Hass, given his interest in translation and in eastern Europe, to think of Boris Pasternak translating these lines. Pasternak is imagined in "Russian summer," but he is imagined as understanding, through his experience with languages, "what persists." I take this to refer to nature, the cycle of the seasons, and the feelings that they invoke in humans. Again, the poem seems both meandering and remarkably coherent.

Ten years separate *Human Wishes* from *Praise*.[12] Hass has clearly become interested in prose, and has recognized his love of stories. Alan Shapiro has singled out the line "And there are always melons" as typical of Hass and his "distrust of intellectuality," but in the poem from which that line comes ("The Beginning of September" [*P* 37]), Hass went on to say, "There are not always melons / There are always stories."[13] *Human Wishes*, a resonant title that invites one to think of Dr. Johnson's great poem on the vanity of such, is largely made up of prose pieces. Initially in the volume, these are composed in little prose stanzas of one to three lines, but they later appear in blocks or longer paragraphs.[14] In "Vintage" (5), Hass indulges in some transparent self-parody. In response to the sight of a blind, crippled beggar in New York City, who is said to have a "hunger for public agony," the speaker (perhaps meant to be insensitive) says, thinking of movies, that after viewing the beggar there should be "a quick cut, or a reaction shot." The poem ends with a liquor store clerk being "appalled"—not at human suffering but at the idea of immediately consuming a Cabernet the couple (?) has picked out. This is easy satire, whether self-directed or not. Later in the volume, in a prose piece called "Tall Windows" (perhaps responding to Larkin's "High Windows"), Hass describes "Riding through the Netherlands on a train" (24) and noting how neat everything was. But here, instead of satirizing this, the speaker notes of himself, "you did not despise the collective orderliness." This is a moral improvement, and closer to the heart of Hass's basically appreciative sensibility (*Praise* includes a good poem on parsnips ["Weed," 33] and a later book, *Time and Materials*, includes a fine poem on the marvel of cucumbers).[15] "Tall Windows" tells the story of a Dutch woman "of strict Calvinist principles" who, in a calm and logical way, was a moral hero (my term, not Hass's)—knowing that she was dying of tuberculosis, the woman took a Jewish woman's place on "the train to the camps." The ending of the piece articulates, with apparent seriousness, a formula for attaining metaphysical complacency that (to me) does not seem fully intelligible ("everything in the world ... would be calm and shine" if you "found its size among the swellings and diminishings"). Perhaps there is something that Hass thinks of as quintessentially Dutch about such a view.

"Museum" (*HW* 18) is another prose piece that avoids satirizing the pleasures of ordinary life, but it is perhaps too schematic, in its juxtaposition of these pleasures (a young couple harmoniously eating, reading the paper, and feeding an infant) against the horrors depicted in Käthe Kollwitz's art ("people with no talent or capacity for suffering who are suffering the numbest kind of pain"). That's a truly brilliant characterization of Kollwitz's work, but the poem ends by coming back to intimacy and the ordinary, with a cosmic turn ("everything seems possible"). Again, one doesn't know if one is supposed to accept this ending (just because it is the ending) or feel uncomfortable at it. In another prose piece ("Conversion" [*HW* 22]), Hass mocks himself for imagining (in Paris) that he would write "grave, luminous meditative poems." He knows that that is not exactly what he is doing. Perhaps "grave" is satirical here, but I am not sure. It may be a genuine ideal, but Hass has too much comic sensibility and too much love of anecdotes to be, for the most part, a poet of that sort. The title poem of the volume

("Human Wishes" [23]) presents a number of profundities afloat in a jelly of trivia. A chimpanzee stirring up an anthill is presented as looking at the ants "as if he were a judge at an ant beauty contest"—a clever but perhaps merely clever line, which continues, "or God suddenly puzzled by the idea of suffering," which is in another register altogether. In presenting himself thinking about "tongue-in-groove" furniture construction, Hass (thankfully) avoids the expected sex joke but says that he finds himself meditating on the phrase "as if language were a kind of moral cloud chamber through which the world passed and from which it emerged charged with desire."[16] That is wonderfully rich and genuinely profound, but the piece ends by merely telling a story about the dubious circumstances surrounding the purchase of some of the wood in question.

Sometimes, when a story is just a story, this works. The piece—which is just over a page long—archly entitled "Novella" (*HW* 19) tells the story of a young girl who modeled for a painter when she was prepubescent, and for whom that memory exists in detail but out of context with the rest of her life. In this case, both the story and the issue implicitly involved (mental continuity) seem worth the attention given to them, and the whole reflection is beautifully told. The ironic title is, in fact, not entirely inappropriate—many of the best moments in this volume could be described as novelistic. The stories recounted in "Paschal Lamb" (27), for instance, are very well told. "Quartet" (31) demonstrates Hass's talent for providing succinct and piquant thumbnail sketches of philosophical positions and structures of belief. In between descriptions of a meal enjoyed by "two couples having dinner on a Saturday night," the poem provides a conspectus of the diners' beliefs about (human) postmortem existence. It starts fairly straightforwardly—"One of them believes that after death there is nothing"; this is not elaborated. The poem warms up when we are told: "Another believes dimly and from time to time not in heaven exactly, but in a place where the dead can meet and talk quietly." That is lovely, but not the end of the sentence, which is: "where losses are made good." That's about as powerful and succinct an evocation of the attraction of the idea of heaven as can be imagined. "Another believes in the transmigration of souls." This seems straightforward enough, but Hass (or "the narrator"—I'm not sure why we need this) then makes a learned and shrewd qualification: "not the cosmic reform school of Indian religion, but an unplanned passage rather like life in its mixture of randomness and affinity."[17] The fourth position described (or postulated) beautifully explains the logic of belief in ghosts. The person to whom this view is ascribed is said to have "felt that consciousness might take longer to perish than the body and linger sometimes as spectral and unfinished grief, or unfinished happiness, if it doesn't come to the same thing." This is extraordinary writing, and I'm not sure why we have to come back to "melon or a poached pear" and "cream-colored cups." After all, there will not always be melons.

"Thin Air" (*HW* 76) is in verse; it's a kind of carpe diem poem addressed to the self, filled with imperatives ("You had better . . . You have to go . . . Hang on") and permissions ("you can . . . you can . . . you can"). It varies in quality (with some undigested "realism"), but its opening, on grand themes, is truly great. It seems as if it is truly going to be one of those "grave, luminous meditative poems." It begins, immediately reminding us of where so many great poems start, "What if I did not mention death to get started," or, it goes on to say—echoing Eliot's self-lacerating mode—"how love fails in our well-meaning hands."[18] Hass is very good at lists of possibilities—the final one here is of true novelistic complexity (Eliotic—but George now, rather than T. S.): "or what my parents in the innocence of their malice / toward each other did to me" (the series of questions ends, interestingly, on a period). Hass's line breaks are often brilliant, and the break after "malice" here is surely so. The reader is busy enough trying to come to terms with "the innocence of their malice" but then has to reorient the thought twice: "toward each other" and "to me." There are many such fine novelistic moments (by which I mean moments of omniscient narrative commentary) in *Human Wishes*. House-hunting is wonderfully described, for instance, as an activity that "figures some tacit imagination of contentment" ("January" [35]).

The best poem in the volume has a philosophical title, "Privilege of Being" (69). It begins by contrasting human passion with the behavior of Rilkean angels:

> Many are making love. Up above, the angels
> in the unshaken ether and crystal of human longing
> are braiding one another's hair, which is strawberry blond
> and the texture of cold rivers.

The poem then gives us the angel-eye view of human sex, "the awkward ecstasy," described somewhat overpoetically ("unbelievably sweet / lubricious glue"). "They hate it." This postulated "distress" of the postulated angels is then seen as having great power, filling the lovers "with unspeakable sadness." This metaphysical vision is then filled in on earth, so to speak.[19] "The woman" tells "the man" that their love does not cure her loneliness; Hass is careful to say that this is not meant in a hurtful way but merely as a statement of fact, which the man accepts ("he understands that life has limits").[20] Hass (or his "narrator") then lists the forms that human sadness within relationships can take, ending on the "merely / companionable." In a final turn, the couples in this condition are presented as "reading magazine articles about intimacy between the sexes / to themselves, and to each other," and, finally and surprisingly, to "the immense, illiterate, consoling angels." "Consoling" is an amazing touch here. I am not sure I understand it, but I am sure that it is the right word.[21]

Hass seems to publish a new collection every six to ten years, and so *Sun Under Wood* was right on schedule.[22] The volume opens with what one recognizes as a "normal" very good Hass poem, not too surprisingly entitled "Happiness" (I have no doubt that Hass would have published a volume called "Sadness and Happiness" if his friend Robert Pinsky had not co-opted the title).[23] The poem purports to explain the title emotion or mood, each section beginning "Because" or "and because." But the experiences cited do not really "explain" the mood. Hass again plays with a kind of poetry that he does not write; he says that the "pair of red foxes" he saw eating looked up at him "long enough to symbolize the wakefulness of living things," and in the second section, the swans that he saw feeding "symbolize mystery"—mordantly adding, "I suppose." The real interest in the poem is not in its descriptive or "symbolic" moments but in its meditative and philosophical ones. The woman in the poem is said to have gone into a gazebo "to coax an inquisitive soul / out of what she thinks of as the reluctance of matter." It is not clear whether the "inquisitive soul" is hers or is in nature somewhere, but the formulation is certainly intriguing. A few lines later, mist is said to rise from the bay "like the luminous and indefinite aspect of intention"—another fascinating idea masquerading as description. It's casually tossed off yet gets richer as one thinks about it and tries to put "luminous" and "indefinite" together and to do so in relation to "intention." Again, I am not sure that I exactly "get" it, but I am sure that there is something there to get. The domestic image of happiness at the end is satisfying enough but expectable and perhaps on the edge of cuteness (which Hass is willing to court in such moments).[24]

The real gain in *Sun Under Wood* is candor. Hass includes a number of poems about childhood experiences with his alcoholic mother (significantly, the volume's title comes from a medieval lyric about Jesus's mother).[25] The poem after "Happiness," "Our Lady of the Snows" (5), introduces the topic; it's mostly low-key but builds to a boyhood fantasy of self-transformation and to a Herbertian surprise ending, a line consisting entirely of two words: "navigable sorrow."[26] The long poem that follows, "Dragonflies Mating" (6), is much more ambitious. It's a poem about what we have already recognized as one of Hass's favorite things (along with nature and sex): stories. The ancestors "told stories," and in the second section, Hass tells a hilarious story about responses to an Indian story that is pretty funny in itself (I won't spoil the joke). But that story reminds him of others about the devastation of the Indians of his area, and also—"in the same thought," he says—about his own childhood devastations. He recalls schoolboy basketball practice (which he loved "more than anything"), and his fear that his mother would show up there, as apparently she sometimes did. He powerfully evokes the feeling of controlling and shooting a basketball, ending the section with a hyperbole that is not meant to be entirely childish: "It was a perfect thing." He then adds, in the same line: "it was almost like killing her." This is breathtaking stuff. But Hass's candor is not yet exhausted. The short following section offers a highly severe perspective on what is going on "When we say 'mother' in poems." The poem ends with a meditation on the title activity (dragonflies mating) and the contrast between this and what, because of our childhoods, "we do." The description of the "insect instructors" is exquisite, but the fine ending is preceded by some unusually cliché and portentous philosophical language (and a weak line break): "the heart goes out to the end of the rope / it has been throwing into abyss after abyss."

"My Mother's Nipples" (12) continues the theme, but mostly doesn't take off. One cannot help but compare it to Ginsberg's *Kaddish*, and Hass's poem does not stand up to that comparison for intensity or memorability (Naomi Ginsberg was worse than Hass's unnamed mother, but that is not the only reason for the difference in power). This poem is interested in "song" as well as story. Hass writes short "songs" for various types. The best are "The melancholic's song" ("They were never there, / les nipples de ma mère. / They are not anywhere") and "The indigenist's song," which is another good story (not humorous) using Indian material. The "nipple" theme does not quite carry through this long piece (which has stretches of interspersed prose), but the theme is continued in an almost too charming account of "The first girl's breasts I saw." The poem becomes one about shame, which is the title and the subject matter of one of the two best poems in the volume (wonderfully and comically billed as an "aria" on the topic).

"Shame: An Aria" (*SUW* 43) is certainly the best poem that I know on the subject of picking one's nose (it's also the only one, but that does not take anything away from it). This activity is a great case for the topic, since one can barely mention the activity without entering into the title state. The poem begins by describing in excruciating comic-novelistic detail the incident that produced the poem, and it then imagines its speaker getting "high-minded" about the topic and delivering a lecture about it. But the imagined lecture turns out not to be nonsensical, gassy, or pompous, though it starts as if it were going to be so: "Nosepicking ... is in a way the ground floor / of being." The "lecture" turns into a paean to (aria on) "The body's fluids and solids, its various despised disjecta." This turns into a reflection on early childhood, on "The most intimate hygienes, / those deepest tribal rules that teach a child ... what can be said (or thought, or done) / inside the house but not out, what can be said (or thought, or done) / only by oneself," which leads to the observation that "the core of the self, we learn early, is where shame lives." This is superb writing, candid and penetrating; self-mockery and comedy have fallen away. The evocation of adult shame is not as successful but has powerful moments; it moves from the physical into the emotional: "small malices, razor knicks on the skin of others of our meannesses." This leads into thoughts about mortality as itself shameful, and then to a final moment evoking, as Hass often does, psychological intimacy between lovers (Hass might be said to be more deeply interested in this sort of intimacy than in the more straightforward one of sex).[27] In this case, the moment is one in which the woman is seen as hoping that her partner can love the face that she normally hides and in relation to which, "if you could love yourself, you would." So shame remains, even in the adult world, at "the core of the self."

Some of the candor in *Sun Under Wood* is about Hass's own poetry. In a rather wandering poem called "English: An Ode" (62)—much less an ode than "Shame" is an aria—Hass acknowledges an objection to one of his own practices, though it sounds, initially, as if he does not take it seriously: "There are those who think it's in fairly bad taste / to make habitual reference to social and political problems / in poems."[28] "Those" who think this are, this implicitly suggests, prissy and limited. But suddenly they get more intelligent, and the thought continues with something like a concession: "To these people it seems a form of melodrama / or self-aggrandizement, which it no doubt partly is." "No doubt" is one of those concessions that barely concedes anything, and "partly" is as far as Hass will go with this. He does not seem really troubled by what seems "like moral nagging." He rightly wants to avoid having "to ironize" everything. But it is not clear that he can successfully include references to "social and political problems / in poems." He finds himself obsessed with José Martí's great poem beginning "Yo soy un hombre sincero," which does bring in social as well as personal concerns ("Con los pobres de la tierra / Quiero yo mi suerte echar" [With the wretched of the earth, I want to cast my lot]), but it is not clear that Hass has written or can write such a poem (or a poem like that by the contemporary female Mexican poet he quotes as the first section of this poem and partly translates as its last).[29]

The final poem in *Sun Under Wood*, and one of the best, is also about Hass's own poetry. In "Interrupted Meditation" (73), Hass presents himself in dialogue with an unnamed "old man" who is eastern European, who knows Hass and his poetry well, and who knows both Hass's devotion to Czeslaw Milosz and Milosz's own poetry and worldview. The poem starts with a description of a creek with amber stones in it that Hass is about to compare with something, but he then stops (we later learn why) and finds himself thinking about a rather devastating comment, quoted in two halves, made by the "old man" who "had seen whole cities leveled": "*We were not put on earth ... to express ourselves*" (italics in the original). Hass recounts something of the old man's wartime experience, and the old man's shame at it and insistence that, in such a context, "self-expression" was not an issue. Hass presents himself, as so often, in nature ("on the mountainside"), recalling this dialogue and more. He recalls himself defending language as responsible to all of "being," however grand and however (apparently) trivial. To this, the old man said (and Hass again shows how good a story and joke teller he is): "Ah ... you've been talking to Milosz." But before countering Milosz, the old man rounds on Hass, noting that "here" (presumably in America, specifically California) *"you can express what you like / enumerate the vegetation."* This latter activity is, needless to say, one of Hass's favorite poetic occupations; the old man presents it not as a gift but as a limitation. We now understand why, in line 5, Hass did not present the simile he was going to. Hass has to "enumerate the vegetation" because, the old man tells Hass, "you don't excel at metaphor." Hass seems to take this calmly, and the old man gives Hass his due—"You write well, clearly. / You are an intelligent man"—before returning to the Milosz problem. Milosz believes in explanations; he believes in the power of language. The old man does not, asserting the primacy of silence. He challenges Hass to provide a "key" to living. But what this makes Hass think about (in the poem) is not poetry but the failure of his marriage. He evokes an emotional scene from that context with almost his usual novelistic precision (*"abysses* of grief" [my italics] doesn't help—that word never does). With some success here—quietly, rather than spectacularly—Hass integrates private and public disastrous ways of being, but comes back to himself as a nature poet and finds himself "ashamed that I want to end this poem singing." But he does, nonetheless, want to do so. And he does do so. But *why* he can end "singing" is not clear.[30] The problem recurs in "Faint Music" (*SUW* 39). Happiness, one might say, becomes less legible as the volume proceeds.

Eleven years later, *Time and Materials* (2007) continues many of the themes of *Sun Under Wood*, though with less intense self-consciousness. *Time and Materials* is much concerned with what language can and can't do ("The Problem of Describing Color" [9], "The Problem of Describing Trees" [10]). It contains a nice, if somewhat sentimental, tribute to Milosz (38); a longish political poem ("Bush's War" [68]) that, again compares unfavorably with Ginsberg's antiwar poetry; and a very rich poem called "Art and Life" (27), which contemplates at length Vermeer's *The Milkmaid*. This bears comparison with Ashbery's "Self-Portrait in a Convex Mirror," and the volume contains a poem in which Hass acknowledges Ashbery's influence ("I Am Your Waiter Tonight and My Name Is Dmitri" [63]).

What captures Hass in the Vermeer painting is its representation of someone paying full attention to a task. After evoking this, Hass turns to contemplating people in the museum cafeteria, wondering which one might be the restorer of the painting. As usual, some of the novelistic touches are wonderful. The man in the brown suit has "A mouth formed by private ironies," which would be a fine line in itself, but continues, "As if he'd sat silent in too many meetings with people / He thought more powerful and less intelligent than he"—a whole professional life imagined from an interpreted facial feature. Hass imagines the fantasized restorer as another paragon of attention, of absorption: "the servant of a gesture so complete, a body / So at peace, it has become a thought, entirely its own." This echoes Donne's claim about the young woman whose early death the *Anniversaries* memorialize that "her body thought," a formulation that intrigued Yeats and Eliot and others, and Hass seems at home in this company.[31] The dismissal of unworldly paradises that follows makes sense, but the poem does not gloss over the difficulties of ordinary life. The speaker shows himself fully paying attention ("not thinking what you're going to say next / When the other person's speaking") and doing so in his shrewdly novelistic way ("she is trying out self-deceptions"). He expresses his ambivalence about relationships, and about the idea of remaking the self. The poem ends with the speaker imagistically becoming Vermeer, and realizing that even the most "realistic" painting takes its power from presenting something "we cannot have."[32]

There are some wonderful poems included in the "new and selected" volume called *The Apple Trees at Olema*.[33] The opening "July Notebook: The Birds" has some lovely moments. In a section about cultivating defense mechanisms, Hass speaks of "a lover perfecting a version / of the silent treatment from some strategy / of anticipatory anger at the failure of love." This is truly (Henry) Jamesian in its subtlety and penetration; it's a beautifully and lucidly expressed picture of a particular human "strategy" complexly understood. Hass can express the effect of nature on us with equal lucidity and complexity; he describes a foggy twilight as taking back "what we didn't know at midday we'd experience / as lack."

Perhaps the best new poem in the volume is an elegy for Hass's older brother ("August Notebook: A Death" [11]). In an unshowy way, Hass presents himself coming upon the form of the opening section of the poem and making a positive feature of "the absence of metaphor" (which the old man in "Interrupted Meditation" saw as a weakness of Hass's poetry). The second section involves some lovely—and relevant—social-historical material, and ends with a superb evocation of the "terrible / tenderness" of a Mississippi John Hurt song about a death ("Louis Collins"). The third section is a fine tribute to the way poets have presented the shadowy world of the dead, but the fourth section is the true climax of the poem. It presents some bits from a series of conversations Hass had with his brother. These are both tender and exasperated, and seem utterly true. If they didn't happen, they should have. The poem ends by acknowledging that Hass is now through and not through with "those arguments" and with "worrying about where you are and how you're doing." This is the plain style at its very best.[34]

We have gotten from 1975 to 2010, but I promised to come back to "Meditation at Lagunitas" (*P* 4).[35] I hope that by now it is clear why this poem has become a classic. It showcases many of Hass's virtues. It begins stunningly, with one of his shrewd observations about a philosophical position or stance: "All the new thinking is about loss." One couldn't say that more accurately or more succinctly. But after one has finished admiring the cogency and lucidity of the statement, one might find oneself demurring on historical grounds: given the *Iliad*, tragedy, much of the Bible, Milton's great epic, and much else, one might feel that such thinking is not so "new." But Hass is already there. The next line states, with almost comic straightforwardness, "In this it resembles all the old thinking." Hass then goes on to give a superb capsule summary of one bit of "the old thinking"—Platonic ontology as a story about loss: "The idea, for example, that each particular erases / the luminous clarity of a general idea." He then, in another turn, makes what could be called reverent fun of the idea that he has (again) so beautifully expressed. He applies the idea to some actual particulars: "That the clown- / faced woodpecker probing the dead sculpted trunk / of that black birch is, by his presence, / some tragic falling off from a first world / of undivided light." This is somewhere between parody and paraphrase. The woodpecker's "presence" hardly seems tragic, and yet "a first world / of undivided light," with its sharp line break, is truly grand and compelling (compare the famous opening of Henry Vaughan's "The World").[36] Hass— or do I have to say "the speaker"?—then moves from Platonic ontology to the fashionable theory of language as loss (we know that Hass has Lacan, among others, in mind from the companion poem in the volume, "Picking Blackberries with a Friend Who Has Been Reading Jacques Lacan" [*P* 36]). An alternative version of the position is then elaborated: "the other notion that, / because there is in this world no one thing / to which the bramble of blackberry corresponds / a word is elegy to what it signifies." This last formulation is even more breathtakingly accurate and succinct than the previous ones.[37]

So far, the poem has been entirely about intellectual positions. But at this point, the interpersonal situation of the poem emerges: "We talked about it late last night." The voice of the friend who has been reading Lacan is described, first poetically—"there was a thin wire of grief"—and then novelistically, "a tone / almost querulous." The "speaker" presents himself as coming to realize that "talking this way, everything dissolves"—abstractions, particulars, persons ("*justice, / pine, hair, woman, you* and *I*"). The italics are meant to suggest, I think, that "everything dissolves" into mere words. But the words *hair* and *woman* seem to lead the speaker into memory, and into the next movement of the poem, a Wordsworthian "spot of time."[38] Instead of everything dissolving for the poet, he recalls a particular woman and a particular relationship in great detail. He remembers her physical presence—not, like the "clown- / faced woodpecker," as a mere fact of matter but as a fact that *mattered*. He remembers and skillfully evokes a tactile experience—"holding / her small shoulders in my hands"—but more than that, he remembers the effect that this tactile experience had on him, an effect at once emotional, psychological, and metaphysical—"a violent wonder" not at her body but "at her presence."[39] "Violent wonder" is a striking phrase, almost an oxymoron, and it leads Hass into a series of analogies—first, a brief physical one ("like a thirst for salt"), and then into a deeper and more psychological thirst, an intense bout of nostalgia, "for my childhood river," aspects of which keep accumulating in his memory. "Presence" here is no longer an abstraction. One might say that the poem has moved from a symbolic to a Real Presence.[40] Another italicized word emerges. This time it is not a generic noun but a local name for an intensely remembered "particular" ("the little orange-silver fish / called *pumpkinseed*").

Hass has gotten caught up in his memories, and he is honest enough to recognize that the feeling he is evoking "hardly had to do with" the woman in question. This is a brave and candid admission of the narcissism of personal associations. The word "longing" comes, logically enough, into his mind, and he makes up a clever false etymology for it as if it were the merest commonplace: "Longing, we say, because desire is full / of endless distances."[41] This would be a joke except that it is dead serious. It sounds as if the speaker has now taken Lacan on board. But in another short and self-contained sentence paralleling "It hardly had to do with her," Hass comes back to the remembered erotic relationship, trying, again bravely if somewhat self-consciously, to acknowledge the erotic other as a person exactly like himself: "I must have been the same to her." This is a gesture of imaginative and intellectual generosity, crediting the woman with the phenomenology that Hass has evoked for himself.[42] But the next line begins with a "But." This recognizes that the focus of the poem is on Hass's memory of the relationship, not on the relationship itself. As the section on Hass's "childhood river" suggests, memory turns out not to be "about loss" but rather to be remarkably full. Hass again remembers physical particulars ("the way her hands dismantled bread"), where "dismantled" seems to capture the particularity of the action and also the intensity and lovingness of the speaker's attention at the time. In the same mode, the speaker remembers emotional particulars, this time with "her" consciousness fully represented. He recalls, in wonderfully plain and plangent language, "the thing her father said that hurt her, what"—in a lovely line break—"she dreamed." And then, after this evocation of a particular person and of real intimacy between persons (sharing mental as well as physical phenomena, emotional wounds and dreams as well as bread), Hass comes to his conclusion.

The speaker of this poem is clearly an intellectual, someone extremely interested in ideas and in words. But the point now is to recover the world from Platonism and words from being Lacanian elegies to what they signify. There are, the speaker says triumphantly, but apparently unsequaciously, "moments when the body is as numinous / as words." He is perhaps returning to "her small shoulders" and the wonder that holding them produced. But the phrasing is very odd. The suspended "as words" is a surprise. Normally, it is not words but things, religious things, that are "numinous"—filled with spiritual presence.[43] The speaker is someone who believes that words can be, perhaps often are, numinous. This is very different from words being markers of ontological absence. But the sentence picks up on "moments" rather than on "words," speaking of "days that are the good flesh continuing." "The good flesh" is a more modest (and less fancy) claim than "numinous"; the line clearly means to affirm something more ordinary—"continuing." The next line, the penultimate one in the poem, picks up on "days that are the good flesh continuing," capturing and praising both the temporal and the affective dimension of the previous line and of the evocation of intimacy—"Such tenderness, those afternoons and evenings." But meanwhile, in all this talk about "the body" and "the good flesh," what has happened to the worries about language? Hass comes back to this after all. We return to an italicized word (this is a poem that is meant to be seen on the page). We contemplate the word three times—"Such tenderness, those afternoons and evenings, / saying *blackberry, blackberry, blackberry*"—but now the word is part of the world, fully immersed and at home in it. The current moment of picking blackberries (evoked in the companion poem) blends into, is perhaps imagined as, a past that is recoverable rather than lost. And instead of the familiar experience of a word losing meaning and reference when the word is repeated, the repetition here seems to connect the word ever more firmly to the thing. This is not exactly what Wittgenstein meant by bringing "home" words alienated by philosophy, but it is not unrelated to it.[44]

This poem is clearly a tour-de-force and deserves, as I have said, its place in the anthologies. It manifests many of Hass's virtues. But it does not show everything that he can do. Hass can be more fully novelistic; can describe the consciousness of another more fully; he can certainly describe nature more fully; and he can use actual dialogue and nonpersonal history. If one were going to read only a single Hass poem, this is not a bad candidate. If one were to do that, one would experience many linguistic and conceptual pleasures and psychological recognitions, but not all such that his poetry offers. I would encourage each reader of Hass's poetry to compile his or her own "new and selected poems."

Notes

I am grateful to Peter Anson, Camille Bennett, Edgar Garcia, Kimberly Johnson, and Alan Shapiro for useful comments on this essay. Roger Greenwald both commented and made detailed editorial suggestions. A discussion at the Poetry and Poetics Workshop at the University of Chicago was very helpful, as was a discussion with faculty and students at Claremont McKenna and associated colleges.

1. For Hass's criticism, see *Twentieth Century Pleasures: Prose on Poetry* (New York: HarperCollins, 1984) and *What Light Can Do: Essays on Art, Imagination, and the Natural World* (New York: HarperCollins, 2012). For the brief essays that he wrote to make poetry reading more widespread and informed,

see *Now and Then: The Poet's Choice Columns, 1997–2000* (Berkeley, CA: Counterpoint, 2007). For his version of something like a textbook, see the slightly ironically titled *A Little Book on Form: An Exploration into the Formal Imagination of Poetry* (New York: Ecco Press, 2017).

2. T. S. Eliot, "What Is Minor Poetry?" (1944), in *On Poetry and Poets* (London: Faber and Faber, 1957), 39–52.
3. It is in relation to Thomas Gray's "Elegy Written in a Country Churchyard" that Johnson states that he rejoices "to concur with the common reader." See the Life of Gray in Samuel Johnson, *The Lives of the Poets: A Selection*, ed. Roger Lonsdale, selected by John Mullan (New York: Oxford University Press, 2009), 461.
4. Robert Hass, *Field Guide* (New Haven, CT: Yale University Press, 1973). Subsequent citations are given in the text with the abbreviation *FG*.
5. This tension is the focus of Wes Davis, "Fear and Loathing at Lagunitas," *Parnassus: Poetry in Review* 31, nos. 1–2 (2009): 275–306.
6. The coeditor of this collection, Robert von Hallberg, has urged me to distinguish between the kind of intelligence I am flagging here, and something like "academic knowingness." Hass certainly does not rely very much on the latter, but, interestingly, it does come into the much-loved "Meditation," whose title itself might signal something more or less "academic." Somehow, though, the "academic" references in the poem do not seem forbidding. This has to do, perhaps, with humor and straightforwardness (see the analysis at the end of this chapter).
7. I don't agree with Alan Shapiro that the poem "turns on the illusion in line five that the 'bearded bird-like man' is the answer to the question, who is Ugo Betti." Possibly this ambiguity is there, but I do not see that the poem "turns on" it or that it reflects Hass's supposed "uneasy sense of culture." Alan Shapiro, "And There Are Always Melons: Some Thoughts on Robert Hass," *Chicago Review* 33, no. 3 (Winter 1983): 85.
8. Shapiro notes the presence of "some days" here but refuses to give it much weight ("And There Are Always Melons," 86).
9. Robert Hass, "The Fury of Robinson Jeffers," in *What Light Can Do*, 149.
10. Joseph Warton recorded that Johnson said this about Swift's style; Johnson partly renounces the claim in the Life of Swift, *The Lives of the Poets*, 340.
11. Robert Hass, *Praise* (New York: Ecco Press, 1979). Subsequent citations are given in the text with the abbreviation *P*.
12. Robert Hass, *Human Wishes* (New York: Ecco Press, 1989). Subsequent citations are given in the text with the abbreviation *HW*.
13. Shapiro, "And There Are Always Melons," 84.
14. Whether these works are to be called "prose poems" or not is a matter of definition. Hass expresses his thoughts about the term in "An Informal Occasion with Robert Hass," *Iowa Review* 21, no. 3 (Fall 1991): 126–32. I will not refer to these works as poems.

15. Robert Hass, *Time and Materials: Poems 1997–2005* (New York: Ecco Press, 2007), 57.
16. In "From Image to Sentence: The Spiritual Development of Robert Hass," *American Poetry Review* 26, no. 2 (March–April 1997): 47–56, Terrence Doody points out the interesting inaccuracy in this metaphor, since a cloud chamber simply tracks particles and does not impart a charge to them (48). Doody does not make anything of this inaccuracy. I am not sure whether Hass was aware of it or not.
17. My colleague Edgar Garcia has pointed out to me how frequently Hass uses discounting formulations, as here with "not in heaven" and "not the cosmic reform school." This can be seen, I think, as part of Hass's commitment to both precision and a rhetoric of precision. It is also, as with litotes in general, a way of saying and not saying at the same time.
18. For Eliot's self-lacerating mode, see, for instance, "Little Gidding," lines 83–89, in *The Poems of T. S. Eliot*, vol. 1: *Collected and Uncollected Poems*, ed. Christopher Ricks and Jim McCue (Baltimore: Johns Hopkins University Press, 2015), 205.
19. Compare Liesl Olson, "Robert Hass's Guilt *or* The Weight of Wallace Stevens," *American Poetry Review* 36, no. 5 (September–October 2007): 37: "Hass examines longing's fold back into the world."
20. On "the aboriginal loneliness of being," see Hass's essay on James Wright in *Twentieth Century Pleasures*, 27–28.
21. Some ways of understanding this word are surely provided by the extraordinary essay called "Looking for Rilke" in *Twentieth Century Pleasures*, 226–68. There, Hass speaks of Rilke's "project" as being "to transform the emptiness, the radical deficiency, of human longing into something else" (233); Hass sees Rilke as having succeeded at this in the *Duino Elegies* and some of the *Sonnets to Orpheus*, which manifest "a positive emptiness from which death flows back into life" (266).
22. Robert Hass, *Sun Under Wood* (Hopewell, NJ: Ecco Press, 1996). Subsequent citations are given in the text with the abbreviation *SUW*.
23. See Robert Pinsky, *Sadness and Happiness: Poems* (Princeton, NJ: Princeton University Press, 1975). Bo Gustavsson links Pinsky and Hass in sharing the ambition to write a "discursive" sort of poetry; see "The Discursive Muse: Robert Hass's 'Songs to Survive the Summer,'" *Studia Neophilologica* 61, no. 2 (1989): 193–201.
24. The poet and critic Angela Sorby is working on the topic of "cuteness" in nineteenth-century poetry and poetry in general. Following the work of Sianne Ngai, Sorby's work should help resuscitate the term as not necessarily derogatory. See Sianne Ngai, "The Cuteness of the Avant-Garde," in *Our Aesthetic Categories: Zany, Cute, Interesting* (Cambridge, MA: Harvard University Press, 2012), 53–109.

25. Hass quotes the entire four-line poem as the epigraph to the volume. It can be found in almost any anthology of medieval English lyrics. See, for example, Robert D. Stevick, ed., *One Hundred Middle English Lyrics* (Indianapolis: Bobbs-Merrill, 1964), 5.
26. For readers not intimately familiar with the poetry of George Herbert, I have in mind moments like Herbert's sonnet on prayer, which, after a long list of images, ends with the words "something understood." For a reading of "Our Lady of the Snows" and some thoughts about how Hass's poetry in this mode relates to that of the confessional poets, see Stephen [now Stephanie] Burt, *The Poem Is You: 60 Contemporary American Poems and How to Read Them* (Cambridge, MA: Belknap Press of Harvard University Press, 2016), 179–84.
27. I owe this observation to a conversation with my colleague Sarah Nooter.
28. In the quite positive chapter on odes in *A Little Book on Form*, Hass notes that in postmodernist poetry, "the form's open-endedness and shifts dissolve into the long free verse poem" (220).
29. In a lyrical essay called "Ode and Empire" (*TriQuarterly*, no. 129 [2007]: 9–19), Linda Gregerson treats "English: An Ode" at some length and makes many shrewd observations about it. I believe that she thinks that the poem works within its announced genre, but since she does not say so explicitly, I am not sure.
30. Wes Davis seems to think that the end of "Interrupted Meditation" works "as a reply to the émigré's challenge" ("Fear and Loathing at Lagunitas," 305), but I am not sure I understand Davis's basis for this claim.
31. The line comes from Donne's "The Second Anniversary" ("Of the Progres of the Soule"), lines 244–46: "her pure and eloquent blood / Spoke in her cheeks, and so distincktly wrought, / That one might almost say, her bodie thought." In *The Complete Poetry of John Donne*, ed. John T. Shawcross (New York: Doubleday, 1967), 298. For the importance of this line to Yeats and others, see Frank Kermode, *Romantic Image* (London: Routledge and Kegan Paul, 1957).
32. I believe my reading here is compatible with that briefly suggested in Olson, "Robert Hass's Guilt *or* The Weight of Wallace Stevens," 39.
33. Robert Hass, *The Apple Trees at Olema: New and Selected Poems* (Hopewell, NJ: Ecco Press, 2010).
34. In 1991, Hass stated, "I'm always most amazed by great plainness in language" ("An Informal Occasion with Robert Hass," 128).
35. This essay was completed before *Summer Snow* (New York: Ecco Press, 2020) appeared. For commentary on that volume, see Charles Altieri, "The Genius of Robert Hass: One Achievement of Summer Snow," *Chicago Review*, forthcoming.
36. Vaughan's poem begins, "I saw Eternity the other night, / Like a great *Ring* of pure and endless light." See *The Works of Henry Vaughan*, ed. L. C. Martin, 2nd ed. (Oxford: Clarendon Press, 1957), 466.

37. Bruce Bond aptly cites Lacan's assertion that "the being of language is the non-being of objects" in "An Abundance of Lack: The Fullness of Desire in the Poetry of Robert Hass," *Kenyon Review*, n.s., 12, no. 4 (Autumn 1990): 47. The assertion appears in Jacques Lacan, *Écrits: A Selection*, trans. Alan Sheridan (New York: W. W. Norton, 1977), 263.
38. Hass might indeed be our Wordsworth, though without a poem of epic length. For Wordsworth on "spots of time" that "retain / A renovating virtue" when we are "depressed / By false opinion and contentious thought," see *The Prelude* (1805 [257–60] and 1850 [208–11]) in William Wordsworth, *The Prelude, 1799, 1805, 1850*, ed. Jonathan Wordsworth, M. H. Abrams, and Stephen Gill (New York: W. W. Norton, 1979). Coleridge's description of Wordsworth's task in the *Lyrical Ballads* as having been to produce poems that give "the charm of novelty to things of every day" can certainly be seen as one of Hass's goals (and accomplishments). Samuel Taylor Coleridge, *Biographia Literaria*, ed. George Watson (London: Dent, 1965), 169.
39. Hass is a kind of connoisseur of wonder. In his "Notes on Poetry and Spirituality," he mentions that his father, when Hass was a child, conveyed "a sense of mild wonder at the [Catholic] church and its doctrines" (*What Light Can Do*, 291). I have not done a survey but am sure that other interesting uses of the word are present in the oeuvre.
40. I owe this formulation to a conversation with Robert Faggen, coeditor of this volume, of Claremont McKenna College. Hass's relation to Catholicism would certainly repay study—in matters like this, not only in overt references like those in *Sun Under Wood*.
41. Doody notes the clever line break here, where, in the course of the enjambment, "full" becomes extremely empty ("From Image to Sentence," 52).
42. One of the things that Hass explicitly values is "that sense that other people's inner lives are as real as one's own" (*What Light Can Do*, 294).
43. Doody, "From Image to Sentence," notes the "reversal" here (between "the body" and "words").
44. For Wittgenstein's desire to bring the words used in philosophy "home," see Ludwig Wittgenstein, *Philosophical Investigations*, trans. G. E. M. Anscombe (New York: Macmillan, 1953), para. 116ff. For useful commentary on this endeavor, see Stanley Cavell, "The Availability of Wittgenstein's Later Philosophy," in *Must We Mean What We Say? A Book of Essays* (New York: Charles Scribner's Sons, 1969), 44–72.

SUBJECT MATTER

CHAPTER 6

Anthony Hecht

Worth the Weight

JONATHAN F. S. POST

ANTHONY HECHT'S SIGNAL, although not sole, contribution to the poetry of post–World War II America was to bring the weight of formal measures to bear on the subject of darkness, especially military violence, with a concentration unequaled among his contemporaries—his contemporaries being, most immediately, Richard Wilbur, James Merrill, and John Hollander, and at a slightly further remove W. H. Auden, Elizabeth Bishop, and Robert Lowell. In this regard, Hecht's seven-book poetic oeuvre is deep rather than wide, the product of a mind reflecting on man's inhumanity to man, in a century that eclipsed all previous centuries in its sheer appetite for brutality. (The present century is, of course, still young.) But it is not darkness alone, or any one of its nuanced, melancholic strains that is the reason to keep returning to his poetry. What modern poet, after all, cannot find something to brood over or complain about? It is the angle or perspective, the shaping of a perception through language that art gives to its subject (whatever the subject), that is always at stake in Hecht's poetry. The frequent disjunction, or tension, that emerges between brutal matter and refined manner is critical to his achievement as a poet.

The central, defining event for Hecht was the Second World War. Memories of it, enhanced by much further reading—Hecht is a capaciously literary poet, who spent much of his life teaching at universities—seep into his poetry and form a seemingly inexhaustible reserve for his musings. Hecht was himself a late participant in the war. He enlisted in the army in 1943, at the age of twenty, but did not see actual ground combat until the final months of the Allied campaign in Europe in the spring of 1945, where he encountered enemy fire, witnessed the killing of fellow soldiers and innocent victims alike, and experienced the gruesome liberation of the Nazi concentration camp at Flossenbürg, located in Bavaria, near the Czech border.

Of the other poets cited above, only Richard Wilbur saw action, and although the two men would form a lasting friendship, their poetry is fundamentally different, not in their respect for received literary forms but in mood and reach, in temperament. Hecht courts an element of tragic pathos and the sublime from which Wilbur instinctively veers away. Hecht, also, can never altogether escape thinking about military violence and the barbaric things people do to each other—what he characterizes, at one point, as the voice that "whispers inwardly, 'My soul, / It is the cost, the cost,' / Like some unhinged Othello, who's just found out / That justice is no more."[1] Just found out (again) that justice is no more is not a bit of facile wordplay but a grim conundrum of a potentially Sophoclean order (see his "Chorus from *Oedipus at Colonos*" in *The Transparent Man*, 1990), one that repeatedly unhinges Hecht's speakers. And, in this poem, it bears emphasizing, it is an earned turn of phrase. "The Cost" is preoccupied with turns, and the eternal turning around of the image of "two thousand raw recruits and scarred veterans" depicted on Trajan's Column and now being replayed, once again, by the United States in Vietnam in 1970, the year when the poem was composed. It is a return for which Hecht offers no political solution, only the moral counter of careful depiction itself, in this case of a poet addressing the endless cycle of "all that ancient pain," the poem functioning in a way the silent column cannot, as "a speaking picture." To the extent that Hecht's poetry delves into the specific, graphic details of violence (not especially prominent in "The Cost"), we might also regard him, in certain moods, as more a poet of atrocity than of military violence, however much military events provide the occasion for reflection.

At the core of Hecht's canon is a trio of great poems that ultimately descend from memories of his war experiences: "'More Light! More Light!,'" "The Venetian Vespers," and "The Book of Yolek." The first and last are frequently anthologized and well known, the middle poem less so.[2] In fact, it is probably fair to say that "The Venetian Vespers" is more often remembered than read since its mellifluously musical title is also the title of the 1979 book of poems in which it appears, but the poem is too long—the longest in Hecht at over eight hundred lines—and baroque in construction and diction to be readily or quickly assimilated by the general reader.

Around this core of poems, a number of others cluster and compete for our attention. The most familiar braid memories of war with bleak family sagas or personal reflections. The best known of this group are probably "A Hill," Hecht's adroit but deliberately diminished Parnassus poem that inaugurates *The Hard Hours* (1967); "Behold the Lilies of the Field," a gruesome "confessional" by a soldier in the time of the Roman emperor Valerian, and the poem that closes the same volume, "'It Out-Herods, Herod. Pray You, Avoid It'" (the title is a line from *Hamlet*); the suite of four sonnets from *Millions of Strange Shadows* (1977) offering a genealogy of simmering male brutality in "The Feast of Stephen"; "Still Life," from *The Venetian Vespers* (1979), as perfect a poem as Hecht ever wrote, an aubade in which he reworks a military situation from a much earlier poem; and "Apprehensions," again from *Millions of Strange Shadows*, one of several dramatic monologues that admits, while also transforming, some of the extreme strategies of confessional poetry. It concludes with the striking image of the concentration camp ovens blazing "away like Pittsburgh steel mills, / Chain-smoking through the night, and no one spoke." Understatement is everything here.

The poems initially listed here have generally enjoyed greater visibility than the last mentioned, the longer "Apprehensions." Again, their appearance in anthologies partially accounts for this situation, one often found in the reception history of poetry more generally that, in Hecht's case, militates against a full response to the poet's narrative powers, especially as these developed in the second half of his career. We might note, too, a cache of poems related more by mood and the general subject matter of violence and loss than by specific reflections on the war. These include the oddly titled but shocking ekphrasis "The Deodand," which juxtaposes, with searing irony, a Renoir painting (*Parisians Dressed in Algerian Costumes*) with the French Algerian war, and some of the midrange dramatic monologues like "The Grapes," in which the chambermaid's recognition of her lonely future is compared to the solitude of a sole survivor in a rubber boat in the Pacific. "The Deodand" and "Behold the Lilies of the Field" are also probably the best candidates for "atrocity" poems in the canon, each characteristically "monstrous" in the extended, grotesque depiction of the human body. Their extravagance, in this respect, seems a feature of their imagined distance from the World War II events that otherwise underlie Hecht's poems.

These are all strong poems in Harold Bloom's sense of openly admitting powerful precursors—Auden, Eliot, Shakespeare, the Bible—into their precincts without being bowed by the weight of authority. Hecht's best readers, among them J. D. McClatchy and Christopher Ricks,[3] have explored how echoes are richly replayed in Hecht's poetry; how allusion, often layered with irony (as we've already partly glimpsed in "The Cost"), becomes a special mark of his verse; and these features are present in the three poems I am identifying at the core of Hecht's poetics. But this trio of poems also brings to the fore certain moments of poetic daring and courage within the larger working of Hecht's canon and the canon of American poetry more generally and therefore possess a further claim on our attention. These are poems that had to be written, not just poems brought into being by the occasion of their writing. Remove them, and Hecht's landscape, almost always well groomed and inviting, becomes suddenly narrower, less dense with meaning. And the same must be said for the landscape of post–World War II poetry more generally. The Pulitzer Prize–winning *The Hard Hours* would be thinner, lighter, without "'More Light! More Light!'" *The Venetian Vespers*, to some readers his finest volume, would become nearly unthinkable, indeed halved, without the title poem; and later Hecht would be more vulnerable to charges of mandarin elegance without "The Book of Yolek." I don't believe any other trio of poems carries the same degree of weight as these three. Although there are many lovely, beautifully crafted poems that reward careful attention, as we might expect from a poet who came of age in the era of New Criticism and who felt, like many of his generation, a special affinity for the great seventeenth-century lyric poets Donne, Herbert, and Marvell, these three poems might be thought of as anchor poems. The fluency of wit is present, in varying degrees and forms, but so, too, is the severity of circumstance and subject matter that gives language special bearing and moral purpose.

"'More Light! More Light!'" is a breakthrough poem in a breakthrough volume of poems. The early Hecht of *A Summoning of Stones* (1954) was created in the shadows of his many mentors, actual and adopted: Yeats, Eliot, Hardy, Auden, Thomas, Stevens, Tate, even the younger Robert Lowell. One of the collection's chief goals is a demonstration of formal abundance amid variety. This is most evident in the shapely stanzas of "The Gardens of Villa d'Este"—a poem that invites comparison with several of Wilbur's including his "A Baroque Wall-Fountain in the Villa Sciarra"—and the fact that none of the verse patterns composed for this volume, even the several sonnets, precisely repeats. (A similar impulse toward shapely variety motivates Merrill's early poetry.) Without dispensing with these formal concerns, *The Hard Hours* is a more decisive redress of previous influences and subjects, a profound reshaping of a poetic identity brought on by personal crisis amid the poet's ongoing strenuous dedication to his craft. If there is an important truth in Frost's pronouncement that "few will dare or deign to dispute that the prime object of composing poetry is to keep any two poems from sounding alike,"[4] it need also be said that the challenge can only be met if a poet is no longer in search of a voice. That change happens with *The Hard Hours*. The various poetic forms are now charged with a basso continuo of suffering, a ground note against which the fuller resources of the lyric air could be sounded, including the sharp wit of mimicry and riposte in celebrated poems like "The Dover Bitch."

A good case could be made that "Rites and Ceremonies" is the crucial poem in *The Hard Hours*. It is certainly the longest. It also occupies a central place in the collection in both its deployment of complex forms and its deliberately ironic revision of Eliot's *The Waste Land* to now include a reckoning of the Holocaust, an insistence on the priority of history over myth, the suffering of a Jewish people after World War II over the spiritual depletion of a generation of people "entre les deux guerres." Although "Rites and Ceremonies" took some thirteen years to complete and has had its notable defenders, the poem can sometimes feel too large and burdened by its mission, can ask too much of form as counterbalance to the terrible events depicted, including the large question of God's having apparently abandoned his people in their time of greatest need, to be altogether persuasive. A chief virtue of the poem might be said, rather, to lie in a different direction. It gave Hecht an extended opportunity to exorcise the ghost of Eliot from his pantheon of influences: to reduce Eliot to one of many voices (to that of "Gerontion," say, in "The Venetian Vespers") instead of continuing to regard Eliot as the dominant Anglo-American sage he had become to many readers by midcentury, especially Hecht's immediate New Critical mentors, Allen Tate and John Crowe Ransom.

The real prize in this willed act of separation of Jewish poet from Gentile authorities is the smaller, more sharply focused, and darkly severe "'More Light! More Light!'" Freed from the need to minister to a surviving remnant in the wilderness, Hecht could concentrate on a single episode of brutality. In fact, not only did Hecht not feel compelled to offer consolation, he also deliberately deployed the idea of redemption as a counterstrategy to trace out the new reality of a post-Holocaust world. To that end, his separation from Eliot and an Elizabethan past in which Christian martyrdom had meaning is more than a legacy of poetic influence. The division fully informs the poem's structure. It is the bleak pivot around which the poem turns:

> Composed in the Tower before his execution
> These moving verses, and being brought at that time
> Painfully to the stake, submitted, declaring thus:
> "I implore my God to witness that I have made no crime."
>
> Nor was he forsaken of courage, but the death was horrible,
> The sack of gunpowder failing to ignite.
> His legs were blistered sticks on which the black sap
> Bubbled and burst as he howled for the Kindly Light.
>
> And that was but one, and by no means one of the worst;
> Permitted at least his pitiful dignity;
> And such as were by made prayers in the name of Christ,
> That shall judge all men, for his soul's tranquility.
>
> We move now to outside a German wood.
> Three men are there commanded to dig a hole
> In which the two Jews are ordered to lie down
> And be buried alive by the third, who is a Pole.
>
> Not light from the shrine at Weimar beyond the hill
> Nor light from heaven appeared. But he did refuse.
> A Lüger settled back deeply in its glove.
> He was ordered to change places with the Jews.

Much casual death had drained away their souls.
The thick dirt mounted toward the quivering chin.
When only the head was exposed the order came
To dig him out again and to get back in.

No light, no light in the blue Polish eye.
When he finished a riding boot packed down the earth.
The Lüger hovered lightly in its glove.
He was shot in the belly and in three hours bled to death.

No prayers or incense rose up in those hours
Which grew to be years, and every day came mute
Ghosts from the ovens, sifting through crisp air,
And settled upon his eyes in a black soot.

Reader's today steeped in the visual effects of violence and perhaps saturated, too, by accounts of the Holocaust may well wonder why all the fuss, but that is to forget the history Hecht is countering here, the general silence still surrounding the subject of the Holocaust in 1960, the year when the poem was composed, and, with the exception of Geoffrey Hill, certainly not the kind of subject that poets in the shadow of Eliot were writing. Eliot's concern with the private soul's spiritual quest seems, literally, to disappear in the closing mute figure of the ghosts emanating from the ovens. The blood of salvation, such as might be sounded in the prayers made "in the name of Christ," slowly drains away from the Pole's belly, disappears without leaving a trace of redemption. The verses spoken in the Tower are said to be moving, and they are, but nothing is as moving as the single line "No light, no light in the blue Polish eye," and nothing quite as terrifying as the simple swivel phrase, "We move now to outside a German wood."

Less is more in this poem but also, purposefully, not enough. The shortest sentence in the poem reports heroic behavior without any applause, "But he did refuse," just as the death itself fails to receive any prayers or incense at the end. The diction in the second half of the poem is particularly terse, factual, functional, in recounting the brief, bleak story involving the two Jews and the Pole. The stanzas throughout are formal without being fancy, the dark ironies finely managed, and also unforgettable, especially the one suggested by the title that forms a leitmotif in the poem. The quotation is a phrase attributed to the German Enlightenment philosopher poet, Johann Wolfgang von Goethe, on his deathbed in Weimar, five miles from where Buchenwald is located and where this incident was reported to have taken place by one of the death camp's survivors, Eugen Kogon, in his *Der SS-Staat* (1946), translated and first published in English as *The Theory and Practice of Hell* (1950). The image of light allows, early on, a cursory play with Cardinal Newman's famous hymn, "Lead kindly light," and a more poignant commentary on the Pole's heroic behavior. We might register, too, a sense of the decline and fall of the German Enlightenment in the metonymic reduction of German thought in the figure of the Lüger and the riding boot, altogether detached from a human body, to say nothing about a named person, and yet, in the dedication to the German Jewish scholars Heinrich Blücher and Hannah Arendt, we might find a crumb of comfort in the fact that not all thought has been eradicated from German culture even if, in this case, it required transplanting to another country. If this is a more (faintly) optimistic reading than is usually accorded the poem, what do we make of the final stanza? Is Hecht just being wistfully ironic? Toying deftly and ironically with the word "crisp," for instance? Or, rather, as I now think, is it an ending that also underscores the long years of silent suffering, during and after the war, in Germany, in Europe, and beyond, a silence finally broken in English in 1960 by the publication of Elie Wiesel's *Night* (now famous but then little known) and also by the author of "'More Light! More Light!'"? The earlier title of Wiesel's work, translated from the Yiddish, was, it should be remembered, *And the World Remained Silent*. We might also recall the quietly purposeful ending of "Apprehensions" cited earlier: "and no one spoke."

If "'More Light! More Light!'" were to have a cinematic parallel today, it would be with a grainy black-and-white documentary recording brutal events from the past and present, with little commentary in between, except for the chilling directive around which the poem pivots. In this context, the poem represents a breakthrough for Hecht, not just in regard to subject matter but also in its means of handling violence: the objective recording, or juxtaposition, of related events, with one event shedding "light" on the other. (It's a technique that will reappear throughout Hecht's later work.) There is no "I" in this poem, no "witness" in Wiesel's sense of an actual survivor of a death camp personally testifying to events,[5] and yet there is an author with an unmistakable point of view, compassionate yet un-fooled by the cruelty the poem confronts and represents. The landscape observed, as it were, is made to speak for itself. In this muted, untheatricalized, impersonal vision, moreover, one could hardly be further from the controversial appropriation of the Holocaust for self-dramatic purposes emerging in the poetry of Hecht's Smith College colleague at the time, Sylvia Plath. For Hecht, the death camps were to be remembered, not made into a dramatic monologue, a script for repeated rehearsals. To the degree that the subject required solemn observance, it raises the question whether the topic reined in or, as I believe, gave further focus to Hecht's facility with words, a matter addressed in different ways in "The Venetian Vespers" and "The Book of Yolek."

"The Venetian Vespers" is the great long poem of Hecht's middle years, vivid and majestic, richly ironic in its use of story and morbidly passionate in image and exposition. Hecht was thirty-seven when he finished "'More Light! More Light!'" "The Venetian Vespers" was written nearly twenty years later, when the author was in his mid-fifties, happily married, and his imaginary powers at their most exuberant. It speaks not to the need to remember past atrocities but, rather, to the problem of not being able to forget them. In this, it distantly resembles "Rites and Ceremonies" and "Behold the Lilies of the Field" but differs significantly from either in the solution it seeks. Ushered into being by a desire to extend the parameters of the lyric in the direction of the novel, "Vespers" revels in an often strange, extravagant idiom, a linguistic creation befitting its baroque setting unmatched anywhere in Hecht's oeuvre or elsewhere in American verse of the period. (Its contemporary long-poem compatriots are John Ashbery's 1975 *Self-Portrait in a Convex Mirror* and James Merrill's *Book of Ephraim* in its first iteration in 1976 as a part of *Divine Comedies*.) The novelization of lyric also affords Hecht an opportunity to anchor his musings in a "character," a speaker more fully developed than in any of his dramatic monologues, causing some readers to regard the poem as barely disguised autobiography. This isn't quite accurate. Hecht, in fact, attributes the speaker's "story" to an American he once met on the island of Ischia, but by the time Hecht finished with the poem, not only did the "source" not recognize himself in the poem, but the poem came to resemble its creator in many of its moods and interests, albeit in exaggerated form. Readers who resist "The Venetian Vespers" also often want simpler phrasing and a more straightforward narrative, but that is to wish Henry James were Ernest Hemingway, although to make that comparison is to suggest that part of the genius of "Vespers" is that it manages to be both Hemingway and James: indirect, syntactically circuitous at times, densely layered with a sense of Venetian culture in its twilight, reflecting a psyche in possession of, and possessed by, a dark secret; and yet, when the poem needs to be, it is remarkably down to earth, even, occasionally, bleakly comical. "The palaces decay. Venice is rich / Chiefly in the deposits of her dogs." Or doges.

At its center lie memories of the war itself, not the Holocaust. The two poems diverge in many respects. The substitution of Ruskin for Kogon as a deep source is especially telling in the turn toward the rich coloration of detail in "Vespers." The story and setting permit Hecht a full demonstration of his gifts of description and exposition, his fluent wit. (See, especially, his lavish account of the interior of Saint Mark's Cathedral in Section III, which is modeled in part on a passage from Ruskin's *The Stones of Venice*.) But the two poems overlap in one important way: the significant role sight plays, with the request for "More Light" now refigured in the speaker's relentless desire to be delivered from the terrifying grip memory has on the present. The suffering soul seeks relief in salvation by sight alone, in the alluring images of art for which Venice is famous, including the image of the city itself. So, too, the coolly observed violence in the earlier poem is now plangently and deeply internalized, turned into a dramatic monologue, into a cosmic hymn of sorts, into a memorable voice. "Vespers," we slowly discover (and slowness is a virtue in this poem), is the lengthy confession of a doubly wounded psyche. As such, it is part of the larger, postwar story of American poetry ultimately indebted to the personal outpourings opened up by Lowell's *Life Studies*, although one steadied and modulated in Hecht by the continuous flow of the poem's blank verse carrying its fantastic booty of images and reflections in unpredictable directions. (That the speaker actually seeks salvation reminds us of the original purpose and meaning of confession rarely sought or realized in "confessional" poetry.) So various, in fact, are the pathways of "Vespers" that it also includes a second story connecting it to one of the ur-myths of American literature as the land of golden opportunity and sullied dreams. The poem's anonymous speaker, of Latvian descent, never knows for sure the identity of his father, and he is as much haunted by this uncertainty as he is haunted by certain memories of the war.

    The most conspicuous of these memories closes off the third of the poem's six sections. Its power is partly a feature of the labyrinthine excursion that precedes it, where the unhinged mind sorts through the many vermiculate particulars of an unnamed malady associated with the death of the speaker's mother. There is a kind of bizarre pleasure here in the willful profusion of imagery, and it helps to establish the contrast with, what seems, the greater source of his dysfunctionality centering on a war memory. Lengthy as it is, few passages in Hecht are more immediately powerful than this one. Its sudden clarity of self-depiction, as if we've just entered the world of a Hemingway novel (the association with *A Farewell to Arms* is difficult to miss), the precise but leisurely pacing of phrase, the cultivation of detail, all are perfectly controlled, right down to the final, shocking image of the corporal's death:

> I was an Aid Man,
> A Medic with an infantry company,
> Who because of my refusal to bear arms
> Was constrained to bear the wounded and the dead
> From under enemy fire, and to bear witness
> To inconceivable pain, usually shot at
> Though banded with Red Crosses and unarmed.
> There was a corporal I knew in Heavy Weapons
> Someone who carried with him into combat
> A book of etiquette by Emily Post.
> Most brought with them some token of the past,
> Some emblem of attachment or affection
> Or coddled childhood—bibles and baby booties,
> Harmonicas, love letters, photographs—
> But this was different. I discovered later
> That he had been brought up in an orphanage,
> So the book was his fiction of kindliness,
> A novel in which personages of wealth
> Firmly secure domestic tranquility.
> He'd cite me instances. It seems a boy
> Will not put "Mr." on his calling cards

> Till he leaves school, and may omit the "Mr."
> Even while at college. Bread and butter plates
> Are never placed on a formal dinner table.
> At a simple dinner party one may serve
> Claret instead of champagne with the meat.
> The satin facings on a butler's lapels
> Are narrower than a gentleman's, and he wears
> Black waistcoat with white tie, whereas the gentleman's
> White waistcoat goes with both black tie and white.
> When a lady lunches alone at her own home
> In a formally kept house the table is set
> For four. As if three Elijahs were expected.
> This was to him a sort of *Corpus Juris*,
> An ancient piety and governance
> Worthy of constant dream and meditation.
> He haunts me here, that seeker after law
> In a lawless world, in rainsoaked combat boots,
> Oil-stained fatigues and heavy bandoleers.
> He was killed by enemy machine-gun fire.
> His helmet had fallen off. They had sheared away
> The top of his cranium like a soft-boiled egg,
> And there he crouched, huddled over his weapon,
> His brains wet in the chalice of his skull.

The passage is wrenchingly serious. If there is a fastidious attention to etiquette à la Emily Post, I don't think that Hecht, or Hecht's speaker, is treating these values ironically. There is too much pressure placed on the witness's role here and the simple confession, "He haunts me here, that seeker after law / In a lawless world," followed by the painfully incongruous particulars of his "oil-stained fatigues." Rather, we are near the center of one of the motivating impulses, the animating "strains," underlying much of Hecht's poetry. In the figure of the Aid Man, the "Medic," we recognize the poet in his burden to "bear witness / To inconceivable pain." As a veteran of the war, Hecht no doubt felt entitled, indeed charged, on this occasion to speak as "witness"; and in the young corporal's attachment to "domestic tranquility" and the ritual forms this impulse lovingly assumes, we glimpse the poet's larger concern with justice: the just placement of objects, that is, whether around the table or in a poem, and the symbolic value of order, the "worthy dream" of *Corpus Juris* ultimately destroyed in the figure of the partially decapitated corporal. The carnage, the waste, is maddening, literally, the savagery registered in the audacious Jacobean or Websterian wit of the skull as chalice. The Aid Man, Hecht's speaker, is shortly discharged from the army for being "mentally unsound," unhinged, like Othello.

Although post-traumatic stress disorder (PTSD) was not officially identified as a syndrome until a decade after Hecht wrote "The Venetian Vespers," there can be little question that his unnamed speaker suffers from this condition. Knowing so gives further pertinence, indeed prescience, to this poem, as timely in its own way as "'More Light! More Light!'" is in its. According to current medical terminology, the specific criteria of PTSD include (1) reexperiencing the trauma (e.g., nightmares, intrusive thoughts); (2) avoidance and numbing (e.g., avoiding reminders, not being able to have loving feelings); and (3) increased arousal (e.g., difficulty sleeping, hypervigilance, exaggerated startle response).[6] All of these conditions apply, at various points, to Hecht's solitary, restive, ruminating speaker, who is also aroused, often desperately, sometimes wryly, by the Venetian sights he sees. It's important to note, as well, that the intruding traumatic images in his case are not simply of randomly distressing thoughts but of the traumatizing event itself, one that cannot be readily dispelled "once it has entered conscious awareness."[7] Images of the helmet, of rain, of the sacrifice of innocence, everywhere haunt the poem, including its two epigraphs respectively, one from *Othello*, tortuously insinuating, the other, quieter, from Ruskin's *The Stones of Venice*:

> . . . where's that palace whereinto foul things
> Sometimes intrude not? Who has a breast so pure
> But some uncleanly apprehensions
> Keep leets and law days, and in session sit
> With meditations lawful?

And

> We cannot all have our gardens now, nor our
> Pleasant fields to meditate in at eventide.

Along with the amplification of meaning generated by quotation, the power in Hecht's poem is twofold. It describes, with surgical detachment, the morbid source of his speaker's disabling wound in the person of the decapitated corporal, one reexperienced, rather than resolved, by the second narrative of a lost "head" of the family in the figure of the missing father. And, in giving voice to the macabre and the morose, it also prescribes, with equal pressure, a wishful drug of choice, not a pharmaceutical like Ativan (although the speaker does report indulging in a nightly aperitif at Florian's in Saint Mark's Square), but a vision of stasis that temporarily lifts the soul, a flight into art that gives the poem and its speaker a knowingly belated, fin-de-siècle feel, in which he is momentarily able to substitute the cool purity and pleasure of looking in place of the pain of remembering.[8]

The happiest of these moments is the brilliantly lit, picturesque description of Venice at midmorning and of the lagoon whose view includes "Palladio's church," San Giorgio Maggiore, floating "at its anchored peace," and Santa Maria della Salute, "the great church of Health / Voted in gratitude by the Venetians / For heavenly deliverance from the plague." The view possesses a Bishop-like concern for surface accuracy, one motivated, though, by the speaker's darker needs for "heavenly deliverance." This is a passage that also gathers its strength gradually, as so many do in Hecht. The section begins almost liturgically, hypnotically:

> Lights. I have chosen Venice for its light,
> Its lightness, buoyancy, its calm suspension
> In time and water, its strange quietness.

And after imagining, in considerable detail, how "Morning has tooled the bay with bright inlays / Of writhing silver, scattered scintillance," the speaker is led to declare, however wishfully, "I am for the moment cured of everything." "For the moment" is a phrase that bears emphasizing. Part of the attraction of Hecht's speaker is that he is a version, in the extreme, of every viewer or reader who has ever experienced art's powers of enchantment, including the reader of this poem. The passage works its magic by drawing us into its beautiful scenery, the serenity of La Serenissima's watery "paysage"—the hypnotic effects of the beginning being ultimately realized in the homely, fantastic vision of art being made, crafted, at the end, in the image of the Vulcan-like glass blowers hard at work at the forge:

> They take the first crude bulb of thickened glass,
> Glowing and taffy-soft on the blow tube,
> And sink it in a mold, a metal cup
> Spiked on its inner surface like a pineapple.
> Half the glass now is regularly dimpled,
> And when these dimples are covered with a glaze
> Of molten glass they are prisoned air-bubbles,
> Breathless, enameled pearly vacancies.

"Breathless" is a word that does double duty here. It voices a sense of wonder over the creation of a work of art but reminds us, too, of the boundary between art and artifice, breath and death. Hecht's speaker yearns for "enameled pearly vacancies," an escape, but the phrase takes thought in a different direction. And so does the poem, which constantly admits "life" into its art, its "passages," a word that Hecht considered at one point in the singular as a possible title for the poem. As with *Paradise Lost*, the blank verse of "The Venetian Vespers" draws the sense variously out, line after line, constantly admitting new light along the way to form the peculiar character that binds together speaker and city, psyche and environment. Although death is the beast in this jungle, poetic abundance is its reward and receives in this poem the fullest airing in all of Hecht.

"The Venetian Vespers" is an anthologist's challenge for more than the usual reasons of length. The poem is constructed out of a series of contrasting visions, the whole being greater than the sum of its parts, its parts carrying, at the level of image and rhythm, variously orchestrated leitmotifs that conclude in an evensong of finely shaded, never-ending wants.

By contrast, "The Book of Yolek," a sestina, is tightly wrapped, complete in itself, a "book," no less, in thirty-nine lines. There is something absolutely definitive about this often reprinted poem. The subject, again, is an incident from World War II. Some of the details Hecht found in a 1973 *Anthology of Holocaust Literature* in an account titled "Yanosz Korchak's Last Walk" by Hanna Mortkowicz-Olczakowa. Korchak, or Korczak, a famous Polish educator, was respected by many Germans in fact and was in charge of the Jewish orphanage in the Warsaw ghetto. When the children were rounded up by the Nazis in 1942—on August 5, 1942, Hecht's poem pointedly reminds us—and marched off to, in all probability, the Treblinka concentration camp, Korchak opted for the hero's choice. Although given opportunities to leave, he elected to stay with the children. They and he were never heard from again. Among the many works honoring Korchak's memory are a statue of him in Warsaw and a 1990 film of his life, *Korczak*, by the great Polish director Andrzej Wajda. He is also the subject of a work of historical fiction by Jim Shepard, *The Book of Aron* (2015), written from the perspective of a young boy, and of much scholarly work besides.

The story, in any version, is a moving, terrifying one, "stomach turning."[9] It was made more immediate to the poet through his own memories of Flossenbürg, as well as of a famous photo from the Warsaw ghetto "of a small boy, perhaps five or six, wearing a shabby peaked cap and short pants, his hands raised and a bewildered, forlorn look on his face as he gazes off at something to the side of the camera, while behind him uniformed, helmeted soldiers keep their rifles trained on him, as one of them looks directly at the camera without the least expression of embarrassment." What makes the poem feel "definitive" to this reader at least is the perfect match between form and subject. The laws of the sestina come now, in concentrated form, to the service of the poet writing about the horrors of the concentration camp, in the manner, as Wiesel says, "of a witness who believes he has a moral obligation to try to prevent the enemy from enjoying one last victory by allowing his crimes to be erased from human memory."[10] And writing about the event, it should be said, with absolute candor and ease of expression. Although the poem possesses, as must all sestinas, significant attention to form, nowhere in Hecht—and in very few sestinas in general—does form feel so natural an extension of thought. (Elizabeth Bishop's "Sestina," beginning "September rain falls on the house," is another pertinent example.) In 1973, Korchak's name had already been remembered in the title of Mortkowicz-Olczakowa's account but, except in passing, not the names of the children. Memorializing Yolek was a way of remembering this otherwise lost boy and, by association, the other children as well and all those children taken in the war and sent to the camps, but more too; for in the sestina, the speaker's memories of boyhood camp mutate inexorably, and shockingly, into those of a soldier coming upon another kind of camp.

That degree of intensely forged identification with the subject, of boy with boy, of soldier with the boy who never got the chance to grow up, is what makes the poem a true witness to the events it describes. You feel the identification in every turn of phrase, in the use of the colloquial "you" as a form of self-address, in the perfectly managed but also terrible logic of the return of those six simple terminal words, the meaning of which even a five-year-old would understand: meal, walk, to, home, camp, day. As the poet says, in the penultimate stanza,

> Whether on a silent, solitary walk
> Or among crowds, far off or safe at home,
> You will remember, helplessly, that day,
> And the smell of smoke, and the loudspeakers of the camp.
> Wherever you are, Yolek will be there, too.
> His unuttered name will interrupt your meal.

"Real war poets are always war poets, peace or any time," wrote Randall Jarrell.[11] And so with Hecht, the poet of "The Book of Yolek." The sestina concludes:

> Prepare to receive him in your home some day.
> Though they killed him in the camp they sent him to,
> He will walk in as you're sitting down to a meal.

Like the speaker of "Venetian Vespers," Hecht cannot but remember his helplessness to do anything but remember; but as an author he can do more than look longingly at "enameled pearly vacancies."

Near the end of his life, Hecht quoted an observation by Seamus Heaney in a review of Heaney's *Finders Keepers*, a collection of essays:

> When a poem rhymes, when a form generates itself, when a metre provokes consciousness into new postures, it is already on the side of life. When a rhyme surprises and extends the fixed relations between words, that in itself protests against necessity. When language does more than enough, as it does in all achieved poetry, it opts for the condition of overlife and rebels at limit.[12]

Sometimes the need for "overlife" is greater than others. Heaney was thinking specifically of Philip Larkin's late "Aubade," a poem Hecht characterizes, rather brutally, as "a bitter, almost resentful meditation on his solitary, mortal condition, a muttered litany of whining complaint." But he found Heaney's fundamental rule, his law, even true here. "In this fundamental artistic way, then," Heaney noted, "Larkin's 'Aubade' does not go over to the side of the adversary." Nor, must it be said, does "The Book of Yolek." In its utter mastery of a complex form, the sestina protests, quietly but strenuously, "against necessity," indeed, in favor of "overlife," as Yolek returns at the end of the poem in the figure of Elijah to assume his seat at the table. One wonders what the unembarrassed German soldier in the photo might have felt had he come upon Hecht's poem in 1981, the year it was composed, or 1990, when it first appeared as part of a collection in *The Transparent Man*.

To a great degree, the angle of this chapter has been to insist on Hecht as "our contemporary," albeit already in some need of historicizing. I think it is important to do so in order to counter the charge that he was, in some regards, the "last Elizabethan," hopelessly out of date in his attraction to form and elegance, to the allurements of a genteel sprezzatura or courtliness, like the corporal in "The Venetian Vespers," or that verse, more generally, cannot speak to matters of great concern, as it has so often done in the past, whether distant or immediate, and still be poetry. This argument could be pressed further by underscoring the timeliness of "The Deodand." A poem with nearly impeccable postcolonial credentials that looks beyond Europe to Africa, it was composed in 1978, the same year that Edward Said's influential *Orientalism* appeared. The poem's continuing relevance is further testified to by its later inclusion in the third edition of volume 2 of *The Norton Anthology of Modern and Contemporary Poetry* (2003), with its postcolonial and transnational slant.

But it's also important not to falsify Hecht's credentials by stressing only what seems most immediately relevant. Hecht could be a remarkably funny poet, as in "The Ghost in the Martini" or "The Mysteries of Caesar," or in long stretches in "The Short End," where both verbal fluency and satiric wit are at his fingertips; and whatever special affinities he felt for the bleakness of *King Lear*, he responded vividly to the subject of love in Shakespearean comedy. His "A Love for Four Voices" is a modern-day riff on *A Midsummer*

Night's Dream, attentive to the orchestration of light and shadow, the folly and humor, the rich wordplay in Shakespeare's drama. "Peripeteia" is a more serious love poem, one constructed, touchingly, out of an evening of Shakespearean theater. Comedy is often easier to read but harder to talk about than tragedy. Nonetheless, Hecht couldn't probe the subject of the barbaric so deeply—in his case, the barbaric is almost always what people do to one another, not, for instance, what humans do to nature or the environment—if he didn't respond so fully to its lively opposite. "A Hill" continues to appeal in part because the speaker's memory of the "plain bitterness" associated with being abandoned as a child, all the cold and silence of loneliness, doesn't blot out, indeed makes more intense, the relief he feels in being "restored / To the sunlight and my friends," in particular to the early-morning commercial bustle of the "warm sunlit piazza" delightfully envisioned and carefully measured at the poem's beginning. And even though we are shocked by the grotesque return of the repressed at the end of "The Deodand," the poem hasn't forgotten the world of human accomplishment represented by the Renoir painting.

The cultural forces against which Hecht's poetry must struggle for a place is culture itself. His poetry, like that of much of his contemporaries, is or was conceived as belonging to a larger world of letters: what used to be referred to as the Western literary canon, although it's important to recognize that, within that tradition, Hecht had an eye for the small fry as well as the big guy. (With the exception of Dickinson and Bishop, and to a lesser degree Marianne Moore, the canon he knew and admired was mostly male.) His moving poem "Coming Home," based on John Clare's journals, was composed in 1976 when Clare was unknown to many and certainly not the celebrated eco-poet he has since become. A line from the minor Elizabethan poet Edmund Bolton will always belong to the footnotes of literary history, but it could be dusted off to form a fitting epigraph to his elegy for the author of *The Changing Light at Sandover*, James Merrill, in which Hecht also quotes, from Milton, the well-known poet's mantra: "Fit audience find though few."

Hecht's ideal reader is someone not put off by allusion or quotation ("'More Light! More Light!'"; "'It Out-Herods Herod. Pray You, Avoid It'"), but, rather, a reader who will see thought growing through references, almost in the manner of an extended conceit, and willingly accept the implied invitation into a life beyond the self that the literary imagines. In this regard,

Google is as much Hecht's friend as the 140-character tweet his foe. The stoning of Stephen, the first Christian martyr, is the subject toward which the four sonnets in "The Feast of Stephen" slowly work their will and way, from "the coltish horseplay of the locker room" to "the rippled heat of a neighbor's field" on to the final, curious insinuating glance at Paul as vicarious spectator to the bloodshed. One reason why Hecht liked lengthy sentences is precisely because they embody an idea in motion. The syntax weaves its sense—sense containing both thought and emotion—in the process of constructing an entire world through its manifold connections. Milton and Stevens are Hecht's chief exemplars here, "Vespers," the principal example—the upward, hieratic celebration of art in Saint Mark's Cathedral gloriously suspended on air, by breath, a prime instance.

A late offering of this kind is the mysterious poem "A Certain Slant" from *The Darkness and the Light* (2001). The poem's title recalls the famous opening line of Emily Dickinson's poem ("There's a certain Slant of Light / Winter afternoons—"), but a footnote provided by Hecht points us toward a source in the short story "The Boys" by Anton Chekhov, and the opening line and closing image seem to allude to Frost, especially the Frost of "The Wood Pile." Perhaps the point of the multiple allusions is to hint at how readily and variously these references can be woven into the fabric of a single vision. Hecht's is a poem that celebrates, like late Stevens, the imagination itself. Light seems to create out of one lengthy sentence a world of its own inside the home, a microcosm that slowly takes the edge off the initial image of "barbarous thistles of frost"; but then, after a short question, a litote masking as a rhetorical question, we're invited to look outside, and the poem suddenly explodes with reflected Promethean light:

> Etched on the window were barbarous thistles of frost,
> Edged everywhere in that tame winter sunlight
> With pavé diamonds and fine prickles of ice
> Through which a shaft of the late afternoon
> Entered our room to entertain the sway
> And float of motes, like tiny aqueous lives,
> Then glanced off the silver teapot, raising stains
> Of snailing gold upcast across the ceiling,
> And bathed itself at last in the slop bucket

> Where other aqueous lives, equally slow,
> Turned in their sad, involuntary courses,
> Swiveled in eel-green broth. Who could have known
> Of any elsewhere? Even of out-of-doors,
> Where the stacked firewood gleamed in drapes of glaze
> And blinded the sun itself with jubilant theft,
> The smooth cool plunder of celestial fire.

Inside and outside, "barbarous thistles of frost" and "celestial fire" are part of a single continuum or vision. The end is in its beginning, in much the same way that the gleaming product, the finished poem on the page, owes its origins to the inner mix of ingredients, the brew or "eel-green broth" that precedes it in time but is also somehow, inexplicably but triumphantly, constitutive of its final being. Hecht is uncovering metaphors for the mysterious working of the inspired mind; for how a poem thick with sources can become its own jubilant work; how Robert Frost even comes out sounding like his near opposite, Wallace Stevens.

Hecht's poetry, in short, insists that we include the barbarous thistles as part of the business of poetry but not to the exclusion of forsaking the medium for the message. A small case in point: the story of the Christian martyrs in "'More Light! More Light!'" is based on the lives of Nicholas Ridley and Hugh Latimer as reported by John Foxe in his *Acts and Monuments*. Neither wrote poetry, as Hecht knew, but in his version his suffering speaker does. "Composed" is the poem's first word, signaling an initial act of agency, an imploration against which all else in this poem is measured, even silence. A final, thrilling example, is his late ekphrasis, "Matisse: Blue Interior with Two Girls—1947" from *Flight among the Tombs* (1996). All thought—"if we but take thought"—is generated by what Hecht sees in the painting. Indeed, so intense is the poet's identification with the painting that the painting itself becomes the thought, "becomes our thought," the connection with us, the reader, now even more deeply interfused in the second half of the poem as we enter the interior Matisse has painted and poet has imagined. But as deep as we go into this twisting spiral of beautiful reflections, Hecht will never quite let us forget the larger world from which we have momentarily departed. The poem's epigraph about Matisse quoted from Robert Hughes, *The Shock of the New*, begins, "[H]e lived through some of the most traumatic political events of recorded history, the worst wars, the greatest slaughters, the most demented rivalries of ideology, without, it seems, turning a hair." In other words, quite literally in the words of another, even this most civilized of poems about art has a barbarous edge to it.

A chapter as discursive as this one should risk a simple takeaway, a fortune cookie of sorts. Mine reads: "The air is sweetest that a thistle guards." The line, pitch perfect iambic pentameter, appears as a refrain from a poem of Hecht's called "A Pledge."[13] That simple, proverbial phrase—here it is again, "The air is sweetest that a thistle guards"—might well serve as Hecht's motto, his *pledge*, his personal mantra, and my conclusion.

Notes

1. "The Cost," from *Millions of Strange Shadows* (1977). Quotations from Hecht's poetry are from Anthony Hecht, *Collected Earlier Poems* (New York: Alfred A. Knopf, 1990); and *Collected Later Poems* (New York: Alfred A. Knopf, 2003).
2. Recently published anthologies consulted for Hecht's poetry include Margaret Ferguson, Mary Jo Salter, and Jon Stallworthy, eds., *The Norton Anthology of Poetry*, 5th ed. (New York: W. W. Norton, 2005); Jahan Ramazani, Richard Ellmann, and Robert O'Clair, eds., *The Norton Anthology of Modern and Contemporary Poetry*, 2 vols., 3rd ed. (New York: W. W. Norton, 2003); David Lehman, ed., *The Oxford Book of American Poetry* (Oxford: Oxford University Press, 2006); J. D. McClatchy, ed., *The Vintage Book of Contemporary American Poetry* (New York: Vintage Books, 1990, 2003); and Elizabeth Hun Schmidt, ed., *The Poets Laureate Anthology* (New York: W. W. Norton, 2010).
3. J. D. McClatchy, introduction to *Anthony Hecht: Selected Poems* (New York: Alfred A. Knopf, 2011); and Christopher Ricks, *True Friendship: Geoffrey Hill, Anthony Hecht, and Robert Lowell under the Sign of Eliot and Pound* (New Haven, CT: Yale University Press, 2010).
4. Robert Frost, *The Notebooks of Robert Frost*, ed. Robert Faggen (Cambridge, MA: Harvard University Press, 2006), 308.
5. Elie Wiesel, *Night*, trans. Marion Wiesel (1958; New York: Hill and Wang, 2006), viii.
6. Emily J. Ozer, Daniel S. Weiss, Suzanne R. Best, and Tami L. Lipsey, "Predictors of Posttraumatic Stress Disorder and Symptoms in Adults: A Meta-Analysis," *Psychological Bulletin* 129, no. 1 (2003): 53.
7. Ibid.
8. On this topic in particular, see Gregory Dowling, "'Pearly Vacancies': The Venice of Anthony Hecht's 'Vespers,'" *Il Bianco e il Nero* 4 (2000–2001): 49–64. For

a more general discussion of this poem, see my book, *A Thickness of Particulars: The Poetry of Anthony Hecht* (Oxford: Oxford University Press, 2015), ch. 5.
9. This and the following quotation are taken from *Anthony Hecht in Conversation with Philip Hoy*, 3rd ed. (London: Between the Lines, 2004), 101.
10. Wiesel, *Night*, viii.
11. Colm Tóibín, "Places Never Explained," *London Review of Books*, August 8, 2013, 22; quoted in Post, *A Thickness of Particulars*, ix.
12. Anthony Hecht, "Seamus Heaney's Prose," in *Melodies Unheard: Essays on the Mysteries of Poetry*, by Anthony Hecht (Baltimore: Johns Hopkins University Press, 2003), 215.
13. In the refrain, Hecht is repurposing, to great effect, the title line from an early James Merrill poem, "Variations: The Air Is Sweetest That a Thistle Guards," in *First Poems* (New York: Alfred A. Knopf, 1951).

CHAPTER 7

Ecovaluation

JOHN SHOPTAW

WHEN WALLACE STEVENS'S "Of Mere Being" was first published in 1957 by Samuel French Morse in *Opus Posthumous*, it began this way:

The palm at the end of the mind,
Beyond the last thought, rises
In the bronze distance,

Then in 1971, in *The Palm at the End of the Mind*, Holly Stevens changed "distance" to "decor" and appended a note: "'Decor' is the word appearing in the original typescript, and has been restored here."[1] This change was adopted by Milton J. Bates in his revised edition of *Opus Posthumous* (1989) and in subsequent editions of Stevens's poems. My first question is—"distance"? This can't have been a misreading; the words are too far apart. And I don't believe Morse would have taken it upon himself to replace "decor" with "distance." I know of no other such emendations (speaking of which, I would if I could put a period after "decor"). Stevens himself then most likely (orally?) revised "decor" with "distance." Which raises the more fundamental question—which word is better? Readers have weighed in on either side of the question. The poet James Reiss, for instance, prefers "distance": "the simpler, earlier version seems to me a lot better than the fussy 'decorator's' version."[2] I favor "decor" because the mind in this poem is a decorated interior, and because "bronze distance" inadvertently echoes Stevens's earlier tropical poem, "The Idea of Order at Key West": "Theatrical distances, bronze shadows heaped / On high horizons . . ." Whichever you choose, the question is one of evaluation, and the answer depends on what you mean by the word. For Reiss, evaluation is aesthetic, relying in his case on the time-honored principle of elegant simplicity; for me, evaluation depends on poetic context. If "distances" is better for "The Idea," "decor" is better for "Of Mere Being."

I am arguing that revision in general is evaluative, and evaluation contextual. Contextual evaluation holds also for larger poetic units. The individual—word in its poem, poem in its book, and book in the hands and heads of its reading public—adapts itself more or less successfully to its environment. Evaluation has been traditionally conceived as an objective consideration of what is inherent in poems themselves. Once the worldly dust of biography, history, and culture more or less settles, one may properly judge what poems and poets are "really good." But as many have objected, evaluation is never disinterested. We who evaluate, and we all do, have hidden or unconcealed agendas. Yet it does not follow that evaluation is arbitrary and hence pointless. Evaluation is relative and it is relatively significant.

If the best word best fits the poem, what are the best poems and their poets good for? The context within which this question finds its answer is what I will call (after Stanley Fish) an evaluative community: a transitional and evolving group of readers, including poets, forming (reforming and reevaluating) around a nodal poet or a group of poets gradually defined by their stylistic and thematic features and poetics. Poundians form an evaluative community; New York Schoolers another. Their judgments will be more authoritative within their communities than outside them. I've resorted to this model partly to account for the situation familiar to poets and poetry fanatics: the mystifying divergence in expert judgments of valuing who is "important" and who is "uninteresting." I know Poundians who skip Ashbery, New York Schoolers who have no use for Heaney, Irish and Scottish poets who don't see the point of Stevens or Ashbery, Stevensians who groan over Language poets, and post-Language innovators who balk at Pound. However discordant, these evaluations are not arbitrary. Like all evaluations, they are a declaration of values. One can dispute about taste within a community; for example, about what in Pound is overlooked or undervalued. And many communities share members and sympathies. Poets and poems will normally matter for more than one group, but they will matter differently.

The evaluative community that I'm going to dwell on here is the one flourishing around what is now often called ecopoetry (or ecopoetics, a distinction attracting somewhat different evaluative communities). Ecopoetry, which I have discussed elsewhere,[3] is a divergent movement of mainstream, renovative, and innovative poets emerging (from different evaluative communities) in response to global environmental crises resulting primarily from climate change and global energy production and marketing. What does poetry of the twentieth century have to offer readers and writers of ecopoetry in the twenty-first? The currents of influence merge. Gary Snyder, for instance, has taken rhythmic cues, juxtapositional composition, and Eastern and archaic cultures from Pound and adapted all that to a poetics of wild(er)ness (adding the geological, for instance, to Pound's historical and cultural frames of reference). Juliana Spahr has adapted the continuous presentation of Gertrude Stein's *The Making of Americans*, and Timothy Donnelly in his long poem "Hymn to Life" has extended the personalism and the painterly pastiche of the New York School to address species extinction. But whatever their genealogies, these poems are not evaluated by form or style alone. The evaluation of environmental poetry isn't merely aesthetic; what also matters is the poem's fitness for the world. On a planet increasingly wasted and stressed by environmental crises, ecopoetry will, I believe, become increasingly relevant.

To see how a familiar poem might adapt to an ecovaluative climate, let's return to "Of Mere Being":

The palm at the end of the mind,
Beyond the last thought, rises
In the bronze decor[.]

A gold-feathered bird
Sings in the palm, without human meaning,
Without human feeling, a foreign song.

You know then that it is not the reason
That makes us happy or unhappy.
The bird sings. Its feathers shine.

The palm stands on the edge of space.

The wind moves slowly in the branches.
The bird's fire-fangled feathers dangle down.

For environmental poetry readers, "Of Mere Being" would be a watershed poem for its thinking about the influence of animal upon human feeling. What really does a bird's singing have to do with us? In his second tercet, Stevens grants his ultimate bird an inhuman autonomy. If the bird means or feels anything by its song, it is utterly "foreign" or inaccessible to us humans. This inhuman bird may remind us of Yeats's golden bird singing upon a golden bough in "Sailing to Byzantium." If birds are natural, Stevens suggests, it is unreasonable to feel that their nature is ours; they might as well be artificial. Stevens thus limits his following descriptions to the merely objective—the bird sings, shines, and dangles downward; the palm stands, the wind moves it—without implying any inwardness.[4] "Of Mere Being" stands then as a corrective to Keats's "Ode to a Nightingale," the poem Stevens here had most in mind, in which the dis-eased, sore-throated poet says that his heart aches not from envy (though it sounds a lot like it) but from a too intense identification with the bird's happiness:

'Tis not through envy of thy happy lot,
But being too happy in thine happiness—
    That thou, light-wingèd Dryad of the trees,
        In some melodious plot
Of beechen green, and shadows numberless,
    Singest of summer in full-throated ease.

Stevens revises his Romantic precursor not just with a more contemporary form (e.g., an abstracted rather than a detailed seasonal landscape) but primarily by introducing a fitter idea of our proper relation to the natural world. Instructed by anthropomorphism and in particular by John Ruskin's pathetic fallacy, the post-Romantic poet reasons that we humans are not made "happy or unhappy" (painfully envious, for instance) by a bird's song, since that bird's own conjectured happiness or unhappiness is not to be found in its "mere being" but is merely our projection.[5] Instructed in turn by experimental ornithology and genomic biology, postmodern ecopoets might object in turn that a bird's merely being does in fact include its being happy in song, which may make us human singing animals reasonably happy, too.[6] But to write such a poem, a poet may want to turn to Stevens, as Stevens turned to Yeats and to Keats. So let's add a seventh revisionary ratio to Harold Bloom's half-dozen: an appeal, beyond the last formal artifice, to the planet the table is on.

As the palm-bird in "Of Mere Being" sings at the end of the mind, the woman in "The Idea of Order at Key West" sings at the end of the land. Her song takes place on a peninsular coral reef "acutest at its vanishing." The poem could take place nowhere else. As Stevens put it in "The Comedian as the Letter C," "his soil is man's intelligence." "The Idea of Order" might then be valued by ecopoets as a modernist poem of place. One far-spreading development in the environmental poetics of the last century has been the rethinking of our place in the place around us. After World War II, the forester and ecologist Aldo Leopold urged an extension of ethics beyond the human: "The land ethic simply enlarges the boundaries of the community to include soils, waters, plants, and animals, or collectively: the land." Humans would no longer hold biblical sway over the planet: "[T]he land ethic changes the role of *Homo sapiens* from conqueror of the land-community to plain member and citizen of it. It implies respect for his fellow-members, and also respect for the community as such."[7] To this influential formulation I would remark that the human, endowed with a special capacity for species extinction and preservation, is no "plain member" among other species, and that with respect comes the responsibility to promote the well-being of species and habitats. In the same year, 1947, Robinson Jeffers proposed a similar reorientation or broadening of (Christian) concerns: "'Love one another' ought to be balanced, at least, by a colder saying.... Turn outward from each other, so far as need and kindness permit, to the vast life and inexhaustible beauty beyond humanity."[8] An environmental poetics would derive from an environment. As Dickinson phrased it in "The Robin's my Criterion for Tune—," "I see—New Englandly—."[9] In her poetics of place, one's native region is not a noun (person, place, or thing) but an adverb—a way of experiencing and of singing the world.

What then does this ethical decentering among other species on the land (air and sea), this outward turning from the life within us to the life abroad, have to do with poetic evaluation? Might poems, too, be valued for reaching beyond their white margins, and might differently placed poets reach in fundamentally different ways? Ecocritics will be invited, if not challenged, to appreciate not just poets who come from various regions but those who come to those regions differently. Native American poets, for instance, whose peoples have been repeatedly displaced and confined when not exterminated from these United States, will necessarily have different criteria for tunes; they will experience and sing otherwise. To help nonnative Americans imagine how a Native poet might see and say things differently, I want to take up "That's the Place Indians Talk About" by the Acoma Pueblo poet Simon Ortiz. This poem, from his 1980 volume *Fight Back: For the Sake of the People, For the Sake of the Land*, is prefaced by a note:

> At a meeting in California I was talking with an elder Paiute man. He had been a rangerider and a migrant laborer. He spoke about Coso Hot Springs, a sacred healing place for the Shoshonean peoples, enclosed within the China Lake Naval Station. Like Los Alamos Scientific Laboratories in New Mexico, the naval station is a center for the development, experimentation, and testing of U.S. military weapons. The elder man, wearing thick glasses and a cowboy hat, said, "That's the place Indians talk about."[10]

Ortiz's poem gives us yet another environment, tuned to the speech of the Paiute elder, whose laconic pentameter—"That's the place Indians talk about"—serves as his poem's understated refrain. The aboriginal sense of place here is distinguished by its unfenced and indefinite sense of time. And this sacred time is what I value most in Ortiz's poem, which begins this way:

> We go up there and camp.
> Several days, we stay there.
> We have to take horses, wagons, or walk.
> And we would stay for the days we have to.

The duration of present-tense "We go up there" and of the generative phrase "Indians talk about" is always—always have and always will. To parse this as the habitual present is not enough to account for this intergenerational continuity, the poetic use of which I will call the ritual present or the present indigenous. In this instance, the land ritual involves immersion in the springs (not a symbolically endowed but a particular sacred place), and talking (presumably in a sweat lodge) with the hot stones. The Paiute elder speaking through this poem believes that when you offer a "flint" to the Coso spring, the spring responds. "Something . . . / from down in there is talking to you." This sacred dialogic time is disturbed, though not destroyed, by the occupation of Coso Hot Springs by the navy, who restrict their access to their own sense of time and number. Within this enclosure, Ortiz's anaphoric lines mark their boundaries:

> And now,
> they have a fence around the Coso Hot Springs.
> We go up there, but they have a fence around.
> They have a government fence all around Coso Hot Springs.
> . . .
>
> We go up there to talk with the hot springs power
> but the Navy tells us we have to talk to them.
> We don't like it, to have to do that.
> We don't want to talk to the government fence,
> the government Navy.
> That's the place the Indian people are talking about now.

The section ends with a key variation of the refrain from an ongoing present to an intervening present progressive ("now" in the present indigenous means "for now"), which leads into the poem's final movement, from the confined present into the restored future. There is no future tense in English, no morphological change beyond past (talked) and present (talk). Here, the fenced present (from 1947 up to now) is displaced by a very different time frame: "for a while" and "pretty soon":

> We don't like to talk to the fence and the Navy
> but for a while we will and pretty soon
> we will talk to the hot springs power again.
> That's the place Indians talk about.

Beneath the present progressive flows the present indigenous, the return of the original refrain to the poem, the enduring now of the temporarily displaced "Indian People."

Like Native Americans, African Americans have suffered involuntary displacement; unlike them, their relation to their "new homeland" may be uniquely fraught. Let's consider the modernist Sterling Brown's "Children of the Mississippi." Appearing first in the journal *Opportunity* in 1931, Brown's poem was composed in the aftermath of the great Mississippi flood of 1927—before Katrina, the worst environmental disaster in US history. Born and raised on the east coast, Brown was teaching at Lincoln University, in Missouri and on the Missouri, during this unprecedented flooding of the lower Mississippi. Here is the magisterial opening sentence of "Children of the Mississippi," freely versed anapestic and iambic lines:

> These know fear; for all their singing
> As the moon thrust her tip above dark woods,
> Tuning their voices to the summer night,
> These folk knew even then the hints of fear.
> For all their loafing on the levee,
> Unperturbably spendthrift of time,
> Greeting the big boat swinging the curve
> "Do it, Mister Pilot! Do it, Big Boy!"
> Beneath their dark laughter
> Roaring like a flood roars, swung into a spillwater,
> There rolled even then a strong undertow
> Of fear.

One novel feature of Brown's antediluvian stanza is his description of group psychology; the latent fear of the children of Lincoln's "Father of Waters" is imagined as the river's "undertow." Readers today (not to mention tomorrow), in the age of ever more violent river deluges, rises and storm surges, may very well feel uneasy reading such flood-lines as "Past highwater marks, past wildest conjecture." I was struck by Brown's simile, in which the Black Mississippians' "dark laughter" is compared to a flood roaring into not a bank but a "spillwater." Brown must have been thinking of the Bonnet Carré Spillway, built to divert floodwater into Lake Pontchartrain, Louisiana, begun after the flood in 1928 and not completed till 1931. (The spillway would be opened for the first time in 1937, in time for Eliot's "Dry Salvages.") How might we appreciate Brown's anachronism? The spillway construction was prompted by a similar collective fear for the sunken Crescent City (cf. "moon thrust her tip"). Along with the overtowering levees, the spillway not only reduces the risk of flooding but allows inhabitants in the floodplain to forget about the river's fearful might.

As Ortiz tuned his poem to the Paiute's speech, so Brown tunes the poems in *Southern Road* to the spirituals and blues of Mississippi River bottomlanders. Which is where his funny dissonance, his sour or blues notes, may be heard. Brown can adapt the music to the region's inhabitants, but his poem, with its dreadful ironic undercurrent, sounds out of tune:

De Lord tole Norah
Dat de flood was due,
Norah listened to the Lord
An' got his stock on board,
Wish dat de Lord
Had tole us too.

The dark humor at the end of this italicized song in "Children" brings to the surface the undertow not only of fear but of disbelief, a confronting of what these devastated people now realize: "These know no Ararat; / No arc of promise . . . / No dove, . . ." These children are not "my people," and their promised land is no Beulah: "These know / Promise of baked lands, burnt as in brickkilns, / Cracked uglily," a parched and unseeded barren clay bottom. Brown sees "uglily" a Mississippi Black culture stripped of romance. So he tunes his poem into a still darker key, a complaint worthy of Job: "*What we done done to you / Makes you do lak you do? / How we done harmed you / Black-hearted river?*" To gauge the difference between the senses of place in Brown and Ortiz, think how unimaginable such a complaint would be for the Pueblo poet, and how unsingable the enduring magic of place would be for the New Negro poet.

One thing I imagine this century's readers will look for in the previous century's poetry of place is an exploration, at least an acknowledgment, of the physical and mental place of technology: the fence in Ortiz; the levee and spillway in Brown. Technology, of course, is advertised as not a fence but a bridge, a tool that connects and enables rather than divides. How does it change our relation to the natural world? Green readers won't want to forget these lines, which open T. S. Eliot's "The Dry Salvages":

> I do not know much about gods; but I think that the river
> Is a strong brown god—sullen, untamed and intractable,
> Patient to some degree, at first recognised as a frontier;
> Useful, untrustworthy, as a conveyor of commerce;
> Then only a problem confronting the builder of bridges.
> The problem once solved, the brown god is almost forgotten
> By the dwellers in cities—ever, however, implacable,
> Keeping his seasons and rages, destroyer, reminder
> Of what men choose to forget. Unhonoured, unpropitiated
> By worshippers of the machine, but waiting, watching and waiting.

Eliot's opening lines may be valued, first of all, for their anapestically expanded pentameters ("I do nót knòw múch about góds; but I thínk that the ríver") in which strong stresses may span any number of syllables ("Úseful, untrústwòrthy, as a convéyer of cómmerce"). As such, these verses emulate not only the Mississippi, swollen and browned at St. Louis from its confluence with the Big Muddy, the Missouri, but the miraculous Mississippi River bridge, constructed of fire-fangled steel and stone pilings by James Eads in 1875 (and still in operation), at the time the world's largest suspension bridge. Eliot's suspension lines don't roll on so much as they soar over. Yet like Brown's, they are ironic. By tuning his vaulting lines to the suspension bridge, Eliot doesn't mean us to imagine the strong silver machine as the new god of progressive Mastery. That worshipful identification is impeded by the cool abstraction of the engineer ("then only a problem . . ."). The reverence due to the strong brown god is forgotten in the technological progressive "then," during which nature is water under the bridge.

American poetry and poetics didn't always see technology this way. As Emerson envisioned it in the 1830s, when the Mississippi was still the nation's western "frontier," the modifications of technology or "Art" could simply be averaged into the balance of Nature: "a little chipping, baking, patching, and washing . . . do not vary the result."[11] Many modernist poets felt free to leave technology out of their poems. Stevens took the Florida Railway out to Key

West; the young Langston Hughes wrote "The Negro Speaks of Rivers" on the train passing over the Mississippi on the Eads Bridge. For Hart Crane in his "Proem" to *The Bridge*, the Brooklyn Bridge is a triumph of the imagination, a symbolic reconciler of east and west, past and present, earth and heaven (ecopoets, I think, have more to learn from his less sublime poem, "The River"). The quixotically masted boats tilting at the Gulf of Mexico at the end of "The Idea of Order at Key West" point toward the domestication of the ocean mapped with imaginary parallel and meridian lines and climactic zones that "portioned out the sea." For Eliot, by contrast, such mastery entails enslavement and then neglect of the natural world, the "strong brown god" chained in steel.[12] As Eliot knows, the triumph of the machine does not mean the death of the river. In a time increasingly subject to artificially induced natural upheavals, the god still waits to remind technological progressives of its presence.

Poetry readers in our dawning decades will search among modern and postmodern poets for traces of an awareness of environmental injustice: the toxic and ruinous devastation dumped upon mostly poor and minority communities and peoples. Environmental justice, or ecojustice, poetry has been almost unavoidably anthropocentric. But such poetry has the advantage of turning nature poetry back toward cities and (nonwhite) local populations, diversifying both subject matter and writing subjects. One poet readers might revisit in this connection is Elizabeth Bishop, particularly her Brazilian poems, in which we find a branch of ecojustice known as ecofeminism, in which the domination of the land is often paired with the sexual subjection of its women. Bishop, who lived in Brazil for fifteen years, describes the country's colonization both in her poem "Brazil, January 1, 1502" and in her surprisingly ironic travel essay *Brazil*, written for Time-Life Books. Beginning with the Portuguese discovery of "Brasil" (named for its red-dye trees), Bishop draws on Pêro Vaz de Caminha's travel journal and a contemporary map:

> On the first maps it is either "Brazil" or the "Land of Parrots." Along with dye-wood, macaws were sent back to Europe, and their brilliant colors, large size, and loud shrieks obviously made a deep impression.... On a mapus mundi published the year after Cabral's voyage ... Caminha's groves of trees are there, lined up as formally as in a Portuguese garden,

and under them sits a group of giant macaws, to give explorers some idea of what to expect.¹³

The map with its "pale-green broken wheel" of Brazil furnishes Bishop with her own description of the unspecified macaws: "perching there in profile, beaks agape, / the big symbolic birds keep quiet . . ."

Four hundred and fifty years later, the North American poet would discover Brazil for herself. But her poem opens not from an outraged feminist perspective but from the ironically compromised position of the colonizing tourist: "Januaries, Nature greets our eyes / exactly as she must have greeted theirs." Nature, the unabashed welcoming female, is gendered in the poem as a breeding lizard:

> The lizards scarcely breathe; all eyes
> are on the smaller, female one, back-to,
> her wicked tail straight up and over,
> red as a red-hot wire.

Straight or queer, we readers find ourselves on no one side. Bishop's shifting alliances teach the primary lesson of ecojustice poetry: moral complicity. After a stanza break, we seem to extend the simile—"Just so the Christians [like the lizards?], hard as nails"—till with the words "came and found it all [like us], / not unfamiliar" we are returned to the poet's modern perspective. In her essay, Bishop includes among Brazil's resources the "Indians . . . friendly and docile, too docile for their own good,"¹⁴ and quotes from Caminha's description of the native Tupi women, a self-interested argument for a Eurocentric natural design: "Our Lord gave them fine bodies and good faces, as to good men, and He who brought us here I believe did not do so without purpose."¹⁵ Bishop's poem ends with the Catholic soldiers seeking to act on their divinely sanctioned beliefs:

> Directly after Mass, humming perhaps
> *L'Homme armé* or some such tune,
> they ripped away into the hanging fabric,
> each out to catch an Indian for himself—
> those maddening little women who kept calling,

calling to each other (or had the birds waked up?)
and retreating, always retreating, behind it.

What later became the ecofeminist likening of colonial conquest with sexual violence is distinctly audible in the crypt word beneath "ripped," *raped*.[16] Also enlightening and instructive is Bishop's association of the "maddening" (a colonizing irony) women with the birds, which are here not merely or entirely symbolic but actually part of the jungle's "hanging fabric," so that the ravishment of the Tupi is both imagined as, and seen as part of, the exploitation of the rainforest.

Closely allied with ecojustice poetry is the recently emergent urban environmental poetry. Modern instances are scarce. If twentieth-century urban poets, "the dwellers in cities," seemed to forget about nature, suburban and nonurban environmental poets have in turn seemed to forget about cities. The place-based *Four Quartets* more or less omits St. Louis, Boston, and London (an unseen backdrop in "Little Gidding"), and Rio de Janeiro barely reverberates in "Januaries," the first word of Bishop's "Brazil." A number of especially male poets—Jeffers, Berry, Merwin, Snyder—followed Thoreau's lead into homemade rural homes and grounds. Indeed, from the vantage point of the country, the city may appear a lure and trap, no more sinisterly so than in Robinson Jeffers's much anthologized 1937 poem, "The Purse-Seine." Thinking of the way phosphorescent sardines are caught in a large net drawn shut, the poet turns his gaze from his "night mountain-top / On a wide city" (presumably San Francisco, north of Monterey Bay, where sardines were fished and canned):

> I thought, We have geared the machines and locked all together into
>   interdependence; we have built the great cities; now
> There is no escape. We have gathered vast populations incapable of free
>   survival, insulated
> From the strong earth, each person in himself helpless, on all dependent.
>   The circle is closed, and the net
> Is being hauled in. . . .[17]

Like the phosphorescent sardines and the glittery metropolitan catch, the poem is "beautiful . . . and a little terrible." Reading these lines today, when the bulk of humanity lives in cities, Jeffers's view strikes me as uncomprehending and reactionary (the western US politics of manly independence is ever more familiar). Jeffers will still find his adherents and his descendants, but I don't think readers will find this particular simile of Jeffers sustainable.

Future readers will, I believe, find more of value and use in Gary Snyder, an environmentally attuned poet who sets his eyes on, and feet in, the technologized postmodern metropolis. I find his most fruitfully environmentally urban poetry in the farfetched collection *Mountains and Rivers Without End*, in which he walks both Los Angeles and New York City. Let's follow the east coast poem, "Walking the New York Bedrock Alive in the Sea of Information." First published in 1987, the poem lies on the border or threshold between the manufacturing and the information economies, the city of human know-how and of electronically processed data. When Snyder wrote "Walking," the word *information*, which had meant education, was acquiring a new meaning: processed and transmitted data. (The luggable desktop computer was introduced in 1984.) For instance, the former merchant marine sees Manhattan's steep "Heartbeat buildings" marvelously as "ships stood on end on the land," where in the boiler rooms human minders are replaced by digital monitors:

> ex-seamen stand watch at the stationary boilers,
>   give way to computers,
> That monitor heat and the power
>   webs underground; in the air;
> In the Sea of Information.

Manhattan in "Walking" is a coastal range of lordly buildings, "layered stratigraphy cliffs." (Less in evidence here are the "Rivers that never give up," audible in "Trill under the roadbed, over the bedrock.") But where in this informational urban island is the actual landscape? One way of answering this question is by considering the poem's grammar. We make our way across Snyder's 128-line[18] city-poem without any easygoing Whitmanian guiding "I" or even a Crane-like apostrophizing night-walker ("Under thy shadow by the piers I waited"). Snyder instead begins his ambulatory poem with a scene recognizable as Central Park, but with no discernable vagabond:

Maple, oak, poplar, gingko
New leaves, "new green" on a rock ledge
Of steep little uplift, tucked among trees
Hot sun dapple—
   wake up.

Roll over and slide down the rockface
Walk away in the woods toward
A squirrel . . .

The poem's title identifies the waking walker with the poet. But how are we to parse the pronoun-less phrasal verbs, which continue throughout the poem? We may think of them as imperatives, but as we proceed, for instance, to "Move, pause, move" through museum gallery rooms, such classification becomes strained. Nor will it work to call the poetry, though it is ongoing, stream of consciousness, which would still leave us with multiple self-directives. It's better to parse these verbs as the elliptical first-person present, formed like those in Chinese or in Latin(ate) languages without the need of pronouns. The verbal persona makes the walker a focalizer, a camera eye reminiscent of *Man with a Movie Camera*, Dziga Vertov's 1929 documentary film of a day in the life of Soviet cities. Like Vertov's cameraman, Snyder's I-less eye knows but does not explicitly feel.

The poem culminates when the peripatetic poet meets some equally singular personas:

Street people rolling their carts
. . .
Eyeballing arêtes and buttresses rising above them,
   con domus, dominion,
      domus,
condominate, condominium
Towers . . .

Rather than have these peaks of the privileged scrape the sky, Snyder (somewhat awkwardly) mixes his metaphor to have them rise in the sea. This way he can register the stratification of the feeding web, where those aloft in their condominiums "get more sushi," while "the street bottom-feeders with shopping carts / Slowly check out the air for the fall of excess." The recently current figurative use of "bottom-feeders" as scrounging people was snapped up by Snyder, who leaves behind its derogatory connotation. In between, picking up his own bits of information, is the poem's godlike avatar:

> —Peregrine sails past the [condominium's 35th-floor] window
> Off the edge of the word-chain
> Harvesting concepts, theologies,
> Snapping up bites of the bits bred by
> Banking
>   ideas and wild speculations
> On new information—
> and stoops in a blur on a pigeon

When homelessness exploded in Manhattan in the 1980s, people began sleeping and waking, like Snyder's persona, in parks along with other animals. The irony is inescapable in the contrast between the technological and engineering triumph of the towering buildings, steel with their magically weightless floating curtain walls, and the enterprising survival of the city's fittest. Snyder's poem is a brilliant indictment of the economically stratified city of the 1980s. Yet where in this poem, ecopoets might wonder, is the environmental injustice inextricable from the economic injustice? The Hudson River was in the 1980s extensively polluted by General Electric and other industries; their runoff was killing actual bottom-feeding fish and sickening the people who ate them. Pete Seeger (along with whom, Snyder told me, he once sang) launched his sloop *Clearwater* to call attention to the disaster, and in 1983 the newly organized Environmental Protection Agency designated the PCB-laced river a superfund site. It will be a continuing challenge for the poets of this century to understand and represent ecosystemic and economic injustices together.

Among our fellow citizens and souls on land and sea, to whom not only love but justice may be extended, are the nonhuman animals, an untold number of which we have sentenced to extinction. Innumerable species are currently stressed by habitat loss, air-transported invasive species, and global marketing. Modernist poets such as Marianne Moore (in "He 'Digesteth

Harde Yron'"), Robinson Jeffers ("Hurt Hawk"), and William Carlos Williams (in "The Sea Elephant") were aware of the threat we pose to our fellow species. But not till the rise of ecology and the environmental movement of the 1960s did poetry become politically environmentalist. Let's consider, for example, W. S. Merwin's 1967 poem on the gray whale, "For a Coming Extinction." As I type, the conservation status of this species is listed as "Least Concern." But the gray whale is locally extinct in the Asian (Japanese and Russian) Pacific, following its earlier collapse in the Atlantic. Merwin may have learned of the human impact on the whales from an alarming 1966 article by Scott McVay.[19] In any case, the movement to "Save the Whales," emblazoned on T-shirts and bumper stickers, led to active opposition by Greenpeace in the 1970s, which led in turn to the (loopholed) global regulation of the whaling industry.

Here's the beginning of Merwin's poem:

Gray whale
Now that we are sending you to The End
That great god
Tell him
That we who follow you invented forgiveness
And forgive nothing[20]

The poem is an envoi employing an apostrophe not ecstatic, as in Keats's "Ode to a Nightingale," but ironic. Even his assumption of the trope is self-aware: "I write as though you could understand / And I could say it." The poet's knowing attitude here is not one of ecstatic engagement or prophetic detachment but of an engaged complicity. Merwin's limpid language should not then be confused with "plain style." We find here no individual speaker, for instance, but a human chorus that addresses not a specimen but a species. Keats, too, shifted his attention from "a Nightingale" to its species at the poem's climactic revelation:

Thou wast not born for death, immortal Bird!
    No hungry generations tread thee down;
The voice I hear this passing night was heard
    In ancient days by emperor and clown

The specimen dies but the species is immortal. And since the nightingale's "self-same song" survives any individual songbird, perhaps the poet's ode will as well. Merwin's chilling postmodern realization, that species themselves are mortal, is underscored with an unnerving time line. The gray whale will ultimately join "The sea cows the Great Auks the gorillas." What we now call Steller's sea cow went extinct in 1768, and the great auks in 1844, a quarter of a century after Keats's ode. But the sea cow and great auk did not go the way of the dinosaur; we slaughtered them from the earth. Like the whale, the gorillas survive, for the time being, among their human extinguishers.[21]

When humans die, the story goes, they go to heaven. Merwin might have imagined dying whales also to be sent to heaven, reunited with their "whale calves trying the light," and not to a "black garden." But as Merwin knows, the nonhuman species is promised no land after death. It is fundamental to Christian philosophy and theology that animals be kept out of heaven. In his widely influential fifth *Discourse on Method*, René Descartes argued that animals had animal spirits but no "rational soul," and that only human souls could enter the kingdom of heaven.[22] But Merwin, after Jeffers and Leopold, denies immortal status to the human spirits as well. Instead, the poet laces his elliptical title with an irony. The ambassadorial gray whale is sent (in preparation) "For a Coming Extinction." The mission of the gray whale is to prepare the way for the human species, who till its dying day believes in its god-given dominion:

> Join your word to theirs
> Tell him
> That it is we who are important

In the pivotal war year of 1863, Emily Dickinson wrote this long-metered quatrain of visionary wit:

> Funny—to be a Century
> And see the People—going by—
> I—should die of the oddity—
> But then—I'm not so staid—as He—

And yet, surveying the twentieth century from our portion of the twenty-first, readers may suffer from just such a weird "oddity—": a centurial perspective. First, we may experience a proleptic nostalgia, a painful urge (if not an uncomfortable regret) to return to a status that has not (yet) disappeared. Let's return once more to Merwin's chronological line, "The sea cows the Great Auks the gorillas." If the gray whale is currently abundant, most species of gorillas are critically endangered. So Merwin's addition of them to the line of extinctions becomes increasingly sad and frustrating (if not motivating)—with each decade of habitat loss, poaching, and disease that passes. We can't but value this line from the 1960s, and the poem that gives it meaning, because it reminds us not only that extinction is historical as well as geological, but that extinction itself is not extinct, and foreordains our own.

If Merwin's poem is valued for its proleptic nostalgia, other poems accrue an uncanny significance from what may be called anachronistic anxiety. Consider Frost's "Once by the Pacific," a sonnet of recollected alarm:

The shattered water made a misty din.
Great waves looked over others coming in,
And thought of doing something to the shore
That water never did to land before.
The clouds were low and hairy in the skies,
Like locks blown forward in the gleam of eyes.
You could not tell, and yet it looked as if
The shore was lucky in being backed by cliff,
The cliff in being backed by continent;
It looked as if a night of dark intent
Was coming, and not only a night, an age.
Someone had better be prepared for rage.
There would be more than ocean-water broken
Before God's last *Put out the Light* was spoken.

One thing we know about "Once" is that whatever Frost intended, he did not mean us to think of a tsunami, or some other increasingly common overheated storm system brought on by climate change. The poem with its super-closural couplets (reminiscent of Shakespeare's Sonnet 126) is indeed apocalyptic, but it is not revelatory, nor its poet visionary. He placed "Once" first in a group of poems in his 1928 volume *West-Running Brook* to which he gave the decreative title "Fiat Nox" ("Let there be night"; cf. *"Put out the Light"*), and for its epigraph he borrowed a line from the previous section's last poem, "Acceptance": "Let the night be too dark for me to see / Into the future. Let what will be, be." In *West-Running Brook*, "Once by the Pacific" was followed by a chronological note: "*As of about 1880*," which would place the poem in the San Francisco Bay of the poet as a child, living hazardously with his frightened mother and his drunken, violently abusive father, a domestic tragedy cued by the closing allusion to *Othello*.[23]

Frost is imagining an actual, if remembered, ocean below Cliff House, near the Golden Gate Bridge. If, in spite of what we know, we feel "Once" to be about something a real ocean might do to an actual shore, I believe we would not be entirely wrong. Frost's poem, if not intentionally revelatory, may be valued for its trans-historicity, its openness to future associations, dark intents unintended by the poet. As Merwin was canny in his apostrophe, Frost was self-conscious about his post-Romantic prosopopoeia. In his influential 1856 essay "Of the Pathetic Fallacy," Ruskin wrote of the hazards of describing ocean storms: "An inspired writer, in full impetuosity of passion, may speak wisely and truly of 'raging waves of the sea foaming out their own shame'; but it is only the basest writer who cannot speak of the sea without talking of 'raging waves,' 'remorseless floods,' etc."[24] Frost's rhetorical face-making hinges on the ambiguous word "look" (see, appear), so that God the Father's "dark intent" may be ascribed merely to a terrified recollection, a "pathetic fallacy" factually false but emotionally true. Yet even at its most human, when the "hairy" storm clouds look "Like locks blown forward in the gleam of eyes," we can still discern the reality of rain-streaming clouds lit by lightning gleams. So a literally false but poetically true reading of the poem may nevertheless overwhelm us. But what in Frost's poem invites our future-oriented misreadings? Should it be valued, in spite of Frost's antiprophetic poetics, for its visionary insight into the life of the belligerent Pacific? Does twentieth-century nature poetry worth our attention see future tendencies in the present? Certainly, and yet a single poem may get as much wrong as right. Who can be stirred by the octave of Hopkins's "God's Grandeur" ("And all is seared with trade") and not be saddened by its sestet ("And for all this, nature is never spent")? Both for what it says, and for what it misbelieves, the poem is precious to me.

But what about Moore, Ammons, Berry, Oppen, Niedecker, Brooks, and

Silko, among others? Are they denied admission to my rocky Parnassus? And what about animal cruelty, pollution, and habitat loss? I'm not aiming here to establish a definitive canon or theme park of proto-ecopoetry or an ecological subspecies of immortal poets. Poets, readers, and critics, unavoidably selective, will find their models and their concerns where they will. At the turn of the century, I myself might have focused instead on nouveau New York School or post-Language poetry. But I don't think now, any more than I did then, that formal innovation is all that matters to poets, realist or surrealist or idealist, or to readers. Poets have always made the world over in their poems, and evaluation should take that, too, into account. Otherwise, how can we learn from them now when (once again) we need them most?

Notes

1. Wallace Stevens, *The Palm at the End of the Mind: Selected Poems and a Play* (New York: Random House, 1967), 404.
2. "Not What I Call a Hail-Fellow-Well-Met-Person: James Reiss on Wallace Stevens's Selected Poems," Gently Read Literature, posted January 1, 2010, by Daniel Casey, https://gentlyread.wordpress.com/tag/wallace-stevens/.
3. John Shoptaw, "Why Ecopoetry?," *Poetry* (January 2016), http://www.poetry foundation.org/poetrymagazine/article/251640.
4. In my 1987 doctoral dissertation on Ashbery, I recorded my discovery (from Herodotus) that phoenix in Greek denotes both "fire-fangled" phoenix and palm tree.
5. I appreciate that Stevens's unidiomatic syntax has been construed differently, as Paul Mariani recently did in his biography: "[O]ne knows it is not reason that makes us happy or unhappy" (*The Whole Harmonium: The Life of Wallace Stevens* [New York: Simon and Schuster, 2016], 394). But I don't think such a reading is responsive to the poem. First, Stevens wrote "the reason," not "reason" (as in the faculty of Reason). Second, "You know then" implies that the third tercet follows from the second: the reason you know then that birdsong doesn't make us happy or unhappy is that its conjectured meaning and feeling is strictly inhuman. I don't think the poet's point can be that we can't identify with feelings in the world. If a solitary reaper or a Key West singer sings a song, that song may make us feel reasonably happy or unhappy. But a bird's song, in Stevens's view, cannot please us, not without our anthropomorphic projection. As Helen Vendler put it in *Wallace Stevens: Words Chosen out of Desire* (Knoxville: University of Tennessee Press, 1984), 42, "The foreign song of the sensual earth will always need to have human meaning and human feeling added to it by

those fictions of intelligibility and desire we all project upon it." Keats felt otherwise; Stevens thinks he knows better.
6. For evidence that singing birds do in fact experience happiness, see Jennifer Ackerman, *The Genius of Birds* (New York: Penguin, 2016): "A song well sung offers its own reward, a 'bolus' of feel-good chemicals such as dopamine and opioids" (154).
7. Aldo Leopold, "The Land Ethic," in *A Sand County Almanac* (New York: Oxford University Press, 1949), 204.
8. Robinson Jeffers, "Preface to *The Double Axe and Other Poems* (1947)," in *The Selected Poetry of Robinson Jeffers*, ed. Tim Hunt (Stanford, CA: Stanford University Press, 2002), 719.
9. Emily Dickinson, *The Poems of Emily Dickinson*, ed. R. W. Franklin (Cambridge, MA: Belknap Press of Harvard University Press, 1998), Fr 256.
10. Simon J. Ortiz, *Woven Stone* (Tucson: University of Arizona Press, 1992), 321–24. China Lake in California's Mohave Desert was named for the Chinese laborers who mined borax, familiar perhaps from Ronald Reagan's commercial pitch for "20 Mule Team Borax" in *Death Valley Days*. The vast Naval Air Weapons Station China Lake, larger in area than Rhode Island, was the established in 1947 by the US Navy and the California Institute of Technology. It is the birthplace of the heat-seeking missile named, with a nod to local color, the Sidewinder.
11. Ralph Waldo Emerson, introduction to *Nature*.
12. Eliot would in 1941 have had in mind the catastrophic flooding of the lower Mississippi in 1927, especially for the toll it took on low-lying and forced labor ("the river with its cargo of dead Negroes, cows and chicken coops"), and also the 1937 overflowing of the Ohio and consequently the lower Mississippi, which led to the grand opening of the Bonnet Carré Spillway. In his commentary, Christopher Ricks quotes Eliot's remark in 1930 to Marquis Childs: "The river also made a deep impression on me; and it *was* a great treat to be taken down to the Eads Bridge in flood time." *The Poems of T. S. Eliot*, vol. 1: *Collected and Uncollected Poems*, ed. Christopher Ricks and Jim McCue (London: Faber and Faber, 2016), 965.
13. Elizabeth Bishop, *The Collected Prose* (New York: Farrar, Straus and Giroux, 2011), 174–5. The map is available online: https://upload.wikimedia.org/wikipedia/commons/9/9c/Cantino_planisphere_(1502).jpg.
14. Ibid., 176.
15. Ibid.
16. For my theory of the process whereby a poet revises a "crypt word" not by seme but by sound, see my "Lyric Cryptography," *Poetics Today* 21, no. 1 (Spring 2000): 221–62.
17. Robinson Jeffers, *Rock and Hawk: A Selection of Shorter Poems*, ed. Robert Hass (New York: Random House, 1987), 190–91.

18. I'm counting only capitalized lines.
19. Scott McVay, "The Last of the Great Whales," *Scientific American*, August 1966.
20. W. S. Merwin, *Collected Poems, 1952–1993* (New York: Library of America, 2013), 304. The entire 1967 volume from which this poem is taken, *The Lice*, truly a watershed in environmentalist poetry, also contains his folk allegory of the deforestation of Easter Island, "The Last One."
21. For the story of the great auk and the history of the idea of "species extinction," see Elizabeth Kolbert, *The Sixth Extinction: An Unnatural History* (New York: Henry Holt, 2014), 47–69.
22. René Descartes, *Discourse on Method and Related Writings*, trans. Desmond M. Clarke (New York: Penguin, 1999), 30–42.
23. For biographical background, see Jay Parini, *Robert Frost: A Life* (New York: Henry Holt, 1999), esp. 12–14.
24. John Ruskin, *The Literary Criticism of John Ruskin*, ed. Harold Bloom (New York: Da Capo Press, 1986), 68. Ruskin is quoting from the epistle Jude (1:13): "Raging waves of the sea, forming out their own shame; wandering stars, to whom is reserved the blackness of darkness for ever." The poet of "Who goes with Fergus" would also remember this verse.

CHAPTER 8

Sharon Olds and the Work of the Body

SARAH NOOTER[1]

SEX AND THE body have evoked some of poetry's most striking metaphors through the ages. Homer offered dew falling on flowers to evoke the ejaculation of Zeus, and Sappho gave us the tradition of roses and fragrances standing in for bodies and their satisfactions; Anacreon contributed extended and titillating horse metaphors, Catullus added a sparrow, and we were off.[2] Closer to our own era, John Donne envisioned his lover as the far-off wilds of America, and Pablo Neruda presented his woman as a white-hilled landscape, both implying their own imminent invasions.[3] There is no end to the names and images one might add to this list, but I will leave off here. My interest is not in the metaphors used to express (usually enthusiastic) thoughts about sex but rather an opposing mode of staring down sex and the body through anti-metaphoricity in the poetry of Sharon Olds.[4]

Olds's poetry proposes, displays, and then dismisses metaphors for sex and other intensely embodied experiences. Most significant, I will suggest, is her display of the act of dismissal. She insists on the literal, as does Anne Sexton in the poem "The Touch":

> The hand had collapsed,
> a small wood pigeon
> that had gone into seclusion.
> I turned it over and the palm was old,
> its lines traced like fine needlepoint

> and stitched up into the fingers.
> It was fat and soft and blind in places.
> Nothing but vulnerable.
>
> And this is all metaphor.
> An ordinary hand—just lonely
> for someone to touch
> that touches back.

Both poets provide a corrective to traditions of representation. Sexton interrupts her series of symbols for her hand (her hand a metonymy for a whole set of haptic and sexual experiences) with a rebuke, "all this is metaphor," and then switches to the literal, while the speaker takes an apologetic tone ("just lonely"). This rebuke of metaphor is important in Olds's poetry, too. It forms part of a dialogue between metaphor-as-distance and an intense preoccupation with the haptic: the body is stripped clean of figurative veils as if of clothes (it is hard to leave the figurative), as Olds faces sensory experience without protective distance. Her poetry captures an experience of thrilling vulnerability and a heady sense of mortality felt in the body as its feats and failures come into language. It is common to attribute to Olds a commitment to portraying embodied experience, in particular her own. In regard to explicit descriptions of sex and the body, she follows Sexton, e. e. cummings, Allen Ginsberg, and many others. While I describe this element here, I claim that her importance is not so much located in her subject matter or its source material as in her search for language fitting to the life of her body.

Language

Olds has published about a dozen books of poetry (including several compilations of prior and new work) since 1980. This is a sizable and varied body of work. I will write in detail only of several poems in her first collection and then of a few poems from her more mature work, specifically from the collection *Blood, Tin, Straw* (1999) and then two more recent books. I have chosen poems, particularly those from *Blood, Tin, Straw*, that make the strongest case for her literary survival. Many of Olds's preoccupations are laid out clearly at the start. The title of her first book, *Satan Says*, is also the title of the first poem in the collection; both name and poem center on precisely the tension that I identify throughout her poetry: the question of when to use and when to avoid metaphorical language. The poem locates its speaker, presumably as a little girl, "locked" in a box made of cedar, while she "tr[ies] to write [her] / way out of the closed box." At this point,

>Satan
>comes to me in the locked box
>and says, *I'll get you out.* Say
>My father is a shit. I say
>my father is a shit and Satan
>laughs and says, *It's opening.*

Here Olds poses a fairly straightforward equation in regard to the psychologically charged autobiography of the poet: to escape the pain of her abusive past, she must write her "way out," but it is an emotionally onerous and guilt-laden process. She must allow a voice that is devilish (from the perspective of her religious upbringing) to speak through her, and this voice must be inflected with vulgarity, committing such crimes as calling her terrifying father "a shit." The voice of Satan will go on to prompt the speaker to utter a number of such blasphemies.

Yet the moments of free speech and scatological breakout are intercut with prosaic lines of resistance: "I love them but / I'm trying to say what happened to us / in the lost past." Satan remains initially undeterred. The language he offers grows more rebellious in his voice, and then in the speaker's recitations of his words. When Satan speaks, his words are in italics ("*Say: the father's cock, the mother's / cunt*, says Satan, *I'll get you out*"). When the speaker obliges, her words are in regular typeface, like the other words in the poem ("When I say / the magic words, Cock, Cunt, / Satan softly says, *Come out*"). And then, as the poem nears its end, the speaker draws back with apparent finality, proclaiming again that she loves her parents, too, and ending with these lines:

>*It's your coffin now*, Satan says.
>I hardly hear;

> I am warming my cold
> hands at the dancer's
> ruby eye—
> *the fire, the suddenly discovered knowledge of love.*

One could hardly frame an inner conflict more clearly, with the voice of Satan contending with a conciliatory, measured voice, given to metaphor ("*the fire, the suddenly discovered knowledge of love*"). The poet's use of italics to accentuate the words of Satan keeps his voice separate; the anger he expresses, the darkness of the truths he speaks, and the need to utter taboo terms (cock, cunt) are *of* the poem but also held away from the mouth of the narrator. The speaker says the "bad" words but then rebukes them. Abandoned in the end by Satan, who is evidently irritated by her more proper and acceptable set of emotions (loving mom and dad), she turns to metaphor, "the dancer's / ruby eye" and "the fire." It is notable that metaphors appear just when the poem slides once and for all into a conventionally acceptable set of values (filial love). It is also important of course that metaphor encases the entire poem, as a "cedar box" encases the girl at its center. Metaphors and enclosures are of a piece in Olds's poetry, one side of a divide.

This dialectic between the metaphorical and the vulgar is meant to apply not only to Olds's particular experience of trauma and memory, as has been asserted elsewhere.[5] Her greater poetic project, as articulated in her first volume, is to seek out forms of language that will bring the sensory experience of the female body into literary representation. Her ambivalence about metaphor's purchase on the corporeal experiences of some women follows a long line of poets rejecting idioms as antiquated or insufficiently raw to describe embodied, gritty human experience: Hesiod's apparent rebuke to Homer, Euripides's answer to Aeschylus, and, in our own language, the "plain style" polemic of Ben Jonson, Dryden, Wordsworth, and the modernists.[6] These poets announced their stylistic intentions in prose.[7] Olds's rebuke of the figurative is in her poetry itself.

From her first collection, "Language of the Brag" and "Prayer" both represent the act of giving birth as momentous. This is not metaphorical birth, as in Plato's *Symposium*, but the literal, corporeal achievement of pushing a person into the world. In "Language of the Brag," the speaker proclaims that she has wanted "some epic use for my excellent body" and refers to the "language of blood" that covers a baby when it is born. All this leads to high bravado:

> I have done what you wanted to do, Walt Whitman,
> Allen Ginsberg, I have done this thing,
> I and the other women this exceptional
> act with the exceptional heroic body,
> this giving birth, this glistening verb,
> and I am putting my proud American boast
> right here with the others.

The gesture of arrival here hardly requires explanation, but the concentration on language does, with "giving birth" configured as a "glistening verb," an act of language whose right to inhabit poetry as *just what it is*—not as a metaphor, nor hidden in abstraction—is asserted. Similarly, in "Prayer," the speaker implores that she will "be faithful to the central meanings" and starts with the "birth-room" before turning to her first experience of sex. She ends the poem with the lines: "let me not forget: / each action, each word / taking its beginning from these." In both poems, the acts of giving birth are asserted to be verbs above all else. Nor are they just any verbs, not even verbs of bodily effort (e.g., to push), but verbs of language: to brag, to boast, to pray.

Pain

Blood, Tin, Straw epitomizes Olds's mature work. Here we see the poet fully in control of a dialectic between a metaphorical voice of high literature and one of cutting literalism. These elements strain against each other in a poetic arc or plot and, at the same time, display the mental processes of the speaker in the course of sensory experiences. Two poems from this collection especially exemplify this dynamic: "After Punishment Was Done with Me" and "You Kindly." Both poems narrate a process of coming in and out of physical sensation while finding ways to cope with prodigious corporeal intensity—to absorb, understand, and fit it to other sensations. "After Punishment" narrates the moments following a beating by the speaker's mother:

> After punishment was done with me,
> after I would put my clothes back on,
> my mother's hairbrush scansion done,
> I'd go back to my room, close the door,
> and wander around, ending up
> on the floor sometimes, always, near the baseboard[8]

The "punishment" here is told in the passive form and contrasted with the speaker's series of active physical responses. The mother's "hairbrush scansion" of spanking suggests a poetic rhythm that almost of its own will sounds through the world, yet the description is precise and only lightly figurative. The speaker skips the core of the experience, and she does not attempt to describe the sensory impact of pain on her body. Elaine Scarry speaks of the "near-absence . . . of literary representations of pain." According to Scarry, in place of representing pain, literary artists resort to "analogies to remote cosmologies" and other such "fictional analogues,"[9] much as I am suggesting that metaphors in Olds's poetry provide an escape from a direct encounter with the sensory. Scarry contrasts pain's lack of "referential content" ("It is not *of* or *for* anything"[10]), which renders it practically incommunicable between subjects, with the radically object-full state of imagination:

> There is in imagining no activity, no "state," no experienceable condition or felt-occurrence separate from the objects: the only evidence that one is "imagining" is that imaginary objects appear in the mind.[11]

In keeping with Scarry's view of pain as something that cannot be shared in language, Olds does not try to share her pain in "After Punishment." Rather, physical pain is almost an atmospheric setting to the poem that the reader must intuit. Instead of confronting pain, then, the reader is plunged into a narration of the post-punishment, imaginative actions of the speaker that soon give way to a catalog of what the speaker sees on the ground where she lies. This catalog starts as an amalgam of the starkly literal but swiftly shifts to small similes: "cocoons of slough like tiny Kotexes / wound and wound in toilet paper," "a larval casing waisted in gold / thin as the poorest gold wedding band," "a fly curled up, dried, / its wings like the rabbit's ears, or the deer's." With each image (and several others like it), the reader is led through a process of a small item (dust, a larval husk, a dead fly) being transformed into a larger one, often (though not always) one that is highly gendered.

The speaker then draws the focus back from these configurations to explain the mental process just displayed:

> I would look at each piece of lint
> and half imagine being it,
> I would feel that I was looking at
> the universe from a great difference.

We are shown here the mental act of imagining expansion from the smallest, most insignificant thing ("nothing the human / would go for") to "the universe," in which she then describes "play[ing] / house," concocting "weddings and / funerals . . . / awful births." This portrait of the child-speaker in the act of imaginative creation—transmuted by the poet-speaker into poetic creation—recalls a literary history of attempts to show how both art and emotion construct worlds within worlds, as in Rilke's evocation of Orpheus's love that arises from his lyre in the form of lament:

> A woman so loved that from one lyre there came
> more lament than from all lamenting women;
> that a whole world of lament arose, in which
> all nature reappeared: forest and valley,
> road and village, field and stream and animal;
> and that around this lament-world, even as
> around the other earth, a sun revolved
> and a silent star-filled heaven, a lament-
> heaven, with its own, disfigured stars—:
> So greatly was she loved.

The steps of transmutation are practically obscured here by lyricism, but one can understand (if the process is slowed) that Orpheus is imagined as loving his lost Eurydice so deeply that his love, transformed to lamentation, gives birth through his lyre to a new universe in which Orpheus himself does not figure. The new world is created by his pain: "forest and valley, / road and village, / field and stream and animal." Pain becomes poetry.

In Olds's poem, the speaker's body is a site of pain, but it is not seen or described except in the initial act of "put[ting] [her] clothes back on." Pain has slipped out of the text. The reader might not even have maintained the context of physical suffering at the forefront of her mind in reading, since the poem has traveled over forty lines with no mention of it. At the end, however, comes an explanatory turn:

> Without desire or rage
> I would watch that atom celestium as the pain
> on my matter died and turned to spirit
> and wandered the cloud world of home,
> the ashes of the earth.

As often, Olds takes a step back here to tell the reader what has been shown: that the speaker herself, as a child, has been waiting out the pain on her body ("my matter") while watching what appear to her as little deaths (with the "celestium" seemingly a cemetery) that she has also created through her gaze. The pain itself, now made an active force through metaphor, has "died" and become a "spirit" that wanders through the "cloud world" and among the "ashes" that the speaker's own gaze has created. She has made a world of death for her pain to inhabit, a place at a remove from her own body. As in Rilke's poem, Olds imagines pain as a generative force. In Rilke's poem, a world created implicitly takes shape through music. In Olds's, a world takes shape through the figurative transmutation of dust, dead insects, and other detritus.

The process displayed is one of metaphor-making as escape from pain, isolation, and humiliation. Metaphor is at work here; indeed, metaphors that imaginatively expand are a vehicle of escape for a child in pain. Yet the process is put on display, not simply enacted, as if to say: here is how abuse makes one long to leave the body. The description at the end of "the pain / on my matter"—pain that has not been mentioned until this point—jars the reader into realizing that pain was the subject all along. The speaker's imaginative gaze has given an incomplete account, a story told to divert attention from the real story. Such metaphor-making typifies the sort of language that the voice of "Satan" in the first book would urge the poet to rip away so as to show the body in pain, a process that Scarry sees as ultimately generative of "the birth of language itself."[12] Olds's attention to pain as a movement into, and then away from, figurative language suggests that she, too, sees the articulation of pain, performed painfully, as a birthing of poetic language.

Sex (Death)

The dialectic of metaphors and anti-metaphoricity becomes still more complex when the physical sensation at play is not pain. The poem "You Kindly" in *Blood, Tin, Straw* very nearly reverses the dynamic described in "After Punishment." In patient, lengthy lines, a scene of sex between the speaker and a man ("you") is described in terms that could hardly be more literal. It begins,

> Because I felt too weak to move
> you kindly moved for me, kneeling
> and turning, until you could take my breast-tip in the
> socket of your lips

With the exception of the "socket" of lips, there is nothing figurative here. The language brings us bluntly in medias res to an extended erotic encounter. The beginning is acutely intimate, launching the reader into a scene before there is time (as it were) to understand its nature. The lines almost jokingly evoke the beginning of the famous poem by Emily Dickinson:

> Because I could not stop for Death—
> He kindly stopped for me—
> The Carriage held but just Ourselves—
> And Immortality.

Dickinson's iconic poem moves immediately into the figurative: the experience of dying is envisioned through the personification of Death paying a visit. This arrival is imagined as an act of kindness, as if Death, who enters the poem in a carriage, is to be congratulated for his gentlemanly behavior. Something of the suddenness of his arrival is transmitted into the sudden entry of Olds's poem; the speaker's partner "kindly" swivels to take her nipple into his mouth. The spiritual lines and patter of Dickinson are a stepping stone here toward raw description of sexual activity. Poetic allusion shows starkly how little Olds's opening lines resemble the heavily figurative lines of Dickinson, though this poem, like Dickinson's, concerns death.

Olds's poem is as patient as Dickinson's Death ("He knew no haste"). The physical sensations described are complemented by slow observations of mundane elements of the scene, without metaphorical embellishment:

> I saw your hand, near me, your
> daily hand, your thumbnail,
> the quiet hairs on your fingers—to see your
> hand in its ordinary self, when your mouth at my
> breast was drawing sweet gashes of come
> up from my womb made black fork-flashes of a
> celibate's lust shoot through me.

The partner's hand recalls Sexton's own "ordinary hand" quoted at the start of this chapter. The ordinary quality of the hand also signals a break from metaphor, a slightly contrite turn to bare emotional content. In Olds's poem, by contrast, her partner's "hand in its ordinary self" stands in sharp relief against the extremity of physical pleasure that she is at pains to display. To gussy up the hand with metaphor would only detract from the juxtaposition between the everyday and the erotic extraordinary. But could metaphors accurately describe the speaker's sexual pleasure?

There are, after all, small figures here: "sweet gashes of come" and "fork-flashes" of lust. Yet they are so brief, their sudden, fissure-like quality so powerful, and their rhyming so intrusive (*gashes, flashes*) in otherwise not notably consonant lines that the words here seem better understood as sensory objects than as small metaphors. A "gash" of come and a "fork-flash" are hard to imagine literally. Not semantic reference but their gulping senselessness is what makes them apt to this moment of abandon. The line breaks are similarly off-kilter, often occurring sharply between a possessive pronoun and the body part it modifies ("your / daily hand," "your / hand," "my / breast") as these body parts are fixated upon, one by one, performing a dislocation from a normal sense of embodied boundaries. At the same time, there is an increasing sense of abandon of conventional meanings and verbal arrangements, as verb phrases are split ("come / up") and articles come apart from nouns ("a / celibate's"). The intensity of sex is transmitted to Olds's words by syntactic rupture rather than by metaphor.

Yet metaphor has its place. As the couple initiates penetrative intercourse, Olds's poem slows to four distinct stages. The first is largely figurative, characterized by a complete embrace of metaphor:

> It seemed to
> take us hours to move the bone
> creatures so their gods could be fitted to each other,
> and then, at last, home, root
> in the earth, wing in the air. As it finished,
> it seemed my sex was a grey flower
> the color of the brain, smooth and glistening,
> a complex calla or iris which you
> were creating with the errless digit
> of your sex.

The first metaphor is grand: bodies are "bone creatures" who honor gods that must be "fitted" to one another. Then comes a brief line of flailing, as though the speaker's voice—caught in the moment—is grasping for the right sort of image: is it "root / in the earth" or "wing in the air"? *Where* is the feeling? Utterly connected or transcendently unloosed? The speaker resolves upon a flower as an image for her "sex," a traditional figure, as old as Homer, and oddly described, since this flower is "the color of the brain" and is created by her partner's erection. The off-kilter originality here lies in Olds's importing of the "brain" into the convention of woman-as-flower. This resulting perspective intrudes upon an image that might otherwise fall back into its standard place as an object of gaze, a role that women-as-flowers and women-as-landscapes have tended to play.[13]

Olds's next move, and what I am calling the second stage of sex, is to dismiss the metaphor she just presented:

> But then, as it finished again,
> one could not speak of a blossom, or the blossom
> was stripped away

The past tense of the image is marked (one *could* not, it *was* stripped away) and suggests that the speaker is forming these images during the act of sex itself, not afterward when she is writing the poem. The act of formulating an image, and then rejecting it, is told as part of the experience of sex itself. The speaker in the act rejects the clothing of her sensation in imagery; it must be stripped down to bare reference.

And yet this rejection of the blossom image quickly settles into a simile itself, which capitalizes on the words "stripped away." Olds dramatically rejects the image by stripping it down to an even more naked reality, below both clothes and skin:

> as if, until
> that moment, the cunt had been clothed, still,
> in the thinnest garment, and now was bare
> or more than bare, silver wet-suit of
> matter itself gone, nothing
> there but the paradise flay.

The mental stripping down of language echoes the speaker's sensation of orgasm and loss of numbness. The language becomes explicit, even coarse: the "cunt" is now "bare / or more than bare." The process of metaphor dismissal that I have outlined appears complete: metaphor has been tried on and then stripped off to reveal raw language intended to embody truth.

But the speaker is not done describing the intensity of this experience. The third stage involves a departure from the body itself:

> And then
> more, that cannot be told—may be,
> but cannot be, things that did not
> have to do with me, as if some
> wires crossed, and history
> or war, or the witches possessed, or the end
> of life were happening in me, or as if
> I were in a borrowed body, I
> knew what I could not know, did—was
> done to—what I cannot-do-be-done-to

Some experience is impossible to relate. The speaker has exhausted her resources: "then / more, that cannot be told." (Fitting, since the poem also begins on a note of physical exhaustion.) Or she *says* she has, before trying once again to spell out the meaning of *not telling*, or of telling things that language has not yet articulated to her satisfaction. In this mode, she imagines herself entering a slipstream of "war" and "witches possessed," and then imagines the feeling of dying ("the end / of life . . . happening to me") and separating from her body. Finally, language unwinds in tautologies ("did—was done to—what I cannot-do-be-done-to"), as if to show that as metaphorical images have failed, so has language, and extreme arcs of narrative too have failed to capture the experience of the body. Only the failures of these many attempts seem adequate to her sensory experience.

The fourth and final stage of sex is configured as a return to life, the body, and human-scale emotions. The mundane is welcomed back:

> so when
> we returned, I cried, afraid for a moment
> I was dead, and had got my wish to come back,
> once, and sleep with you, on a summer
> afternoon, in an empty house
> where no one could hear us.

This is an imaginary realm in which the speaker herself is as if dead, returned only to be at peace once more with her partner. The specter of death is again in play: sex has made her again feel near to the end of life, and then fear that it has indeed happened. These two imaginary encounters with mortality prepare the speaker for an even more searing interface.

The third appearance of death is more concrete. The speaker strokes her partner's hair, and that leads to the end of the poem:

> I did not think of my father's hair
> in death, those oiled paths, I lay
> along your length and did not think how he
> did not love me, how he trained me not to be loved.

These negations suggest their opposites: if the speaker did not relate her lover's hair to her father's in death (and maybe she did), the poet has done so; if the speaker did not relate this haptic impression of her father's hair to his lack of love for her (and maybe she did), the poet has done this, too. Critical to the pain of this passage is the father's death; his lack of love is irremediable now.

The complicated grief that attends the death of this parent is ongoing, signaled even by the lover's kind face. Just as sex conjures death, in this instance, the present lover's touch refers to the (now terminally) absent father. A trap inheres in even the most pleasurable of embodied experiences, or perhaps in the poetic act of articulating them, with the body and mind aligned by touch and memory working in concert. The imaginative instrument strips back associative images (the flower) to describe (feel) the experience, but the poet becomes transported by other associations, forced to confront the inevitability of death and one especially difficult death. Olds's poetry represents intense physical sensations as inroads to fresh forms of language. Yet the poems also turn in response to unwanted associations, through metaphors and memories, back to experience.

Metaphor, after all, means "carried across." It is often conceptualized as a cognitive reach from one thing to another, a displacement of one meaning that brings another meaning closer.[14] Olds sometimes replaces such metaphorical discursions and connections with associations made across time. In the case of her transportation back to her father's death at the end of "You Kindly," we may look to the end of a poem from an earlier book, *The Father* (1992), which chronicles the death of her father.[15] "The Exact Moment of His Death" closes with these lines:

> as if the purely physical were claiming him,
> and then it was not my father,
> it was not a man, it was not an animal,
> I ran my hand slowly through the hair,
> lifted my fingers up through the grey
> waves of it, the unliving glistening
> matter of this world.

The "claim" of the "purely physical" at the moment of death needs no elaboration. I would only point to the bareness of the lines. The "as if" signals the entrance of personification, a suggestion that physicality has a will. The description of the dead father is all negation: "not my father /... not a man ... not an animal" and "unliving." He is now an "it," silver hair that glistens, outside the categories of family, humanity, or fauna. He has become "matter of the world," stripped of identity, unequal to himself. In contradistinction, she runs her hands through his hair. An earlier version of the poem is even more centered on the speaker's actions, drawing them out in time and description: "plunged my fingers into it gently and / lifted them up slowly."[16] As he loses human characteristics in stark language, her activity gains adverbial contours; her touch is gentle and slow. A reader of the body of Olds's work will see that this act is a marker of many meanings: a haptic metaphor triggered by the fingers' movement through the "matter of this world." This touch becomes a metaphor (a sign of departure and return) when it is accessed again much later in "You Kindly" and meaning is carried between two sensory points and outward into language.

Abstraction

In Olds's *Odes* (2016), the traditional English ode, to which she hews closely, establishes some distance from its subject matter through the formality of direct address. Olds's work did not always exhibit such formal distance; these odes seem to push her toward attempts, sometimes awkward, to compel the minute to serve as broadly representative of the general and categorical. Each poem is figured as a meditation; often, the abstracted form of the address is facetiously invoked ("O general idea of the penis, do you mind / being noticed?").[17] Against this push toward the conceptual, Olds strains to find new ways to maintain the sensory and material aspects of her poetry, now experimenting with doodles on the page ("Spoon"), then offering a poem whose bifurcated shape across lines imitates its subject matter ("Split Ode"). She ends the book with a poem shaped into a triangle made from the ancient incantatory term "abracadabra," thus evoking the early use of the word on amulets and a time when a sonic word-object was thought capable of healing. Is there nostalgia and longing for the elemental in these lines? A reach toward materiality that her stark verbal style no longer provides?[18]

The tension between the conceptual and sensory is echoed in a tension between the universal and the autobiographical. Materiality and autobiography come together as Olds draws her partners' voices into her poems, specifically their (imagined, remembered) complaints, and gives responses to them. One is a sympathetic account from her previous book, *Stag's Leap* (2012), of her ex-husband as weighed down by the books written about him.[19] Another is from a poem saucily titled "Second Ode to the Hymen":

> My partner says that what I write
> about women is self-involved—"You're sixty
> something years old," he exclaims, "and still
> writing about the first time you got laid!"
> But it isn't just my hymen—
> people get to talk about Beauty and Truth,
> why not address, directly, the human
> maidenhead, the Platonic form
> of her, the putting off intercourse until
> the girl will not be torn apart by full-term birth,
> why not lament the hymen being hunted
> and plundered, impaled on a pike in a public
> square like a tiny severed head.

Her partner's critique is circumstantially framed (as if it had been stated in just these terms on one particular day) but stands in for a common criticism of Olds's poetry: she is self-involved, even self-obsessed. The speaker has already said that what she writes about is "women" in general, anticipating her more explicit defense: "But it isn't just *my* hymen."

When she says that "people get to talk about Beauty and Truth," the "people" in question are likely men, such as Plato (cited a few lines later), who made a strong and influential claim for abstraction as an overarching goal. Can't the hymen stand in metonymically for the "human / maidenhead, the Platonic form / of her"? As if to show how this Platonic procedure might work in service of the hymen, and the heteronormative female experience more generally, the poet gives us a metaphor of the hymen in bad straits, "being hunted / and plundered, impaled on a pike in a public / square," which soon transforms into a simile, "like a tiny severed head." Female embodied experience is thus invested with the cognitive heft of a "head" (if a severed one). Another way that Olds shows how one hymen could stand in for many is to gesture at the long history of abuse received by hymens that have often been battered and broken without the consent of the persons whose bodies they occupy. Olds's reach for a metaphor and, still more showily, for similes to suggest the importance of the hymen is a condensed response to her critics. Anne Keefe has praised Olds for her insistence on "the very 'bigness' of smallness."[20] Yet the case for the universal within the minute is made even more strongly in Olds's poetry when it is shown rather than said, when she has the courage to pull her metaphors.

Now for evaluative claims. Olds's poetry does not offer every kind of poetic good. She is not, for one thing, a poet who works much with sound; her verse is not metered and she rarely does much with consonance, such as alliteration, rhymes, or puns. She does not push back against the boundaries of language by using sonic resources to invite unexpected or illicit meanings to surface from their linguistic depths; she does not evoke the musical parentage of poetry. The result is that if I had to choose just one poet to represent all poetry to future generations, even all contemporary poetry, I would not choose Olds. She leaves too many tools on the table.

Yet this does not present a problem necessarily: I do not demand singularity or absolute superiority of poems or people. An exciting encounter with a person—whether a single conversation or a relationship of many years—can alter one's view of the world and what sort of existence is possible within it. Poems can have the same effect. I chose to write about Olds's poetry because my encounter with it adjusted my sense of embodied experience: how it can be communicated, aestheticized, shared, and made literary, while remaining singular. Her poetry prompts me to consider the relations between discursive and nondiscursive experiences (like sex, pain, death), particularly those experiences that seem more likely to silence the semantic, logical, linguistic, and cognitive. This is poetry that loosens the boundary between feeling and language. How are we to decide what ought to be framed as significant, memorable, and poetical? Olds asks what is worthy of poetic attention and suggests lending subjecthood to bodies in which it has not previously resided.

Her poetry also implies that a startlingly raw form of language is needed to give voice to these bodies. Her struggle against poetic metaphor stages the figurative and frank in locked battle. As such, it is not actually a repudiation of metaphorical or poetical speech but an underlining of its powers and limitations. The various poems I have examined in this chapter press the reader to interrogate the use of the figurative: when does it reveal and when, instead, does it cast a veil over the truth of experience and expression? After all, the mode of language that expresses experience is crucial to determining how that experience is understood and remembered. The reader of Olds's poetry is expected to wonder alongside with the poet: what does language do? How must it be wielded? In what terms should we express, remember, and tell? Olds's poetry, in other words, lays bare her own experiences but also asks the reader whether and in what terms experience can and should be laid bare. The value of this poetry thus arises from its confrontations with the meaning of experience and its interrogation of language.

Notes

1. I offer thanks to Richard Strier for bringing me to this project and his sharp-eyed reading, to Robert von Hallberg for his insightful comments, and to Norman Ware for excellent editing. I am grateful also to Clifford Ando, who made me see the poetry of Sharon Olds in a new light and provided inspiration for this essay.
2. Homer, *Iliad* 14.346–51, Sappho 94, Anacreon 287 and 417, and Catullus 2 and 3.
3. John Donne, "To His Mistress Going to Bed"; and Pablo Neruda, "Cuerpo de mujer."
4. In this chapter, I use "metaphor" to stand in metonymically for a range of forms of figurative language: not just metaphors but also similes and even allegorical images.
5. Anne Keefe provides a very thoughtful and subtle example of this trend: "It is in the body that Olds locates her voice, her poetic creation, and her resistance and power in the face of difficulty and trauma." Anne Keefe, "'The Day They Tied Me Up': Serial Return, Punishment, and the Phenomenology of Memory in the Work of Sharon Olds," *Contemporary Women's Writing* 9, no. 2 (July 2015): 275.
6. See Timothy Steele, "Tradition and Revolution: The Modern Movement and Free Verse," *Southwest Review* 70, no. 3 (Summer 1985): 294–319 on the rhetoric of recurrence used by poets to contextualize revolutions in poetic language. See Wesley Trimpi, *Ben Jonson's Poems: A Study of the Plain Style* (Stanford, CA: Stanford University Press, 1962), 95, for a helpful delineation of "plain style" as "that style in which the distinction between the denotative and connotative qualities of language is least apparent, in which content and the feelings

expressed about the content qualify one another to the exclusion of all irrelevant material, in which the division between the conceptual statement and the feelings properly associated with the statement is most nearly healed."

7. See Steele, "Tradition and Revolution," for examples of such intentions in the prose of Dryden, Eliot, Pound, and others.
8. See Keefe, "The Day They Tied Me Up," 266, on this poem as part of a larger project of "serial lyric return" to a memory of trauma.
9. Elaine Scarry, *The Body in Pain: The Making and Unmaking of the World* (New York: Oxford University Press, 1985), 10, 4.
10. Ibid., 5.
11. Ibid., 162.
12. Ibid., 6.
13. Cf. Olds's "The Love Object" from *Satan Says* on this point.
14. See, for example, Paul Ricoeur, *On Metaphor* (Chicago: University of Chicago Press, 1979), 142–43.
15. Here the melding of speaker and poet becomes clear. Olds's work is adamantly autobiographical, allowing the reader to feel confident that the speaker's father who dies in a poem from *The Father* is also the speaker's father who is recalled in a poem from *Blood, Tin, Straw*.
16. "The Moment of His Death," from *The Matter of This World: New and Selected Poems* (1987).
17. This change perhaps reflects a more general experiential shift that plays with Kant's idea of the "categorical imperative": "the longer I went without him, / the more the longing was general, cate- / gorical, and imperative," from the poem "Celibate's Ode to Balls" in *Odes*.
18. In an interview in the *New Yorker*, Olds suggests that she was influenced by the odes of Pablo Neruda and "excited" to introduce the conceptual into her poetry more robustly than she had before. Alexandra Schwartz, "Sharon Olds Sings the Body Electric," *New Yorker*, September 22, 2016.
19.   And when I wrote about him, did he
    feel he had to walk around
    carrying my books on his head like a stack of
    posture volumes, or the racks of horns
    hung where a hunter washes the venison
    down with the sauvignon? Oh leap,
    leap!
    —"Stag's Leap"
20. Keefe, "The Day They Tied Me Up," 260.

CHAPTER 9

"A Kind of Life"

On Lucille Clifton and Community

JONATHAN FARMER

THE FIRST LUCILLE Clifton poem I ever read remains my point of entry for her work. Published in her first book, 1969's *Good Times*, "if i stand in my window" (which, like many of her poems, is actually untitled, and which seems to play with the freedoms of William Carlos Williams's "Danse Russe") is structurally simple—a prolonged "if/then" statement—and persistently surprising, driven by wit that manages to be both sharp and disarming, often at once.

The terms of her argument are historically loaded—the "my" that appears in each of the poem's first three lines ("if i stand in my window / naked in my own house / and press my breasts / against the windowpane"), and then again either by itself or in the phrase "my own" another four times in a poem of just nineteen short lines, insisting on her rights as a property owner and insisting, too, on her exclusive right to control her own body ("being property once myself / i have a feeling for it," she would write a few years later); and the "his" that stands against it in the phrase that sets up the poem's turn, "his // Gods," which are, of course, historically loaded too, and which set up the final stanza:

> let him watch my black body
> push against my own glass
> let him discover self

> let him run naked through the streets
> crying
> praying in tongues[1]

Characteristically—at least in terms of her earlier work—Clifton deploys those terms in ways that both make their burden easily visible and, through the same gestures, lessen their weight. If all successful poems succeed in part because of their confidence—their ability to move with confidence, even in their embodiment of doubt—in Clifton's poems confidence is not only a means but, often, an end. Her command, in the poem's final stanza, over "the man" (subservient now to her logic and imagination) who wanted not only to see her, "naked in my own house," her breasts pressed "against my windowpane," but to stop her there, to carry his offense, his standards, through her window and into her house and insist on its significance, becomes a power to reach outside her window into the streets that she, with lordly condescension ("let him," her new anaphora, replacing "if"), will send him into, having seen her body ("let him watch," she says, this time being even more explicit about what he should see: "my *black* body"—the adjective had previously belonged to a metaphor: "black birds"—which will now "push against my own glass," even the medium through which she will let him see, she insists, hers), now naked himself, now "crying / praying in tongues."

It's a joyous poem, one whose obvious investment in fantasy ("the man" has again and again proved remarkably capable of making his offense matter) doesn't make it any less real. Whatever happens in the actual streets, Clifton has created a place in which we can come together over our delight in making a joke—in Clifton's making a joke that we are invited to share in—out of the grotesque imagination that elsewhere insists on its preeminence. Notably, when I say that "we" are invited, I mean me, too, even though I am, in my identity and experience, far more like "the man" than I am like her. It's of secondary importance, but it nonetheless says something about Clifton—the person who wrote the poems and the person who is so present within them—that I, even when I first read this poem in the early 1990s, maybe nineteen or twenty, white, male, coddled by my good fortune, equal parts arrogant and insecure, in no way inclined to imagine value that didn't begin with my needs, read this poem with so much delight. In small poems Clifton creates large spaces; beginning from the historical and personal particulars of her life—and of a relationship to language that seems thoroughly untroubled by the dominant culture's assumptions of linguistic propriety—she creates a life's work whose welcome still feels wide and deep.

But that's not to say that the poems compromise to make a white audience feel at home. The invitation is only absolute within its very specific terms. "won't you celebrate with me," which came out in those same early 1990s, is not, I think, among Clifton's most impressive poems, but it's nonetheless a poem that continues to do essential work in the world, and one in which the terms of Clifton's invitation are clear. In an admiring and insightful review of the *Collected Poems* for the *Nation*, the critic Jordan Davis claimed, responding to one poem he takes to be of particular merit:

> When Clifton writes such poems, she is among the very few true poets of our times. But one has to read a lot of her work to find that poet. She is not the Clifton found in the anthologies, and until *Next*, she was not the Clifton who would usually turn up in her own books. More characteristic of the first third of her new *Collected Poems* are the kinds of general, earnest poems that, playing to her public persona as a nonthreatening wise woman, work well with large audiences at readings but wouldn't stop a solitary reader for more than a few seconds.[2]

That seems accurate up to a point, but it's the wrong point for many of these poems. More personable in her poems than other poets of such talent, Clifton wrote her poems for persons. And the phrase "nonthreatening wise woman," with its coding and condescension (a rare moment of both in the review), is also insufficient in its description of that persona. That opening line, "won't you celebrate with me," which, in isolation, feels a little generic, something you could safely put on a greeting card, becomes more particular in the following lines: "what i have shaped into / a kind of life?" The poem is partly an ars poetica—that shaping describing in part the work of creating a body of poems (in which context "kind of life" is less bleak than its other, more immediate meaning); the subsequent claim to have "had no model" both a slight exaggeration and an obvious truth.

It is also an attempt, in the continuous present tense of its encounter with others, to give people something of worth in their attempts to live their lives. It is generous in a more social sense of that word than we usually mean when we apply it to poems. Clifton believed in poetry, and her poems often achieve their literary significance in concert with a concern that feels more fundamental to their being—the need to help those who are in need of help, especially, though not exclusively, those who have suffered as she has suffered, at the hands of racism, of sexism, of sexual violence, disease, cruelty, lasting grief... The African American poets who referred to her later in her life and still refer to her now as "Miss Lucille" are legion, as are, I imagine, even more people who weren't poets, even many who didn't read much poetry, who say and feel the same. The suffering that her poems frequently configured into beauty and humor, that they frequently make palpable, as well as the love for others (sometimes cumbersome) and the far from inevitable, sometimes despondent love for herself, drove her both out and in; and the other potentials of her poetry—beyond its potential to help, to heal—often played out either through or against that potential, with the not always easy marriage between them often making both more visible and more complex.

The poem's invitation does require me—in particular—to accept that I am not its principal concern. It is not forbidding in that insistence, merely confident, determined to stand at the center of a language and identity—and, as always with Clifton, a body—wherein blackness is a given, as is its history.

The poem ends, as many Clifton poems do, with a kind of punch line, returning in this case to the initial invitation in order to make the nature of the celebration both more terrible and, again, in the same move, more delightful:

> come celebrate
> with me that everyday
> something has tried to kill me
> and has failed.

That final sentence achieves its particularity via movement. It opens at first into the implication that we are celebrating the forces that have tried to kill her. The syntactically complete "celebrate / with me that everyday / something has tried to kill me," landing at the end of the line, *sounds* resolved, the two modifications in "with me that everyday" slowing the poem before it straightens out in the next line to set up a sense of completion. And so the extra line, which brings us back to something more sensible, that we are celebrating her daily triumph, becomes itself triumphant, a swerving into victory. And it's the specificity of that movement that makes the openness of its meaning persuasive, allowing it to encompass a host of threats without dissolving into generality. The particularity of this person, of the way she writes, of her ability to turn the forces that have put her life and health at risk into emblems of her strength, and the way you can almost hear her laughing with delight, a little mischievous, there at the end, allows her to create something that others can inhabit and feel more real, more consoled, and, yes, more strong. If you think that's an invalid end for poetry to serve, you'll probably never be completely at ease with Clifton's poems; you'll probably never stop feeling suspicious, wary that she's going to use your pleasure, her skill, for some human purpose. But hopefully you can at least see how important it is for something that does these things this well to exist—for our collective inheritance of language to encompass, with this much vitality, a part of the collective experience it has often been engaged in never thinking even to think about. Hopefully you can accept that every use of poetry is a human use.

Davis is right about the moment when Clifton's poetry changed—and right, too, to point out that it was not a complete alteration but rather a shift in proportions. At that moment, it seems, some greater confidence about her centrality, her representative importance, as well as, quite likely, the loneliness that followed her husband's death three years earlier in 1984, let her go more deeply, more often, into her own body, and further out into mythology—and to come into greater contact with the violence in both. A more tragic sensibility took root, a feeling for her body that was fleshier, clotted, further in, the earlier symbolic freedom yielding, in many cases, to a sense of just how inescapable, how full of grief and organs, blood and pain, her body was. Still readily comprehensible, but less clear, the poems, in many cases, became more private, their welcome more often offering admission into a dark intimacy, more astonishing, more perilous, less careful of the audience it still intends, if not to heal, then at least to make less lonely, more at home in a legacy of suffering and love that for Clifton was longer than a life. (The dead that speak in her poems are the actual, still articulate, dead, ancestors whose own welcome was inseparable from despair, despair inseparable from hope.)

Cancer (and, later, kidney failure) stalked Clifton as she aged, and the disease—both *of* her body and *destroying* her body—inspired a kind of metaphorical and sonic density, a strangeness that seemed to sing from within. In "lumpectomy eve" she ends, "all night it is the one breast / comforting the other." In "scar" she refers to "empty pocket flap / edge of before and after." In "poem to my uterus" she opens:

> you   uterus
> you have been patient
> as a sock
> while i have slippered into you
> my dead and living children

In all of these lines, metaphor makes her body more tangible, more flesh, parts. There's a violence to the comparisons, the wrenching of the uterus, the breast, the scar where a malignant part of the breast had been, out of their familiar names, out of their belonging, but still regarded with care, her body now, such writing suggests, only capable of being honored if it can be named as something potentially destructive, potentially grotesque.

Published in the same book as both "scar" and "lumpectomy eve"—*The Terrible Stories*—"1994" is explicit in its speaking to an audience; it's also explicit in declaring who that audience is, but not immediately. Before that specification, Clifton writes:

> i was leaving my fifty-eighth year
> when a thumb of ice
> stamped itself hard near my heart
>
> you have your own story
> you know about the fear the tears
> the scars of disbelief

The shift from the first to the second stanza, from Clifton to "you," is abrupt, the strangeness of "a thumb of ice" yielding to "story," "fear," and "tears," fueled more by speed than surprise, and even "scars of disbelief" is fairly generic by comparison. The change is immediate; "you have your own story" is a humbling before the knowledge of others' suffering. It stands out not because it is unique, but because it deliberately refuses the imaginative complexity of the preceding lines; at the same time, though, even as it defers, the shift from "i" (the first word of the first stanza) to "you" (the first of the second) introduces a new kind of confidence, an almost commanding tone. The yielding is also a kind of power here.

It's a few lines later when she finally says who "you" are, and as she does so the three-line stanza, for the first time, falters as a syntactic unit:

> you know how dangerous it is
>
> to be born with breasts
> you know how dangerous it is
> to wear dark skin

It's generalization as specification, the categorical placing limits on the audience who will hear this poem spoken to them. The moment is not unwelcoming to others, to me—or, it doesn't feel that way—but rather an indication that the stakes are too high right now to heal us all. It's an image, from another angle, of all that Clifton needs, in poetry, to do, of the people, including her, who need her help—and, eventually, of the challenge of holding any kind of community together in the midst of so much pain. After "dark skin," she goes back to the beginning, repeating the first line before reentering the metaphor of ice in different terms, more complex and finally more strange, as the three-line stanzas collapse into sets of two and, in the couplet below, "the one mad nipple" seems, in one reading, to be both the object of "hanging off" and the subject of "weeping," whereas in another "hanging off" and "weeping" are a compound of two verbs that fall far short of parallelism, the latter having no object at all:

> i was leaving my fifty-eighth year
> when i woke into the winter
> of a cold and mortal body
>
> thin icicles hanging off
> the one mad nipple weeping

There are just two more couplets left after that, the first a simultaneous attempt to speak, for the first time, for "us" and a hopeless calling out, rhetorical questions echoing the perennial, childish protest, "why me?" And then, out of those, the final couplet, which in speaking to "you" seems to push you away:

> but you must know all about this
> from your own shivering life

The "must" there makes the line less commanding, less certain, than "you have your own story," but the loss of command is also, it seems to me, a loss of hope. Clifton seems almost to turn away from the audience, slightly disgusted, the narrowing of audience a constriction now. If, like any poem that suggests poetry is not enough, its existence (its having been written, its having been published) partly undermines the claim, poetry's value, in *this* poem, still feels narrower, more thoroughly (though not comfortably) constrained to something private and lonely. It stands out for its achievement in making despair audible. It is not, ultimately, a social act—that is merely its form. Its consolation is that someone could make something like this, out of this. It runs deep, not wide.

In "grandma, we are poets," from the early 1990s, Clifton makes a case for that less social imagination, concluding,

> say rather i withdrew
> to seek within myself
> some small reassurance
> that tragedy while vast
> is bearable

She sets up the lines with one of several phrases she's taken from a definition of autism, "*by disregard of external reality, / withdrawing into a private world.*" It's probably no accident that, in this apologia, she feels compelled to answer to a definition of privacy as antisocial and even symptomatic of illness. In an early, unpublished poem, "let them say," she wrote, responding to the titular phrase:

> that she had going for her

a good ass and six children.
that she obeyed her daddy
and her husband
and looked like her mama
more and more.
that she thought god was
a good idea.
that she cried when she saw
she wasn't beautiful
and tried to be real nice.

I assume Clifton is wearing a mask here. I can't imagine her aspiring to be a woman who "obeyed . . . her husband." (She frequently cited the story of her father disapproving of her mother's writing, and her mother burning her—her own—poems in response.) But it's hard to put away the echo between these lines and the much later ones above. (Clifton did that sometimes; a late poem ends, retrieving the conclusion of "won't you celebrate with me," with her statement that "we" have come to love a world not paradise for, among other things, "how, each day, / something that loves us // tries to save us.") I wonder how often she meant to be that thing that "tries to save us" (and how much the gap between trying to save and saving haunted her), much as I wonder how often the desire to be "real nice" and the impulse to withdraw, "to seek within myself / some small reassurance / that tragedy while vast / is bearable" (note how she works to diminish both), were in conflict for her, and how often that tension provided some of the energy of her work (an energy that often and artfully played over pacing and line, the depleted landing of "is bearable" collecting the hurry that rushes into it).

It seems worth noting here that Clifton always claimed to have forgiven her father for abusing her. In "june 20," another poem of the early 1990s, she begins by making plain his betrayal:

i will be born in one week
to a frowned forehead of a woman
and a man whose fingers will itch
to enter me.

It's appalling, the way his body waits to violate her even before she has passed into the world. It's hard to imagine those lines as the starting point for compassion, much less that compassion would come as quickly as it does. But the poem continues,

> she will crochet
> a dress for me of silver
> and he will carry me in it.
> they will do for each other
> all that they can
> but it will not be enough.
> none of us will know that we will not
> smile again for years,
> that she will not live long.
> in one week i will emerge face first
> into their temporary joy.

Already, in the second stanza, his hands have been transformed, not outside of the knowledge of what they will do, but into something that will also carry her, and the awareness of what's coming does not wipe the present away. (Nor does the dangerous echo of her body in her mother's: "enter" and "emerge.") Instead, like the "temporary joy" the poem ends on, out of all the future it faces, it is more worth cherishing for the terrible failures that depend from it. Elizabeth Alexander wrote in the *New Yorker*, just after Clifton died, that "she elucidates the ironies of history without using an ironic tone."[3] Even at such a small and appalling scale as this, that doubling (that additional irony) persists. Clifton's achievement—her ability to create a communal space and present a private self—is at its heart contradictory, but the contradiction is itself an image of reality—the reality, in particular, of an African American culture that has found joy and made family out of materials (including history; including family life itself) that the dominant culture continued (and continues) to tear apart, and that, like all cultures, like many families, encompassed (her father, that itch) its own terrible, particular rending, too.

Family, the possibility of it, the violations of it, the ways in which it uses bodies, even its continuities beyond death, was fundamental to Clifton's life as a poet. (Especially in the early poems, both her Dahomey ancestry and her birth with twelve fingers, something she shared with her mother and her first daughter, were recurring symbols.) And her own family life was never clear of suffering for long—her father's sexual abuse of her; her mother's early death; her husband's early death; the early death of two of her children. Her sense of humor preceded most of these, but it also proved essential to her ability to fashion a world of aesthetic redemption out of a life that often argued for despair. "man and wife"—which also comes from the same volume as "june 20" and "grandma, we are poets"—is the rare poem in which that humor doesn't figure (except, perhaps, as an echo of something unavailable here), and the rare one in which no specific person—Clifton or persona—speaks. It instead stands outside, seeking order, its orderly pairings from the first to the second stanza accentuating the inevitability of his death and their powerlessness to serve each other well, looking out on each other from their different forms of suffering—her grief, his pain—the isolation that itself still seems to live, in the poem's grace, inside their care:

> she blames him, at the last, for
> backing away from his bones
> and his woman, from the life
> he promised her was worth
> cold sheets. she blames him
> for being unable to see
> the tears in her eyes, the birds
> hovered by the window, for love being
> not enough, for leaving.
>
> he blames her, at the last, for
> holding him back with her eyes
> beyond when the pain was more
> than he was prepared to bear,
> for the tears he could neither
> end nor ignore, for believing
> that love could be enough,
> for the birds, for the life
> so difficult to leave.

The poem is, in many ways, an inverse of "june 20," the long happiness of their life together rendered in the final moment of sorrow. The poem's final swerve, so characteristic of Clifton, feels exhausted, the wit recognizable but also wanting, there at the end, more synopsis than surprise. The poem's power is heartbreaking. It's the power, simply, to make one feel—to feel, in strange communion, alone, to know love by having seen clearly what love can't keep. All the invention, almost unadorned, of "for / backing away from his bones / and his woman," of "from the life / he promised her was worth / cold sheets," has waned by the final line. "for the life / so difficult to leave" is sad, is plain, its art gone into the awareness that he is leaving it anyway and the way their shared pain pulls them apart even before he's gone, and the sense that it matters because of the love, the beauty, the poem lifts them toward.

In his afterword to *The Collected Poems of Lucille Clifton*, from which I've taken the text of all the poems quoted here, including the previously unpublished ones, Kevin Young associates Clifton's early poetry with the Black Arts movement, observing, "Black Arts sought many things but above all a public poetry—one aware of and even pitched toward a newfound audience that it was both meeting and making." That appeal to a nonliterary audience often sits awkwardly in the critical responses to her work—and likely goes some way toward explaining the relative paucity of serious responses. Toni Morrison, in the introduction to the same book, complained:

> Accolades from fellow poets and critics refer to her universal human heart; they describe her as a fierce caring female. They compliment her courage, vision, joy—unadorned (meaning "simple"), mystical, poignant, humorous, intuitive, harsh and loving.
>
>   I do not disagree with these judgments. Yet I am startled by the silence in these interpretations of her work. There are no references to her intellect, imagination, scholarship or her risk-taking manipulation of language. To me she is not the big mama/big sister of racial reassurance and self-empowerment. I read her skill as that emanating from an astute, profound intellect—characteristics mostly absent from her reviews. The personal courage of the woman cannot be gainsaid, but it should not function as a substitute for piercing insight and bracing intelligence.

Such omissions are, inevitably and in part, a function of race. Clifton's work in a demotic vein is read differently than Wordsworth's, say, or Frank O'Hara's, or William Carlos Williams's. But there's more to it, as well. Because Clifton (like O'Hara) so frequently succeeded in creating the impression of an actual person speaking in an actual moment (and because, unlike O'Hara's, her actual moments weren't intertwined with high art and white, metropolitan sophistication), and because she often took care, as Young suggests, to reach and serve an audience that was not exclusively literary (and, I suspect, because her poetry is often fun), the stereotypical responses—to treat her as a sort of natural poet, a storyteller with line breaks engaging in something less sophisticated or complex than true, serious poetry, someone whose wisdom was cultural rather than concentrated—come more readily to mind for those of us who already have them there.

In support of her claim, Morrison points to the opening lines of "brothers," a sequence in which we overhear the words of Lucifer (a sometime stand-in for Clifton, who loved to play on the meaning of her first name) from a conversation he and God are having "long after":

> come coil with me
> here in creation's bed
> among the twigs and ribbons
> of the past. i have grown old
> remembering the garden,
> the hum of the great cats
> moving into language, the sweet
> fume of the man's rib
> as it rose up and began to walk.

It's probably no coincidence that the opening line resembles the beginning of "won't you celebrate with me" from the same book. But it's easier here to see the complexity of Clifton's imagination, her ability to work beyond the possibility of satisfactory paraphrase. Phrases like "the hum of the great cats / moving into language" and "the sweet / fume of the man's rib" foreground Clifton's inventiveness, her ability to keep turning the metaphor while sustaining its forward motion. When a more ordinary phrase like "moving into language" shows up, it does so within the unlikeliness of the specific entering into abstraction intact, Adam's invention recovering some of its original marvel—and "language" retrieving a little bit of luster in the bargain, too.

Mythology, including Christian mythology, often allowed Clifton to showcase her skill in a way she was less likely to do elsewhere, and those mythological poems can serve, along with their own unique virtues, as places to more easily observe the talents Morrison describes—and to then better detect their presence in her more personal and communal work, where they are at times more muted, supporting some other goal. A relatively early poem, "mary," captures some of the physical density and distress that would show up more often later in more personal poems, the conclusion's symbolic import growing thick and heavy as it violates Mary's body: "i feel a garden / in my mouth // between my legs / i see a tree."

"leda 3" appears just a few pages before "brothers" in *The Book of Light*, part of a section of poems that pull from Greek and Christian mythology and create space (as such subjects typically did) in which Clifton could take her talent out for a spin. Clifton describes "leda 3" as "a personal note (re: visitations)," but it also inevitably (and concurrently) talks back to Yeats's "Leda and the Swan." (She was a fan of Yeats.) The poem reads in full:

> always pyrotechnics;
> stars spinning into phalluses
> of light, serpents promising
> sweetness, their forked tongues
> thick and erect, patriarchs of bird
> exposing themselves in the air.
> this skin is sick with loneliness.
> You want what a man wants,
> next time come as a man
> or don't come.

The double meaning of "don't come" is unmistakable, as is the poem's more persistent mocking of masculine entitlement and masculine display. That such entitlement was a terrible wound in her childhood does not define the poem's tone, nor does it seem to hamstring in any way the muscularity of her writing here. Clifton's persistent transformation of the scene's elements into penises manages to stand (no pun intended), tonally, in multiple places at once—playful and tactile, the mocking of it neither weighed down by heavy-handedness nor thinned out by a singularity of purpose. "their forked tongues / thick and erect" is, in addition to its sonic richness (the way saying it forces you to feel, if not necessarily think about, the thickness of your own tongue), at once disturbing and marvelous, too real to dismiss, too surprising to stop the sentence's pleasurable motion, in which each broken phrase extends a little closer to the line ending, until "air" ends both sentence and line, clearing room for something smaller, sadder, and more fierce—Zeus stripped of his disguise, yes, but Clifton, too, stripped of the cover she had taken up until then in her mastery of the scene.

The final sentence makes me think of Coleridge: "had I met these lines running wild in the deserts of Arabia, I should have instantly screamed out 'Wordsworth!'" It's so audibly her, the perfect little machine she made for her wit at the end of some of her best poems, the last line dropping the sentence into something sharper even as it collects the sentence's energy. But the energy, here, is more diminished from the outset. The wit is just as sharp, but you can also hear the loneliness it leaves behind—the slight formality of diction that so often ran through her poems, unremarked, relenting as the poem settles into the lines, more fierce but also more subdued—having sent the visitation away. There's fun to be had here, as at the end of "if i stand in my window," but there's also Clifton there with you, creating the fun—making fun, as we say—and her loneliness inside that achievement deepens it, and complicates it, and serves as a reminder of how much it means to have her there in the poems, so often, and the way her confidence came increasingly to encompass, to embody, her doubt.

It's interesting to set that awareness up against one of her more social poems, "wishes for sons," which appeared just two pages after "poem to my uterus" in *Quilting*. Structurally, the poem resembles "if i stand in my window," down to the concluding repetition of "let . . ." And tonally, too, it's not that far removed from the earlier poem, which preceded it by nearly two decades, except that here, as in "leda 3," the sorrow underneath the outrage that is itself underneath the poem's conquering wit peers through—so that the public act stays more personal and Clifton appears less triumphant, more ready to stand in the middle of her vulnerability and lead from there. The first stanza shows just how good Clifton was at pacing a poem, the blunt almost-in-media-res first sentence followed by a sentence that spreads out after the second line break, then the third sentence returning, mostly, to the bluntness of the first, except that the extra syllables crack apart the blunt dimeter of the opening line, as well as the almost-pattern of concluding spondees in the second and third:

> i wish them cramps.
> i wish them a strange town
> and the last tampon,
> i wish them no 7-11.

Throughout the next two stanzas, the poem keeps gathering energy only to disperse or check it. Unlike "if i stand in my window," "wishes for sons," until the final stanza, never lets a sentence go on longer than two and a half short lines. Both of the sentences that do go on that long are in the third and penultimate stanza, the only one in which syntax and line don't agree, and the one in which "i wish" gives way to "let":

> later i wish them hot flashes
> and clots like you
> wouldn't believe. let the
> flashes come when they
> meet someone special.
> let the clots come
> when they want to.

The last stanza is just one sentence, but that sentence, the poem's longest by far, restores the decorum of line and syntax that the stanza before it disrupted, as well as allowing for a logical extension of the sentence's first wish, causality—another kind of order establishing itself as the poem imaginatively expands the universe of people who must suffer at the hands of masculine entitlement in an apparent attempt to ward off masculine entitlement:

> let them think they have accepted
> arrogance in the universe,
> then bring them to gynecologists
> not unlike themselves.

I say "apparent attempt" because even as the poem moves from "wish"—a kind of curse, a power given to the earthly; but also something smaller, something outside of reality—to the unearthly authority of "let," it retains the knowledge that it has no power to do anything it imagines. What it does instead is to create a community of countervailing pleasure, one shot through not only with awareness of the imperviousness of male arrogance but also with an ongoing frustration, worn lightly, that the outrage of this extends even to one's own (though the title doesn't quite say so) sons, another emblem of the loneliness out of which the poem laughs—that intensely social response.

In a 1999 interview with her longtime friend and colleague Michael S. Glaser, Clifton said, "I think that writing is a way of continuing to hope. When things sometimes feel as if they're not going to get any better, writing offers a way of trying to connect beyond that obvious feeling . . . because you know, there is hope in connecting, and so perhaps for me it is a way of remembering I am not alone."[4] And then, in answer to the same question she posed to herself in the early unpublished poem "let them say," she explained, "I would like to be seen as a woman whose roots go back to Africa, who tried to honor being human. And who tried to do the best she could, most of the time. My inclination is to try to help." The two answers, pointing in different directions, come remarkably close to alignment. Her early, slightly self-mocking conclusion, that she "tried to be real nice," puts that impulse on equal footing with but second in sequence to "she cried when she saw / she wasn't beautiful," suggesting that she chose kindness only after being denied something more appealing. The much later, less leavened assertion that she "withdrew" seems at first, here, like the outlier, in apparent opposition to her seeking assurance that "I am not alone." And to some extent it was. Those impulses had the potential to answer each other, but only in tension with each other, and her work often shifted along a spectrum between the two, with the separation sometimes serving, as in "1994," to make the collective experience of loneliness ring more true.

In "here be dragons," from 1992's *The Book of Light*, Clifton asked "who / among us can imagine ourselves / unimagined." In "the times," the opening poem in *Blessing the Boats* eight years later, she entered the state of unimagining: "another child has killed a child / and i catch myself relieved that they are / white and i might understand except / that i am tired of understanding." The "tragedy" that Clifton sought to bear was, indeed, vast, and she consistently worked to navigate, sometimes visibly, sometimes trying to erase the distinction, her sense of herself as both singular and representative, and sometimes the burden of that became a part of the portrait, another way in which she weighed the world.

If we define a political poem as one that puts aside the particularity of a lyric speaker to address a collective injustice, then she wrote those, including an untitled curse from *Mercy* in 2004 that begins "the air / you have polluted / you will breathe" and goes on, with distressing consistency, in that vein; there's a hinge halfway through, the lines "when you come again / and you will come again," which launch the poem into a word-for-word repetition of what preceded it. And if we define a political poem as one in which a lyric speaker is intended to drive home a point about injustice, she wrote those, too, including "jasper texas 1998," a response to the death by dragging of James Byrd Jr. That poem begins:

> i am a man's head hunched in the road.
> i was chosen to speak by the members
> of my body. the arm as it pulled away
> pointed toward me, the hand opened once
> and was gone.

And if we define a political poem as one that is simply aware of its historical situation, then Clifton never stopped writing those. In "to the unborn and waiting children" she wrote:

> i went into my mother as
> some souls go into a church,
> for the rest only. but there,
> even there, from the belly of a
> poor woman who could not save herself
> i was pushed without my permission
> into a tangle of birthdays.
> listen, eavesdroppers, there is no such thing
> as a bed without affliction;
> the bodies all may open wide but
> you enter at your own risk.

And in *The Book of Light*, she wrote of her mother. "thel" (the poem's title and first word):

> was my first landscape
> red brown as the clay
> of her georgia.
> sweet attic of a woman,
> repository of old songs.
> there was such music in her;
> she would sit, shy as a wren
> humming alone and lonely
> amid broken promises,
> amid the sweet broken bodies
> of birds.

In a 1998 interview with the critic Hilary Holladay,[5] Clifton insisted on her shyness, complaining with good humor that no one ever believed that about her—not even, she claimed, her kids, though one of her kids walked through just after that and said "No, you're shy; you're about the shyest person I know." I keep thinking about what Clifton told Glaser: "My inclination is to try to help." I'm grateful for the smallness of that statement—and I'm inclined to line it up with that marriage of "vast" and "bearable." To say that Clifton was a practical poet is not to say that her imaginative achievement was any less than other important poets of her time, nor her ambition any smaller. Rather, it is to say that her imagination encompassed her audience in a way and to an extent that seems exceptional to me—at least among those whose poems so far exceeded what an audience could imagine wanting from them. Among those she imagined most fully was, of course, herself—both as someone in need of help and as someone capable of offering it, with the latter sometimes answering the former. Though that person, both in her poems and out, was prone to despair and often, I suspect, profoundly alone, even in company, I find myself, even as someone she may have been less compelled to imagine, consoled by her presence in poems—less alone in my own loneliness and despair, which is both private and, lately, increasingly, cultural as well. The tendency, in writing about Clifton, given the compression of her work, is to place her on the side of Dickinson in the imaginative divide of

American poetry's ancestors. And yet, reading those poems that seem to me to stand at the mobile heart of her achievement—poems like "if I stand in my window," "man and wife," "wishes for sons," "june 20," "leda 3," "lumpectomy eve" and "1994"—I think of her much more in terms of Whitman, an eccentric and extraordinary figure determined to stand at the center of experience, containing multitudes, determined to heal the world with unlikely images of itself.

Notes

1. Lucille Clifton, *The Collected Poems of Lucille Clifton 1965–2010*, edited by Kevin Young and Michael S. Glaser (Rochester, NY: BOA Editions, 2012). All quotations are from this volume.
2. Jordan Davis, "Unsparing Truths: On Lucille Clifton," *Nation*, June 19, 2013.
3. Elizabeth Alexander, "Remembering Lucille Clifton," *New Yorker*, February 17, 2010.
4. Michael S. Glaser, "I'd Like Not to Be a Stranger in the World: A Conversation/Interview with Lucille Clifton," *Antioch Review* 58, no. 3 (Summer 2000): 310–28.
5. Hilary Holladay, "She Could Tell You Stories," interview with Lucille Clifton, Poetry Foundation, https://www.poetryfoundation.org/articles/68875/she-could-tell-you-stories. The interview took place on April 11, 1998.

CHAPTER 10

Ed Dorn's Vulgate

KEITH TUMA

IS THERE A critical consensus about the best recent American poetry? No, nothing is likely to be settled soon. I have confidence in the diversity of poets and poetry readers and in future readers who will find something to value in poetry ignored today. The proliferation of poets has made it more difficult to survey the field, as Craig Dworkin and Ron Silliman have written, but that should mean that conversations about evaluation are helpful. Silliman estimates the number of poetry books now being published yearly in the United States at one thousand and the number of publishing poets at forty thousand.[1] With such numbers, claims about what counts as the most innovative, engaged, or significant poetry—pick your criteria—are inevitably suspect, partial in both senses of the word. But that is only a problem for those who imagine an ideal world of disinterested judgment. The poetry world has always been messier than that.

I began reading Edward Dorn's poetry while studying with Robert von Hallberg at Chicago. He is the author of the most explicitly evaluative essay about Dorn's poetry.[2] Few critics in recent decades have been as interested as von Hallberg is in criteria for evaluating poems, although other critics have indicated what they value in Dorn's work. Donald Wesling praises Dorn's skill with the line and sound patterning, his wit as it alternates "comic understatement" with "preposterous hyperbole," and his expansive lyric practice, which is "always *bringing things back in*." He contrasts stanzas by Dorn and Richard Wilbur and shows Wilbur's writing to be musty with tradition.[3] He is smart about the jostling of registers of diction in Dorn's poetry, which "yok[es] . . . seemingly unrelated ideas by means of alarming suggestion and strenuous intellection" (37). But Wesling has little to say against Dorn's poetry, and of course the poetry is uneven; there is no point in ignoring its weaknesses. For example, "The World Box-score Cup of 1966" (1966) is interesting as an early effort to employ a vernacular form in satire—it mimics a sportscast rather than a box score, describing a contest between the Haves and the Havenots, the former including the English, the "Major Christian Nations,"[4] and the Russians—but it is considerably less subtle and funny than *Gunslinger* and written in a flat prosaic verse. It counts as a warm-up for *Gunslinger*, presenting a range of characters and voices, but the voices run together. It should be of interest to scholars following the history of Dorn's thoughts about class, race, and other topics, including sexual promiscuity, but few who are not Dorn scholars are likely to be entertained by it. The skill with the line that Wesling rightly celebrates is not always evident in Dorn's earlier poems or in the late fragments of *High West Rendezvous* (1997). Similarly, when Wesling says of the long poem "Oxford" in *The North Atlantic Turbine* (1967) that Dorn is "[n]ot overwhelmed by the prestige of the English poetic tradition" (38), he might have noted that Dorn himself described the book as "overreached" and "vague."[5] It is not unusual for the first academic essays about an author to be light on criticism. Michael Davidson's essay about *Gunslinger* is provocative for its reading of the poem's philosophical sources, but other than remarking on the "relentlessly obscure" language of the section of the poem called "The Cycle," he, too, is reluctant to criticize Dorn.[6]

Von Hallberg's essay ends with a speculative passage claiming that Dorn seemed poised—the essay was written in the early 1980s while Dorn was alive—to attain recognition as a major poet. It argues that Dorn's work cannot be adequately represented by a few poems, as Eliot said minor but not major poets can be represented.[7] Dorn had already completed *Gunslinger*, and this was a decade when long poems were highly valued and much studied by scholars. But Dorn finally does not rank as a major poet for von Hallberg. Dorn is not for him among the very best of recent American political poets, for one thing. Hopes for a poetry that serves civic discourse do not prevent him from praising Dorn's commitment to "the correction of taste" (84), but Dorn's discursive modes, and especially his irony, make his work less important than Robert Lowell's. Von Hallberg writes with close attention to changes in Dorn's poetry between early poems, where "[s]entimentality is a principle, a disciplined unraveling of a tangled ideology" (49), and later poems less elegiac and more committed to satire. But satire simply does not make for major poetry for him because it has to do with "vivacity" and "surprise" rather than the "guidance" he looks for in poetry. The then very recent poem that I remember him valuing most in those days was Robert Pinsky's *An Explanation of America* (1979), whose title suggests what poetry might be designed to do. Von Hallberg's criteria were Arnoldian, as Pinsky's were Horatian: "If we ask of political poetry only that it be surprising, opinionated, extreme, we would sell poetry short indeed, because along with such a notion goes the belief that prose, not poetry, bears the greatest intelligence and utility in regard to our collective public life" (66). Dorn "tries to be fresh, unpredictable, severe—not wise, or even right" (66), he adds, in a comment that is unfair to Dorn, however much wit and surprise mattered to the poet.

I don't doubt that upsetting conventional liberal pieties with idiosyncratic irony was one of Dorn's objectives, especially in his later work, much as expressions of solidarity with America's poor and dispossessed were in his early work. Dorn was a reactive poet, prepared to respond to events, though his mode of commentary varied across the years and eventually picked up speed in his epigrams. But there is analysis and truth-seeking in his poems, too. That can be difficult to see for academic critics. Although he taught at universities later in his life, Dorn's writing was never so governed by academic conventions as von Hallberg's, or Pinsky's, has been, unless it is correct to say that some of its discursive modes were a reaction to those conventions. Von Hallberg makes Dorn's poetry, especially the late poetry, seem the pursuit of controversy, as if Dorn set out to be "a stunning maverick" (66), as he calls him. An English friend once said to me that he thought a lot of Americans try to be eccentric, but few really are; the same goes for mavericks, I suppose. For some time, it has been hard to find a poet who wants to be the caretaker of the guild; that goes for critics, too. But to focus on Dorn's independence and outsider status, on his style and critical posture as it was cultivated or principled, is to slight his conversation with the Protestantism of his youth. Dorn was less of an outsider than some have thought; he took seriously the claims of Christian belief, and critics have not seen that their secularity was not his. His poems end in the place that they began, expressing confidence in his "tribe," to use the title of a great late poem.

In reviewing Tom Clark's biography of Dorn, Skip Fox describes "the influence of a bleak and often fatalistic Methodism on Dorn's stance of stoical resistance."[8] No doubt Dorn's experience of poverty also had much to do with the "stoical resistance" of his poems, but it is his work's Christian roots that have been most neglected. If it is possible to read his work as bleak, it is also possible to read it as hopeful, although his hopefulness has apocalyptic dimensions. His is not liberal optimism. It depends on nothing he sees, on no evidence past or present, on no circumstances. One of the longer discursive poems recently uncovered by the editors of the posthumous collection *Derelict Air: From Collected Out* (2015) demonstrates the extent to which the Christian fatalism that Fox identifies figures in Dorn's thinking. "Something Small, and Ignominious," which apparently dates from the mid-1950s, is about the search for "a house / larger than the house I now dwell in, for which I have no foundation / either in my head or hand."[9] In those years, Dorn was often on the move searching for work, but the house and its "foundation" refer to material *and* spiritual being, the two forever at war:

> The spiritual world cannot win. And should not, in the sense
> that mortal reason commands. The human saying—give your riches
> to the poor and follow me, is the *only* radical postulate
> ever put before the world upon which our foundations and structures
>
> are laid. (*DA* 86)

I don't want to represent this as Dorn's best writing in a discursive mode, and neither are the poem's propositions unfamiliar. But we have seen few American poets in recent decades, especially on the Left, cite the Bible in terms this generous.

Dorn's Christianity is not sentimental. It doesn't stand a chance in a world of "mortal reason," and he knows it. In Matthew 19:21, Christ tells the rich young man who has informed him that he already follows the commandments that if he wants to be perfect, he will give away his wealth and follow him. His treasure will be in heaven. This news makes the young man sorrowful, and he goes away. Christ is left to his disciples, who are amazed to hear how difficult it is for the rich to enter into the kingdom of God, how demanding a religious commitment for all. In Dorn's poem, it is possible that *nothing* one possesses will put us at ease (or redeem us); that possibility "plagues the material world" (*DA* 85). The poem considers news from friends who are building a house; Dorn wonders how they have come to believe that the world is "built on a firm foundation" (*DA* 85). He fears that they have become complacent in their pursuit of material comfort and thinks about his own search for a house:

SOMETHING SMALL, AND IGNOMINIOUS

I thot as I plucked the stem of grass
is one such a crass hand and ignominious
to scatter seed, prior to the given time,
and I thot of the letters that have come, lately
and the searches I have made small as they are, for a house
larger than the house I now dwell in, for which I have no foundation

either in my head or hand.

A letter from friends who are building a foundation
to a house, and thus forever I guess desolated from me
become wage earners and inhabitants of the world proper. (*DA* 85)

The poet is aloof—wasting time, scattering seed, distressed that his friends have settled, which is to say conformed, even if they haven't gone all the way over to television and picnics. Dorn quotes part of their letter after offering his thoughts concerning the death of a moth he has crushed between his fingers; "the dry wing under the nail makes death commonplace / ... a misfortune of the spirit" (*DA* 85). His images of poetic vocation are histrionic. He is establishing what it is to be a poet: as hard as to be a disciple of Christ.

If what is small and ignominious is the desire for material comfort, this "settling" that is like coming to terms with crushing the moth, Dorn is honest enough to acknowledge that he, too, has been tempted to settle. He wanted a house on the water, coveted his neighbor's pear; here, he remembers the story from Augustine's *Confessions*. He knows that if he imagines that he stands apart from a world made up of Sancho Panzas and Iagos, the world only ridicules him. That is the fate of poets, as of the disciples. Perhaps he's "the only fool alive," he continues, and he should buy the "shack on the water" (*DA* 86) after all. But he cannot afford it; the issue is already settled by economics. The real estate agent has told him that the shack is a special place, and he shouldn't get his hopes up about his chances to purchase it. But that is the material house—what of the other? We come to the crux of the poem: "I knew I was lost. / For remember: All I have is Hope" (*DA* 86). Hope is a currency, like grace; the famous hymn echoes here. It's good for the house in heaven, but not for the one on the lake.

This isn't the conclusion of this odd, mannered, agonized poem struggling to articulate some of the ironies that dominate Dorn's later writing. A prose paragraph follows, as if a footnote on hope. The poem is "an attempt at atonement," Dorn writes, for his lack of clarity and resolve, for a weakness that desires material comfort and the house on the water. The poem

> is an advance in the purity of my soul because yesterday I fancied that everyone was exactly created in the image of Bertrand Russell, in that they all believe there is hope for the past (which is Satanism). You see, they think the world hasn't already ended, and when they hope that thermonuclear devices wont be used because of some political fix they are placing their hope in the past. I want it to be understood my Hope is strickly Christian, i.e. for the future. (*DA* 87)[10]

What a strange note this is! Bertrand Russell was then famous (as philosophers go) for professing rational atheism, and that is the point of mentioning him here with ironic reference to the idea that we are created in the image of God. It is hard to believe that Dorn's remark about Satanism is altogether earnest, since like the phrase about "the purity of my soul" his language mimics pulpit oratory. Yet the larger point about the futility of hoping for a political fix seems earnest. Our bombs will be used eventually because we use our bombs; that is our history. It is indeed bleak (though hardly unprecedented) to consider diplomacy feckless and thermonuclear war inevitable. And what to make of the note's last sentence, with its reference to an afterlife? Just because many readers do not take seriously the concept of evil or the inevitability of nuclear disaster does not mean that Dorn is not serious.

From this poem recovered from the archives we can read Dorn's work forward, even though he either had forgotten about it or chose not to publish it in his lifetime. It should be put beside "The Garden of the White Rose," apparently his last poem.

> Lord, your mercy is stretched so thin
> to accommodate the need
> of the trembling earth—
> How can I solicit even
> a particle of it
> for the relief of my singularity
> the single White Rose
> across the garden will
> return next year
> identical to your faith—
> the White Rose, whose
> house is light against the
> threatening darkness. (*CP* 912)

No satire here but instead the humility with which he began. Protestantism was part of his work in many early poems; his citation of the hymns that serve as epitaphs on tombstones in "The Air of June Sings" is another important moment in this record. Christianity never really disappeared from his work, although in *Gunslinger* and the epigrams it is not part of the discourse but rather of the implicit ethical foundation of satire. Dorn's irony, even at its most caustic, is supported by a large vision of salvation that is familiar to most Americans, however unlikely such a vision is for an academic sensibility. I don't know if there is another recent American poet whose last poem is a prayer.

This white rose in the last poem, whether it points to a flower in Dorn's Colorado backyard or alludes to the movement of the young German pamphleteers who dared to speak out against Hitler and lost their lives for it, is run up against "singularity" without the punctuation the poem seems to demand. The pronouns are odd, too: it is the Lord's faith, Christ's faith, not the speaker's, in which the poem confides. Mercy will not be casually solicited ("Lord have mercy"), nor will the poet rest assured of its arrival. The return of the rose, as also the survival of dissent in the darkest hours, confirms the Lord's faith in the world: that is the light that opposes darkness.

Dorn identified as Protestant, but he surely knew Dante's white rose in *Paradiso*; Hans Scholl, whose last words before being executed in 1943 were "Long live freedom," and his sister Sophie are thought to have taken the name of their oppositional student movement based at the University of Munich from a poem by the German poet Clemens Brentano or the 1929 novel *Die Weiße Rose* by B. Traven.[11] Dorn visited cathedrals during a year at the University of Montpellier in the 1990s and wrote about Rome and the Cathars in his late unfinished work "Languedoc Variorum," subtitled "A Defense of Heresy and Heretics." His readers can sort out how various traditions of dissent influenced his criticism of institutions and people, but their first task is acknowledging the extent to which his dissent was girded by faith.

Dorn described himself as a theoretical poet who felt an obligation to keep his distance from power, and argued that a poet's responsibilities are to the "Divine," to Spirit, by which he appears to have meant something like the truth.[12] That trumps whatever is owed to civic discourse. Some truths override others. This bears on even the smallest, most topical or occasional of his poems. At the end his prayer is reluctant to impose, deeply earnest. All of his late work but especially "The Garden of the White Rose" and "Tribe," his celebration of his ancestry and community, sits uneasily beside von Hallberg's claim that "[j]udgment and understanding are not, for Dorn, ends in themselves; they are the vehicles of wit, which is his true muse" (86). Admittedly, von Hallberg was writing years before these poems were published. But there is a lot more than wit in Dorn, and where there is wit it is rarely playful. Von Hallberg describes Dorn's late, topical epigrams about mass culture as "a modest form of writing," though he adds that Dorn's subject matter, "the mind and manners of the nation, is major indeed" (86).

While Dorn's poetry has admirers, few have much to say about his epigrams and later work. Alan Golding's essay is an exception to the view that the late work is either best ignored or vulnerable to serious criticism.[13] The early scholarship about Dorn was written in the United States, but recently there has been more and often better work on the poetry coming out of England. Even there, we lack a strong reading of the later poetry.[14] There are younger writers publishing on Dorn in both countries, including Kyle Waugh, Dale Smith, Reitha Pattison, and Justin Katko, and Penguin brought out an American edition of new and selected poems by Dorn, *Way More West*, in 2007. Meanwhile, several dissertations about his work have been written at Cambridge, and *Collected Poems* (2012) and the volume of uncollected poems, *Derelict Air: From Collected Out* (2015), were both published in the United Kingdom. Dorn's fortunes are improving there faster than in the United States. He is still a part of the conversation among young poets in Britain. Cambridge is the home of his friend J. H. Prynne, and for many years Tom Raworth, another friend, lived there, too.

Dorn's correspondent David Southern wrote in an issue of the *Chicago Review* dedicated to Dorn's work that Dorn's career resembles Thomas Carlyle's, though Carlyle had more influence. Both were helped by powerful mentors—Charles Olson in Dorn's case—and soon established "a unique voice that would be received as unusually animated and conspicuous in originality." Both made their mark quickly, and both experienced "a lessening among their early enthusiasts."[15] The poems in Donald Allen's landmark anthology *The New American Poetry* (1960) put Dorn on the map, and across his early books including *The Newly Fallen* (1961), *Hands Up!* (1964), *Geography* (1965), and *The North Atlantic Turbine* (1967) and up through the several volumes of *Gunslinger*, published entire in 1975,[16] Dorn's stock was rising. Wesling's collection of essays, *Internal Resistances*, was published in 1985, by which point Dorn was already publishing his epigrams. Meanwhile, the usual story about Dorn's career, which I hear in conversation, is that a decline began after *Gunslinger*.[17] Southern writes of the "critical scorn" that was increasingly the response to his "astringent opinions," and there was controversy following a series of cruel statements concerning several of his contemporaries; these were published in his and Jennifer Dorn's magazine *Rolling Stock*. The epigrams in *Abhorrences: A Chronicle of the 1980s* (1990) show Dorn at his most intolerant. He found poverty to be a bigger problem than the AIDS crisis and said so. The latter distracted attention, he thought, from more urgent concerns. He made the point in a manner that did nothing for his cause and came off as a macho poet who wanted to blame AIDS on licentiousness in the gay community. It was easy to take him only for a reactionary, and the anger of Kevin Killian and others about the epigrams and about the *Rolling Stock* "awards" is justified.[18] Dorn's attacks were ad hominem and misunderstood both the gravity and the causes of the AIDS crisis.

But there is another issue with late Dorn. Few readers value epigrams and topical poetry, which von Hallberg is typical in viewing as a minor genre. Many view satire itself as a minor mode, the recent praise for the late cartoonists of *Charlie Hebdo* notwithstanding. What von Hallberg says of Dorn is true of much of his work from *Gunslinger* forward—Dorn was "more an ironist than an explainer" (66). But even if we understand the epigram as a minor form, Dorn deserves credit for reimagining its contemporary use. J. V. Cunningham wrote satiric epigrams, but they don't challenge the form or vary the content of the epigrams of Ben Jonson or Robert Herrick. Cunningham's epigrams snap shut in a witty, bitter turn that allows the eloquence of well-managed syntax to override statement. We admire the perfection of form and pessimism and quickly move on, sickened by the thought that we hadn't thought to put the matter so perfectly. Dorn rather bends the epigram out of shape without sacrificing economy, and while taking on an impressive range of subject matter and opinion. His success with the epigram does come down to surprise, as art always does, Ford Madox Ford said, but there is little that is merely clever or only bitter about these poems. Dorn's effort is to think differently, to imagine the unfamiliar logics generated by recent public events. Herrick's epigrams skewered the character flaws of a small circle; Dorn's take up subjects as different as Alaska and Barry Manilow. They were timely, however heterodox. The epigrams are models for poets who seek to address public events with the alacrity of other media. As Dorn says somewhere, they could be bumper stickers. (What would he have done with Twitter?) Quick little poems might seem appropriate to a culture with the attention span of a goldfish, but Dorn's epigrams turn over issues as no journalist or Twitter junkie does. They require thought and reflection. They can be subtle (they are not always so). Not that he had anything against journalists, I should add. "I admire journalism," he told Stephen Fredman, while adding that "[p]oetry seeks to incandesce for a longer period."[19] But few poets have been as eager to take up the role of commentator.

Dorn's epigrams would be less worthy of our attention without the success of *Gunslinger*, which offered him a larger audience and the authority that comes with completing a big poem celebrated for originality and spirit. He never had the audience of Allen Ginsberg, but *Gunslinger* reached more readers than his earlier books, and the epigrams should have, too. They are virtually called for in Book II of *Gunslinger*, where a "Literate Projector" is introduced, "a revolutionary medium / . . . sure to turn everything around" (*CP* 463). Film an event (the question asked, troping on Shakespeare's, is whether the whole world is cinema) and play it back through the Literate Projector and one discovers its text, the logics that shape it. Add acerbic commentary and one has the epigrams. Even fewer would have bothered with them if they didn't know about *Gunslinger*'s struggle with global capitalism and its stylized, hip verse. Dorn adds characters throughout the books of his long poem before his band disbands for eternity, closing with reference to a famous Frank Zappa song about moving to Montana and a series of good wishes, the last of these in Spanish and offering hope for a better life. Nobody else has written a poem that makes it so obvious that the cosmic and the comic are separated only by a letter, with characters as familiar as those in black-and-white Westerns who utter words stranger than Heidegger's, a poem capable of mixing the most vulgar puns with lyric passages out of Shelley: "I see cars drawn by rainbow-wingèd steeds / Which trample the dim winds: in each there stands / A wild eyed charioteer urging their flight / On a long take-off roll, this is the purging of the beads" (*CP* 478). Beads are balls, the poem's "SLLAB" backward. These lines, the first three of them from Shelley's *Prometheus Unbound*, adorn the opening quatrain of "The Cycle," a visionary poem uttered by the Slinger (one of many poems within this poem) telling of the journey of the quasi-mythical Howard Hughes disguised as the cheese in the burger. As an ecstatic, stoned, hilarious though angry account of the culture, and for the energy of its collisions of idioms and of lyric and narrative, *Gunslinger* was and still is unmatched in American poetry.

Dorn merits our continuing attention for the range of his work, and for his ambitious hopes for poetry and poetic vocation, the latter best represented by the instrument the poet in *Gunslinger* plays, the abso-lute, which points to the allegiance of the poet to "truth." He published memorable short poems that should be good anthology pieces in the future, including "The Air of June Sings," "On the Debt My Mother Owed to Sears Roebuck," "In My Youth I Was a Tireless Dancer," "If It Should Ever Come," "A Fate of Unannounced Years," "Thesis," "Ode on the Facelifting of the 'Statue' of Liberty," "Sketches from Edgewater," and "Tribe," to name my favorites. Many of these feature a signature "density of syntax and clustering of sound values," and a "wrenched, singing line," to quote Wesling (18). But technique cannot be distinguished from rhetoric in Dorn's poetry. These poems speak of the dispossessed, of Native Americans and also his own people of "a far midwest recrudescence of Appalachia" (*CP* 893), of Serbians, Iraqis, and others demonized by world governments, by the United States. We have had too few poets who have spoken so passionately of the poor and fewer who have understood as well as Dorn did the international movement of capital.

Dorn's work is most important for its effort to renew poetry with conspicuous vernacular idioms and forms, as borrowed from ballads but also from spaghetti Westerns, country and western songs, the video scrolls of CNN, and the ticker tape of Wall Street, as also the sports broadcast I mentioned earlier. There is eclectic reading behind Dorn's work, in science, philosophy, and political theory, but by contrast with Pound and Olson he wears his reading lightly. One often hears him locating the sharpest analysis in commonplaces. These are the vernacular, too. The English critic Ian Brinton writes at his *Tears in the Fence* online magazine of the "wonderful merging of the colloquial with the analytic" and "the anger and directness of statement" that characterizes the writing of Dorn and Prynne.[20] This makes most sense as a description of Dorn's earlier work, which Brinton is reviewing, but science, theory, and Westerns also merged in *Gunslinger* just when the "great divide" between mass and elite culture that Andreas Huyssen has described seemed about to disappear in the United States, Britain, and Europe.[21] It was especially the youth who followed Bob Dylan from folk to rock for whom the divide seemed about to disappear. While Dorn's writing followed a trajectory similar to that of Dylan's music, it is important to add that he never flattered the young as Lowell, Levertov, and Rich did.[22] The hope among many was that dichotomies such as that between the intellectuals and the streets (between analysis and colloquialism) could be overcome by art. On this count, Dorn's work bears comparison with the poems of Charles Bernstein, whose engagement with popular culture includes borrowing from popular genres, even such commercial genres as ads and consumer surveys. The pratfalls and puns of Bernstein's poetry, its Situationist *détournement*, have been read as a critical engagement with language. But if Bernstein wants poetry to unsettle and transform language, he has less confidence than Dorn does in the adequacy of the vernacular. Denise Riley also incorporates lines from pop songs in order to indicate their power to define us. But Dorn neither ironizes nor lionizes the vernacular. For him, it is all resource.

As I try to identify what is admirable about the best of Dorn's poetry, I should mention the obvious: at its best it is funny. That cannot be said about recent poetry, Bernstein notwithstanding. Laughter is liberating, or it can be:

"Entrapment is this society's / Sole activity, I whispered / and Only laughter, can blow it to rags / *But* there is no negative pure enough / to entrap our Expectations" (*CP* 543). These are Dorn's most famous lines. Laughter helps us escape that which would contain us. But the third clause requires analysis. At its best, satire is not only about indignation and subversion but also about fellow feeling and sympathy, or the expectation of change. At its best, it is hopeful. Dorn did not always remember that, to be sure. It is worth noting that his second clause—about laughter blowing "it" to rags—is borrowed from Mark Twain's least hopeful book, *The Mysterious Stranger*, a story about the earthly exploits of an angel boy named Satan. Twain, like Wyndham Lewis, W. B. Yeats, and John Clare, is rarely mentioned when scholars cite Dorn's numerous influences. It makes sense to think of Dorn as the Mark Twain of American poetry—although he was never so bitter as Twain is in *The Mysterious Stranger*.

Back to the streets. In 1977, two years after Wingbow Press published *Gunslinger*, Dorn talks about the "quicker, harder, more inexorable precision of the vernacular, which at the same time seems very, very loose and offhand. That's where its power comes from, because there are no themes, really. There's no story . . . In fact, if it has a salvation, that's it."[23] He is referring to a passage in *Gunslinger* that derives from John Randolph Lucas on space-time:

> Time is more fundamental than space.
> It is, indeed, the most pervasive
> of all the categories
> in other words
> theres plenty of it.
> And it stretches things themselves
> until they blend into one,
> so if youve seen one thing
> youve seen them all. (*CP* 393)

Dorn is serious about the torpor of duration and asks us to read his concluding commonplace anew—not as a joke, not ironically, but for its wisdom, which has to do with the relationship of the particular thing to its category. But the vernacular is so much more forceful, so much more precise than such an abstraction. History and experience pour out of it inside this poetic frame as they would not if I used the phrase in conversation. The passage leads into another that is also vulgar: "I held the reins of his horse / while he went into the desert / to pee. *Yes*, he reflected / when he returned, that's less" (*CP* 393). Lowbrow humor of the body as it meets science and philosophy also belongs in the poem. A discourse concerning genetics and mutation given to (carried by) a talking horse is a metaphor for the possibilities of cultural change and revolution. Opposition to global capitalism and the value of purportedly consciousness-raising activities like drug use and the modes of thought that reflect embodied being are figured in the poem among layers of Kleenex that encase the feet of the arch-capitalist Howard Hughes. *Gunslinger* tracks the counterculture of the late 1960s and early 1970s in real time up to and including its failures. If its first book is its best for many readers, that has a lot to do with its date of publication, 1968. As the Vietnam War and the struggle against the war carried on, the poem's stylized, high-spirited writing had to take on new complexities and disappointments. It turns out that the "shit" really is "TOTAL" (*CP* 513) and the "sublime" really is "sold out" (*CP* 511).[24]

In a lecture at the Naropa Institute, Dorn talks of his discovery that Olson's "too turgid and complicated" verse line was of no use to him in writing *Gunslinger*, which instead has lines that vary from "not quite short to very little beyond medium" and also "a hard, distant rhyme, which happens a lot."[25] Olson's free-ranging, prosaic line was never altogether forgotten, but Dorn's interest in song was more persistent than his attraction to discursive prose, more persistent even than his ironist's taste for kitsch. There are two strains in Dorn's work, one discursive and the other song-like. When they are working together, Dorn is at his best. *Gunslinger* is big enough to contain both strains. The books in a more purely discursive mode, *Geography* and *The North Atlantic Turbine*, count as efforts to modify Olson's discursive style, but they are lesser books.

In *Gunslinger* and occasionally thereafter, Dorn makes more of rhyme and sound play than he did even in early poems such as "The Rick of Green Wood" and "Vaquero," or in the circling sentences and thick repetitions of "On the Debt My Mother Owed to Sears Roebuck." Von Hallberg admires the concluding strophe of this poem about debt, which acknowledges not only its ravages (likened to locusts eating the crops) but also its benefits: the poet got to school and the American war was won. He finds Dorn's metaphors too familiar but admires the poem's ability in its last strophe to recognize the lived contradictions of capitalism. His criteria are novelty of figurative language and self-reflexivity, though as a figure in the poem the locusts are more complex than he suggests; they are crunched under the poet's boots, like the mechanical heart mentioned earlier in the poem. The poem works like that, circling back to develop its thought, as if amid passionate speech. Apophasis and occupatio are terms for the insistence that a speaker has nothing to say about something he has been talking about. Dorn's accomplishment is in making such rhetoric seem conversational even as it is highly worked and structured, as if writing a poem were as easy as a lazy man trying to avoid the work of pumping the family well for the horses.

No generalization about American speech patterns will hold across the nation and its history, but like a lot of Dorn's best writing, "On the Debt My Mother Owed to Sears Roebuck" is true to what Dorn describes to Fredman as an American "articulation . . . quite different from other people's; we arrive at understanding and meaning through massive assaults on the language, so no particular word is apt to be final."[26] It is Robert Creeley's stuttering rhythms and common diction that the poem most suggests, though its lines are longer than Creeley's, and anxiousness is not Dorn's tone. Taciturnity might have attracted him, in its Western mode, and enigma. The temptation was always to be smarter than the next guy, faster.

It would be wrong to suggest that his poem accurately represents working-class speech. But its gestures toward commonness assert a social allegiance, even if that is momentary, and both the early and (to a lesser extent) the very late work has the speech of Dorn's first and closest communities in sight. The poems are literary artifacts, sure. He makes a related point about the very different language and style of *Gunslinger* when Robert Bertholf asks if its rapid, jokey banter reflects his own cadence: "Well, in a poem of that kind it's highly artificial. I don't think that's my speech cadence. It was meant to strike a kind of artifice of speech and maintain it, except when it was supposed to 'be' natural."[27] The point was never to imitate a speech that is really used but rather to expand what counts as expressive in poetry. There is no effort to restrict or purify diction, as Dorn's English friend Donald Davie once asked poets to do; Dorn went in the opposite direction. If the earlier poems gestured to the conversation of a community that Dorn knew well, *Gunslinger* refers to no community except the hip and initiated, who know that in the right context anything goes, including the most archaic poeticisms and words such as "garmlees" (*CP* 478).²⁸ Without calling attention to his borrowing with quotation marks or otherwise, Book III and Book IIII include everything from a phrase taken from country-pop singer Roger Miller's "England Swings" to a line from Kipling's *The Winners*.²⁹ *Gunslinger*'s vernacular reaches out to a coming community wherein distinctions between poetic and common diction do not promise or signify a specific identity.

There are several varieties of pop in *Gunslinger*. Dorn's readers knew about pop art and about writers like Thomas Pynchon who drop song lyrics into their narratives. *Gunslinger*'s Book I features among its Homeric cast a drifter singer, and the boldfaced notation of "**strumming**" suggests a movie soundtrack beyond the attention of the poem's characters, who are capable of responding to their narrator. (They don't answer the soundtrack, which is the background that makes everything possible.) Rock 'n' roll (to use a quaint term) dominates, but there is also the song the Gunslinger sings echoing *Alice in Wonderland*, with its hints of limerick:

> Oh a girl there was in the street
> The day we rode into La Cruz
> And the name of the name of her feet
> Was the same as the name of the street
> And she stood and she stared like a moose
> And her hair was tangled and loose (*CP* 402)

But for the most part, "This roll's as hard as a rock" (*CP* 536), as Dorn has his Howard Hughes character Robart say late in the poem. Dorn wanted to affiliate his poem with the conspicuous triumph of the most popular music of the moment. Amiri Baraka's celebration of John Coltrane and Miles Davis expresses another affiliation.

Dorn would insist on the low even more in later poems such as "Montana and Montaner":

> Big winds, big clouds
> Big grass, big rain
> Big road, big load
> Big railroad—big caboose

Elk jerky, deer jerky
Jerky de moose (*CP* 871)

This is country and western, though tighter in its turns. *Gunslinger* begins with an echo of "Streets of Laredo" and within a few pages comes to the ballad refrain of "Lord Randall," as if to remember the older modes of poems such as "The Hide of My Mother." Or perhaps he took the refrain from Dylan's "A Hard Rain's a-Gonna Fall," although Dylan probably also got it from "Lord Randall":

But when you have found him my Gunslinger
What will you do, oh what will you do? (*CP* 394)

So much for modernist difficulty! Even *Gunslinger*'s most difficult section, "The Cycle," is thick with rhyme.[30] Dorn's borrowings do not suggest nostalgia; they indicate the breadth of the poetic culture.

When Dorn says that *Gunslinger* means to "vernacularize," he refers especially to his engagement with the language of philosophy and cultural theory, from Heidegger to Schumpeter. He sets Schumpeter's theory of capitalism's "creative destruction" among the poker chips and whiskey of Hollywood Westerns: "Lo que pasa he breathed / this place is / in the constructive process / of ruin" (*CP* 404). Some critics read *Gunslinger* as mock epic, a cartoon Western critical of the genre's imperialist ideology, but Hollywood Westerns at their best are critical of the myth of the West, as Robert Pippin has shown.[31] Of course, the poet *likes* Westerns. He wants to "vernacularize" not only philosophy but also its vehicle of expression. *The Cycle* was first published as an oversize comic book, *Bean News* as a newspaper. After decades of high modernist esteem for literary tradition and the wonders of the archaeological West, a little engagement with pop culture was refreshing. This is not to say that *Gunslinger* does not reach for other registers, as for example in the "Prolegomenon" to Book IIII or the opening lines of Book II: "This tapestry moves / as the morning lights up. / And they who are in it move / and love its moving" (*CP* 433). Few poets move so swiftly between registers.

The risks attending the evaluation of poetry—the possibility of appearing only self-interested—are one reason this critical function has been eclipsed by interpretation. Dorn is ironic about the need for the evaluation of poetry in "Whereas" from *Yellow Lola* (1978):

> Poetry is now mostly governmental product
> the work of our non-existent critics
> is unnecessary, the grades assigned
> to meat will do nicely:
>
> > Prime
> > choice
> > food
> > commercial
> > utility
> > canners[32]

This must have been written in one of the fatter years of NEA money supporting poetry publishing. The study of poetry in public universities is likely also on Dorn's mind, as it is on Tom Raworth's in his "University Days." Subsidies promote orthodoxies of both sentiment and style. Dorn preferred to publish with independent presses. That seems a small matter but it is not. Poets should "stay as removed as possible from all permanent associations with power," he said to Fredman, adding that "among our people the taste for poetry is rather an amusement of the fancy than a passion of the soul."[33] Most of that second sentence is borrowed from Edward Gibbon, who is describing a "barbarian" Germanic culture; Dorn was not friendly to literary cultures that declined judgment and attention to distinctions. "Not to Mention Names," an outtake from *Abhorrences* uncovered in *Derelict Air*, skewers M. L. Rosenthal and Sally Gall for their inclusiveness: "American poetry is a little like / Poland in that respect: just get in line anyway" (*DA* 417). This was written before the Wall came down, but with forty thousand poets the lines are even longer than they were.

John Ruskin thought that it was "the imperative duty of all who have any perception or knowledge of what is really great in art, and any desire for its advancement in England, to come fearlessly forward" to offer "knowledge of what is good and right" based upon "the authority of the Beautiful and the True."[34] You don't have to believe that poetry and art advance or imagine that a critic can do much about what Ruskin describes as the "degradation" of public taste to admire the ambition of a statement like this, and yet, as Lawrence Rainey writes in his essay about the publication of *The Waste Land*, "the question of aesthetic value is inseparable from commercial success in a market economy."[35] We are salmon swimming upstream when we hold out for standards of taste. This is the kind of basic truth that Dorn was given to insisting on sarcastically, as a poet who knew little commercial success: "Chicken Relativity / Two thighs are better / than one / where one is better than none // majority remains / the clearest / standard of value" (*DA* 384). He had a gift for aphorisms like this, and for rough severity.

Dorn wrote little criticism, and the idea of a major as opposed to a minor poet does not figure importantly in his work, although to be true to his many contradictions I should note that he seems to have thought of Pound as the greatest poet of his century.[36] But he also valued writers who now and then got something right. He described Matthew Arnold's "Dover Beach" as "the greatest single poem ever written in the English language . . . by a guy who wrote volume after volume of lousy, awful poetry." The ability of a man with a "rather pedestrian mind, but a very serious past" to write a poem like "Dover Beach" was "an extremely hopeful thing in the world," he said.[37] Vigilance might help a writer stay alert, but success is not predictable. The modernist idea that a poet should operate on the language has not often been thought to mean that a poet should take up commentary on topical concerns, but perhaps it should. The Austrian writer Karl Kraus is famous for exactly that. Dorn told Fredman in 1977 that he thought it was "important for poets to be as varied as possible, since the instrumentation is the language."[38] In 1999, he told Peter Michelson much the same thing: "There's just no way to use poetry unless it's constantly searching within itself for a new way to be read. . . . I can't understand how people who write poetry aren't constantly or incessantly searching for new manners of approach to the poem, because that's about all we can do now."[39] Dorn never sat still in a form, never softened his solidarity with the poor, and never lost faith in the vernacular. This is why I keep returning to his writing.

Notes

1. See Silliman's blog entry for March 23, 2015, at http://ronsilliman.blogspot.com. Craig Dworkin remarks on the critical difficulties created by the acceleration of poetry publication in his introduction to his edited volume, *The Consequence of Innovation: 21st Century Poetics* (New York: Roof Books, 2008).
2. Robert von Hallberg, "'This Marvellous Accidentalism,'" in *Internal Resistances: The Poetry of Edward Dorn*, ed. Donald Wesling (Berkeley: University of California Press, 1985), 45–86. Further citations are included parenthetically. Von Hallberg's essay is also included in his book *American Poetry and Culture, 1945–1980* (Cambridge, MA: Harvard University Press, 1985).
3. Donald Wesling, "'To Fire We Give Everything': Dorn's Shorter Poems," in *Internal Resistances*, 18, 41, 26. Further citations are included parenthetically.
4. Edward Dorn, *Collected Poems*, ed. Jennifer Dunbar Dorn with Justin Katko, Reitha Pattison, and Kyle Waugh (Manchester: Carcanet Press, 2012), 217. Further citations are included parenthetically as *CP*.
5. See Barry Alpert's 1972 interview with Dorn in Edward Dorn, *Interviews*, ed. Donald Allen (Bolinas, CA: Four Seasons, 1980), 24. In a 1981 interview, Dorn again describes his dissatisfaction with "Oxford." Interviewer Gavin Selerie tells him that the English needed to hear its criticism of English culture and writing, but Dorn says, "[T]here was a kind of chauvinistic Americanism lodged in it that I have since repudiated almost entirely." Edward Dorn, *Two Interviews*, ed. Gavin Selerie and Justin Katko (Bristol: Shearsman Books, 2012), 79.
6. Michael Davidson, "'To eliminate the draw': Narrative and Language in *Slinger*," in *Internal Resistances*, 133, 149. Sam Ladkin discusses the sources and language of "The Cycle" in his essay "'as they wander estranged': Ed Dorn's *Gunslinger*," *Edinburgh Review* 114 (2004): 59–98.
7. T. S. Eliot, "What Is Minor Poetry?" (1944), in *On Poetry and Poets* (London: Faber and Faber, 1957), 39–52.
8. Skip Fox, review of *Edward Dorn: A World of Difference*, by Tom Clark, *Jacket* 23 (August 2003), http://jacketmagazine.com/23/fox-clark-dorn.html.
9. Edward Dorn, *Derelict Air: From Collected Out*, ed. Justin Katko and Kyle Waugh (London: Enitharmon Press, 2015), 85. Further citations are included parenthetically as *DA*.
10. Katko and Waugh indicate in *Derelict Air* that the poem belongs to an unpublished manuscript titled "Poems of Washington, Idaho, & Mexico" (1959). "Strickly" and "wont" are Dorn's spellings.
11. See https://en.wikipedia.org/wiki/White_Rose. The version of the poem in the *Collected Poems* adds capital letters to White Rose, which suggests an allusion to the German student group.
12. In "Road-Testing the Language," his interview with Stephen Fredman, Dorn likened the poet's role to "divining," mentioning Stephen Hawking's "divining" of the "formula for black holes." Neither self-expression, which von Hallberg

rightly notes that Dorn had no interest in, nor civic discourse describe poetry's function for him. Dorn sought "not so much [to] write poetry as to compose the poetry that's constantly written on air," viewing the poet as the antennae of the race, to borrow a phrase from Pound. The language of "divining" suggests the poet as soothsayer or "vates." Dorn, *Interviews*, 66.

13. Alan Golding, "Edward Dorn's 'Pontificatory use of the art': *Hello, La Jolla* and *Yellow Lola*," in *Internal Resistances*, 208–34.
14. I tried to make my case for a few of the later poems, particularly "Sketches from Edgewater," in an earlier essay: "Late Dorn," *Chicago Review* 49, nos. 3–4 (Summer 2004): 237–51.
15. David Southern, "Forensics in the Provinces: Collecting the Correspondence of Edward Dorn," *Chicago Review* 49, nos. 3–4 (Summer 2004): 92–93.
16. I should recognize here the publication of *Gunslinger* "satellites" in *Derelict Air*, and also note that scholars think that *Bean News*, a satirical newspaper with contributions by Dorn, Prynne, Raworth, Tom Clark, and others, belongs to *Gunslinger*, in which case we still lack a complete edition of the poem.
17. Ron Silliman and August Kleinzahler are two writers who have articulated a view of Dorn's decline. A strong contrary response published on the web by Brian Richards on May 15, 2007, is archived here: www.writing.upenn.edu/epc/mirrors/tomraworth.com/bric.html.
18. Killian writes in a letter to the editors of *Apex of the M* about the "AIDS Award" that *Rolling Stock* assigned to the poet Steve Abbott. His letter was widely circulated but not published until December 2014, when it appeared in the samizdat British journal *Materials* 4. Eliot Weinberger also criticized the *Rolling Stock* awards in "A Case of AIDS Hysteria," published in *Sulfur* 9 in 1984. Among Dorn's most intolerant poems concerning the AIDS crisis is "Aid(e) Memoire" in *Abhorrences*, in which the crisis is blamed on licentiousness. There are a variety of equally intolerant and ignorant references to AIDS in the previously unpublished poems gathered in *Derelict Air*.
19. "Road-Testing the Language," in Dorn, *Interviews*, 64–106.
20. Ian Brinton, *Tears in the Fence*, July 2, 2015, http://tearsinthefence.com/blog/page/2/.
21. Andreas Huyssen, *After the Great Divide: Modernism, Mass Culture, Postmodernism* (Bloomington: Indiana University Press, 1986).
22. Nor did Dorn follow Dylan into Christian evangelism. *Derelict Air* includes his parody of Dylan's "Gotta Serve Somebody" as "Gotta Hurt Somebody."
23. Edward Dorn, "On the Authority of Root Meanings, the External, and the Making of *Gunslinger*, circa 1967" (1977), in *Ed Dorn Live: Lectures, Interviews, and Outtakes*, ed. Joseph Richey (Ann Arbor: University of Michigan Press, 2007), 16.
24. James K. Elmborg writes that *Gunslinger*'s Book IIII "has long frustrated those who expected the narrative to culminate with a confrontation between

Robart [Hughes] and the Slinger. No such confrontation occurs, and the poem lacks the dramatic climax such a showdown might provide. Some critics and interviewers have considered the final book anti-climactic because it eschews the 'high-noon' effect; Robart rides away toward 'Siberia' as the Slinger dozes beneath his hat-rim. . . . While the poem sets up expectations of a confrontation between two opposing forces, a more important action has been the development of an alternative consciousness, one that will serve to resist the seduction of power." For Elmborg's "consciousness," one can also read modes of linguistic and poetic action. See James K. Elmborg, *"A Pageant of Its Time": Edward Dorn's "Slinger" and the Sixties* (New York: Peter Lang, 1998), 105.

25. "On the Authority of Root Meanings, the External, and the Making of *Gunslinger*, circa 1967," in Richey, *Ed Dorn Live*, 17.
26. "Road-Testing the Language," in Dorn, *Interviews*, 100.
27. See the conversation with Robert Bertholf titled "The Poetic Line" in Dorn, *Interviews*, 61. Dorn mentions "women's speech," thinking of *Gunslinger*'s Miss Lil character. He says: "I have some trouble, because I don't know any one woman's speech I came actually to record in that sense. It becomes composite. It's a little bit of my mother, you know, vernacular quips, and other women I have known. It would be a hybrid of that determination." Later in the interview Dorn says, "[T]his poem seeks to reproduce as faithfully as possible the condition of a group of men hanging around" (71).
28. Scholars have glossed "garmlees," which the poet "releases" as he begins "The Cycle," as referring to the demons of Norwegian myth, but Justin Katko believes the word to be Dorn's neologism: "My take is that the word is basically Dorn's own invention, a neologism built on 'Garm,' the wolf-dog of Norse myth who was chained up by the gods of Asgard. His howl signifies the beginning of Ragnarök (Götterdämmerung), fall of the Norse gods." Justin Katko, e-mail to the author, September 28, 2015.
29. See Stephen Fredman and Grant Jenkins, "First Annotations to Edward Dorn's *Gunslinger*," *Sagetrieb* 15, no. 3 (Winter 1996): 57–176.
30. The best reading of *Gunslinger*'s sources in "The Cycle" is in Ladkin, "'as they wander estranged.'"
31. Robert B. Pippin, *Hollywood Westerns and American Myth: The Importance of Howard Hawks and John Ford for Political Philosophy* (New Haven, CT: Yale University Press, 2010).
32. Edward Dorn, *Way More West: New and Selected Poems*, ed. Michael Rothenberg (New York: Penguin, 2007), 198.
33. "Road-Testing The Language," in Dorn, *Interviews*, 65.
34. John Ruskin, "Preface to the First Edition," *Modern Painters* (1843–1860; New York: John Wiley and Sons, 1879), x–xi.
35. Lawrence Rainey, "The Price of Modernism: Publishing *The Waste Land*," in

The Waste Land, by T. S. Eliot, ed. Michael North (New York: W. W. Norton, 1999), 99.
36. See "Dismissal" for Dorn on Pound: "The Greatest Poet of this expendable century / was also its greatest, must public heretic" (*CP* 848).
37. "Poetry Is a Difficult Labor," in Richey, *Ed Dorn Live*, 132.
38. "Road-Testing the Language," in Dorn, *Interviews*, 66.
39. "Waying the West: The Cooperman Interviews," in Richey, *Ed Dorn Live*, 110.

NATION

CHAPTER 11

Strange American Heart

August Kleinzahler

PATRICK MORRISSEY

AUGUST KLEINZAHLER'S POEMS began appearing in the late 1970s and early 1980s in little magazines such as *Origin* and *Sulfur*. Today they appear regularly in the *London Review of Books*, and his collections receive reviews in the *New York Times*. Such success in the literary marketplace is unusual for a contemporary poet, especially one whose career began in magazines associated with the New American Poetry. Remarkably, Kleinzahler's style has been more or less intact since the beginning, so it seems his success is not a matter of "selling out" but of gradually reaching a wider audience. The poet owns up to influences both "high" modernist (Basil Bunting, Ezra Pound) and countercultural (the New York School, the Beats, Thom Gunn), yet he has crafted an idiom that communicates to many readers. He speaks one moment of Bartók, the next of gas stations and liquor stores. Critics often focus narrowly on the hard luck and tough talk in some of his poems (rarely have the adjectives "pugilistic" and "pugnacious" been so frequently applied to a poet), but toughness is neither the most important nor the most interesting thing about him. More important is that hard luck is only one of many subjects in his poems, tough talk only one of their many verbal textures. He writes about all sorts of people and places, and within a single poem he typically ranges in diction and register. His poetry embraces both high culture and the culture of people living on the margins, and it does so as a matter of course. Kleinzahler is unabashedly erudite, yet he writes about poor people and poor places—the "other half" of American life—without condescension or romanticism. He does not make an explicit project of his regard for run-down districts, homeless people, and addicts—he simply includes them with everything else his attention encompasses. They are all parts of the same world. Furthermore, Kleinzahler writes in a lucid style that makes the work available to readers who live outside the institutions of poetry and higher education. The source of the work's wide appeal (at least for poetry) is also its enduring value: it represents the variety and strangeness of life in late twentieth- and early twenty-first-century America with singular veracity and capaciousness, and it does so in a poetic idiom that is both egalitarian and aesthetically sophisticated.

If inclusiveness is one distinctive value of Kleinzahler's poetry, another is its craft. He writes with a precision rare among contemporary poets—precision of observation and image, precision of diction and syntax, precision of line and stanza. His technical finesse and formal ingenuity are notable not only because they give great pleasure but also because they underwrite the generosity of his attention and reference. What allows him to be capacious without becoming incoherent, unintelligible, or boring is his flexible yet controlled management of diction, syntax, and line. The critic Kenneth Cox, writing about Kleinzahler's first book, *A Calendar of Airs*, sized the poet up presciently in 1980: "The poems combine broad sweep with deft tactics. . . . The writing has one general and unfailing characteristic: whatever features it may show at any moment (syntax smooth or angular, diction simple or far-fetched, handling close or loose) they command at the moment assent. Unimprovability of the execution: that is what marks the artist."[1]

Kleinzahler's great variety makes it difficult to draw up a comprehensive survey of his poetry, so here I will focus on one sort of poem—a place-based or loco-descriptive poem, often about New Jersey or San Francisco—as a way to enter his work. There are other sorts to choose from: Kleinzahler has written dramatic monologues, character sketches, historical panoramas, dream narratives, faux-classical epistles, elegiac songs, and verse essays on music history, to name a few. But the loco-descriptive is perhaps the one to which he returns most frequently, and the one in which he has written some of his finest poems. His poems of place also help us locate him in the history of poetry in the United States. When he writes about the places he knows and the people who inhabit them, he makes his inheritance of Walt Whitman and especially William Carlos Williams richly evident. In his combination of adventurousness and availability, the poet he most resembles is Williams, his fellow New Jerseyan. Both are poets of compact technical dexterity and of American speech—capable both of rapid, surprising swerves and of talking plainly to cats and dogs. And like Whitman and Williams, Kleinzahler is a democratic realist with a lyric gift, one who believes that ordinary people and things are suitable subjects for poetry. Yet where Whitman and Williams prized immediacy and planted their feet firmly on home terrain, Kleinzahler is a poet of both proximity and distance, writing from an airplane as often as from home. An American in the age of globalization, he writes in and of transit. His poetry is marked by a sense of doubleness—here and there, self and others, now and then—and a sense of how one place, person, or time might become or be haunted by another.

The poem "Snow in North Jersey," which first appeared in Kleinzahler's 1999 collection *Green Sees Things in Waves*, is a formal homage to Whitman, a rangy litany of ordinary people and locations—everyone and everyplace the snow falls upon—joined by anaphora and the accretion of simple conjunctions. Its homage to Williams is even more explicit: "and they're calling for snow tonight and through tomorrow / an inch an hour over 9 Ridge Road and the old courthouse / and along the sluggish, gray Passaic / as it empties itself into Newark Bay."[2] Kleinzahler names the doctor's address and quickly sketches the itinerary of his *Paterson*, the long poem that followed the Passaic River over the Falls and out to sea. But while Williams's approach to North Jersey is archaeological, excavating what he called "the elemental character of the place," Kleinzahler's is cinematic, panning with the weather across the region.[3] The poem provides something like an extended aerial shot that zooms fluidly in and out. Consider its opening lines:

> Snow is falling along the Boulevard
> and its little cemeteries hugged by transmission shops
> and on the stone bear in the park
> and the WWI monument, making a crust
> on the soldier with his chin strap and bayonet (137)

Kleinzahler begins with a cartographer's distance, yet a brief survey of the landscape quickly establishes a sense of temporal depth. The dead and the auto mechanics who survive them are intimate with one another, lovingly occupying the same turf. Then the time scale broadens to include world-historical events: in the finely rendered face of the WWI statue, a familiar representation of local boys who died abroad, North Jersey's past is integrated into the global twentieth century. Kleinzahler continues by shifting scales again:

> It's blowing in from the west
> over the low hills and meadowlands
> swirling past the giant cracking stills
> that flare all night along the Turnpike
> It is with a terrible deliberateness
> that Mr. Ruiz reaches into his back pocket
> and counts out $18 and change for his lotto picks
> while in the upstairs of a thousand duplexes
> with the TV on, cancers tick   tick   tick
> and the snow continues to fall and blanket
> these crowded rows of frame and brick
> with their heartbreaking porches and castellations
> and the red '68 Impala on blocks
> and Joe he's drinking again and Myra's boy Tommy
> in the old days it would have been a disgrace (137)

In the space of a few lines, the poem sweeps back out to encompass a natural terrain overlaid by highways and oil refineries, then zooms into Mr. Ruiz's pocket and the pathos of his careful count of bills and coins, a tiny hard-luck narrative. From there the poem expands and contracts at once, giving us the deadening endlessness of "a thousand duplexes" and the particularity of a single upstairs room lit blue by the TV. And then the most dramatic zoom yet, down to the cellular level, as Kleinzahler unsettlingly imagines cancer proliferating in thousands of bodies, the result perhaps of overexposure to petrochemicals, while they watch sitcoms or the evening news. Out on the wintry street again, Kleinzahler plays "castellations" off of "the red '68 Impala," achieving a sort of tragicomedy in the juxtaposition of a multisyllabic archaism with the name of a best-selling Chevy sedan, a jalopy decaying in front of run-down duplexes adorned (or defended) by castle-like parapets. The shift of verbal registers and the sharp observation of socioeconomic class markers are both signature Kleinzahler. "And Joe he's drinking again and Myra's boy Tommy / in the old days it would have been a disgrace": in these lines Kleinzahler ventriloquizes local speech, the language of rumor and resignation, integrated seamlessly into the poem's movement but also marked as impersonation by its difference from words like "castellations" or the playful literary formality of a clause like "It is with terrible deliberateness."

Whitman sought a new poetry appropriate to what he believed was the infinite breadth of American democracy, and Williams wanted to find poetic form for the American idiom and the humble particulars of everyday life. Both held utopian hopes for their poems, believing that poetic innovation could bring readers into closer contact with the "reality" of their lives. Kleinzahler seeks a similarly capacious, realistic rendering of contemporary American life, but he is more doubtful about its transformative potential. "Snow in North Jersey" ends with this image:

> It's snowing on us all
> and on a three-story *fix-up* off of Van Vorst Park
> a young lawyer couple from Manhattan bought
> where for no special reason in back of a closet
> a thick, dusty volume from the '30s sits open
> with a broken spine and smelling of mildew
> to a chapter called Social Realism (138)

After an earnest note of Whitmanian solidarity—"It's snowing on us all"—the poem takes an almost satirical turn. At first the joke seems to be about yuppies moving into the neighborhood, but then it turns on the poem itself. This faithful recording of an evening in North Jersey—its cemeteries, oil refineries, convenience-store gamblers, junked cars, tumors, and dead poets—might end up as an example of an outdated art form in an old book. Its realism might become just another mildewed object of study or curiosity for the young college types who gentrify working-class streets. Yet the poet persists in his witnessing, and he does so without condescension, sentimentality, or pulled punches. The reality he depicts includes the possibility that bearing witness to what's passing finally won't matter much, but he writes it anyway, out of something like love for the world.

Kleinzahler's lyric "Poetics," first published in the 1985 collection *Storm over Hackensack*, is another poem of his native North Jersey, though here he works in a more compact, imagistic mode common to his early poems:

> I have loved the air outside Shop-Rite Liquor
> on summer evenings
> better than the Marin Hills at dusk
> lavender and gold
> stretching miles to the sea.
>
> At the junction, up from the synagogue
> a weeknight, necessarily
> and with my father—
> a sale on German beer.
>
> Air full of living dust:
> bus exhaust, airborne grains of pizza crust
> wounded crystals
> appearing, disappearing
> among streetlights and unsuccessful neon. (88)

A few well-chosen words specify the landscape and let it expand in our imaginations. "Shop-Rite Liquor" names a package store of certain vintage, concerned not with refinement but with cost effectiveness, its parking lot or curb lit by a familiar sort of sign. There are at least two senses in which its neon might be "unsuccessful": business is slow at Shop-Rite, and the sign itself might be on the blink. We can begin to construct a local economy. "At the junction, up from the synagogue"—these prepositional phrases casually locate us by landmark, like directions from someone who knows the area. "Synagogue" offhandedly signals a certain religious and ethnic milieu, one that's relatively comfortable here in Jersey. The temple's proximity to the package store and the faint verbal echo of "Shop-Rite Liquor" in "synagogue" give us a wink: there's as much family ritual in a beer run as there is in worship.

"Poetics" doubles this primary landscape with another more distant one—"the Marin Hills at dusk"—to which, perhaps surprisingly, New Jersey compares favorably. Kleinzahler plays this surprise for humor, but the development of the first stanza's transcontinental comparison also allows him simultaneously to expand the poem's scale and to make its primary location seem all the more particular. The description of "lavender and gold / stretching miles to the sea" quickly transports us from neon-lit asphalt to sweeping grassy vistas bathed in late western sunlight. Yet by a slight shift in register, from the brassy particularity of "Shop-Rite Liquor" to the more ambrosial, generically "poetic" description of "lavender and gold," Kleinzahler makes his beloved New Jersey pop. The four-line second stanza narrows the scale again, cutting rapidly back to the poem's kernel scene, a thumbnail narrative of the poet and his father. Within this scene, the third stanza, five-lined like the first, initially seems to narrow the scale further by zooming in on "living dust: / bus exhaust, airborne grains of pizza crust," but this minute focus also enacts another kind of expansion, as the particulars of the scene—buses and pizza joints—become particulate matter suspended in the atmosphere, drifting into the evening lit by streetlights and neon. Kleinzahler pairs this physical expansion with a metaphorical one, recasting "living dust" as "wounded crystals." New Jersey's polluted, pizza-dusted air is made to glimmer as preciously as a Marin breeze, but it also now evokes the vulnerability and disappointment of the people who breathe it.

This short poem has a remarkable power of expansion in time as well as place, owing almost entirely to its only verb: "I have loved the air . . ." The present perfect tense locates the poet's love in both the present and the past, and thus "Poetics" resonates with both praise and remembrance at once. We sense that he has lost yet still breathes the air outside Shop-Rite Liquor. The feeling that past and present are somehow simultaneous grows stronger in the second stanza, where a lack of verbs makes it impossible to determine whether he is recalling boyhood trips to the package store or is a grown man accompanying his father in the acquisition of German beer. The poem lays one possibility over the other, powerfully rendering the strange temporality of an adult child's relationship with his parent: it's different than it used to be, but it's also pretty much the same. The son has gone away and come home: he now also knows and loves the Marin Hills, which are both beautiful and populated by rich people, but New Jersey remains constant and constantly unsuccessful. If this poem is a statement of Kleinzahler's poetics, he proposes that writing poetry is the composition—the putting together—of seemingly distinct times and places. It involves both love and disappointment.

The poems in Kleinzahler's first several collections are typically fairly short, often with compact stanzas and relatively clipped lines, and these short poems are sometimes organized into sequences. With 1995's *Red Sauce, Whiskey and Snow*, his first book published by the trade press Farrar, Straus and Giroux, Kleinzahler began to work in more expansive forms. While he continues to write some short lyrics and sequences, his poems of the past twenty years have tended to be longer, often stretching across multiple pages with more extended lines. The poems take different shapes, but Kleinzahler's sensibility and concerns remain constant, as we can see in the poem "San Francisco / New York," which inverts the orientation of "Poetics." Now the poet is in San Francisco, his adopted hometown, thinking of New York:

> A red band of light stretches across the west,
> low over the sea, as we say goodbye to our friend,
> Saturday night, in the room he always keeps unlit
> and head off to take in the avenues,
> actually take them in, letting the gables,
>
> bay windows and facades impress themselves,
> the clay of our brows accepting the forms.
> Darkness falls over the district's slow life,
> miles of pastel stucco cancelled
> with its arched doorways and second-floor businesses:
>
> herbalists and accountants, jars
> of depilatories. Such a strange calm, the days
> lengthening and asparagus already
> under two dollars a pound.
>   Is New York fierce? (115)

With its image of evening light stretched across the sky and an announcement of setting out, the poem's opening stanza might be a pastiche of "The Love Song of J. Alfred Prufrock." Like Eliot's poem, Kleinzahler's is a dramatic monologue—a performance of voice that supposes its own virtual auditors. Eliot's "I" has its "you," and Kleinzahler speaks of "we"; both lead their companions into the city streets. But once out the door, Kleinzahler quickly diverges from Eliot. The "certain half-deserted streets" of "Prufrock" serve mainly as material for the speaker's extravagant figurative language to transform. He projects etherized patients, tedious arguments, and feline forms upon the cityscape, drenching it in his pathos. Kleinzahler's speaker, meanwhile, seeks not to project but to receive the impressions of the city around him, which he hopes will be quite physically pressed "into the clay of our brows." Aside from this metaphor, Kleinzahler's description of the streets is vividly reportorial but free of figurative language. Thus his San Francisco appears as an actual place, whereas Eliot's city is a more generic representation of urban alienation, its "one-night cheap hotels" and "sawdust restaurants" functioning as atmospheric touches rather than actual, particular locations. With the wonderful detail that "asparagus [is] already under / two dollars a pound," Kleinzahler signals his speaker's lived intimacy with this "district's slow life," his attention to its ordinary rhythms.

This detail also tells us that while "San Francisco / New York" might be a monologue, it's not really a dramatic one. The "speaker" is Kleinzahler, and he's walking through his own neighborhood. He isn't playing a part, or if he is, he's playing the part of himself. And his "you" isn't an imaginary one, it's a real person—someone who's not with him but whom he has in mind. Prufrock, we realize as his monologue goes on, is talking to himself, and if his "you" refers to anyone, it's the reader he invites into his confidence, as if into his own head, a sort of spectral auditor. Prufrock is lonely because he can't get out of that highly sensitive head, but Kleinzahler is lonely because the person he's thinking about is in New York, far away from him. The cut from the asparagus to the question "Is New York fierce?" comes upon us with abrupt intensity, as the pang of another's absence might suddenly seize a person. Is one alone in such moments or not? The poem's pronouns go wobbly:

> The wind, I mean. I dream of you in the shadows,
> hurt, whimpering. But it's not like that, really,
> is it? Lots of taxis and brittle fun.
> We pass the shop of used mystery books
> with its ferrety customers and proprietress

behind her desk, a swollen arachnid
surrounded by murder and the dried-out glue
of old paperback bindings. (115–16)

For a few lines, the "we" of the first three stanzas breaks apart into "I" and "you," and the elegant, literary discourse of the poet's tour through the neighborhood momentarily disintegrates into a slightly disjointed conversational mode. The clarification—"The wind, I mean"—oddly upsets the theatrical illusion of the monologue. Kleinzahler worries about the confusion his sudden interjection might have caused, as if he had briefly lost control of the poem. We realize that his "we" is neither an actual plurality of people nor a stylized literary "we" but the poet and someone he cares about, absent in body but present in mind—present enough for Kleinzahler to chat with as he walks around the neighborhood. He addresses this unspecified other as though he or she is beside him even as he acknowledges the distance between them, "I" in San Francisco and "you" in New York. As quickly as the gap between the two singular pronouns opens, they converge again and the tour continues: "We pass the shop of used mystery books."

Kleinzahler's memorable sketch of the bookshop is at once funny, tender, and merciless:

>   What is more touching
> than a used-book store on Saturday night,
>
> dowdy clientele haunting the aisles:
> the girl with bad skin, the man with a tic,
> some chronic ass at the counter giving his art speech?
> How utterly provincial and doomed we feel
> tonight with the streetcar appearing over the rise
>
> and at our backs the moon full in the east,
> lighting the slopes of Mount Diablo
> and the charred eucalyptus in the Oakland hills. (116)

Kleinzahler has a good storyteller's knack for conjuring a "type" in just a few words. But what makes this passage more remarkable is the way he identifies with these characters even as he pokes fun. His inventory of book shoppers slides right into his lament—"How utterly provincial and doomed we feel"—so that "we" takes on new meaning, momentarily expressing his solidarity with these other lonely hearts "haunting" a Saturday night at the edge of America. The poet is one more "type"—the solitary middle-aged flaneur looking into shop windows. The question of "What is more touching" is simultaneously sarcastic and sincere. The poem's sense of loneliness only grows more acute as the scene broadens with beautiful efficiency, the streetcar carrying in passengers from other districts and the city giving way to the wilderness at its edges. Then we are swept upward toward the moon, from which vantage New York comes back into view, and Kleinzahler wonders whether his absent companion is looking upward, too:

> Did you see it in the East 60's
> or bother to look up for it downtown?
>
> And where would you have found it,
> shimmering over Bensonhurst, over Jackson Heights?
> It fairly booms down on us tonight
> with the sky so clear,
>   and through us
>
> as if these were ruins, as if we were ghosts. (116)

Kleinzahler's questions are about the moon, but he's also asking something else: are you thinking about me as I'm thinking about you? On New York's busy streets, down among its tall buildings, do you "bother" to think of me? Is elsewhere even visible, or thinkable, from there? Are you as haunted as I am? Here Kleinzahler risks becoming maudlin, and whether intentional or not, the poem seems almost to comment upon its wager. As sentiment crescendos, color and life drain away. The moonlight of the poem's final sentence blanches these characters and their distinctive landscapes with audible force; its emotional power washes away the previously vivid particulars of place and person. Book shoppers, the poet, and his companion—the moon makes ghosts of them all. There is a sort of beauty in this ghostliness, but there is also something lost.

Like "Snow in North Jersey" and "Poetics," "San Francisco / New York" makes plain Kleinzahler's talent for observing and rendering specific places. The poem is about being in one place while thinking of another, and its force depends upon his rendering of each city in its particularity, even though its final lines imagine both as "ruins" leveled under the moon. By contrast, the long poem "Above Gower Street," collected in *Sleeping It Off in Rapid City*, takes place nowhere in particular. The poem is written from an airplane, suspended between cities. Rather than faithfully depict a single location, as he does in "Snow in North Jersey," or a relation between two locations, as he does in "Poetics" and "San Francisco / New York," here Kleinzahler seems to meditate on the experience of place itself—or perhaps more accurately, on the experience of placelessness. "Above Gower Street" sustains a ghostly drift across six pages, briefly touching down in cities remembered or glimpsed out the window but just as quickly shifting elsewhere. Particular people appear and disappear, but in the poet's traveling consciousness, both places and people become spectral, almost interchangeable with one another. The very construction of the poem's lines and stanzas conducts this ghostly interchange. Consider its opening:

Rain   a cab   you
Standing there on the sidewalk, in the dark
The gathering thrum as the city awakens

A field of clouds below
Below the clouds the sea
On the screen overhead a movie

Across the great city
They are moving, the two of them
The freeways nearly empty
In pursuit, being pursued
Down ramps, among warehouses
A girl in jeopardy
A beautiful young woman in jeopardy
Before dawn, before the city awakens (14)

The initial capitalization of each line and a lack of terminal punctuation are crucial to this poem's composition. In each of the previous poems I've discussed, Kleinzahler stretches phrases and clauses across multiple line breaks, using varying degrees of enjambment to pull us through the poem and down the page. "Snow in North Jersey," for instance, is a barely punctuated run-on sentence containing many clauses, and "San Francisco / New York" unfolds in a series of elegantly hypotactic sentences. "Above Gower Street," however, accrues phrase by phrase. Even as they begin to coalesce like so many brushstrokes, each line retains its autonomy, floating in and out of relation to the lines around it. The only independent clause here is "They are moving," and it does not decisively subordinate the other phrases. This poem's movement is directed not by verbs, which are scarce, but by the proximities of nouns and prepositions.

The lightness of the poem's phrasal construction allows it to shift places and pronouns almost without detection. The first stanza begins dispersed among three nouns—"Rain a cab you"—simply placed next to each other without grammatical syntax, as though tracking the movement of the eye or a memory gradually coming into focus. With the second line we find ourselves in a street scene, waiting for a cab, and then finally in the expansive acoustic environment of an entire city. But then the city's "gathering thrum" gives way to the huge humming of a jet engine as the poem simply layers another trio of phrases: "A field of clouds below / Below the clouds the sea / On the screen overhead a movie." The poem's logic here is gently paratactic, rendering the disorientations of air travel with appropriate quickness. We cut from street level to an aerial window and then toward another sort of pane, a television screen—from memory to transit and then into fiction. With "Across the great city," the third stanza shifts into an action movie's chase scene, described in such generic terms that this city could be any city, this "beautiful young woman" any woman in any movie. Kleinzahler's trick, though, is to make this fictional city a double for the city in his memory, this "girl in jeopardy" a double for the "you" in the first line, hailing a cab "Before dawn, before the city awakens." There's comedy in imagining the poet and his lady friend caught up in a chase scene, but there's also perhaps a more puzzling thought here about the nature of aesthetic representation: once it's filmed in a movie or remembered in a poem, a particular city may easily become any city, interchangeable with any other, real or imaginary. This is also, the poem seems to suggest, the condition of air travel.

Yet rather than worry about this slippage of the realism he seeks and achieves in other poems, in "Above Gower Street," Kleinzahler settles into the blur, as one settles into a long flight and whatever entertainment is available:

On wet streets
The melting greens and reds of traffic lights
A cinematographer's trick with a lens

An access road, the belly
Of a jet, so low overhead
You can read, within its logo
A message:

    Why am I here? Who are you?

Because you chose to be here
I am who I appear to be

Across that great city
No, not that one, another
They are moving
Not those two, we
Not you and I
A friend and me, on foot
—Am I not a friend?

We are moving slowly
You can track us from on high
an aerial shot (14–15)

The principal entertainment here is Kleinzahler's play with pronouns. The poem becomes a chamber of barely embodied voices, emerging from memory or imagination, shading into one another, drifting away. It's unclear where exactly we're located: on the street of the first stanza, waiting for a cab in the rain? On a street in the movie? Suddenly somehow outside the city, on an access road near the airport? The scenes of travel collapse into one another, as do the rapidly proliferating pronouns. It's unclear who's speaking to whom at any given point in the passage. The pronoun "you" reappears, though it's not clearly the "you" from the first stanza. It could be an impersonal "one," or it could be the poet talking to himself. And what about the italicized voice that speaks out from the jet's logo: "*Why am I here? Who are you?*" Is this the poet talking to himself? Or the earlier "you" wondering why she's still in the picture? Or somehow the voice of travel itself, calling the poet's identity into question? This "I" and "you" can hold a conversation and constitute a "we" but are otherwise difficult to distinguish from one another. With a sort of Laurel-and-Hardy turn, the scene shifts into yet another "great city," yet another "we," a memory of an adventure with some other friend. Kleinzahler's internal dialogue veers briefly into comic shtick, but then he's up to camera tricks again, taking us from a ground level memory back up into the sky, back into the movies. The second half of "Above Gower Street" does take place mainly on the ground, among "Brick   sky   pastureland," en route from a city that seems to be London to the Midlands home of a friend who seems to be the poet Roy Fisher, with "His cat and his piano" (17). Yet even on the ground, Kleinzahler keeps looking up at passenger jets and remembering other people in other cities, as if in a jet-lagged reverie. He's still not entirely sure where he is: "We are in the north of the country / And in the eastern part / I forget which country / It may come back to me, perhaps not" (18).

The strangeness of travel and the intimacy of home turf—these are Kleinzahler's twinned, persistent preoccupations. Travel poems are as common in his books as poems about New Jersey or San Francisco. Sometimes, as in the beautiful poem "Gray Light in May," from *Green Sees Things in Waves*, a travel poem becomes a poem about home, flickering between intimacy and strangeness. Here is the first of the poem's two long stanzas:

The soft gray light between rains
This enveloping light
Under a canopy of green
Oak   chestnut   maple
Last night the moon, orange and full

Over Manhattan's West Side
Edgewater below so sleepy
The neighborhood asleep
My family asleep
Coming back here how many years now
And the ride in from Newark
Manhattan looming over the meadows
The beauties of travel are due to
The strange hours we keep to see them
This soft windless air
Away now thirty years
You can smell the tidal flats below
Passenger jets silent overhead
In and out of Kennedy, LaGuardia
As if gliding across the night
My heart abrim
A glass of wine, spilling over
The air like wine
I am a stranger to myself (152–53)

The italicized lines, a quotation from Williams's 1917 suite "January Morning," are talismanic for Kleinzahler. They appear first in this poem and then reappear in the title poem and epigram of his 2003 collection *The Strange Hours Travelers Keep*. It isn't hard to understand why Kleinzahler would identify so strongly with these lines, which in Williams's poem prompt a celebration of the sights of New Jersey:

I have discovered that most of
the beauties of travel are due to
the strange hours we keep to see them:

the domes of the Church of
the Paulist fathers in Weehawken
against a smoky dawn—the heart stirred—
are beautiful as Saint Peters
approached after years of anticipation.[4]

The heart-stirring effects of travel, Williams suggests, are induced not by great distances but by the peculiar temporality of transit. At the right hour, the homeliest, most familiar places might rival pilgrimage sites; here we can recall the evening transfiguration of the Shop-Rite Liquor in "Poetics." As a physician, Williams traveled widely in Jersey; his strange hours were those of a doctor called before dawn to the hospital or the home of a patient. Kleinzahler's are the jet-lagged hours of airports and train stations, of the prodigal son returning home. Whether in January or in May, transit makes both poets unusually alert to ordinary facts and happenings, and they sustain that strange alertness in the act of writing, Williams in the fifteen numbered snapshots of "January Morning," Kleinzahler in the hushed rapture of "Gray Light in May."

Like "Above Gower Street," Kleinzahler's poem of homecoming accrues line by semi-autonomous line, but he uses this technique to different effect here. While the loose joining of lines in "Above Gower Street" enables sudden yet seamless shifts in place and time, in "Gray Light in May" it creates a sort of reverberant stasis, the expansion of a single experience in a single place. And while repetition of words and phrases induces a sense of disorientation in the former poem, one city blurring into another, in the latter poem repetition produces absorption and focus. "The soft gray light between rains / This enveloping light": from the first line to the next, "light" expands beyond its visual aspect to become an atmosphere, a palpable medium, a substance to sink into "Under the canopy of green." As the poet recalls his arrival the previous night, the landscape expands under the moon (a favorite motif) to include Manhattan but then in three steps narrows down through the suburbs to the Kleinzahler family: "Edgewater below so sleepy / The neighborhood asleep / My family asleep." The variant repetitions of "sleep" lull the poem into a pervasive hush, conjuring a sense of stillness across the breadth of North Jersey and within the rooms of his family home. The poem's grammar contributes to this hushed stillness as well; the first stanza accumulates almost entirely without verbs, gradually gathering into a "windless" tableau. The only disturbance comes at stanza's end, with the delicate, finely focused image of wine lapping over the lip of a glass. In the stillness of the house, we can almost hear a drop hit the table. Here, too, repetition is crucial to the poem's work, establishing overlapping figurative associations: "My heart abrim / A glass of wine, spilling over / The air like wine / I am a stranger to myself." The poet's heart is a glass, overfull with feeling; the air, too, is rich as wine; the very atmosphere of his childhood neighborhood is the feeling that spills over. The experience seems to absorb his actual body, its sensations and emotions. So powerful is this immersion that Kleinzahler becomes strange to himself, or perhaps more accurately, realizes how thirty years away have estranged him from some original part of himself. Keeping traveler's hours and returning from a distance, he both identifies deeply with the sensorium of home and experiences it with defamiliarized intensity. Homecoming becomes a moment of self-confrontation.

In its second stanza, "Gray Light in May" loops back on itself, repeating and varying the set of phrases and images established in the first stanza, even citing another apt line from Williams's "January Morning":

> The soft gray light
> The still moist air
> The azaleas in these yards
> Under the canopies of leaves
> Fiercely abloom in this gray light
> Between rains
> Almost stereoscopic
> The broad green leaves overhead as well
> Painters know it, photographers too
> The smell of lilac
> Nudging my chest like the muzzle of a dog
> The manner in which this gray light
> Wraps itself around things
> Saturating them
> Bringing up their color
> So much a part of me
> So much of what is dearest
> I can barely stand upright under the weight of it
> The song of the wood thrush
> Reverberates through the heavy air
> And around its hidden columns
> *Who knows the Palisades as I do*
> Lilac and dogwood

> Flowering pear blossoms, mingling
> Drifting in gutters
> How many years
> For how many years
> A stranger to my own heart (153–54)

With its emphasis on the aesthetics of this particular gray light—the way it alters or accentuates the ordinary aspects of things, creating a "stereoscopic" or realer-than-real effect—this stanza offers visual art as an analogy for what Kleinzahler attempts in this poem. Like a photographer or a painter, he seeks to draw out certain qualities of physical reality by rendering them artificially. The poem's repetitions and formal symmetries are a poet's attempt to arrest and sustain a single moment as a visual artist might. In this moment of absorption, his physical and emotional worlds become indistinguishable. The emotions summoned by sensory experience in fact become physically overwhelming: "So much a part of me / So much of what is dearest / I can barely stand upright under the weight of it." The plain vulnerability of these lines is disarming and quite moving. Here is Kleinzahler at his most earnest, admirably unafraid of feeling. He is always a poet of emotion, but he often mingles emotion with wit, playfulness, or trenchant self-mockery. Even in a poem as direct and deeply felt as "Poetics," the opening declaration of love for the air outside Shop-Rite Liquor winks at certain "poetic" conventions. In "Gray Light in May," however, there are no winks, no tough-guy mugs. Kleinzahler confronts himself head-on: "How many years / For how many years / A stranger to my own heart." There is deep loss in these lines, even as the poem achieves great fullness. If his heart is an organ that pumps Jersey's "air like wine," there is a sense in which Kleinzahler can never know himself away from home.

So far my selection of poems has emphasized the personal side of Kleinzahler's work. They are poems of home and memory, affection, desire, and loss. This is not to say that Kleinzahler is a confessional poet; as much as he writes *as* himself, he rarely writes *about* himself. From reading his poems, one might be able to reconstruct a rough itinerary of his life, as well as a discography and a bibliography, but not much of a biography. (The interesting biographical material can be found, however, in *Cutty, One Rock*, his excellent collection of memoirs and literary essays.) What's personal about the poetry is the direction and quality of its attention. Even when Kleinzahler's "I" is absent, as it is in "Snow in North Jersey," the choice of place and the intimacy with which he renders it reveal the authorial presence of a Jersey boy. But Kleinzahler is not always so personal. For instance, "The Tartar Swept," the long poem concluding *The Strange Hours Travelers Keep*, rambles impressionistically alongside the Tartar conquests; "Fridge Magnet Nippon," in *Sleeping It Off in Rapid City*, playfully cuts up and rearranges language from Paul Claudel's *Cent phrases pour éventails*; and "The Rapture of Vachel Lindsay," from Kleinzahler's 2014 collection *The Hotel Oneira*, dramatizes Lindsay's travels across the United States. In these historical and literary investigations, we can recognize Kleinzahler's characteristic craft, curiosity, and wit, but fewer references to his own life.

He has also written loco-descriptive poems of more public significance. "Sleeping It Off in Rapid City," the title poem of Kleinzahler's *Poems, New and Selected*, is not about any of the poet's familiar haunts in New Jersey or California, nor is it about absent companions or friends visited. It is a dispatch from Rapid City, South Dakota—"the heart of the heart of America"—where the poet happens to be spending the night in "a heritage hotel." At just over five pages, it is one of Kleinzahler's best and most sustained poems, a masterpiece of local-color writing that grows into a meditation on the history and spiritual life of America. (It seems fitting that he read the poem at Harvard's Phi Beta Kappa ceremony in 2013, fifty-two years after Williams read his long travel poem, "The Desert Music," at the same event; what the graduates might have made of either as a valedictory poem is something to ponder.) Alertness to the luminous details of a place, a capacious lexicon, skillful verse phrasing—the poet's distinctive talents are all on display in "Sleeping It Off in Rapid City":

On a 700 foot thick shelf of Cretaceous pink sandstone
Nel mezzo . . .
Sixth floor, turn right at the elevator
"The hotel of the century"
Elegant dining, dancing, solarium
Around the block from the Black Hills School of Beauty
And campaign headquarters of one Jack Billion
("Together we can move forward")

The exact center of the Oglala known universe
Cante wamakoguake
Or only 30 miles away, southwest, off Highway 87
I waken to the sound of the dm & e
Rattling through this sleeping town
Sounding its horn as it snakes its way through
Hauling coal from nowhere, through nowhere, and then some
Old rocks and distance, a few hawks overhead
4 a.m.—*per una selva oscura*
—*Kwok, kwok, kwok*, shrieks the velociraptor
In the closed dinosaur shop
                    —*Vroooom*
Roars the Triceratops, like Texas thunder
They keep the tape-loop going through the night
Always have done, no one knows why
The Bible Store respires in its sanctum
As if in an outsize black glass humidor (3)

Here again Kleinzahler uses the semi-autonomous, lightly punctuated, mostly end-stopped line of "Above Gower Street" and "Gray Light in May," this time to create a palimpsest of historical periods atop a "shelf of Cretaceous pink sandstone." In the space of eleven lines he establishes the geological bedrock, then layers atop it the early twentieth-century boom years of luxury hotels, the pre–Westward Expansion age of the Oglala Sioux, and the present day of beauty schools and storefront campaign offices. (Jack Billion was the unsuccessful Democratic candidate for governor of South Dakota in 2006.) Kleinzahler quickly conjures contemporary Rapid City, shifting easily among different scales, from the wide open "Old rocks and distance, a few hawks overhead" to the surreal, closely focused image of the Bible Store humidor. Pink sandstone extends fifty stories below the landscape's surface, putting "The hotel of the century" in humbling perspective. We can hear the train's horn in the air and its clanking along the ground, the hotel's carpeted hush and the strange dinosaur calls from the lobby. Coal extraction, vocational training, religion, and kitsch—with just a few images, Kleinzahler vividly evokes a small American city perched on the edge of today's economy.

Yet imagery does only part of the work in "Sleeping It Off in Rapid City." Kleinzahler's collage-like arrangement of quotations is also crucial to the poem's rendering of the place. The italicized words are drawn from widely various (and not always human) sources: the opening lines of Dante's *Inferno*, publicity material for the luxury hotel, the simulated mouths of dinosaurs, and the Lakota Sioux language (*Cante wamakoguake* means something like "the heart of the universe," a sacred site in the Black Hills also known today as Pe' Sla). The layering of these diverse quotations is another way the poem creates a sense of historical depth in the present: in Kleinzahler's Rapid City, the sounds of dinosaurs, the language of the now-marginalized indigenous people who once flourished there, and the advertising copy of American economic expansion all coexist. Simultaneously we can hear prehistory, precolonial history, and American prosperity fading into history. In parentheses Kleinzahler drops in a bit of vapid contemporary political sloganeering; later in the poem he quotes from Custer's memory of his soldiers picking prairie flowers—"*It was a strange sight*, he wrote / *To glance back at the advancing columns of cavalry / And behold the men with beautiful bouquets in their hands*"—and recounts Kevin Costner's learning of the Lakota word *Tatanka*, for buffalo, in the movie *Dances with Wolves* (6–7). The mash-up is surreal but entirely real—screwball, satirical, and poignant all at once.

But what is Dante doing in the mix? With the allusion to *Inferno*, Kleinzahler casts himself as a wayward pilgrim in the long literary tradition, and he likens this South Dakota locale either to a dark wood or to Hell—to the place where one gets lost or to the place that shocks one back onto the path. But this poet has no Virgil and no particular itinerary; instead of seeking God, he's just "sleeping it off." By invoking Dante, Kleinzahler manages both to poke fun at Rapid City and to suggest that it might be a place of epic spiritual significance. Like *Inferno*, Kleinzahler's poem is comedic in a deep sense. He's joking around, but he's also serious, hence the elusiveness of the poem's tone. His reverence for Rapid City is a bit like his love for the air outside Shop-Rite Liquor—simultaneously wry and sincere. The divinity of Kleinzahler's comedy is uncertain, shifting among multiple cosmologies. He's not exactly at the center of the Oglala universe, but he's just a short drive away. There are other spirits in the air too:

This old heritage hotel, this is a sacred place

> The tour buses are lined up outside it
> Awaiting the countless pilgrims
> On the floor, my shoe, under the bed
> Even my shoe is blessed
> The Lord's blessing is everywhere to be found
> The Lambs of Christ are among us
> You can tell by the billboards
> The billboards with fetuses, out there on the highway
> Through the buzzing, sodium-lit night
> Semis grind it out on the Interstate
> Hauling toothpaste, wheels of Muenster, rapeseed oil
> Blessed is the abundance, blessed the commerce
> Across the Cretaceous hogback
> Hundred million year old Lakota limestone, clays, shale, gypsum
> And down through the basins of ancient seabeds
> Past the souvenir shops and empty missile silos
> The ghosts of 98 foot long Titans and Minutemen
> 150,000 pounds of thrust
> Stainless steel, nickel-alloy-coated warheads
> Quartz ceramic warheads, webbed in metal honeycomb
> 8 megaton payloads
> Range 6,300 miles
> *Noli me tangere*
> God bless America (4–5)

In this kaleidoscopic passage, evangelical Christianity and Sioux sacred geography mingle with the spirit of capitalism. Commerce and its relics become sacred while religion becomes a source of profit. The boom-time hotel attracts pilgrims, and interstate trucking signifies sacred plenty. Instead of a church, we have the Bible Store, and anti-abortion evangelicals rent billboard signage. Kleinzahler relishes the strange juxtaposition of linguistic textures, playing "fetuses" off "toothpaste" and "Cretaceous." With a sudden swerve into the specialized language and statistics of the Cold War missile defense system, he summons the ghosts of the military-industrial complex. (The National Park Service maintains the Minuteman Missile National Historic Site about an hour east of Rapid City.) "*Noli me tangere*" figures the body of the American state as the risen body of Christ or as one of Caesar's stags, and with "God bless America," Kleinzahler echoes the State of the Union address and cues the music.

With its antic incantation of sacred stuff, "Sleeping It Off in Rapid City" reveals ways in which the spiritual is historical and satirizes the way America spiritualizes its national history. Soon after quoting Custer, the poem moves on to Mount Rushmore and the unfinished Crazy Horse Memorial (which is *not* a national park): "The Great White Fathers dwell in these hills / Noses and foreheads blasted out of granite / Crazy Horse too, 30 stories high / An enormous pod of migmatite glowering east" (6). Around Rapid City, Kleinzahler tells us, there are "Big chiefs everywhere" in the form of civic statuary. One of these bronze street-corner chiefs is Richard Nixon, "Seated, hands folded on his lap, the way he did / In the midst of 'delicate negotiations with Mao' / This is what it says at the base / Bless them, Nixon and Mao both" (6). The litany of so many historic figures, delivered with faux-piety, deflates their spiritual authority and reveals the basic, violent logic of power that lies beneath it. Whether it's the Sioux fighting the Pawnee, the US cavalry fighting the Sioux, Cold Warriors brandishing their nuclear missiles (or, for that matter, railroads moving extracted minerals, truckers hauling goods, or evangelical Christians campaigning against abortion), all these sacred forces just want to claim as much territory for themselves as possible. Kleinzahler seems both skeptical and truly astonished. By the end of the poem, what he seems to be sleeping off is several hundred years of American history, and what he finds beneath its shifting regimes is the physical fact of rock: "Here, yes, here / The dead solid center of the universe / At the heart of the heart of America" (8). We might almost believe him when he says that he finds "Surcease here from all doubt," though he seems to place his faith not in any particular spiritual or national authority but in the wide-awake witnessing of what has happened here—and what continues to happen.

Indeed, here and in all of his poems, Kleinzahler is more concerned with bearing witness than with critique. It is not surprising, then, that his work gravitates toward comedy—a genre that acknowledges fault but remains generous to what's faulty. His wit might make us laugh, but the deeper comedy is in his attempt to hold opposing forces in proximity to one another. Note how frequently I have used the word "both" in describing Kleinzahler's poetry and sensibility. Comedy is well suited to that inclusive doubleness and the even more expansive multiplicities he entertains in "Sleeping It Off in Rapid City." Christianity and capitalism, Crazy Horse and Custer and Costner, missile silos and spiritual sites, Nixon and Mao—he is concerned first to register and even to revel in their coexistence, not to adjudicate among their competing claims. The poem's political and historical satire never resolves into self-satisfied judgment; Kleinzahler refuses the attitude of superiority that would allow such certainty. He writes from within the world he depicts, not from someplace outside it. His poetry affirms that the poet belongs down inside the mess, not commenting upon it from above. The truth he has to tell is that America somehow accommodates an astonishing variety of persons, places, and problems. That's why American life is interesting.

Kleinzahler has over the past forty years refined a repertoire of verse techniques uniquely suited to witnessing the strange realities of contemporary life in America. Whether compact or expansive, his poems reverberate with the diverse sounds of American speech and vividly render the particulars of the places we inhabit. His craft, which is rarely showy but always evident, permits attention to almost anything, anyone, or anyplace. In their ranginess and technical invention, his poems are sometimes demanding, but they always ask to be understood. Kleinzahler seeks to communicate. He is not especially political, nor does he seem hopeful about the prospects of poetry or of American public life, but his work aspires to a sort of democracy, to be open to anything and available to anyone who's interested. It's poetry that takes an interest in the world and makes a good case that we should get interested, too.

Notes

1. Kenneth Cox, "August Kleinzahler," in *The Art of Language: Selected Essays*, ed. Jenny Penberthy (Chicago: Flood Editions, 2016), 241.
2. *Sleeping It Off in Rapid City: Poems, New and Selected* (New York: Farrar, Straus and Giroux, 2008), 138. All quotations of Kleinzahler's poems will be drawn from this book and cited by page number hereafter in the text.
3. William Carlos Williams, *Paterson*, rev. ed., ed. Christopher MacGowan (New York: New Directions, 1992), xiv.
4. William Carlos Williams, *Collected Poems*, vol. 1: *1909–1939*, ed. A. Walton Litz and Christopher MacGowan (New York: New Directions, 1986), 100.

CHAPTER 12

Robert Pinsky's Affirmations

ROBERT VON HALLBERG

SOME WRITE POETRY, more than poems, to fashion an alternative world or, at least, a manner of speaking. Blake, Whitman, Pound, Olson, and Duncan are examples. They are understood and evaluated in terms of large, long-term projects. Others make poems, one by one, distinctive, bounded off from others. About these poets, there is a question concerning minority, T. S. Eliot famously argued, because usually they are adequately represented, by a selection of poems in an anthology. Bishop and Merrill are minor poets, on this view. It is a pleasure to fetch one of these poems for a friend or student—"One Art," or "Lost in Translation"—to coordinate a poem with some topic under discussion, loss, say. This is one kind of literary life: sharing one's finds, poems, songs, novels, giving away one's books. Poets who write for such a literary culture have every reason to hew to common idioms. Being understood, at least partly, on a first reading, facilitates exchange; a first reading repays attention, then invites a second one. The art of such poems is often in close phrases that depart slightly but meaningfully from familiar locutions. Robert Pinsky is such a poet.[1] Hopkins and Dickinson, too, wrote singular, memorable poems, many of them, but in unfamiliar idioms. The writing of stand-alone poems does not require a plain style, but plainness does encourage a collaborative literary culture. Those who treasure this collaboration will not settle easily for the notion that the writing of exceptional poems is an achievement properly called minor. One wants to know whence this success. Pinsky's success as man of letters—poet-critic, translator, advocate for the art—has been remarkable. But his success as a maker of shapely, short-ish, stand-alone poems is likely to be more lasting. In what follows, I will say why.

His art is evident to those who struggle with the craft of prose. At the level of the sentence: point and apparent ease, or fluency. One can imagine excisions, but not without sacrifice of local pleasures and of a distinctive and coherent manner of self-presentation. A sense of plenitude is central to his vision—and he does have a vision. He writes of life repeatedly remade by immigrants, those who, for whatever reason, leave familiarity behind. The poems appreciate seekers of change, and still more the nation's effort, flawed and intermittent, to measure up to a heterogeneous and fast-evolving heritage. At its best, our collective life encourages magnanimity—at its worst, bigotry and greed. The best is written into laws, but also poems, songs, and even jokes.

Pinsky took the title of his 1996 collected poems from a magnificent poem published a dozen years earlier, "The Figured Wheel." That poem develops a single figure, derived from Jack Kerouac's "211th Chorus" from *Mexico City Blues* (1959). (Kerouac rails against avarice, or the meat-eating consciousness—not Pinsky's concern.) Here are the first four of Pinsky's twelve quatrains.

> The figured wheel rolls through shopping malls and prisons,
> Over farms, small and immense, and the rotten little downtowns.
> Covered with symbols, it mills everything alive and grinds
> The remains of the dead in the cemeteries, in unmarked graves and
>   oceans
>
> Sluiced by salt water and fresh, by pure and contaminated rivers,
> By snow and sand, it separates and recombines all droplets and grains,
> Even the infinite sub-atomic particles crushed under the illustrated,
> Varying treads of its wide circumferential track.
>
> Spraying flecks of tar and molten rock it rumbles
> Through the Antarctic station of American sailors and technicians,
> And shakes the floors and windows of whorehouses for diggers and
>   smelters
> From Bethany, Pennsylvania to a practically nameless, semi-penal New
>   Town.

In the mineral-rich tundra of the Soviet northernmost settlements.
Artists illuminate it with pictures and incised mottoes
Taken from the Ten Thousand Stories and the Register of True Dramas.
They hang it with colored ribbons and with bells of many pitches.²

It is an engine of change and a monument to the imaginations of those it has milled while rolling, in time, through space; both a force of destruction and an archive of all that aspires to be preserved in memory. One recoils at the thought of graves being ground up—as if this monstrous power were like Ginsberg's Moloch. But morality is simply missing here. Like Whitman, Pinsky loves the pairs of antithetical terms (malls and prisons, small and immense farms) because they express acceptance of life itself, of rivalries overcome. That is what artists do: praise and preserve images of it all, the particularity of the world as we find it, which all comes to gravel, as the representations of life wheel on toward no particular destination. In line 8 the single Latinate word "circumferential" slows the verse so that each of the word's five syllables can be brought to clear utterance. That interruption of the line's rhythm expresses the poet's pleasure in (and insistence on) the comprehensiveness of the process. The sound of the word demands that serious consideration be given to the admiration summoned by the poem. It's a spectacle of change known broadly as culture, or people living in time. The richness of reference expresses the adequacy of human life. All of it rolls over the earth grinding everything down as time surely does. And the artists' adornments honor mere life. This is a democratic sublime, terrifying but not to be challenged, changed, or avoided. Admiration is what as democrats we owe to the contests of expression around us. Even the poet's sweet self is more gravel. Humility and humor are just responses to the process.

Samuel Johnson's "The Vanity of Human Wishes," an imitation of Juvenal's Tenth Satire, is the great articulation of an Enlightenment concept of universality that underlies our national democracy.

Let Observation with extensive View,
Survey Mankind from China to Peru;
Remark each anxious Toil, each eager Strife,
And watch the busy Scenes of crowded Life. (ll. 1–4)

Johnson, too, represents heterogeneity but in connection with moral choice. What draws people together, in his view, is their confrontation of alternatives, though "How rarely Reason guides the stubborn Choice" (l. 11). Wealth and social station systematically corrupt reason. Intellectuals now resist the appeal of generality in favor of various categories of identity that claim to render others visible and knowable. Pinsky presents a vision of generality that suspends morality and pathos too—this last, a challenge to the thought of our time. To regard human changes in time with equanimity, as Pinsky does here, one must get beyond political, moral, and humane compunctions. That, the poem suggests, is the reasonable price of a bird's-eye view. He imagines, as many do, that community is fortified not by judgment but by stories, even by those that glorify brutality and indifference to the suffering of others, to the devastation resulting from our own acts. One distinction of the poem is its frank acceptance of the inevitability of destruction we fondly consider peculiar to the twentieth century. Within this style, the apparent specificity of Pinsky's phrasing—Ibo dryads, pampered, a street in Iași—cues readers, as Whitman did too, to interpret particulars as instances of familiar general categories. The language is as much instructive as indicative.

I start with this poem in order to show that despite Pinsky's development of the particularities of his own life, he aspires, as Whitman did, to a general address. That includes, in some poems, a focus on nationality, but the aspiration is grander. There is a sense in which the voices of all poems are general.[3] But few poets answer for the art's generality by stating why a poem's call to others deserves to be accepted as plausible or just.[4] Nor do many express so clear a sense of what must be held in abeyance in order to allow general language to do its work. Johnson's language is closely analytical; it expresses firm moral, political, and social judgment. Pinsky has foregone ethical and political judgments in order to sustain a general perspective that is now less accessible than it was for Johnson and, more important, in order to affirm life as it is, not as one might wish it to be. For Pinsky, a general address and acceptance are two faces of one kind of poetry. Moral judgments are plentiful, divisive, and in time without effect. Big wheel keeps on turning.

I mentioned the familiarity of Pinsky's style. One easily imagines his sentences as prose running right past the jagged right margin. Remember that when Wordsworth advocated speech as a model for poetry, he had in mind prose usage: idioms that might be uttered, but in proximity to the diction and syntax preserved in print. As prose, "The Hearts" (1990), for instance, is vigorous, lean, especially where it departs from prose convention: the opening "sentence" is a fragment, but the comma after "troubles" indicates, with grammaticality, that the troubles cling like mussels. That last detail matters because the figure recurs throughout the poem (ll. 22–23, 34–38, 44–45, 51–52, 62–66), so its significance should be definite. The poem's prosodic measure is relaxed: a four-beat line in which only the major stresses count. That is the plain ground of his art. Consider the poem's opening phrase:

> The legendary muscle that wants and grieves,
> The organ of attachment, the pump of thrills
> And troubles, clinging in stubborn colonies

An odd but exact modifier for that first noun! The point is that so many stories take as their subject the ways of the heart. Which are later said to be "almost certainly invented" (l. 31). The stories of the heart are constructed, imposed on more than derived from this muscle. And however prose-like the language seems on first reading, the poet is so alert to the sonic undersong that a homonym can determine the course of the poem: muscle→mussel takes it from stanza 1 to stanza 2. Its second stanza calls from a different register, against the prose idioms:

> Like pulpy shore-life battened on a jetty.
> Slashed by the little deaths of sleep and pleasure,   5
> They swell in the nurturing spasms of the waves,
>
> Sucking to cling; and even in death itself—
> Baked, frozen—they shrink to grip the granite harder.
> "Rid yourself of attachments and aversions"—

The second stanza is sonically compact, a bit of Shakespearian pastiche. Beneath his phrasing stirs the sexual energy that drives hearts on: swelling, nurturing, spasms, and sucking. The command of the Buddha, announced by quotation marks (l. 9), is set in contention with Pinsky's recollection of Shakespeare's Romeo, who even in the first act surrenders to Juliet.

> But in her father's orchard, already, he says 10
> He'd like to be her bird, and she says: Sweet, yes,
> Yet I should kill thee with much cherishing,
>
> Showing that she knows already—as Art Pepper,
> That first time he takes heroin, already knows
> That he will go to prison, and that he'll suffer 15
>
> And knows he needs to have it, or die; and the one
> Who makes the General lose the world for love
> Lets him say, Would I had never seen her, but Oh!
>
> Says Enobarbus, Then you would have missed
> A wonderful piece of work, which left unseen 20
> Would bring less glory to your travels. (*FW* 47)

The poem is a study in desire, generated, one imagines, by worry; ardent desire has its abjection and destructiveness. Pinsky elsewhere noted that wanting is about both acquiring and lacking. Desire is an engine of both life and death. The great tenor saxophonist and heroin addict Art Pepper is cited to substantiate the point; then Marc Antony and Enobarbus. "If only I had known what would follow from my acts" is what Marc Antony means, and that is too easy. Romeo and Art Pepper knew: knowledge is no bulwark against ardent desire. I appreciate the economies of Pinsky's style—the abbreviation of connective tissue—and yet the allusions to Romeo, Marc Antony, and Lee Andrews and the Hearts all substantiate one claim about the destructiveness of erotic desire.[5] Economy normally proposes that one allusion suffice. Pinsky's parsimony is felt consistently at the level of phrasing; at the level of larger forms, he is expansive. The poems I single out are nearly all fifty lines or longer. Moreover, his expansiveness has a particular character. When the Buddha speaks in "The Hearts," he is heard as enigmatic because he contradicts the other texts adduced to support the notion that ardent desire is personal, particular: it must be Juliet or no one else. The Buddha speaks very briefly, but from another direction. Pinsky taps the power of modernist collage. But he is also an essayistic poet with points to make. His amplitude is intended to fortify his claims, but the life of the poem (and prudence too) depends on a pull away from ardor, and that is what the Buddha provides. The little rifts between the texts he appropriates are summonses to interpretation. And therein lies the poem's latent topic: fear that desire might bring the speaker to breaking faith, losing hope, and uncharitably betraying one beloved for a new ardor.

The conceit of crystal tears covering a window is attributed to Romeo, though it derives still more from "Venus and Adonis" and the tune "Teardrops," performed by the Philadelphia doo-wop group Lee Andrews and the Hearts. The notion of tears as crystals descending in a shower turned into a rain of skepticism, leaving the apish heart with the shattered illusion of a particular beloved. Pinsky's method is not to argue his way to clarity, though his writing is consistently clear: one instance would suffice if clarity were the only objective. Instead he makes of diverse texts a single memorable and coherent artifact. Here we have a song attached to two plays, a Renaissance writer to a recent one, canonical to vernacular poetry, religious to secular tastes, Benares to Philly. That is central to the vision he presents of people joined to strangers by common illusions, not by their essential beliefs. Chief among illusions is particularity. The poets turn illusions variously and thereby generate renown, glory (ll. 41–42)—a point made earlier by "The Figured Wheel" and of course Plato. That is human culture, the world over. We imagine particularity, our grandeur and folly. "Teardrops" is a song not of longing but of remorse: "I know you'll never forgive me, dear, for running out on you . . ." Lee Andrews knows how mobile desire is, and he regrets abandonment of the first gal for the next. He's on the side of the Buddha, and he ends the poem. Pinsky loves the particularity of things and recollections, too, but his poetic project, even his style at the level of the sentence, depends on rising to a generality beyond the fond charms of proper nouns.

Taking what is inherited or otherwise available, like the air, and making it a means of self-expression—that is Pinsky's model of culture. Although the saxophone was invented in Paris in the mid-nineteenth century by a Belgian named Adolphe Sax, it became an African American instrument in the mid-twentieth century when Coleman Hawkins, Johnny Hodges, Lester Young, and Charlie Parker made it their instrument. Genius appropriates freely, bends time and space. In February 1958, Stan Getz and Cal Tjader recorded "Ginza Samba," a tune written by Vince Guaraldi, who played piano on this version. Billy Higgins was on drums, Scott LaFaro on bass, Eddie Duran on guitar, Cal Tjader on vibes, and Stan Getz on tenor saxophone. The self-taught Swedish American vibraphonist was then the most famous non-Latin Latin percussionist. Stan Getz's grandparents on both sides, the Gayetskis and the Yampolskys, left the pogroms of Ukraine behind in 1903. Neither Getz nor Tjader could be fond of boundaries or proscriptions. They made a good living in a competitive field by touring constantly, gathering resources for US music. Ginza is the name of a luxury shopping district in Tokyo; samba, a dance and musical genre with roots in the West African slave trade. The mix is jazz.

The first lines of Pinsky's "Ginza Samba" (1996) introduce an anecdote to support a thesis.

> A monosyllabic European called Sax
> Invents a horn, walla whirledy wah, a kind of twisted
> Brazen clarinet, but with its column of vibrating
> Air shaped not in a cylinder but in a cone
> Widening ever outward and bawaah spouting
> Infinitely upward through an upturned
> Swollen golden bell rimmed
> Like a gloxinia flowering
> In Sax's Belgian imagination . . . (*FW* 5)

A "monosyllabic European" sounds like a taciturn person, a Garbo maybe, though the literal sense is that Adolphe Sax's family name is a single syllable, the one that names the ostensible subject of the poem. And the European version ought to be Sachs, but in time it was probably phoneticized, as Gayetski was. Taciturn, though, in that his invention is in sound not language. The horn's sounds, Pinsky stresses, make it over inexactly into near words: "wah," "bawaah." The elegance is in the device, "a cone / Widening ever outward . . ." Those "Swollen golden" syllables approximate its sumptuous eloquence; he is a sax player.

The rhythm is composed of three- and four-beat lines, with varying numbers of unstressed syllables; this is Pinsky's inconspicuous departure from traditional accentual-syllabic measures. Each strophe runs into the next. Enjambment is also a prominent feature of his verse: contestation between different levels of order: sentences versus lines and strophes. The poem collects a surprising assortment of references. Better, it weaves them together in a manner that affirms the creativity of immigrants crossing from one life to another. Combinations are made in tunes, in chambers of memory, in the valves, wires, and circuits of the saxophone, in the body's cells, too. They generate oddities and apparently stimulate genius.

Puns and cognates bubble up, summoning one another, as phonemes and syllables get swapped, reversed, and otherwise altered. Ginza→gloxinia; walla→wah→waah; upward→upturned; swollen→golden; bell→Belgian. Exuberant with echoes, the words do not stand alone, nor do people. The poem tracks strange crossings in folds of time and space. The first sentence (nineteen lines) is an elaborate compound of people and things, to the effect that the saxophone flowered both in Sax's imagination and in the bodies and memories of slaves and slave dealers from Africa. The sentence arrays sites of significance but not historically. What is time to art? "Calicos and slaves"—they come together in trade. Engineers and artists come, too, eventually and abidingly. "Two / Cousins in a royal family / Of Niger known as the Birds or Hawks" rhyme with two grand masters of the instrument, one up-scale, up-tempo, the Bird, Charlie Parker; the other down and slow, Hawk, Coleman Hawkins. They stake out the range of what time does in this art. The connections are not exactly material, even though slaves are exchanged like baubles. It's the air vibrating that generates the poem's music.

Across generations, between continents and languages, people connect—and are compelled to connect—and remake the present into a future. From servants and slaves come generals and poets, musicians—not by plan. Whitmanesque optimism here, yes, but without state support. The poem is about reproduction, change, life starting over, taking from the past, moving on to something quite different. Families grow by exogamy, reaching out to others. Their points of origin and destination—Niger, Baltimore, Rio, Tokyo—are little affected by ideology. Place-names are not states. People move as cells do, seeking advantage, survival, but not ideas. Pushkin's family is founded by the czar's release from servitude of a Russian African. True ennoblement derives more from the acts of the dandies, courtiers, generals, and poets than from the czar's edict. The institutions that generate decrees and regulations do not foresee all that is possible in what Pinsky calls the choruses of time. The future is rich in surprises. A light hand on immigrants is the glory of a nation.

Although Pushkin dies in a duel, Africans are sold as slaves, and one woman, raped, dies in childbirth, yet this is a joyful poem. Reproduction generates new combinations that delight the world. No hope hangs on the realization of justice. The notion that time and reproduction will change the world is a hard one for contemporary readers to accept. Which institutions change lives? Legislatures and courts are the common answers among Pinsky's contemporaries, though the poem dissents from that view. Its implicit answer is the family, because that is what shapes reproduction. He recited the poem in a lecture hall at Boston University with collaboration from three musicians playing Vince Guaraldi's sprightly tune "Ginza."[6] Laurence Hobgood did keyboards; Stan Strickland, alto and tenor saxophones; John Lockwood, bass. Pinsky there made the point that music is free to establish any relationship, ironic or not, to the semantic sense of a poet's words and subject. However horrible rape and slavery are, musicians, improvising, not following a score, can make of those subjects something different, light even. What seems the major issue to most readers—rape, murder, slavery—may obstruct an artist's oblique angle on something to affirm. How wide, then, is a poet's liberty with the paraphrasable sense of a text, or the morality of a topic? Very wide, Pinsky claims. Are poets to be constrained by decorum—conventions of what is fitting—in joining sound and sense? No such constraint generated the inventions of Parker and Thelonious Monk.

There are two poles of Pinsky's diction: the particularity of pearls and calicos, Baltimore and Seminole, copper, stirrup, and anvil; and the indefiniteness of infinitely, unfathomable, aether, and unimaginable. The ballast of particularity allows him some range beyond the proscriptions of Pound: toward words that dissolve boundaries. This is more than a detail of style. The last strophe of the poem comes as a surprise.

> It is like falling in love, the atavistic
> Imperative of some one
> Voice or face—the skill, the copper filament,
> The golden bellyful of notes twirling through
> Their invisible element from
> Rio to Tokyo and back again gathering
> Speed in the variations as they tunnel
> The twin haunted labyrinths of stirrup

And anvil echoing here in the hearkening
Instrument of my skull. (*FW* 6)

What is "like falling in love"? The poem seems to draw to a close with an unsettling non sequitur. But not really: particularity is the pertinent illusion. Seen from the aether, the suffering of individuals, their joys too, are barely discernable. What matters is the movement of sounds and generations, the demography of art. The tangle of unlikely causation behind the inventions of jazz geniuses makes it hard to feel confident that social policies formulated to remedy the predations of racism are adequate to the task of reinventing a culture of equality.

"Poem with Refrains" (1996) is Pinsky's strongest poem. Here are its opening lines:

The opening scene. The yellow, coal-fed fog
Uncurling over the tainted city river,
A young girl rowing and her anxious father
Scavenging for corpses. Funeral meats. The clever
Abandoned orphan. The great athletic killer   5
Sulking in his tent. As though all stories began
with someone dying.

                When her mother died,
My mother refused to attend the funeral—
In fact, she sulked in her tent all through the year
Of the old lady's dying. I don't know why: 10
She said, because she loved her mother so much
She couldn't bear to see the way the doctors,
Or her father, or—someone—was letting her mother die.
"Follow your saint, follow with accents sweet;
Haste you, sad notes, fall at her flying feet."   15

She fogs things up, she scavenges the taint.
Possibly that's the reason I write these poems. (*FW* 7)

The first words allude to the opening of Dickens's *Our Mutual Friend*.

Gaffer Hexam and his daughter Lizzie are scavenging for corpses in the polluted Thames; Gaffer makes a living by salvaging debris and also particularly coins on the corpses he pulls up. His daughter reluctantly assists him. He defends the work as utterly distinct from that of those who take money from the living. "Has a dead man any use for money?" he asks. Lizzie remains ashamed of their activity. Her father reproaches her directly: "As if it wasn't your living! As if it wasn't meat and drink to you!" The meat is the link to Hamlet and the twisted forms that grieving takes. The first allusion runs deep. In telling of his mother's erratic behavior, Pinsky is taking a kind of gold—poetic resources—from her. He resembles both Gaffer and Lizzie, for he feels shame in putting his disturbed mother on display. This is a tough representation of one who must nonetheless have been dear to him.

Like most of his memorable poems, it is an assemblage, conspicuously a poem of parts. There are first the diverse memories of his mother: her reclusiveness during her own mother's final year (ll. 7–24); her skeptical remarks about religious authority (ll. 25–40); her retreat from his bar mitzvah (ll. 41–58); her amusing remark about a representative of the Nation of Islam (ll. 59–68); her attendance at the placing of her mother's gravestone (ll. 69–82). Each passage is memorable and moving. The feelings evoked are indefinite, hard to name, because conflicted. She is, as Pinsky says clearly, one who seeks trouble, but she is also deeply troubled by forces the poem does not name. She is enigmatic, hurtful but in pain herself, confused but very intelligent. This is a rich, delicate portrayal of character, a great elegy for a peculiar person, as is Johnson's elegy for Dr. Levet, but Pinsky's subject was his mother. Moreover, she was alive when he published this poem. There is a vague violation associated with the poem—vague because repeatedly suggested, but never articulated. The opening with *Our Mutual Friend* suggests this sense of shame, the feeling that moves Lizzie to hide under her hood. It is there too in the difference between the first and second refrains. The first, from Thomas Campion, might be best understood as the poet's expression of his effort to honor his mother, or saint. But the second, from Fulke Greville, seems spoken by Pinsky's mother, who, below the surface, complains that her son/sun is against her. The exact relation of the refrains to Pinsky's statements in the poem is open to conjecture. He has left some blanks in the poem for the things he doesn't know; this is why it seems to me to rise above his other poems. In publishing this before she died, he was declaring her dead. He refused to engage any longer in the conflicts that were life with her. He too was tented, and by the logic of sounds (different from sound logic) tainted.

The poet Tom Sleigh speaks of the "different registers of speech" in the poem. He probably had in mind several passages where midsentence Pinsky's voice moves into the voice of his subject, known by different rhythms and grammar (e.g., l. 13). One may recognize these shifts through syntax and allusion. The opening strophe is composed mostly of noun phrases substituting for sentences, as if nothing adequate might be predicated of these things. That is true in that the noun phrases are allusions whose pertinence to Pinsky's words, their fit with the portrayal of his mother, emerges belatedly. That his mother is like Achilles is explicitly stipulated in line 9. That she seeks out trouble, that Pinsky does too, that his poems are instances of that drive—all that emerges in lines 16–17, when he returns to the fragmentary syntax of the opening strophe. Hamlet was orphaned from an abstract point of view. He lost both parents because Gertrude ceased to be his father's widow; she took a new familial identity as wife of Claudius. Achilles too was a kind of orphan. Pinsky's suggestion of these nonliteral senses of orphanhood indicates that his strain to embellish his own adversity (with memories of Dickens, Shakespeare, and Homer) is meant as part of the experience of the poem. The poet's voice is generally measured, restrained. He selected the anecdotes with an eye to their humor and charm. But there is also an irreverent and unattractive element of the speaker's voice, as when he refers to his grandmother as the old lady (l. 10), and to his bar mitzvah Hebrew recitation as babble (l. 44). One of the pleasures of reading Pinsky is tracking these shifts line by line. This is especially true of this poem. For all the prosiness of the diction and syntax, there is no question here of the fact that this is poetry, that grammatical rules concerning pronoun reference, for instance, will not take one through this poem. The poem moves at a deeper and less predictable level, and that warrants a degree of conjecture in one's reading as well as a sense that one is unlikely to hit bottom in interpreting the sources and references of the verse. But one will be drawn along in contemplation of the richness and amplitude of the mind—not just Pinsky's mind, but mind itself—and the supposed aberrations of family life.

I referred to Pinsky's collagist techniques in "The Hearts." He often places together sentences that do not apparently lead one to the next. When this technique is dialed up, one faces a non sequitur, or apparent error of composition; when dialed down, one recognizes without difficulty the aptness of a juxtaposition. Usually the effect is somewhere in between. Decades after Eliot's *The Waste Land* and Pound's *Cantos*, readers can find their way. "Poem with Refrains" makes this technique a predictable element of its form in that six of eight strophes conclude with a lyrical quotation from another poem, and the poem's last strophe consists entirely of a quotation. No single quotation recurs as a refrain conventionally does, but the concept of a verse quotation does recur, and in that sense the title is accurate. The collage effect is in the cognitive and stylistic gaps between Pinsky's words and those of the poets he cites. This poem takes his use of collage to another level. The quoted lines are gorgeous and their relation to Pinsky's lines about his mother, moving and elegant.

In Pinsky's *Gulf Music* (2007), he experiments with a still more abrupt collage effect. "Poem of Disconnected Parts" and "Poem with Lines in Any Order" are extreme cases of foregone coherence. But here I want to focus instead on an experiment in topicality, "The Dig," an uncharacteristically lean poem: only fifteen lines of accentual verse, mostly trimeters. He did not include this 9/11 poem in his recent *Selected Poems*, I think, because he is not satisfied with his treatment of its theme; but it is excellent and indicative of the direction he wants to take. Its theme is depth.

> Under the ruins, a steel
> Mirror, intended to expose
> The true faces of governors.
>
> Beneath that rubble,
> Inscriptions: annals of   5
> Atrocities of the righteous.
>
> Still deeper, the submerged
> Foundation, dream-dark piers
> Of speech, a chamber of clouds:
>
> Atomized parables   10
> Of descent, exhaled syllables
> Of workers, victors, victims,

> Dead languages alive,
> Contagions of dust, mute
> Parliament of each thing.⁷   15

What he considers deep, in the sense of abiding? Utterances and the contention they arouse. The first level of analysis concerns the duplicity of political leaders: their character, one wants to know, presumably in order to assess the actual nature of the state and its likely constraints. The governors, not surprisingly, are damaged, not noble. Steel mirrors are for inmates of hospitals and prisons, those at risk of hurting themselves. These are the appropriate institutions for governors: where they might be segregated and, even, rehabilitated. That is the level closest to the surface. The second and deeper strophe has one great phrase: "annals of / Atrocities of the righteous." Terrorists call themselves righteous, though their victims' families say zealots at best. Pinsky's good phrase refers more generally still, I think, to the wrongdoing of proudly careful people, even those who *are* in some measure righteous. One recalls here "The Childhood of Jesus," a brief narrative that handsomely presents the extremism of the Gospels in a tone of equanimity (though Pinsky's source is the Apocrypha). The true face of Jesus: egotism and the severity of children are built in, it appears, to the idea of religion. The Jew Jesus founded a sect that has cost Jews dearly. "Religion is nearly always a terrible thing," Pinsky says in "In Defense of Allusion"—a plausible claim in face of the implicit site for the poem (*GM* 51). There is actually little hope of escaping responsibility for atrocities. One goes on, bearing the suffering atrocities entail. This is the only peace reasonably to be expected.

Philology is an archive, largely of malfeasance—and not just of others' deeds. Our grievous verbs—murder, kill, knife, stab, shoot, spear, choke, strangle, club, crush, burn—derive from Old and Middle English, not from the invaders' French. Insofar as a hybrid nation has common roots, they lie in law and language; the Germanic etymons identify the precinct of English that literary critics since Dryden have called native. With these familiar terms we entertain ourselves and administer at best talion justice. All English speakers (even nonnative ones) have nourished the roots of our fierceness. Wicked foreign zealots have played a smaller role. The term for throwing someone out a window, "defenestrate," has its Latin etymon in clear view (*fenêtre*, French for window) and is not a concept for which English speakers must take much responsibility, though neither is it on many lips. Philology has given Pinsky an understanding of words as assemblies of unreconciled voices. The bluntest term for matter in English specifically refers to unresolved contest. The last two lines of the poem, the deepest, draw on an earlier passage in *Gulf Music* in which he presents a surprising etymology of "thing": "From an assembly or law court comes the sense of a matter at hand, an issue for debate." The nub of materiality itself is seen in English as a site of quarrel. Dust comes down to debate. This sense of "thing" is familiar; even its etymology is not legible. In the vernacular, one says, "Let it go. Don't make a thing of it." Pinsky returns to this claim in several poems from *Gulf Music*, trying repeatedly to get the one right poem from this provocative notion. This particular etymology calls to mind how essentially different people are from each other, how inevitably their interests diverge. To speak of anything, on this view, is to challenge others to a counterstatement. How inappropriate, then, to complain of dissension; and naïve, to seek harmony in poems, courts, or the streets. Any long-term claims one advances should accommodate a state of constant contest.

Every household has a pair of pliers for moments when the one right tool is not at hand; "thing" is like a lexical pair of pliers. Pinsky's poem on this homely tool for making-do, is an etymological study. To "ply" is an Anglo-Norman term that means to make a person fold or bend; hence "pliant" in ordinary usage still, and *plié* in ballet. "Pliers" is also an expression of one brought low, bent, bowed, and for no particular reason. How to write from there without endearing pathos? Formally, "Pliers" is intricately devised: composed of couplets, though the linkages are made variously on exact repetition, on consonants, or on rhymes. The couplets pull against the grid of tercets, but they do so methodically: the tug comes after the second, fourth, sixth, eighth, and tenth tercets, and only then. Each tercet is linked to another, but to only one other. The tercets all display a prominent variation in line length. The first has two long lines (four major beats), and one short (one major beat); the second has two short and one long. The third, two long and one short, and so on. In a villanelle, the terminal terms are repeated and their sense extended, developed by rhetorical invention. Pinsky has improvised a ghost form in which terms are turned and reexamined by means of philological connections. The topic is a feeling one cannot get past without some antiseptic drill. But instead of asking for a remedy for despair, as one normally would, he seeks an origin, as a philologist does.

The origins of a word, even one so plain as "pliers," clarify connections between one's disparate thoughts, feelings, and (above all) oversights. That is what Pinsky's engineered form in fact manages to do. An etymology, once legible, lends authority to one particular line of signification among the various senses of a word.

> What is the origin of this despair I feel
> When I feel
> I've lost my grip, can't manage a thing?

One loses one's grip and seems to others on the edge. Unable to manage, we say, of one requiring a custodian. To grip is to clutch, to grasp and hold. To "manage" comes from a Latin word, *manus*, for hand. Handle, we say, manage. The opening lines seek the source of a particular despair in the roots of words. This is an austere form of introspection.

> Thing
> That means a clutch of contending voices—   5
> So my voice:
>
> When my mongrel palate, tongue, teeth, breath
> Breathe
> Out the noise *thing* I become host and guest
>
> Of ghosts: 10
> Angles, Picts, Romans, Celts, Norsemen,
> Normans,
>
> Pincers of English the conquered embrace.

To be both host and guest of words indicates how modest is a speaker's agency. Choose one's words well, we say, as if that made all the difference. Care alone, however, cannot entirely control the significance of one's utterances. Words have powers of their own; they allow us all to say more than we know, because they retain, to no fixed or predictable extent, prior usage. In "The Dig," Pinsky speaks of the history of language as "a chamber of clouds," suggesting the uncertainty of signification (l. 9). A cloud chamber refers as well to a device for rendering visible the trail of subatomic particles in motion. Words, too, move from speaker to speaker, context to context. The *OED* tracks their migration through literary history. Philologists labor to identify the residue of prior usage that has become obscured from view. Pinsky's point in "The Dig" is that the residue is enormous and heterogeneous; nothing, however arcane, is entirely lost. The word "thing," for instance, does not render legible its sense of an assembly; awareness of that usage comes only from philological inquiry. The etymon for "arms" that is evident to readers of French (*bras*) renders apparent and sensical Pinsky's transition from "embrace" in line 14 to the anecdote of the woman who strangled her sister and then held the corpse in her arms through a night of moaning (ll. 15–17)—and then to "pliers" (ll. 18–19).

> Embrace
> Of the woman who strangled her sister one night, 15
>
> All night
> Moaning with the body held in her arms.
> The arms
>
> Of the pliers I squeeze hard squeeze its jaws
> And my jaw 20
> Clenches unwilled: brain helplessly implicated
>
> In plaited
> Filaments of muscle and nerve. In the enveloping
> Grip of its evolution
>
> Chambered in the skull, it cannot tell the tool 25
> From the toiler
> Primate who plies it. Purposeless despair
>
> Spirits
> The ape to its grapples, restless to devise
> In the vise- 30
>
> Grip *Discontent*, the grasper's bent. (*GM* 43–44)

One thinks that arcane etymological connections—as, for instance, "thing" to contention—survive only in the pages of learned journals. The anecdote of the bad sister leads, though, to "unwilled" conformity to the deep shapes of words. He squeezes the tool and his jaw clenches—also without apparent intent. Opposition, our thumbs indicate, is our nature. Muscles, nerves, and brain collaborate in pushing back. We know this from experience, even if we are ignorant of the script for this concerted effort, even if we forget it long enough to invest hope in consensus. Philologists remind poets of the experiences recorded in words themselves.

This notion of contention at the basis of even our sense of materiality—this takes us back to the themes of heterogeneity and immigration. That is the red thread through Pinsky's thinking. I have called this a vision, and that seems fair. Reduced to a proposition: differences do more for the health of the nation than union does. His best poems urge one to back away from notions of wholeness and harmony, even from justice. Equality is no spur to change; rather, strange combinations of exotic elements help new art emerge. This is not to say that what we commonly speak of as diversity—meaning particular combinations of race and ethnicity—promises social stability. Stability itself is not to be had in an open society, nor to be sought. Argumentativeness is a defining feature of a democratic republic. I am speaking of Pinsky as if he were a social theorist. Whatever authority he has comes from his ability to give pleasure to readers of poems like "Poem with Refrains," "Ginza Samba," "Hearts," and "Impossible to Tell." The value of this work comes first from its surprises, shapeliness, and clarity. But he is a poet whose work is well measured by a contemporaneity standard. His is an art of his time in the sense that he does speak with independence of mind to matters of common concern to his contemporaries. One would not say that as a poet he is representative. But as a writer he is especially responsive to his moment. To his credit, one knows from his poems what he does think and one recognizes that he speaks for no particular party, and to none's ongoing satisfaction.

People change, we say, to cover grief, broken lives. They change partners, loyalties, affiliations, objectives, their thinking, names, jobs, nations. They do this constantly, because desire is agile, promiscuous. Against the turbulence of lives that charm the poet is the shapeliness of memorable lines, stanzas, poems that arrive like handsome gifts. They are affirmations of not only the language and craft that birthed them but also of the chanciness of things that come out better than expected. What have walls and embargoes ever done for you or me? Porous boundaries serve us well. To them we owe our food and music at least. For their children, most Americans want mobility; the colleges are full. We mean to remain a nation of wall-jumpers. Finally one has to say that Pinsky, like Williams and Ginsberg, is an insistently American poet—a celebrant of immigration.

Notes

1. My list of Pinsky's strongest poems includes: "History of My Heart," "Figured Wheel," "The Hearts," "The Shirt," "From the Childhood of Jesus," "Ginza Samba," "Poem with Refrains," and "Impossible to Tell."
2. Robert Pinsky, *The Figured Wheel: New and Collected Poems* (New York: Farrar, Straus and Giroux, 1996), 105; subsequent references to this volume abbreviated as *FW*.
3. See Mark Payne, "On Being Vatic: Pindar, Pragmatism, and Historicism," *American Journal of Philology* 127, no. 2 (October 2006): 159–84.
4. For a formulaic effort to discredit poetic efforts at general address, see Ben Lerner: "The lyric—that is, the intensely subjective, personal poem—that can authentically encompass everyone is an impossibility in a world characterized by difference and violence." Ben Lerner, *The Hatred of Poetry* (New York: Farrar, Straus and Giroux, 2016), 62. Wordsworth, Dickinson, and Eliot evidently enjoyed peaceful, harmonious times.
5. Art Pepper speaks of his corrupt erotic desires, his voyeurism in particular, just before he discovered heroin. He was playing with the Stan Kenton band and peering in windows on breaks. "What's happening to me?" he asked himself; "What would Stan think and the guys in the band?" He could not imagine how to overcome his prurient habits. "Heroin stopped it for me," he reports. When he had his first heroin high, he knew what would follow: "I knew that I would get busted and I knew that I would go to prison." Art and Laurie Pepper, *Straight Life: The Story Of Art Pepper* (New York: Schirmer Books, 1979), 82–86.
6. Here is a link to their performance: http://www.bu.edu/buniverse/view/?v=Cbto1WG.
7. Robert Pinsky, *Gulf Music* (New York: Farrar, Straus and Giroux, 2007), 55; subsequent references to this volume abbreviated as *GM*.

CHAPTER 13

On Michael O'Brien

AUGUST KLEINZAHLER

IN A SHORT essay on the brilliant, little known British literary critic Kenneth Cox, Michael O'Brien quotes Cox on the work of the poet Lorine Niedecker, almost as obscure a figure in her lifetime as Cox:

> Her silences derive from an intellectual conviction that art, like science, demands
> total concentration on the object of attention.

And again, further along in the essay, Cox on Niedecker:

> At length her versification came to consist of nothing but syllables placed one
> under another at different angles and different distances.

As is often the case, when one writer discusses or quotes the work, in an admiring fashion, of another writer, he is likely telling you something about what he aspires to in his own work.

Very few significant American poets have received as little attention in their lifetimes as Michael O'Brien. Niedecker is another. And, as with Niedecker's poetry, O'Brien's poems are so delicately and quietly intricate, "small," that they could hardly be calling less attention to themselves, at least at first glance. Ironically, O'Brien's poetry is, above all, about *attention*, attention to the smallest, most fleeting details, more often than not of an interstitial, liminal nature, in the world at hand; and the world at hand in nearly all of O'Brien's city poetry, when not pastoral—New England or the western Catskills—is Manhattan: the Upper West Side during his years at Columbia, Chelsea, where he has lived for decades, to the financial district near the foot of Manhattan, where he worked at an office job for many years, and midtown, where he spent the last decade or so of his working life. These are the city poems, which, to my mind, are among the finest in the language. They are cinematic, in a flickery, stroboscopic manner that, by the unlikely juxtaposition of particulars, captures something of the speed and density of urban life at the end of the twentieth century:

> Mahler ripens in the bookstores
> Upstairs a jet is icing the sky
> Across Spring Street a man pours ice from a sack
> Into a bucket, precise as a drumroll
> Down Sixth three buildings glow like ingots
>
> The Morgan darkens, an old tooth
> Doors of sound on 42nd Street
> Where I sit in the reading room
> At the window the sun comes and goes
> Like a heart pumping light

This is from a poem entitled "The Days," published by Cairn Editions in the collection *The Floor and the Breath*.[1] Cairn Editions was an imprint that O'Brien felt the need to create in order to get out his own work and that of his friend, the poet Frank Kuenstler, because, quite simply, no one else was interested in publishing it. In all, O'Brien published six books under the Cairn imprint.

The sequence "The Days" and another, "Four Choruses," from the same volume, were originally published in chapbook form, also from Cairn Editions, eight years earlier in 1986, by which time O'Brien, born in 1939, had forged his mature style. What is somewhat different about the two aforementioned sequences, a form he was drawn to early on through his readings of George Oppen, René Char, and Jack Spicer, is that O'Brien here is exploring a somewhat longer line than is his custom, although he has a number of poems in prose and mixed configurations. If one observed at arm's length how the majority of O'Brien's poems sit on the page, one would be reminded of any number of other contemporary poets—far too many, in fact, overly reliant on enjambment—and the influence of traditional Japanese short forms—the waka, tanka and haiku—along with the minimalist modernism of W. C. Williams and his successors, most particularly the objectivist and Black Mountain poets. One would not be entirely wrong in citing these influences, but at the same time would be discounting the influence of late nineteenth/early twentieth-century French poetry, with its extreme transitions and discontinuity, the associative flaring and synesthesia of the symbolists, alongside the multiple points of view and crowding one identifies with cubism, most especially its offshoot, collage; and the surrealist influence, with its dream-like logic and unpredictability, the unlikeliness in the way disparate images are made to mingle with one another. The influence, more significant and less obvious, is the poetry of O'Brien's friend and contemporary Frank Kuenstler, also an experimental filmmaker, who, more often than not, tends to be more radical in his procedures and whose work seems to have encouraged the aforementioned cinematic qualities in O'Brien's work. Kuenstler has a short film entitled *El Atlantis* (Manhattan's IRT Third Avenue El), which can be found online and serves as a kind of visual analogue to both poets' work, with its jump-cuts, its densely layered quality, a deliberately cultivated grainy, "static-y" field of vision, what's called "snow" or "noise" in analog video, "fast-flickering black bugs on a white background," which all contribute to the sense of instability, movement, pressure—something approaching, overall, a kind of synaptic assault, which might seem familiar to anyone who has spent time in midtown or lower Manhattan, especially during the workday hours; an effect amplified by the proliferation of reflections and refractions from the windows of the moving trains. Another tendency both poets share, and which lends an instability and juddered quality to their work, is wordplay, especially punning. Words and phrases are subject to disruption from ambient pressures before they arrive where they'd conventionally be headed, coming apart and then regrouping in unintended, surprising ways.

Here's Kuenstler from his volume *In Which*:

> In which the big wig. In which a new brooms sweeps streets. In which from wench I came.

In which rain on rain. In which Lucy Lippard's slippers. In which nouns,
    calendars. In
which the garter belt & Bible Belt.[2]

Here's O'Brien:

You got a kiss like the Grand Concourse
You got a kiss like Chicago
You got a kiss like Chopin the Polish Scarlatti
O baby, don't you step on my blue dissuade shoes!

Thanks for the candied remarks. Thanks for the losssuit.
"Thanks for the mammary." "My sediments." "Exactly."
Sex is ephemeral, rabbinical, clockwork.
O, baby, don't you step on my blue dissuade shoes![3]

It's far easier, I believe, to capture the quality of instability, the "randomly pixilated," at least insofar as it relates to the frenzy and cacophony of city life, through the visual arts or music than, say, poetry. Frank O'Hara is the best known of those who have tried, and often succeeded, in poems like "Second Avenue," to capture the random energy of modern New York and its onslaught of undifferentiated *information*, visual, auditory, psychological, conceptual ... Kuenstler is another, both poets more extravagantly inclusive than O'Brien, who somehow achieves an equivalent effect in relatively few words and in a far more restrained, even austere fashion than O'Hara or James Schuyler, say, and denuded of that quality of "voice," so essential to the poetry of the so-called New York School:

Chambers Street ends in rain. Civic Fame's gold laurel catches the eye, but the day damps down. The man who lives in Warren Street settles in his duck blind. Four men stand like empties outside the Stanley Employment Agency. A television set left on in a shop tips its huge alphabet into the street. It is not speech but the parts of speech. Likeness joins what was separate, then the unwanted information pours in; a surd, a swarm ...[4]

Or:

> So much eyelid in a girl's downcast gaze
> Washington Square powdery with dusk
>
> cicada-song of the nervous system
> crossing the day's vacant places
>
> 37 floors of parallel lives
> little bell of the coffee-cart
>
> Landowska's harpsichord, a clatter of wings[5]

Or:

> Sun's eye at cloud rift like the ideogram for speakeasy. Big A. Scarlet Letter. Everything must be sold. MOMMIE DEAREST. BODY HEAT. "Is this in 4/4 or 3/4?" *New Criterion*. Old regime. A drugstore window full of jockstraps and vitamins. Academy Safe Warehouse Co. Century Iron Works. Punch. Once. Commodity & Tragedy. The teeth were the alphabet. A trail of lost erections. BRAS HALF OFF...[6]

Baudelaire writes in a letter to his friend Arsène Houssaye in 1862:

> Which of us has never imagined, in his more ambitious moments, the miracle of a poetic Prose, musical though rhythmless and rhymeless, flexible yet strong enough to identify with the lyrical impulses of the soul, the ebbs and flows of revery, the pangs of conscience?
>   The motion of such an obsessive ideal has its origins above all in our experience of the life of great cities, the confluence and interactions of the countless relationships within them. Have you not yourself, dear friend, endeavored to transmute the Glazier's strident street-cry into a song, and to express in lyrical prose all the saddening implications that such an utterance throws up to garret and attic throughout the mist-bound streets?

Young man had a sweet tooth for jelly-roll
gone down to make his long home with King Mole

Heart, utensil, old laborer,
the adorable springtime has lost it fragrance.[7]

If O'Brien's New York poems were the extent of his achievement, he would still be a figure of importance. His city poems, begun a century after Whitman's and Baudelaire's pioneering poetic engagement with the overwhelming new fact of the modern city, constitute a significant formal advance in creating poetic structures that can accommodate the torrent of sensory information. The volume of information encountered at noon, say, at the corner of Thirty-Fourth Street and Seventh Avenue in late-twentieth-century Manhattan is of another order than mid-nineteenth-century Paris or Whitman's New York. O'Brien is indeed a flaneur, but not the dandified kind on a leisurely stroll gazing into restaurant and shop windows, anonymously adrift in the crowds we encounter in *Paris Spleen*, but rather a sort of ambulatory Sony 4K Ultra HD Camcorder HC-X1000 that can capture 60 fps (frames per second) at 150 Mbit/s.

But that's not the half of it. "I'm a hick," O'Brien cheerfully describes himself. He was born in Granville, New York, in 1939, population 2,500, on the Vermont state border, 225 miles from NYC. He left in 1956 to attend college in the Bronx. O'Brien is among a long line of "hicks" from Upstate who made their way to the big city and realized notable achievement in the arts. John Ashbery, a poet whose work O'Brien particularly disapproves of—"the poetry of programmatic inconsequence," "the wallpaper of dreams"—arrived in NYC fifteen years earlier than O'Brien, from a farm near Lake Ontario. The poet Maureen McLane is another Upstate "hick," arriving in NYC some thirty years after O'Brien from Minoa, New York, near Syracuse, via Harvard, like Ashbery, and whose work O'Brien doesn't at all disapprove of; in fact, Ms. McLane has interviewed O'Brien for Zoland Books and commented on the work in general, with the original insight she brings to all her critical writing.

An equal share of O'Brien's poems could be characterized as "nature" or "pastoral" poetry:

The sea still patiently
playing its cards, turning
them over, one by one,
breaking up the pattern,
laying them out again,
unhurried, nothing to
lose or gain, only the
course of the possible . . .[8]

. . .

a bird like two stones struck together
(bird of reproof) through leaf-shimmer
a moth-spot of white light sky washed
an intense blue by yesterday's rain, no vein of opal

near the spring a red leaf-colored frog the size of an eye[9]

Tree—wraiths in
fog, wind-clatter, a

rash of
lichen-flowers.

Many clouds marry
the one mountain.[10]

The lens (zoom/macro) and shutter speed (slower) tend to be different, predictably, in the nature poetry, but the eye/mind is still made to jump around, *un*-predictably, each poem operating as if on an elaborate set of tiny hinges (spacing, pauses, juxtaposition, enjambment), turning one's attention first here, then . . . The shorter nature poetry conveys the sense of the words emerging from silence and disappearing back into it. Many of them, particularly the poems from 2007 on, have a spectral quality.

Delicacy of observation, oblique precision, and subtlety of movement, word by word, syllable by syllable, are the hallmarks of O'Brien's artistry in these poems, which seem much informed by the masters of haiku poetry, as do any number of the shorter city poems.

> dusk, Ninth Avenue, face
> bathed in cellophane glow, cowboy
> Narcissus, at his tasks[11]

It is not an accident. Around 1969/1970 O'Brien met and became close friends with the master translator of Japanese poetry, Hiroaki Sato, the two men collaborating on a number of translations from the Japanese. There are a variety of influences at work in O'Brien's work as a whole, but it is not too much to say that the primary influences on the mature work are the French modernists, whom O'Brien first came across on a junior year abroad in Paris while at Fordham; George Oppen, whom he became friendly with in the mid-1960s, around the time Oppen had begun writing again after a long silence; Kuenstler; and the poets of Donald Allen's 1960 anthology, *The New American Poetry*—Olson, Duncan, Creeley, and others—which hit O'Brien, at the time under the sway of the 1957 anthology *New Poets of England and America*, like a bolt of lightning. "I was still reading, or trying to read *The Mills of the Kavanaughs*," O'Brien later wrote. "Oppen pointed a way out." Sato, who would later introduce him to the world of Japanese poetry and sensibility, both traditional and contemporary, seems to have been the final piece in the puzzle.

Since 2000, when Zoland Books published O'Brien's *Sills: Selected Poems*, his most inclusive and important collection, the poet has enjoyed support from solid, if small, publishers. Flood Editions of Chicago has published three of O'Brien's collections since 2007: *Sleeping and Waking*, 2007 (which fetched an extended, smart review from that unlikeliest quarter, the *New York Times*, written by David Orr); *Avenue*, 2012; and *To the River*, 2017, which alternates the city and nature poems with remarkable effect:

> tips his newspaper
> gently back &
> forth as he were
> fanning his heart[12]

Shadow

    cars pumping out their
    plasma of music

    ash language
    junk cantos

    Sunup

    unplug the
    dream jukebox

    ragged figures
    cross a field[13]

The hynogogic realm, between sleep and waking (*Sleeping and Waking*) here and elsewhere, serves as a favored vantage throughout O'Brien's poetry, again the *liminal*.

Finally, there are those poems that, as pure lyrics, go beyond locality; the first of these two is ostensibly of a pastoral nature but covers a good deal more terrain than many of the more purely imagistic nature pieces tend to do:

[THE SONG . . .]

    The song the torso sings

    in February
    in the cold

    in a thawed field

    shallow pools standing
    beside the corn stubble

nothing else near
all the way up

THE LOOM

The snow's turned dross

The city's gloss wears thin
As a Bible's onion-skin

Or needle's eye

Her body
Is a kind of mirror writing

There
In its cockpit of air

Its ration book of days

Two sons
Two ways

Out

Cold quickens the ear
The lungs fill and fill

The will
Rests

At 25 below
Each step's like rosin on a bow

The second poem, "The Loom," a poem of return, is reminiscent—in its sparseness, how it does its work and sits on the page, the ground it covers—of a good deal of Oppen's best poetry, and in the best of ways. George Oppen, both the poet and the man, was of large importance to O'Brien. The two met during a propitious time for each of them. Oppen and his wife Mary were just back from Mexico, George writing again and curious about what was going on. O'Brien, at that point, the mid-1960s, was part of an Upper West Side art collective, centered on Columbia, that called itself the Eventorium and included, among others, Frank Kuenstler, Michael Benedikt, Serge Gavronsky, and Rachel Blau (DuPlessis). There were open readings in a loft every Sunday and later a magazine and press, which published five books, including O'Brien's *The Summer Poems* (1967). O'Brien was at that stage much under the influence of Hart Crane. The professor at Columbia who meant the most to him, John Unterecker, was at work on a biography of Crane at the time. O'Brien's mature work was still a long way off—*Veil, Hard Rain* (1986)—so there was little if any immediate direct influence of Oppen evident in the poetry he was writing during the time of their friendship. But O'Brien was most taken by the man and poet, and Oppen seems to have taught O'Brien a great deal, lessons the younger poet would take to heart in the later work:

A kind of plain-spokenness about inner things.

Not to simplify. To know as precisely as you could just how complicated things are, and not to make them either more or less so.

Patience. That there are things you can't rush.

"Paradise of the real." That it was here, if anywhere . . . How resonant that word "real," was for Oppen, for Duncan, for Jack Spicer.

That there was no part of one's life that couldn't be part of one's poem.

Clarity. That clarity was possible.

That you could employ prose or verse as needed.

That writing poems was a serious business. Not that you had to be a bloody owl, but that it mattered.

RADIO

A forced synecdoche, a voice insisting that you infer its body from one sense only, at you, at your ear. You forget this, the sound seems to issue from a tap you control, speech poured out like water, abolishing the membrane between plenum and vacuum. Sometimes you hear radio over the telephone, a denatured music, twice-removed. Sometimes the tuner drifts, and you hear the friction between stations. A sound like the sugaring of marble. A landslide of cells.[14]

In the Elevator

creaks like a mast
her leather jacket
as her body stirs

You can hear a bit of Oppen in this following statement about his poetry that O'Brien had meant to appear, though it didn't, in his collection *Sills*:

From the beginning I wanted presence and music, and I came to want concentration. I learned these things as I went along: that words were physical [viz. Oppen]: that irony finally isn't much protection; that music is a kind of description; that some things should not be lost. When Lady Murasaki is asked by the Prince why she writes she says, *So there will never be a time when people don't know these things happened.* Sometimes a page will light up, like the one on which Whitehead says, *The objectivist holds that the things experienced and the cognizant subject enter the common world on equal terms.* Or the one on which Gertrude Stein says, *Writing wants to go on. The poems dance their dance of stillness and motion.* Lately they have more space, more silence. They employ prose or verse as needed. Their art is in the measure they keep between the instant-by-instant life of the world and that of their words. The issue is a quiet, patterned music, animated, disciplined, ecstatic; not closure but recognition.

In a recent email exchange, Michael O'Brien sent me this quotation from William Carlos Williams's *Autobiography*:

It is ourselves we organize in this way not against the past or for the future or even for survival but for integrity of understanding to insure persistence, to give the mind its stay.

Notes

1. Michael O'Brien, *The Floor and the Breath* (New York: Cairn Editions, 1994).
2. Frank Kuenstler, *In Which* (New York: Cairn Editions, 1994).
3. Michael O'Brien, "song & image," in *Veil, Hard Rain* (New York: Cairn Editions, 1986).
4. Michael O'Brien, "Chambers Street," in *Sills: Selected Poems 1960-1999* (Boston: Zoland Books, 2000).
5. Michael O'Brien, "A Quarry," in *Sills*.
6. Michael O'Brien, "Perceptual Difficulties," in *Veil, Hard Rain*.
7. Michael O'Brien, "Baudelaire Young, Baudelaire Old," in *To the River* (Chicago: Flood Editions, 2017).
8. Michael O'Brien, *Avenue* (Chicago: Flood Editions, 2012).
9. Michael O'Brien, "East Branch," in *Sills*.
10. Michael O'Brien, "In Maine," in *Sleeping and Waking* (Chicago: Flood Editions, 2007).
11. O'Brien, *Avenue*.
12. Michael O'Brien, "Subways," in *To the River*.
13. Michael O'Brien, "Urns," in *To the River*.
14. O'Brien, *Sills*.

POWER

CHAPTER 14

Barbara Guest and Jorie Graham

CAL BEDIENT

I ASK MYSELF, what do I look for in poetry? A better question is, what does poetry look for in me? Do I have enough openness for it, a plastic enough sensibility to take its imprint, a need for what it "says"? Does it make me feel inwardly alert, alive, befriended, exposed to an astonishing intimacy, challenged, scared? Does it run over me, are we together on a dark road? Does it take me apart and reassemble me? Do I flow and change in it, done with the imperialism of absolutes and *I swears*? Do I dance in it to a new rhythm, speak a new code, enter the space and pace of a new form, walk on a new layer of language placed like sod over the scraggy old? How long and old and big and new am I when I read it? Would it lead me up a mountain, rock me on the ocean? What possibilities does it discover in us? What wild welter do I harbor? What is the weight and scope of my humanity? Besides my capacity to be extrahuman?

But for the present purpose, I must commit to a few considerations. I will go so far as to claim for the best poetry (hoping I don't regret it later), three qualities. First, a renewing vitality of temperament, perspective, and style, which (granted) may by themselves be three qualities. Second, as described by the angelic late nineteenth-century American writer John Jay Chapman, a drawing out of the soul from its recesses: "[T]he truth is that art and letters speak a language that comes from behind the work, not from within it. What makes us happy in art and letters is the power in them that has been unconsciously absorbed by the artist, and is unconsciously conveyed to us by his work." I will call this unforced power "depth." And third, to quote again from Chapman's *Letters and Religion*, work that does not prevent "our seeing life in the enormous perspectives in which it really looms." And call this height and breadth. It puts me in mind of Walter Pater's distinction between "great art," which has large scope and scale, and "good art," which settles for patch views and less awesome pleasures.

But leaving the term "great art" aside, I will simply say that for me these three criteria go a long way toward defining major poetry, that thing you know when a strong, decidedly new thing ("voice") enters poetry. All three are abundant in the work of, for instance, Barbara Guest and Jorie Graham, at the same time that the two poets stand forth as opposites. Which is to say that the criteria do not form a groove, a chute, for delivering poetry in a set mold.

Guest's style is oblique, Graham's strenuously direct. Guest's perspective is deconstructive, limited to subjects and objects that, with her radical reactive will and (one finally comes to see) brilliant imaginings, her writing stays aside from. Graham, on the other hand, attacks description and discourse with a powerful demand that world-reality yield itself to her, that is, cease to shut her out, there where deconstructive time-reality, the "minutes," eat her with their "rat teeth." Guest is cool, poised, bizarre but calmly declarative. Graham is all clamor and gaping vulnerability. The defining word for Guest is distance—distance that does not suffer. Emotional distance, imaginative distance, distance from expected continuities and transparency of style. A defining term for Graham is the impossible. She suffers from the undeliverable gift of love for, and a terrible need to be of ultimate use to, existence conceived in the largest way, as a great reality bearing a destiny, a tormenting "x." To Guest's horizonal world set off by distances, which are temporary terminations more than continuations, shields against nothing, Graham opposes a global reality that could not be larger or less protective than it is.

Guest is not without a general idea of reality, namely reality as precisely a general phenomenon in which particulars are of small moment and as subject to substitution as one word is by another, a denotation by a metaphor. She alternately denies perspective itself (in a critical reaction to the hegemony of the point of view) and intimates an abstracting picture of the world as a musical circulation of energies coming and going—a perspective totally indifferent to history, to the singularity of objects, and to the misfortunes in life, as well as to the pangs and hopes of a possible transcendence. By contrast, Graham takes on history, time (the devouring "minute"), psychological struggle, love, and death. Driven to break totality open, she is epic and tragic, while Guest is comic, a poet with a blithe temperament and enchanted by the dodges of the eccentric.

My formula of comic poet vs. tragic poet is of course a thing of easy handles and is not meant to obscure the fact that both poets work the abyssal side of the great modern divide between artists who hold—who simply feel—that dissonance must now be the truth of art (we are here in the domain of Freud's "death drive") and those who stay on the traditional side of solutions and harmonies and trust to a dominant Eros to conquer skepticism and its driftings and randomness.

"Comic," even though the atmosphere of Guest's work remains difficult, "contrary," aloof, as said, from the small activities of those who live in history. Comic in that Guest accepts the dissonant abyss with a sort of glee that she can meet it with an aristocratic superiority of attitude, a limber sword of style, whereas Graham tries to climb, to think and feel, her way out of it, the drama of the effort forming a large part of the substance of her poems.

Apprised of the knowledge of "the difficulties of property on sand," Guest puts herself at the periphery of the passions, is minus empathy, keeps a distance from people and time's toy chest of objects, much like the airborne swan-mounted knight in her brilliant comic extravaganza, "Knight of the Swan," who looks down and finds "strange" the things he sees below. She practices a defensive (or simply superb) notational quirkiness, imbued with muted feeling but not emotional, not sexy. Her imaginative play is scattered and glitters, but seldom deep or expansive. Depth, after all, is created by organic roots that are better mimicked by, say, the tonal system of music, or by painting with a vanishing point.

By contrast, Graham, philosophically turbulent, works this side of the objective world at the conjecturable edge of its boundaries. The world looms over her. She desperately wants to cross the ontological divide, she can almost smell the secret, smell it right through the transparent glass wall of language that, together with time, its architect, keeps her from entering it. She won't turn her back on it, not altogether, and give way to "the nomadism of the death drive" (Jean-François Lyotard), even if the effort makes her feel haggard.

There they are, then: Guest a comic poet who does not admit of any failure or even that there is anything to fail, and Graham a tragic poet of an always withheld full existence, a poet of failure. Temperament, of course, plays into this contrast. Each poet writes as the history of her spirit always already drives her to write.

Guest's poetry was slow to catch up with the lyric abstraction of painting after World War II. She became a part of the New York art scene in the mid-1950s, but her radically experimental work was delayed until *Moscow Mansions* (1973), after the new painting's creative furor had died down.

In order to approximate to what Gorky or Pollock had done, she would need to abandon the dianoia of the syntax to which she clung in aggressive bad faith at the start. She was eventually to perfect the no-sense (well, hardly any) of a verbal chromatism and randomized arrangements of fragments. She would go well beyond her New York cohorts Frank O'Hara and (leaving some early work aside) John Ashbery in taking a long breath and swimming under the rules of discourse with almost total fearlessness, yet emerge with breath intact. She wrote sparse pieces (not really *whole* poems) with a restraint whose principle was obscure, but likely a matter of aristocratic reserve and taste. Often, and always on first reading, there is little apparent sense, but there is never bacchic delirium. Odd as it may be to say, her art is cool and classical, but the classical riddled with holes, the target just reeled in for inspection in a shooting range. In fact, the lack of strong charge, of excitement or urgency, is a limitation in the work. The poetry does not easily carry over. The reader must go to it (not into it; there is no "in") and try to parse it (or not: the conclusion that it cannot be understood may come quickly, too quickly).

Guest became the queen (she loved the idea of royalty) of deconstructive poetics. It was an aristocratic thing to do. Art is not work, not utility. The aristocratic principle of her deconstruction (and not only hers) bears the Joycean motto, *I will not serve*. She would not endow the line with the energy of a developed rhythmic figure or of regularized description; she would not devise formal beginnings, middles, and ends, a single point of view, or often any point of view at all. She veered only intermittently into scenography, realist space, perceptual space, sensory space, plastic space, conceptual space. At her most distinctive, she created a new space, a non-place, much as her friend Helen Frankenthaler had done, and as Pollock had done in a densely buzzing atomism of spots and strings.

If Guest broke rules, it was not so that "the beast fur" might shine "in this light of twelve tones" ("East of Omsk"), but to eliminate the beast altogether. Let the poem be a "composite" without the accents of vitality; but let it consist of multiple movements (like the frequent turns in dressage), and in that way oppose "marble," which includes "all orthodox movements" (this noted already in an early poem, "The Blue Stairs" in the book of that title, published in 1968). Guest was in agreement with Foucault that, instead of being a sculptural Subject, the apparently singular person is a creature of many folds (children have twenty-two to unfold, said Henri Michaux). Subjectification can be a constant production, made of will and creativity, nothing "orthodox." This instancy of created subjectivity licenses incoherence. In Guest's work, the seriality of change is her constancy and coherence.

Guest begrudges that there is indeed a world of natural appearances—in *Rocks on a Platter*, IV (1999), she writes (typically, as if in a marginal note), "flotsam of the world of appearances"—but the motions of time see to it that the appearances are not guaranteed. Physics has not settled on a theory of Time. Time appears to be implicated in thermodynamics and quantum fluctuations. Essentially, it has nothing to do with the clock. It may be hazarded that reality is above all (or, better, below all) a seething series of interruptions, snapped entrances and exits, so many that an enumerable succession of instances does not exist. A sense of this instability can color one's relation to the accidents of surfaces. Guest would no more write "Light thickens, / And the crow makes wing to the rooky wood"—not that anybody but Shakespeare could—than she would count syllables. Particulars are not ultimate accuracies. Guest often implies a point of view precisely in abandoning points of view, and, in keeping, she sometimes gestures beyond ineloquent and diced up "locality" toward a faraway frosty horizon. *Enter (after all) a large perspective*, one associated with Nietzsche and Deleuze, among others—namely, as intimated earlier, that everything is "constantly replayed, the dice are recast, the Throw of the dice returns" (I quote Alain Badiou's paraphrase of Deleuze in his little book *Deleuze, The Clamor of Being*, first published in French in 1997).

The notion of an Appearance-dissolving cyclicity is, then, Guest's concession, such as it is, to the *actuality* of Appearance. (She once even underscores the solidity of objects: "solid objects are merciless" [*Rocks on a Platter*, II].) For her, Apparition has more appeal than Appearance does. Hence her affinity for the Gothic genre. Her detachment from singularities obviously negates intimacy with objects and emotion: "cold tears splashed acre is intimacy" (*Rocks on a Platter*, III). Her *long* and *cyclical* view of things, flocking to "distance and disappearance," is the source of the all but total indifference to death in her poetry, as well as to the surface effects of time. She is effectively in agreement with Emmanuel Levinas's statement that, "among the elements of this world, . . . change only transforms, safeguards, and presupposes a permanent term." If death is "a break," Levinas adds, it "does not interrupt the 'monadic' Being qua being, the 'existing' in existents."

By the 1980s, distance was Guest's Eden, far from commercial "edens of soap and fat." Far, too, from "the sinking afternoon in a fleet of taxi-cabs" in New York City and "rose Nabiscos," gaudy consumer crap (I quote from "Seeing You Off," in her first book, *The Location of Things*, 1960). Built-in distance is the rule of her mature work, until, as will be noted, a break and turn near the very end. The concept of distance as rapture recurs in it. Stand back and you see that reality is not a congeries of objects, a clamor of bodies or beings, but an inevitable generality of movement that makes of the passing parts secondary phenomena, the equivalent of apparitions. This relieves the soul of being, so to speak, a soul, terrible with gravity. It frees feeling to enjoy romance, hence occasional references to medieval kings, knights, and castles. Plain American nature can do the same, as in "Santa Fe Trail" (*The Location of Things*): "O mother of lakes and glaciers, save us gamblers / whose wagon is perilously rapt." (It was rare for her to admit the perilous, and when she does, it is rapt!) Distance is also a not unwelcome muting of dissonance. Also a sort of winter in which she delights to play: "In the dark sits / the first Angel of snow / tomorrow in the outraged sky / his form," she wrote in an early poem, "Snow Angel" (*The Location of Things*). The imagination outrages what would have been its death by universal frost. She treats it with grateful positiveness again in "Landing," in the same book: "I watch the egg / Unhatched. I am the sight / Over the egg, like an aviator."

At the peak of her deconstructive "rapture," cold rapture though it may seem to the puzzled reader, she perfects her aristocratic disdain of rational sense. She sometimes wrote without direction, steadied only by a fidelity to distance and disappearance as the touchstones of what is finally real. She created driftwork, work in which cathexis is withdrawn and currents swirl and rule. In his book *Driftworks* (1984), Lyotard spoke of the seriousness imposed by the capitalist system—that which Gertrude Stein had treated with sincere unseriousness in "Patriarchal Poetry" (1927): "Patriarchal Poetry one two three. / Patriarchal Poetry accountably . . . / Patriarchal Poetry administratedly." Driftworks are "examples of the reactive art of discontinuous procedures and distorted figures." Guest was clearly "reactive" in her close-to-nonsensical inventions. Anticapitalist? Implicitly, but hardly passionately. Feminist? Not particularly. A comic Inhumanist, rather.

Whatever her motivations, other than originally to keep up with the new painting in New York, her bold practice of discontinuity gradually came to influence younger poets, perhaps especially women in the Bay Area, as Brenda Hillman mentioned to me, though Guest exceeds them in a rather wonderfully *superb* attitude in her use of fragments, a playful but adamant invulnerability. She has the value, then, of being one of the markers of what Lyotard in *Driftworks* calls the "fulgurant junction" of theory and practice in an era still lit by Picasso and Jules Breton.

"The function of the artist," Lyotard remarks, "was no longer to produce good forms [those formerly grounded in religion], . . . but on the contrary to deconstruct them systematically and accelerate their obsolescence . . . , [to] attack these good forms on all levels"—as in the dodecaphony of Schoenberg (one of Guest's touchstones) and in Cage's music made up of noises, not notes. Lyotard points to artistic practices outside the signifying official organization of things, practices that contest systems of libidinal repression and are happily inutile. *Comic*, as de Kooning is comic. As Klee is. As Picasso is. As Guest was finally able to be.

"The position of art is a refutation of the position of discourse," Lyotard states in *Discourse, Figure* (2011)—especially random art that abandons Eros or at least makes desire "cunning" (as Rimbaud advised). Radical art disconcerts us, Lyotard elaborates, by pointing to a non-locus, an unidentifiable space. Following Freud, such art exposes the social nature of "reality" as a "bound set of perceptions"; it refuses to be an accustomed site of community, even if it obviously appeals to the limited community of those who want to be disconcerted.

Guest shows her hand—the back of her hand—not only in her poetry but explicitly in her prose on poetry and art. In "Radical Poetics and Conservative Poetry" (1990), she writes that "the forms of poetry . . . are restlessly releasing themselves. Having feasted on Modernism they are readying for a new patrol into less inhibited— ... glimpsed as a more fractured—territory" (*Forces of Imagination*). Again, "in the defenestrating process of saying something new, the structure of the poem suffers." The modernist poet—not postmodernist, for "to accept this term," Guest remarked, "we have to believe that Modernism, itself, is finished. Like throwing a bathing cap into the divine flux"—the modernist poet "confronts endless space." (Here is that "large" view again.) The poet trusts to the imagination alone, for "imagination has its orderly zones," even if suffering "the touch of exile" because resisting "clear and absolute meaning." The imagination is not "a conservative toy." Guest chose not to be one of the majority, those "cosseted in the mimic field" (*Stripped Tales*, 1995).

For Guest, poetry is like music, the antithesis of sculpture. The great thing is not to build poetic body but to be on the move, to fragment, to drop lines down the page as if conceivably they could continue off of it. Imagination as a traditional form of empathy is off-road in her most definitive poems. She uses emotion-thwarting "wrong" completions of descriptive phrases and stanzas so as to be a rival inventor to organized systems of reality, one who mixes things up like a mischievous but not malicious god. In "On the Verge of the Path" in *Moscow Mansions* she asked, "What inspires me?" Answer: "Picasso."

Guest, who wrote for *Art News* in the 1950s, observed in her essay "The Shadow of Surrealism" that "painters are the revolutionaries to whom writers turn in their desire to break from the solemnity of the judicious rules of their craft." Gertrude Stein, for instance, in writing cubist portraits, was, Guest says, "seeking an escape from literature, or from 'the literary.'" As for continued adherence to good forms:

> Vanish Vanish *Building*
> Except here on my calendar
> a last iridescent bite[1]

Over two decades later, in the loose, long poem "Stripped Tales," Guest narrativized her animus against "marble":

> She put the pail on her head then moving through wire she called to the Master of Sculpture "to make way for *Softness* I'm pouring it over the torso" then the bronze rain fell (BG 324)

This clever little narrative, finally more than clever, beautiful, has a *pouring* syntax. At a large interval, the isolated word "*moment*" stands above these lines and the likewise isolated phrase "*of ingenuity*" below them. Ingenuity has to be equal to unforeseen moments, "soft" in that sense. At times, Guest's plasticity, her mercurial "spills," might appear to be due to an attention disorder but is of course a principled rejection of the commoner's subjection to rules.

Guest wears some of the preternatural colors of surrealism (she was weaned on the stuff), but she's not a dreamer, she doesn't pursue embowled depths, an inner "world." Her imaginative practice is to separate from realism without adopting desire's recourse to the dream techniques Freud identified: condensation and displacement. Her metaphors, to be sure, displace, but cannily. She's not bound by fantasies in which desire is entrapped and thus always saying the same thing.

Much of what she writes is careful not to make apparent. (Because of a problematic reading experience, memory may magnify the effect of nonsense beyond what a rereading actually confirms.) An example of the problem:

> He wears pleasure trousers
>   olive bird--
>
> nomadic filter--the harsh bridals--
>   sand eclipse Oxus
>
> "Beyond the limit of our world"
>
> we beg for lustered sleep--Argival-- (BG 216)

Is this nonsense? The passage lacks the Victorian devices of nonsense—phonetic substitution, inversion, literalizations, asemantic word combinations, and still more—devices that constitute a game played with rules, as Elizabeth Sewall observed in *The Field of Nonsense*; a game whose breaks in the chain of coherence suggest "a universe out of control, frighteningly akin to lunacy." Moreover, Guest may not often do the one thing necessary in nonsense poetry, and that is write nonhermeneutical lines. Her nonsense can be not only fabulously silly, as in "Knight of the Swan," but also apparently oblivious to its incoherence, its "parts without a ruling unity," as Walter

Blumenthal would put it. But is that what we encounter in the lines just quoted? If so, why does she end the passage so beautifully, with the sketch of a "large" perspective," if she means it to be nonsense? Though the fragments might seem to be, at most, random pieces of some prior narrative, is the passage necessarily nonsense? Yes, if in their totality the pieces are not "dissolvable into concepts," in Ludwig Tieck's formulation.

But frequently, as I have said before, what may at first look like nonsense proves to be, on close inspection, daring obliquity, metaphorical code. Consider the following lines from "Dove" in *Defensive Rapture* (1993):

> sunset
>   venom in rust
>   the small breathing.
> of cowhide.
>
>   employed
> a chalk wing. (BG 263)

Have you actually succeeded in reading the poem if you come to think, "yes, things rust, as if poisoned, and even the sun sets. And in such a decaying world, breathing is small. But at least there is one free wing, the wing of art, if only a 'chalk wing.'" (As regards Guest's own art, chalk, a dry medium, is appropriate, as opposed to oil's potentially traumatic wet medium.) Yet "venom in rust" is excessive in this context, "cowhide" remains unilluminated, and "employed" is flat and uninformative. Guest, you see, will not let you in without some pushing back at the door.

Consider another example of lines ambiguous with regard to their participation in meaning. I quote from the poem "Expectation." The title is accompanied by a dropped-down reference, "(*Erwartung: Schoenberg*)," as if by a helpful clue, but the content is nothing like *Erwartung*'s song-story of a woman hysterically searching for her lover in a forest, where she finally comes upon his body; and it is not like anything else, either. Is it nothing more than an opaque arrangement of words?

>   more liquid
> than eyes adulterous surface—

>   the bruised arch—a sting
>   severely clothed—rich in dynamite—
>   cord to shallows—;
>
>   a fluid haze divides—
>   the rhythm vault—
>
>   —single movement—topped with purple hills—
>   contralto shift (BG 266)

The flagrant polyphony (there is no "single movement" here), the frustration of visualization that is pleasantly if untrustworthily relieved in non sequitur by the romantic phrase "topped with purple hills," the extremely dubious modifications ("a sting / severely clothed," "rich in dynamite," "a fluid haze"), the scissor-snips of the deconstructing dashes, and the agrammaticism of "eyes adulterous surface"—these can be characterized by William Carlos Williams's phrase "untamed aggregates," also as "driftwork." But (so often a "but") the poem resists its own anarchy, and without resorting to the synthesis of "I think," which lacks sovereignty and is posed over against the multiple. Guest's polished anarchy plays with the adulterous lexical surface where words can be disloyal to their long-standing partners and have affairs. This anarchy, "more liquid / than eyes adulterous surface," is destructive of the established architecture of rules and meanings; it bruises the arch. It carries a sting beneath its obscuring clothing. It has denotative power, it can destroy the "cord to shallows," which is all that a denotation is. It avoids rhythmic regularity—*that* rule; it is free to haze up the integrity of a "single movement" topped with corny "purple hills." It shifts at will or on impulse.

The limitation of the metapoetic turn common in yesterday's experimental modernism is of course its incestuous confinement. Guest all but transcended its kiss-art tendency by being brusque and inventive with respect to it. In one of her most winning little poems, the ninth poem in the sequence "The Screen of Distance" (*Fair Realism*, 1989), she diversifies it brilliantly. She alters the game by animating a famous work of art and making *it* do the honors. I refer to

>   The Bride raised the cloud settled on her

aspen head and stepping away from her bachelors
she seized like wands the poems I handed her;

"A life glitters under leaves
piled for anonymity . . ."

She would lead us through glass to view the
enigmatic hill where a castle slung a shadow (BG 230)

An anarchic upset of ekphrasis, the poem, marking a departure in this middle period of Guest's work, takes off from the basis of something everyone can recognize, an object in the known world, Marcel Duchamp's *The Bride Stripped Bare by Her Bachelors*, which is not unrelated to the tradition of representational art (it is a comic twist on the epithalamium). But Guest has no use for that; she ignores Duchamp's conception and, with a somewhat comic narcissism, faces the Bride toward herself, removing her from the feel and look of Duchamp's figures, their machine-design aspect, their entrapment in a dead glass medium. Guest, as poet, must have movement, and so she animates the Bride and summons her to the same place she herself occupies, and further summons her out of geometry and her mineral state to be nothing other and nothing less than an aspen tree, living nature. Great as it is, the change is not enough for the Bride. Coveting the transformative power of Guest's poems, she seizes on them like so many batons to produce other changes not dreamed of by a glass-frozen figure. The poems show the Bride the anonymity of natural change, the impersonality imposed by the ruthless flux and repetition of natural cycles, as opposed to the anonymity the bride illustrated as a figure in the Large Glass, where she was already, it is true, anonymous, a type, *the bride*. But autumnal tree or not, she isn't ready to depart; she wants an expansive prospect: a hill, an elevated castle and its shadow, a sort of enigma drawn from out of a Europe distant enough from modernity to allow for mystery and anonymity. Superb, the castle holds itself above common humanity, it even slings its shadow, as if peremptorily casting it off, wanting to be left alone. The Bride would lead us *through* the glass (for we are all encased subjects) and reveal a marvel; she would take on something of Guest's own role as a poet. (When Guest imagines the goings-on in a castle in "Otranto," the strain after the Gothic fails to impress; the high life of royalty serves her best when it remains remote and emblematic.) The twelve-poem sequence itself ends with the anonymity of distance replacing a narrative figure: "The Baron faded as distance gleamed / a clear jar multiplied by frost." From an unlikely object that is not without kinship to marble, Guest thus frees an organic world of natural growth and death, while retaining her requirement of anonymity.

But even before her posthumous poems, Guest displayed, if infrequently, the strong weakness of faltering in her intransigent practice of "atonal" writing, cold "rapture." She had vacillated over "airlessness" as an aesthetic practice as early as her excellent poem on Juan Gris's *Roses* in *Moscow Mansions*: "There is the mysterious / traveling that one does outside / the cube and this takes place / in air." Now, three full-length collections later, in the major poem "Dissonance Royal Traveller" (*Defensive Rapture*), she abandons the airless writing and driftwork of the first page and a half of the poem for two pages of something close to what used to be called "natural feeling," familiar kinds of affects: joy in nature, exaltation through music. There is, first, music's liberating emotional range,

> the sleeve of heaven
> and the hoof of earth
>   loosed from their garrison. (BG 291)

Next a "tragic," pretty perspective on the cyclical world of the moon and generativity ("a monarch butterfly / touches the season; // by accident grips the burning flowers. // in the stops between terror / the moon aflame on its plaza," where "terror" is the affect of being in a hole outside the productive moment of gripping and pollinating within world-process); but, despite her penchant for generalizing cycles, this hardly sounds like the Barbara Guest of the earlier poems. Then comes a tragicomic variation on the theme of processual change. The poem concludes as follows:

> . . . harsh fists
> on the waterfall changing the season;
> the horse romps in flax
> a cardboard feature
> creating a cycle of flax.

> *music imagines this cardboard*
>
> the horse in cardboard jacket
> flagrant the ragged grove
> red summit red.
> dissonance royal traveller
> altered the red saddle. (BG 292)

This is as close as Guest ever gets to a tragic feeling about time's harsh changes. But she brings art to the rescue. "Music" even *delights* to imagine that the horse is "cardboard." What truly serious harm can come to cardboard? The less there is of bestial life, the less of living substance in things, the more acceptable is the knowledge that they pass. A noble rider, *art arrogates reality to itself*. It cardboards appearances, and that's not a loss, it's play, it's joy. It costs music nothing to picture the cardboard horse as romping in the flax as if it were a real horse acting out the nature of a horse in an innocent demonstration of the drive to destroy.

Already seventy-three when she wrote "Dissonance Royal Traveller," Guest was to continue writing for another thirteen years, into the year of her death, 2006, and in that interval, for the first time in her poetry, and as it were just in time, she warmed, if not consistently, to the common world of things and persons. Here and there in *The Red Gaze* (2005), she openly seeks the solace of an intimacy with nominally actual objects. True, in "A Burst of Leaves," she reiterates her earlier call for a radical poetry:

> A disappointed generation, words collapse around us.
> Like the one who jumped into the sea. But the seas disappoint us, also.
> We do not like to walk on their beaches, lined with laboratories and
>   formula.
> We are ready for a new orientation. (BG 496)

But in thus writing so lucidly in the old orientation of poetry itself, she steps out of the cube of airlessness. She becomes less preoccupied with making of language a "silver hut" in which "Narcissism" lives. Her age, her declining vitality—*something* behooved if not impelled her "to welcome tonality" rather than "succumb to the theme of inharmony . . . / where we once were"

(*Rocks on a Platter*, I). She became much less bent on "clearing the ordinary from the room" ("Modernism").

Guest even softened into nostalgia—an unexpected final relaxation of the battle against conservatism. The leadoff poem in *The Red Gaze* is in fact entitled "Nostalgia." "You began the departure," she writes. "Leaves restrain." The departure is thus punningly delayed by the hold of familiar living things. She revises: "you attempted the departure." Follows "a smile in sunshine, nostalgia.... / I have lost my detachment, sparrow with silver teeth. / I have lost the doves of Milan, floating politely." (Note the strongly felt stops, as opposed to the spotty and distracted periods such as often appeared earlier.) The loss of aristocratic ("silver") detachment explains the nostalgia for the doves of Milan, who mean no harm as they float on *l*'s and a choice long *o* ("floating politely"). "I shall be here," the speaker says, familiarly addressing Nietzsche: "Recognize me in sunshine."

Speaking first of herself and then for her now *divided* self, she says,

>   I am not detached,
> bulletins permit us comb, fish of silver
> A part of the tower
> beckons to us (BG 491)

She still lives in the experimental aristocratic tower of art (she speaks of skipping down three pairs of unnumbered stairs that are "oddly assorted, velvet"), but she can be reached by bulletins from outside and, naming real things (comb, ornamental fish), she drops the most radical project of the modernist painting that inspired her, the dismantling or elimination of objects.

And though one of the six posthumous poems, the short "Hotel Comfort," begins with an extravagant imagining, "Minutes each hour took ostrich leaps on the roof of the Hotel Comfort in Strasbourg," it immediately adds a pinch of sense to the nonsense: these "Surrealist moments cherished each roof a last time." Her extravagant imagining is a farewell to extravagant imaginings (revere nostalgia). In her own turn to late, last cherishings, she can see, even in "the thickened weather of Surrealism the cathedral... / across the street." She nods to the stony, storied art of architecture, which she had earlier threatened to dynamite. The built has survived modernism. How much in the "real world" had radical modernism really challenged and changed?

The poem now takes what is for her an unexpected turn: it accentuates humble material things:

> Wise lettuces exaggerate their claim near the windows of the Hotel Comfort.
> And you have sent your letter of explanation for the pleasure obtained in the wooden jar. Speechmaker, you have sent notes of pleasure in the glass jars.
>
> Tasting of weather and cinnamon. (BG 516)

Both the wooden jar and the glass jars contrast with Guest's earlier image of distance as "a clear jar, multiplied by frost." Someone has sent a letter to her (such is her story) elaborating on some pleasure—sent it in a wooden jar; and, in addition, has sent notes in fragile containers, glass jars. The correspondent is not one who reacts against humble or familiar *forms*, ordinary reality. The words prove to be an invitation to share in words about *things*. Words can convey, as if they held them, the qualities and pleasures of real things: weather, cinnamon.

Still greater, and arguably her masterpiece, is another posthumous poem, a pastoral double poem on the English painter John Constable. Here the references are generalized, but how warm and sympathetic they are. Guest's imaginary Constable (who, like the real Constable, is a painter in wet weather) is not made of cardboard but is, rather, an artist passionately associated with elemental things (rain, water), generic and constitutive things (paint and painting, but here not particular paintings), music (but not particular songs), and the alphabet (not words). In this respect, the general, always Guest's preference, still reigns over the particular. Witness, "He had found an orientation of *rain* that carved *notes* / he made on the bridge. Formerly it was a green *alphabet* of *water*" (italics added). Again:

> He traced with his brushes music. There is no song
> in Constable but there is music, even underground
> when the waters have washed the musical keys
> and paint is waiting. (BG 513)

But the singular is generously welcome within the general. Inclusiveness is the note, plenitude also. Who would have foreseen that Guest would end her career with words that dance in their places with a Mozartian lightness?

In sharp contrast to Barbara Guest's distancing fragments with their air of cheerful experimental hauteur, Jorie Graham's relation to observable reality is aggressively inquiring. For her, the Here is not cardboard, nor tamed, nor does it offer itself to be shattered and recombined into aggregates, for defensive rapture. It cannot be shaken off in favor of a There or a phantasmagoria of cyclical rise and fall. It is a concrete immensity that may, all but must, harbor a meaning, conceal a destiny of knowledge meant for us, or anyway one who could perhaps be seized, a recompense for subjecting us to the treachery of the minutes. If we are only arbitrary beings, we have no purpose, and life tends to turn either cold or vicious in our hands, our blood. This cannot be right; we must be missing something. We must be strong in questioning. But despair keeps working itself into the poet's asking.

Graham is Aristotelian, but she wants to escape from the common oil-like density of thought-and-sensation into a clarity of being-knowing that would be Alpine air in relation to the death instinct—at least there would be no conjectural further, a going beyond. She rejects religious solutions that would too easily belie the constant dissolves of time. More than any other writer who comes to mind, she suffers from time's invisible killing hand, its constant dismantling of "Self" (the securities of the self-reflective "I" and its traces of memory). Graham has, you might say, a fundamental *objection* to time; she fights it. Again and again she is pushed back on herself into a stub-self, not the Self she might have thought she almost was a moment ago—and finds herself elbowed in the ribs by the next minute to come. One glimpse of the transtemporal and she would be rescued. Oh, but it probably doesn't exist. How many times does one have to call to it to know for sure?

What keeps her going? Her powerful analytical drive? Not so, or not well, for it enables her to see only the kill-holes of her mind's redoubt. The trick is to get to the There (which is, however, subjective), from the Here (which is also subjective), without abandoning or being abandoned by the Here, where existence is immediately felt with a pressure and seduction that does not exist in Guest's world, but nonetheless feels incomplete and uncorroborated.

To repeat, Graham's desire for this transit, her rather terrible spiritual famine with regard to it, is fierce. Gifted with the ability, if not the will, to forget past failures, she takes up the problem over and over again. She will not be defeated, though she will be.

Even though consciousness "is the last and latest development of the organic and hence also what is most unfinished and unstrong," as George Steiner said, it *must* be meant to have a destiny, so Graham cannot help but believe: a destiny to coincide with whatever is ultimate in reality. Or what merit, let alone nobility, does it have? What then are we, an animal with an epistemological disease?

As our representative Graham will try to find out if we can be useful in clarifying and helping to further destiny. But, unlike, say, the great Chardin, she lacks a theological afflatus that would lift her above the biosphere. She seldom even looks out to the cosmos, though she feels it in her blood and under her feet. Like Hopkins, a favorite of hers, she is all attentive ear and eye in the here and now. But unlike him she lacks Bible and Church.

I have called her a tragic poet, and certainly her sense of modern history is no different from, if less personally acute than, for example, that of Osip Mandelstam, who wrote, "your backbone is broken, / My beautiful, pitiful century." But she is not a poet of tragic *joy*, except in moments of stunning exceptions (most recently, "Sundown," in *Place*, 2012). She does not feel, at least in the degree that Mandelstam did (let alone that Walt Whitman did), the blood's "grass-like and ringing connection" with everything. She is hemmed in by a pagan atheism and the sense that humanity is the ruin of itself ("Dementia," her latest poem as I write, is tragically scathing about the matter). And she's no aesthete: the world as an aesthetic phenomenon is not enough if it passes by like a phantom caravan on the horizon. No, a spark must fly from the me to the missing other, the foam of the upside-down sea of the Invisible.

For Graham, natural appearances, with their diverse attributes, can feel like clues, but like all clues partial—you might say ungenerous. Though her descriptions can be studiously detailed (no one's more so) and abundant, they are, of course, not those of a naturalist; they are charged with anguish and symbolism, with her passions and ideas. In her work, desire is enmeshed with description. At the same time, thinking tests it rather severely. But Description and Thought (thought's thought and desire's thought) almost never coincide. Description becomes overwhelmed and is abandoned by the thought that asks too much of it. Conversely, when Thought leaves the ground of Description, it doesn't know where it is.

Graham's looking would go further than Thought can go and be "prayer." But a prayer to what, exactly? She resorts to inadequate metaphor: "script" Script, as if prayer were a reading, not an appeal. (It is not in Graham's nature to be a supplicant. She identifies with competence and power.) She looks at the natural world with a perfect readiness to be transported. She presses up as near to a scene as the hungry eyes of her language can go. Bug a poet with prodigious powers of mind, she *thinks* what she sees, and that is already a sign that she won't get as near to it as a fox would.

In contrast to the incarnationist Hopkins, she suspects that nature, as Emerson said in his essay "Nature," may be "but one stuff," ontologically indifferent in its particulars and more radical than can be gleaned from its "dream-like variety." Nonetheless, she regards the *persons* of the Here as preciously particular, and is a poet of moral and political exigencies. "Stuff" is to be differentiated at both this level and at the level of trees and birds. She is far from Guest's happy recourse to cardboard instead of flesh. Recall that Guest does not honor the down-home notion of "stuff"; apparitions within the cyclical flow of reality are substance enough.

Graham is also at one with Emerson in finding that a "disappointment is felt in every landscape . . . [a]lways a referred existence, an absence, never a presence and satisfaction." She is clearly in the great line of Emerson, Thoreau, and Whitman, the American line of pagan transcendence-hunger, but she is more haunted than they ever were by the possibility that the person, unable to wrap Self in the disintegrating moth-wings of Time, is nothing, the more so because Time, stronger than Self, itself equals nothing. Naturally she feels beset, creature as she is whose bit of life wills to break through to vitality's whole wild freedom, where it would be qualitatively superior to time. She is a small bit of life on the earth that would make so bold as to enwrap Time.

Graham can feel guilt for not being open to the natural world as an immanent perfection in itself, as against something from which the mind is free to pluck this and that. The poem "Guantánamo" in *Sea Change* (2008) addresses this guilt vis-à-vis nature along with shared guilt for the *taking capture* of one's supposed enemies. Here it is important to emphasize that Graham is as much a poet of historical crimes, even of history *as* crime, as she is of the dark intent of the existing universe.

> Waning moon. Rising now. Creak, it goes. Deep
>   over the exhausted continents. I wonder says my
>   fullness. Nobody nobody says the room in which I
>   lie very still in the
> darkness watching. Your heart says the moon, waning & rising still
>   further. Where is it. Your
>   keep, your eyes your trigger
>   finger your spine your reasoning . . .

Her room is as a keep in Guantánamo in that there is "nobody there," nobody to answer if she calls out. For who is she, what is her place? At the same time, she is a keeper. There are acts, she says to herself (and of course to the reader), being

>   committed in your name, & your captives arriving
>   at *your* detention center, there, in your
> eyes, the lockup, deep in your pupil, the softening-up, you paying all your
>   attention
>   out, your eyes, your cell, your keep, your hold,
> after all it is yours, yes, what you have taken in, grasp it, grasp
>   this, there is no law . . .[2]

That we use "coercive interrogation techniques," naming, reclassifying, withholding things from themselves in appropriative, deconstructible words—this is to dazzle ourselves with our own nonexistence. Graham thus sums up modernity's discovery of the guilt of being an imperial subject, with a takeover language and a power-will. The poem includes a list of our human abuses of the earth.

The long line that became Graham's specialty beginning with her third book, the great collection *The End of Beauty* (1987), is a "paying out" of space enough for her description and thought to gain traction in the spread of a location. The bunched analytical shorter lines alternating with long lines in "Guantánamo" are, instead, a graph for how little possession of the ground there actually is.

As for Guantánamo Bay, it is itself no doubt consciously *used* in this poem about the horrid human drive to use things, at the same that this use illustrates the drive. Here, Graham (one could be sticky and say a "supposed person," Dickinson's phrase to put off Thomas Wentworth Higginson's sniffings into her privacy) suffers less from being taken from herself by the keeper time than from the moral guilt of being one who keeps. It would be so cleansing to lose oneself in what is truly dazzling, the natural world. Might it not also be what is required of one?

> ... Moon, who will write
> the final poem? Your veil is flying, its uselessness makes us feel there is
>   still time, it is about two now,
> you are asking me to lose myself.
>   In this overflowing of my eye,
> I do.

Here, *seeing* triumphs over *thinking*, sensory neutrality over anxious thought, or so we would believe if the imagined speaker were not still talking. The performative "I do" is, of course, still an act of self-reflection. What is wanted is not to be "grasped"; it must come through surrendering to it.

Graham's sensibility—usually but not always at once ravenous and doubting—is capable of producing exquisite writing; but power is her usual note. She rarely stops, or poses as having stopped, to soak up the moment. With notable exceptions, such as her poem on her father's death, she hasn't felt the necessity to express tenderness, nor is she given to playfulness. Instead, with her impasto syntactical elaborations, she resembles Milton, who, as Hazlitt said, "grapples with and exhausts his subject" ("On Gusto"). She must muscle her way toward disclosing (really *feeling*) the improbable importance of being alive in this place and time, with only a cellular voltage of awareness in the inanimacy of the universe. She would fill "the blank in which one sees," "the blank in which one is," so as to be an "I am" ("Dusk Shore Prayer," *Never*, 2002). From the eye to the soul of things: an Emersonian path.

With the exception of "Sundown" (again, in *Place*) and "Dementia" and "Incarnation" (in *Fast*, 2017), I will continue to bypass Graham's greater poems, a number of which I have touched on elsewhere, and stay with poems that expose in short order her aporias, the holes she can't bridge, as *she* is the first to know—hot spots where (typically) crisis is faced and borne, but not eased, though in "Guantánamo" the struggle to write "the final poem," to be at least *that* useful ("Your veil is flying, its uselessness makes us feel there is / still time") is putatively put aside for a pure act of seeing.

Elsewhere, she reprises Christian and Romantic ardors for connection with a transcendent meaning, or at least a transdescendent reality ("the underneath"). She reprises, for instance, Johann Fichte, who said that to "discern, . . . seize, and live wholly" in the Divine Idea pervading the universe is the condition of all knowledge and freedom (I here re-echo Thomas Carlyle's summary). She is at least as contemporary as Deleuze, a philosopher of a single fold of Being, in which the sensible and the intelligible are united and whose perpetual mutation constitutes the inanimate "Life" of the universe, a "One-All." (Foucault: "Perhaps one day this century will be known as Deleuzian.") At the same time she's even more contemporary than Deleuze in that, unlike him, she is beset by waves of deconstructions (starting from Nietzsche on): all those attacks on the signifying organization of things that make a naïveté of the bright blood. Former spiritual supports—including the assumption of universality inherited from philosophers, strivings for ontological purchase-power in language—have reached her exhausted, barely alive, and expiring. No wonder she goes back to Leibniz and his "folds," lest the universe roll by like a flaming hoop.

The ratio of thought to description changes often in Graham's poems as she tries different ways to find what Paul Celan called "the One sole secret [that] mixes in with the word, forever." Mental power and "a journey-heavy" mouth (Celan again) take turns as desire lives or dies. Her description is love unsatisfied, the analysis is unsatisfied inquiry. Description is a green eye, analysis a black eye. Questions (so many questions) finally overshadow the physical grass and water, the ravens, the flickering fish. By exception, there is a sudden glut of sights and sensations in "Sundown" as a galloping horse and its rider pass the speaker, going into the waves where she stands with her feet in the water and striking thunder into her sensorium and pounding into extinction her tendency to inquire. Instead, she sees; sees "prints on / wet sand deep and immediately filled by thousands of / sandfleas thrilled to the / declivities in succession" as light carves out the declivities "with / shadow," a "glow on each ridge," and still more.

When Graham really sees, she's relentless, as in section 7 of "Impressionism":

> Swollen, thick, pin-cushioned-up with fat and slack-dead open
> pores,
> the bleached-out jumbo turkey-leg and thigh draws up
> knotted to this yellow string—eleven crabs attached, all feeding
>   wildly on their
>   catch, clacking
> their armors onto each other, class embedded . . . (JG 262)

The description makes a mockery of the title. It exposes the brutal oral drive of creatures, sees the rage for destruction in a child who looks got up by an impressionist, the "child's hammer / taken to [the crabs] / one by one—fast— only one scrambling across the bridge today / to get away." Just so, the terrifying poem "Dementia" depicts, thousands of years before "the clenched fist of the present instant," the "first introduction / to what might have been a species—a first try a failure but full of nervous sparks," which evolves into "the pleasures of nihilism," hands that "want to / inflict pain on the powerless the weak the poor," as once they did on the animals they killed and ate ("me stilled and dragged," she says, identifying for a moment with the prey, "opened, shared, meat"; she sees them "scribbling me again on / the walls of the cave").

Rare but not unexpected in her work is the kind of seeing asserted, if not without doubts, in "Dusk Shore Prayer" in *Never* (2002): a seeing avid for a spilled golden writing redeeming the wilderness of the world, much as in the paintings of Frederick Church and other American painters of his era:

>   sun making of each
>   mile-long wave-retreat
> a golden translucent forward downgoing,
> golden sentences writ on clearest moving waters (JG 222)

But she must collect herself and admit that the sentences are "meaninglessness on (not in) the moving of the / waters." "It's a trick," she says in brackets as sharp as thorns—a trick of the eye "wanting . . . to catch and take /

dominant final-hold, feel the thickest rope of / waterlipped / scripting / to be producing a thing that speaks," wanting "to believe this truly, not in metaphor." The poem dizzies one with its tremblings between affirmation and negation. It claims at the least to attain to a "stump interpretation," never mind that a stump is dead, its inner circulation having been terminated. In any case, day and poem end in darkness, "the path back barely findable." Yes, be distrustful—but must you be?—of the feeling that, as Yves Bonnefoy put it, "poetry may be on the verge of knowing whatever presence is capable of opening itself up to us."

But at the very least the horror of existence can make Graham want to experience (that is, to suffer), "the gash of likeness," as she frames it in "Dusk Shore Prayer." It is to settle for wild jouissance: "O then, Desire! father of Jouissance," she quotes from the sixteenth-century *Zepheria* poet. To be close enough to the invisible to resemble it, what masochistic joy! It would mean being violated by ontology, as Donne understood it when he said, "Batter my heart, three-personed God." Wasn't birth itself the first violation?

An extreme example of the acute and dramatic seesaw of description and thinking in Graham's work, as against their entanglement in "Dusk Shore Prayer," is "Prayer," the first poem in *Never*. The poem itself ends in the antithesis of prayer. The immediate subject is the instinctive self-current formed by minnows inside a larger current of water. Wonderful the way the minnows make of themselves a

> visual current, one that cannot freight or sway by
> minutest fractions the water's downdrafts and upswirls, the
> dockside cycles of finally-arriving boat-wakes, there where
> they hit deeper resistance, water that seems to burst into
> itself (it has those layers), a real current though mostly
> invisible sending into the visible (minnows) arrowing
>   motion that forces change—
> this is freedom. This is the force of faith. (JG 219)

But already negativity is poised to enter in. Why note that the minnows' current "cannot freight or sway / by the minutest fractions" the boat-wakes' backwash (the writing here is characteristically thick in texture, the compounds assisting), if you are going to say of their vital current "this is freedom." You say it if you hardly mean it, or you mean only that they are free of doubt in their involuntary staying together.

At this juncture the speaker's brain fires off savagely disappointed statements about life, as if involuntarily, as if such a psychic collapse had been waiting to happen. First comes the blast of the following complaints:

> Nobody gets
> what they want. Never again are you the same. The longing
> is to be pure. What you get is to be changed. More and more by
> each glistening minute, through which infinity threads itself,
> also oblivion, of course, the aftershocks of something
> at sea.

Time, then, is only that through which an arrowing "infinity threads itself," producing moment-by-moment oblivion. There has been a shock followed still, followed forever, by aftershocks. (Graham thus retroactively turns into a figure of the present cosmos, "those finally-arriving boat-wakes"; she wastes nothing in a poem, there must be layers, folds, a self-gathering against time's collapses and scatterings.) Being is trauma.

You might think that the speaker had done now. After all, she has already recognized a spirit-burn from which no one can heal. But she has yet to complete her realization of unfreedom by abandoning hope for her "Self" as a project, an anthology of memories, a collection of meanings. She resigns time:

> ... Here, hands full of sand, letting it sift through
> in the wind, I look in and say take this, this is
> what I have saved, take this, hurry. And if I listen
> now? Listen, I was not saying anything. It was only
>   something I did. I could not choose words. I am free to go.
> I cannot of course come back. Not to this. Never.
> It is a ghost posed on my lips. Here: never.

In a fine pique, she all but throws herself away, sand to sand. She surrenders expectations of a continuous "vital" current in time. (In "Dementia," she says "this minute is pecking at your shell—that's the sound—percussion is / our mind"—as if it weren't punishment enough to be "moleculed to death" from conception onward, as she puts it in "Incarnation," and surrounded by constant ear noise, call it background noise, "like 2000 miles of shorebreak at once.") Thus the speaker underscores and scores on her own lips time's brute behavior. It is her own thought that has done her in, quit her, in the build-up of her disgust at time's ghost-productions. She disowns even her speech: after all, she didn't choose the words just uttered, whether because they were provoked out of her or because, as Nietzsche reasoned, thinking thinks us, our billions of neurons think us. Only action is left, and it is conceived as departure, like a death.

Though these ideas are familiar in Graham's work, there is nothing like this rapid ticking-off of negative thought elsewhere in her poetry, or in any poetry. The minnows become almost instantly an allegory of life in a forced condition. The concluding statements, taking up over half of the one-page poem, explode from the realization the minnows afford. They acknowledge the weight and sway of a cosmic catastrophe whose signature is time.

I have not dwelt enough on Graham's sometimes terrified concern about others and, in quite a different vein, her reasoned-out détentes with the "planet," her eye "staying upon [its] back and riding [it]": "I want to lie here arms / spread / on your almost eternal turn . . . / how huge you / carrying / me are—and there is / never hurry" ("Earth," *Place*), and still other facets and counterfacets of her work; there is simply too much of it, too much wealth in it, to bring satisfactorily forward in a short essay. What I would stress is that, spiritually (and this is a large part of her significance for us), Graham continues, and not by choice, the tragic and epic quality and tonality of the first half of the twentieth century, the shadows of which, after all, have lengthened into the twenty-first, though much contemporary art does not, will not, take its lessons upon its flesh (what little flesh it has); its mode is defense. I have suggested that Barbara Guest is in this category, though she holds an honorable place there. After all, she wrote in "The Hungry Knight,"

> Heavy is the literature
> bred on the rock,
> filled with epiphany
> night has known since infancy. (BG 498)

Graham sees modern life in the "enormous perspectives in which it really looms," to go back to where I began, with the words of Chapman, and suffers from her exclusion from any secret, any reason for exultation, hidden in that immensity. To again paraphrase Chapman, the power in her work is not only a surface articulating power but power that she unconsciously absorbs (not least from the country's will to domination), and that she unconsciously as well as consciously conveys to us.

Gone in her most recent poems is her "dream of the unified field," which provided the title for her first selection and which was anyway acknowledged to be a dream. Gone, even, in the most recent poems, is the desire to dominate the external world, to, as she said, "make it mine": "no more exploding, no more smoldering, no more, / inside, a splinter colony, new world, possession" ("Materialism," 1993). We have seen that in "Guantánamo" Graham still stands self-accused as outrageous in her drive to dominate the reality she inhabits. She is still learning to have done with the desire to do so. But it is hard. Will she then no longer contribute to the last gasp of metaphysics? That remains to be seen. There is a need and a force in her that must go in some direction, even if she has to turn it against herself, her very existence. It is a good thing for her and for us that she can keep writing poems, poems that resound with her clamor and the clamor of Being.

Notes

1. Barbara Guest, *The Collected Poems of Barbara Guest*, ed. Hadley Hayden Guest (Middletown, CT: Wesleyan University Press, 2008), 133; subsequent references to this volume abbreviated as BG.
2. Jorie Graham, *From the New World: Poems 1976–2014* (New York: Ecco Press, 2013), 270; subsequent references to this volume abbreviated as JG.

CHAPTER 15

Ashbery's Power and the Phantom "I"

LAURA QUINNEY

THE GENERAL RECEPTION of John Ashbery identifies him primarily with challenging avant-garde poetics. In a compelling recent essay on the density of poetic language, for example, the philosopher Ronald de Sousa distinguishes Ashbery's poetry for its linguistic experimentation: "there is a dreamlike disconnection between the elements found in any particular sequence of words in a randomly chosen poem," and "words are deliberately located in highly improbable contexts."[1] To stress the dislocations of sense and diction in Ashbery's poetics is to focus on the "postmodern" Ashbery, profoundly influential and imitated, celebrated for innovation, and renowned for obscurity. Yet as many Ashbery imitators have discovered to their cost, linguistic experiment does not in itself create powerful poetry. It is misleading to locate Ashbery's own power, and his originality, in his avant-garde poetics alone. As the poet Allen Grossman once remarked, Ashbery's poetic resources are, after all, "traditional."[2] To my mind, this means that Ashbery remains a lyric poet in the British Romantic tradition (lyric poetry in English from the 1780s to the present), in which a poem dramatizes the experience of a single subject confronting its singular subjectivity—that is, confronting its thoughts and feelings, but also the very consciousness of having them, and undergoing their changes. Ashbery once said that his poetry is about "the experience of experience," and I take him to mean just this: that the poems track the experience of having a consciousness reacting to experience.[3]

Ashbery's poetry has a general purchase, despite appearances. He begins from his own consciousness and its "experience of experience," but takes his individual perspective to stand in for the common, in the grand manner of the "Intimations Ode" and other major philosophical statements in lyric form. However, he does not pursue this Romantic aim with the straightforwardness, the *relative* straightforwardness, of the Romantic or the Victorian or the twentieth-century autobiographical lyric, and this is where the dislocations of sense and diction enter. What makes Ashbery compelling and original is not that he invented a new poetics per se but that he invented a poetics that newly, and stirringly, conveys what it is like to be a subject. In special, it conveys the fundamental experience of subjectivity—its peculiar pathos, one might say—which is its experience of its own insubstantiality. This theme is not unknown to earlier Romantic and post-Romantic poetry, but Ashbery gives it forthright expression and vivid meaning through new poetic form. He gives the intuition more force than it ever had before.

Out of the miasma of rhetorics, a phantasmal "I" surfaces to utter an appeal, and to make a claim on our attention. The "I" remains phantasmal in two senses: first, it brings with it no robust sense of self within the poem—no empirical location or identity—and second, within the poem it comes and goes lightly and, it seems, capriciously. Most Ashbery poems (after the early experiments) are haunted by their own ghostly "I," floated from moment to moment, flickering, disappearing, then reemerging amid the whirling syncretism of language and imagery in which it is expressing itself. Note that I do not say: fighting to express itself, fighting through the thicket of words and the flotsam and jetsam of the cultural collective. It is tempting to think of Ashbery's poetics as taking this form—the struggle of the singular I to clarify its consciousness through the medium of a corrupted tongue—but that is quite wrong: the bewildered subject in Ashbery is bewildered by experience, and by its own subjectivity, not by the inauthenticity, on the one hand, or the chaos, on the other, of the linguistic medium. In Ashbery, intransigence to expression most often stems from the subject's reluctance to see and say what at the same time it is pressed to see and say. To complicate matters, the "I" is sometimes shrouded in impersonal constructions ("It makes hot tears spurt," from "Self-Portrait in a Convex Mirror"), or in the pronouns "we" or "one" and their possessive forms ("To step free at last, minuscule on the gigantic plateau— / This was our ambition," from "Soonest Mended"), and sometimes its existence is merely implied.[4] Yet it is this trace of subjectivity that lifts the poems beyond linguistic virtuosity to poetic power. Ashbery demonstrates—in one of the chief fascinations of his poetry—how vestigial the "I" can be, an "I" barely there in the words, and still succeed in evoking the pathos of subjectivity.

Let us begin our investigation of the phantom "I" with a short poem, in hope that its brevity will bring out the essentials. Here is "This Room," the first poem in *Your Name Here*.

> The room I entered was a dream of this room.
> Surely all those feet on the sofa were mine.
> The oval portrait
> of a dog was me at an early age.
> Something shimmers, something is hushed up.
>
> We had macaroni for lunch every day
> except Sunday, when a small quail was induced
> to be served to us. Why do I tell you these things?
> You are not even here.[5]

The potential for pathos in the poem, though hinted at in the line "Something shimmers, something is hushed up," abruptly emerges in the last two sentences, with their notice of absence and loss. Now readers are compelled to rework their understanding of the previous lines: what had seemed some sort of idle reportage turns out to have been fond recollection—the telling of surreal dreams, the faintly Proustian memory of daily routines—that is proper to an intimate relationship. The speaker, it turns out, was retailing these odd bits in a certain spirit, the expectation of interest and indulgence, which has been brought up short. Of a sudden self-conscious, the speaker catches himself speaking into a void. (The adverb "even" plays its own role, suggesting a hint of self-reproach: the reverie might have failed as a gesture of intimacy even if you were here, but as it is . . .) *Your Name Here* is dedicated to Pierre Martory, the French poet, and Ashbery's lover, who had died a couple of years before its publication. "This Room" may be taken as an elegy for Martory, but it goes beyond elegy by dovetailing the lover's relation to his lost beloved with the poet's relation to his reader. For the paradoxical salutation, "You are not even here," applies to the reader as well as the dead, obviously not in quite the same sense, and yet, as far as the poet is concerned, in something like the same sense. One audience for these stray personal facts is gone, and the other is purely notional: whatever readers the poem may eventually have will not share space or time with the poet.

The pathos of the poem is not lessened, but increased, by the ambiguity of the reference in "You." The same goes for the title of the poem, "This Room," in which the deictic adjective "this," which ought to point to one room in particular, actually points to several, literal and metaphorical: the room in which the poet writes, the room of the poem itself (following the old pun on "stanza"), the moment in which the poem is composed or read, the enclosure of subjectivity (an "oubliette," as Ashbery suggests elsewhere).[6] The phrase "this room" works to delimit—in its singularity and evanescence—any and all of these possible references. The phrase distills; it is a pure poignancy. And so too with the "I" and "You" of the last two lines, stripped down to the bare pronouns, without identity. The memory and the dream, manifestly irreal, funny and so close to nonsense, stand in for what might have been empirical information; they tell us nothing historical about the "I," but rather, as rhetorical ciphers, they stand in for the kind of thing the "I" might have wished to divulge. The "I" is missing its "You." Yet the poem is not "about" that fact. It does not announce but *dramatizes* the movement of thought and feeling in the "I," briefly lulled into forgetting the loss it awakes with a start to remember. More subtly, a customary love inspires it to reminisce, to impart, but then the act of imparting recalls the absence of the one with whom the reminiscence was to be shared. The poem descends from Wordsworth's "Surprised by Joy":

> impatient as the Wind
> I turned to share the transport—Oh! With whom
> But Thee, long buried in the silent Tomb . . .
> Love, faithful love, recalled Thee to my mind—
> But how could I forget Thee?[7]

"This Room" evokes the experience of a singular subject—but the "I" is singular only in the philosophical sense that it is *lone*, not in the empirical sense that it belongs to a specific character, a person, whether of a real or fictional nature. Even though one wants to introduce biographical information about Ashbery and Martory, the subject detaches itself from context. The speaker of "Surprised by Joy" is a man with a particular history he plainly draws upon. By contrast, Ashbery's "I" is an "I" of pure subjectivity: it floats beyond identity, and that is in part why I call it a "phantom" I.

Sometimes the "I" in Ashbery appears to have reached an extreme in which it has become meaningless, a mere dummy in a piece of rhetorical code ("It was great to see you the other day / at the carnival. My enchiladas were delicious, / and I hope that yours were too"). But the trace of subjectivity, the trace of feeling in the banal or clichéd or nonsensical utterance, lingers and in context contributes to the emotional matrix of the poem. "Proximity," for example, the poem whose opening lines I just quoted, continues:

> I wanted to fulfill your dream of me
>
> in some suitable way. Giving away my new gloves,
> for instance, or putting a box around all that's wrong with us.
>
> But these gutta-percha lamps do not whisper on our behalf.
> Now sometimes in the evenings, I am lonely
>
> with dread. A rambunctious wind fills the pine
> at my doorstep, the woodbine is enchanted,
>
> and I must be off before the clock strikes
> whatever hour it is intent on.
>
> Do not leave me in this wilderness!
> Or, if you do, pay me to stay behind.[8]

The banality about the enchiladas takes on some content from the earnest sentiment that follows—"I wanted to fulfill your dream of me"—although this is then deflated by a further banality: "in some suitable way." The poem as it goes on shuttles between abject pathos ("I am lonely / with dread") and undercutting self-mockery ("Or, if you do, pay me to stay behind"), interspersed with lines that are emotionally suggestive if not wholly sensible ("these gutta-percha lamps do not whisper on our behalf"). The "I" is not consistently expressive—it returns to a rhetorical flavor in "I must be off"—and we would expect, in theory, that the first-person perspective and its anguish would be compromised by such rhetorical uses of the word "I," as well as by the self-mockery and near-nonsense. Yet they are not: quite the reverse. The reader has no doubt about the feelings of the subject in the poem: tentative longing, foreboding solitude, fear of death.

But I ought not to imply that it takes an "I" to summon an "I"—in other words, that a poem only creates a first-person perspective by explicitly using the first person. The assumption of subjectivity is basic to the lyric: in the lyric, typically, a "voice," a singular perspective, emerges over the course of the poem, no matter how impersonal the formulations or seemingly "objective" the point of view. Poets who abjure the lyric "I" may still conjure the lyric subject. Stevens, for example, shifts from "I" to "we" and "one," but—depending on context—the evasive pronoun may only veil the "I" it means: "One feels a malady here, a malady" ("Banal Sojourn").[9] Even a whole poem of Stevens written in large, impersonal philosophical generalizations projects a lyric "I" behind them by hinting at the human passion that has inspired them and the consequences for human feeling of believing or disbelieving in them: "Do not speak to us of the greatness of poetry / Of the torches wisping in the ground" ("The Man with the Blue Guitar").[10] What is different about Ashbery? At this point, we should recur to the "postmodern" elements of his poetry. For typically, what creates first-person utterance without the use of the first person is unity of perspective, and the poem's coherence at other linguistic levels, in diction, style, and sense. But Ashbery scatters all of this. His first-person pathos may be traditional, but his poetic modes of generating it are not. He does not make use of the unities—at least not the more apparent ones—that earlier poets do.

I say "not the more apparent ones"—diction, style, sense, point of view—because I do think that Ashbery's poems have *thematic* unity, partly established by subtle connections among seemingly aleatory utterances, and partly by tonal emphases and shifts related to ghostly appearances of a first person. Let us take an example. "Soonest Mended" begins with a hodgepodge of diction and imagery—the jargon of pop psychology, a learned reference to *Orlando Furioso*, an oblique comment about "needing to be rescued," a clip of *Happy Hooligan*. It is hard to find one's bearings until the poem says that "we," who "were always having to be rescued," now find ourselves "confused." The reader does not know who "we" are, nor what "our" trouble is, but he or she does gather that there is a chronology unfolding, booming activity leading over a period of time to disorientation and dismay. Substance begins to cohere over the next number of lines, though they offer no empirical information, imagistic coherence, or perspicuous psychological description.

> Only by that time we were in another chapter and confused
> About how to receive this latest piece of information.
> *Was* it information? Weren't we rather acting this out
> For someone's benefit, thoughts in a mind
> With room enough and to spare for our little problems (so they began to seem).
> Our daily quandary about food and the rent and the bills to be paid?
> To reduce all this to a small variant,
> To step free at last, minuscule on the gigantic plateau—
> This was our ambition, to be small and clear and free.
> Alas, the summer's energy wanes quickly.
> A moment and it is gone. And no longer
> May we make the necessary arrangements, simple as they are.
> Our star was brighter perhaps when it had water in it.[11]

The passage is strong in emotion and in persuasive transition between tones. There is even a narrative, though it does not take the form of recounting facts nor of a logical or verbal development: the narrative is a narrative of feeling, the story of a sentimental education. We follow the sentiments and their progression: from embattled existential longing to disappointment, defeat, self-doubt, and belatedness. An Ashbery sentence need not make propositional sense to communicate emotion (compare Gertrude Stein). "Our star was brighter perhaps when it had water in it" is a moving line, though it verges on the absurd. It conveys the feeling of defeat through basic structures (the comparatives "brighter" and "[once] it had"), and suggestive associations (the Romantic coupling of star, soul, and transcendence; the visual image of an eye bright with tears). Even the qualification "perhaps" has its pathos in context: as a symptom of hesitancy and self-doubt, or as part of an effort to resist self-indulgence. "Alas, the summer's energy wanes quickly. / A moment and it is gone" and "no longer / May we make the necessary arrangements" are moving because, given the rigorously abstract context, the reader understands their meaning to be metaphorical; the subject is not climatology or logistics, but self-loss. (And "Alas" carries its own elegiac freight.) The reader would not expect euphemistic and bureaucratic language like "make the necessary arrangements" to succeed in creating poetic pathos, but the linguistic frame ("And no longer . . . simple as they are") as well as the tone and meaning within the sentimental context transvaluate the banality. (Ashbery has been very successful at finding new techniques for transvaluating banality.) What is striking is that the emotion of the passage should be so strong—and hence, the presence of a singular subject experiencing it (despite the "we")—when the means of evoking it are so fragmentary and allusive.

The phantasmal "I," however, is not merely a literary effect: it is not merely that the ghost of an "I" appears in spite of—or by means of—a scattered utterance. The ghostliness of the "I" expands into a thematic feature of Ashbery's poetry. His poems regularly adumbrate the "I" or self's experience of itself—its own being—as phantasmal, where phantasmal means variable, elusive, insubstantial. A tenuous and flickering thing, the self loses sight of itself in the welter of language, encounter, and event. When conscious of itself, it feels bewilderment. Somehow in arrears of its own experience, it is displaced from agency, comprehension, and self-knowledge. It is submerged, it is drowning, yet still it craves life; it is full of desire. The next lines of "Soonest Mended" convey this floundering passion:

> Now there is no question of that, but only
> Of holding on to the hard earth so as not to get thrown off
> With an occasional dream, a vision: a robin flies across
> The upper corner of the window, you brush your hair away
> And cannot quite see, or a wound will flash
> Against the sweet faces of the others, something like:
> This is what you wanted to hear, so why
> Did you think of listening to something else? We are all talkers
> It is true, but underneath the talk lies
> The moving and not wanting to be moved, the loose
> Meaning, untidy and simple like a threshing floor.[12]

The drift, the uncertainty, the unsettling: these aspects of style are also aspects of feeling. Even where the abyssal experience of selfhood does not provide the topic of an Ashbery poem (as it does in "Self-Portrait in a Convex Mirror"), the poetics makes it a corollary theme. Or perhaps this is putting it the wrong way round: in fact, it seems that Ashbery evolved his style to "answer" what was for him a basic intuition about selfhood. Therefore his style and theme often intertwine to the one end.

For the linguistic anarchy tallies with the existential anxiety of the phantom "I." Consider, for example, how dread interacts with verbal dislocation in the first stanza of "The Inchcape Rock."

> Prop up the "meaning,"
> take the trash out, the dog for a walk,
> give the old balls a scratch, apologize for three things
> by Friday—oh quiet noumenon
> of my soul, is this right?
> You lost the key and the answer is inside
> somewhere, and where are you going to breathe?
> The box is shut that knew you
> and all your friends,
> voices that could have spoken in your behalf...[13]

Poetic anarchy runs through the lines (though less than in some Ashbery poems): dictional clash ("balls" vs. "noumenon"), mixed metaphor ("You lost the key... and where are you going to breathe?"), touches of obscurity ("Prop up the 'meaning'"), sudden eruptions of pathos ("voices that could have spoken in your behalf"). Yet the movement of feeling is unmistakable: the quailing of "oh quiet noumenon," the self-reproach of "You lost the key," the anxiety of "where are you going to breathe?," the bereavement and loss of the past in "The box is shut that knew you / and all your friends." Even the random banalities of the opening lines turn out to be meaningful: they cipher the life of dutiful routine that prompts quiet desperation and the existential query, "is this right?" Like other Ashbery poems, this one speaks not *despite* its linguistic anarchy but *through* it. Still, it is not pat: the anarchy is both anxious and anxiety provoking. It carries the existential anxiety of the subject lost in itself and in the world. I use the word "carries" here rather than "conveys" or "reflects" or "communicates" in order to circumvent what seems, here, an irrelevant distinction between content and form. When it comes to the transmission of affect, the wildness of words *is* the discombobulation of the "I."

I do not know that any amount of close reading can demonstrate this, or that this claim is really susceptible of proof. Also, it obviously does not hold for every moment in Ashbery. Qualifications are called for, chief among them that the discombobulation of "I" and poetry results in humor as often as pathos, or in some combination of the two, as in the final lines of "Gentle Reader":

> Soon there is something to be said for everything,
> he said, whiplash, whippets; why even my identity
> is strange to me now, a curiosity. When someone comes later,
> who will I be talking with? The erroneous vision
> made no mention of this. Its conquering agenda is complete,
> and we, of course, are incomplete, destined to ourselves
> and its fitful version of eternity:
> the one with chapter titles.
> More worldliness to celebrate. And yet, someone
> Will take it from you, needy thing.[14]

The only use of the first-person singular ("who will I be talking with") appears in a quotation ("he said") while the lyric "I" is veiled under a first-person plural ("we, of course, are incomplete"). Yet the first-person perspective flickers in and out of the passage, subtly felt in the personal pathos of "we are ... destined to ourselves" and "yet, someone will take it from you." The humor of self-mockery ("needy thing") complements rather than undermines the existential disappointment ("And yet, someone / Will take it from you"). For the whole passage concerns the failure of the self to be what it seemed to promise it was: now it confronts the elusiveness of identity, the shortfall of knowledge, the apprehension of smallness and weakness, of domination by greater forces:

> Its conquering agenda is complete,
> and we, of course, are incomplete, destined to ourselves.

The poem ends with the expectation that the future will bring more losses, and the use of the second person works to intimate the "I"'s sense of helplessness better than the use of the first person would (try rewriting the line as "And yet, someone / Will take it from me, needy thing," which has a self-assertive flavor). I can identify these thematic meanings well enough; what I am asking you to *hear* is that the rhetorical wanderings of the passage—the shifting pronouns, the inconsistent metaphors, the patchwork of dictions, the apparently mercurial point of view—participate in the self's sense of its incoherence and vulnerability.

But why am I asking this of you? You are not even here, or I am not. The self will be, and is now, absent to itself in a way that remains nonetheless accessible to intuition. Thus the self's incoherence does not cancel out but rather measures its vulnerability. As Ashbery conveys better than any other poet, it is through exposure to the fragility of selfhood that we experience or, in Kierkegaard's terms, "deepen" our subjectivity.[15] For Kierkegaard, deepening our subjectivity, or "becoming subjective," remains an ethical task, the task of willing to be the belated and elusive self one actually is, and though we shirk the task and flee from it, it continues to impose itself upon us through the thin veils of our evasion.

> No matter how much the despairing person avoids [being himself], no matter how successfully he has completely lost himself (especially the case in the form of despair that is ignorance of being in despair) and lost himself in such a manner that the loss is not at all detectable—eternity nevertheless will make it manifest that his condition was despair and will nail him to himself so that his torment will still be that he cannot rid himself of his self, and it will become obvious that he was just imagining that he had succeeded in doing so. Eternity is obliged to do this, because to have a self, to be a self, is the greatest concession, an infinite concession, given to man, but is also eternity's claim upon him.[16]

Kierkegaard's disturbing image of selfhood as a Crucifixion makes it clear that he thinks of subjectivity not simply as pathos, but as Passion. Yet one need not fall in with his Christian apologetics, nor even with his ethics, nor even with his language of "eternity," to grant that "to have a self, to be a self, is the greatest concession, an infinite concession, given to man," poor as it is. Like a rubbing of an inscription in stone, Ashbery's poems bring out the contours of selfhood and communicate its bewildering nature, not in spite of but by means of his avant-garde poetics. The value of his poetry (or one of its values) lies in bringing to the consciousness of his readers the fragility of subjectivity that they already experience. It is inaccurate to say that he dispenses with the "lyric I," and ill-imagined to think he should.

Notes

1. Ronald de Sousa, "The Dense and the Transparent: Reconciling Opposites," in *The Philosophy of Poetry*, ed. John Gibson (Oxford: Oxford University Press, 2015), 52.
2. Allen Grossman, *Against Our Vanishing: Winter Conversations With Allen Grossman on the Theory and Practice of Poetry*, ed. Mark Halliday (Boston: Rowan Tree Press, 1981), 49.
3. A. Poulin Jr., "The Experience of Experience: A Conversation with John Ashbery," *Michigan Quarterly Review* 20, no. 3 (Summer 1981): 242–55, http://hdl.handle.net/2027/spo.act2080.0020.003:20.
4. John Ashbery, "Self-Portrait in a Convex Mirror," in *Self-Portrait in a Convex Mirror* (New York: Viking, 1975), 69; and "Soonest Mended," in *Selected Poems* (New York: Viking Penguin, 1985), 87.
5. John Ashbery, "This Room," in *Your Name Here* (New York: Farrar, Straus and Giroux, 2001), 3.
6. John Ashbery, "Your Name Here," in *Your Name Here*, 127.
7. William Wordsworth, "Surprised by Joy," in *Romantic Poetry and Prose*, ed. Harold Bloom and Lionel Trilling (New York: Oxford University Press, 1973), 229.
8. John Ashbery, "Proximity," in *Wakefulness* (New York: Farrar, Straus and Giroux, 1998), 55.
9. Wallace Stevens, "Banal Sojourn," in *The Collected Poems of Wallace Stevens* (New York: Vintage Books, 2015), 66.
10. Wallace Stevens, "The Man with the Blue Guitar," in *The Collected Poems*, 177.
11. John Ashbery, "Soonest Mended," in *Selected Poems*, 87.
12. Ibid., 87–88.
13. John Ashbery, "The Inchcape Rock," in *A Worldly Country* (New York: Ecco Press, 2007), 32.

14. John Ashbery, "Gentle Reader," in *Wakefulness*, 79.
15. See the chapter entitled "Becoming Subjective," in Søren Kierkegaard, *Concluding Unscientific Postscript*, ed. and trans. Howard V. Hong and Edna H. Hong (Princeton, NJ: Princeton University Press, 1992), 129–98.
16. Søren Kierkegaard, *The Sickness unto Death*, ed. and trans. Howard V. Hong and Edna H. Hong (Princeton, NJ: Princeton University Press, 1980), 21.

Conclusion

ROBERT FAGGEN AND ROBERT VON HALLBERG

At the end of two volumes, one wants to call this collection a just representation of current literary opinion, a roll of the most active candidates for survival, but the essays more accurately indicate poets on behalf of whom critics think advocacy is now warranted. To those who wrote for these volumes, the status of Louise Glück, Robert Duncan, W. S. Merwin, Robert Creeley, Robert Hayden, Allen Ginsberg, Frank Bidart, Robert Lowell, Sylvia Plath, John Berryman, and others not in these pages may stand in less immediate need of explicit advocacy. In that sense, the essays characterize a temporary state of literary judgment but do not constitute a fair summary of the poetic achievements of the past seventy years. The promotional efforts of publishers—in encouraging editors to review their authors, in arranging for books to be signed and sold at readings—take effect in a brief period; ditto for awards. Reviews and blogs directly encourage sales, but are read once and then discarded. Reviewers are unconcerned with endurance. Critical essays have a longer shelf life and promote not a sale but the survival of reputations. Their work is done gradually as general readers, students, literary scholars, and editors find their way to these and other patient assessments.

Evaluative criticism more or less began with Johnson's *Lives of the English Poets* (1779). He came to that labor after a consortium of forty-two London booksellers and six printers solicited his collaboration with an advance. They meant, with his support, to sell anthologies of poets (not selected by Johnson). Within two years of their solicitation of the critic, they issued fifty-eight volumes of poetry; they meant to get their product to market ahead of competitors. Johnson accepted the constraints of commerce, as few critics now do. Colleges and universities provide livelihoods to many critics who can afford, therefore, to orient their work on ideas, with conspicuous indifference to commerce. That idealism is a treasure. Without it, the intellectual lives of readers would be more dependent on the marketplace. How well commerce alone might govern a literary culture, one can estimate. Ginsberg, Bukowski, Plath, Rich, and recently Claudia Rankine are the commercially successful poets of the past seventy years. The marketplace responds to advocacy and representation: songs for social issues express patriotism for a republic of handsome aspirations. Stephen Dedalus says, *non serviam*, but poets do serve, and audiences appreciate service. Critics rightly inquire, as Charles Altieri, Robert Faggen, and Nigel Smith have, when poetry is well served by responsive audiences.

Confidence in the importance of small-sale volumes rests partly on a plausible sense that they reach a fit audience in classrooms. Academic institutions constitute a distribution network: dissenting views are sent to educable audiences of the near future. Is poetry adequately served by an audience composed largely of conscripts? Is it preferable that poems reach an audience of five hundred or five dozen who know that they want them? Jazz musicians would be ill served if large audiences from rock festivals could be conscripted to fill jazz cabarets and concert halls. More realistically: think of a club in the Village where Ron Carter and Cedar Walton play on a Saturday night. Seats all taken, largely by spirited NYU students charmed by their tablemates, indifferent to the music. Fit audiences protect art from sentimentality and monotony. One comes back to the sense in which evaluative criticism is especially idealistic.

Critics argue for poets in relation to contestable and often timely ideas. Intellectual independence is of course a virtue, and partiality too. Critics ask wherein a poem's value lies, a narrower question than what a poem is, or means. Like poets they require only modest material support to see their work to completion. Empson, Winters, Davie, Kenner, Vendler, Perloff, and Bloom: one maverick mind opens alternatives to consensus. Jürgen Habermas described the London coffeehouses of the eighteenth century as places where one went to read the papers and discuss ideas with strangers. One expected to hear differences of opinion, but with evidence and supporting claims. Critics enter a public sphere to say something considerable; otherwise, one reads the paper to the hum of one's own thoughts. A good coffeehouse must have been where one could expect to hear surprising but acute observations. Critical advocacy is properly strenuous. Some critics are thought cranks.

No one believes all ideas equal. Critics are assessed in accord with the quality and provenance of the ideas that engage them. One probably listens with greater alertness, it should be admitted, to those who share one's ideals, though what one wants from critics is less confirmation of one's beliefs than news from the unknown; intellectual exploration more than concepts borrowed from academic discourse. Borrow a little and you will owe still more, because debts entail affiliations—an issue in particular for politically engaged critics. The eventual task of critics is to weave together the poems they love and the ideas that command their allegiance or interest; some do that without acknowledging any difference between the two, as if the forms of poems imply all a critic might say about ideals. Ideas are more often partial than universal; an idealistic reader attends to a part of a poem, one issue, in hope that others may come to share that concern. Evaluative arguments aim to facilitate or confirm community, as F. R. Leavis said. Agreements are in fact struck. Edmund Burke observed that Virgil's excellence is in less doubt than Aristotle's theories. A story is told about Harold Bloom visiting the University of California, Santa Barbara, where Edgar Bowers taught for most of his career. Bloom entered the reception after his lecture, walked past all others, and hailed Bowers as "Maestro!" That was his acknowledgment of Bowers's art, regardless of Bloom's own terms and enthusiasms. One might not have predicted that Bloom would admire Bowers. One might easily have underestimated Bloom's sensibility and intelligence by imagining his theoretical claims as comprehensive where he knew them to be partial. Ideas are essential to criticism, but there is a plane of aesthetic consensus, and poetry critics sometimes get to that golden field without rational argumentation. In face of mastery, humility is good.

—R.F. and R.v.H.

CONTRIBUTORS

Robert Faggen is the Barton Evans and H. Andrea Neves Professor of Literature at Claremont McKenna College. He is the author of *Robert Frost and the Challenge of Darwin* and the *Cambridge Introduction to Robert Frost*. He is writing a biography of Ken Kesey.

Charles Altieri is the Rachael Anderson Stageberg Professor of English at the University of California, Berkeley. He is the author of *Reckoning with Imagination: Wittgenstein and the Aesthetics of Literary Experience* and *Modernist Poetry and the Limitations of Materialist Theory: The Importance of Constructivist Values*.

V. Joshua Adams is an associate professor of English at the University of Louisville. His recent collection of poems is *Cold Affections*. He is finishing a book on philosophical skepticism and literary impersonality.

Oren Izenberg is an associate professor of English at the University of California, Irvine. He is the author of *Being Numerous: Poetry and the Ground of Social Life*.

Peter O'Leary is adjunct professor of liberal arts at the School of the Art Institute of Chicago. His most recent book of poems is *Earth Is Best*. He is the author of *Thick and Dazzling Darkness: Religious Poetry in a Secular Age* and *Gnostic Contagion: Robert Duncan and the Art of Illness*.

Richard Strier is the Frank L. Sulzberger Professor of English emeritus at the University of Chicago. He is the author of *The Unrepentant Renaissance: From Petrarch to Shakespeare to Milton* and *Resistant Structures: Particularity, Radicalism, and Renaissance Texts*.

Jonathan F. S. Post is a Distinguished Research Professor of English at the University of California, Los Angeles. He is the author of *A Thickness of Particulars: The Poetry of Anthony Hecht* and *Shakespeare's Sonnets and Poems: A Very Short Introduction*. *Elizabeth Bishop: A Very Short Introduction* is forthcoming.

John Shoptaw is a Continuing Lecturer in English at the University of California, Berkeley. His most recent book of poems is *Time's Beach*. He is the author as well of *On the Outside Looking Out: John Ashbery's Poetry*.

Sarah Nooter is a professor of classics at the University of Chicago. She is the author of *The Mortal Voice in the Tragedies of Aeschylus* and *When Heroes Sing: Sophocles and the Shifting Soundscape of Tragedy*.

Jonathan Farmer is the author of *That Peculiar Affirmative: On the Social Life of Poems* and the poetry editor and editor in chief of *At Length*. He teaches middle and high school English, and he lives in Durham, North Carolina.

Keith Tuma is a professor of English at Miami University in Ohio. His most recent book of poems is *Climbing into the Orchestra*. He is the author of *Fishing by Obstinate Isles: Modern and Postmodern British Poetry and American Readers* and editor of *Anthology of Twentieth-Century British and Irish Poetry*.

Patrick Morrissey is a lecturer in humanities at the University of Chicago. He is the author of three collections of poetry: *The Differences*, *World Music*, and the forthcoming *Light Box*.

Robert von Hallberg is a professor of literature at Claremont McKenna College. He is the author of *Lyric Powers* and the forthcoming *Monogamy, Its Songs and Poems*.

August Kleinzahler lives in San Francisco. His most recent book of poems is *Snow Approaching on the Hudson*. He is the author as well of *Sallies, Romps, Portraits, and Send-Offs: Selected Prose, 2000–2018*.

Cal Bedient is a professor of English emeritus at the University of California, Los Angeles. His most recent book of poems is *The Breathing Place*. He is the author of *The Yeats Brothers and Modernism's Love of Motion* and *He Do the Police in Different Voices*. He is the coeditor, with David Lau, of *Lana Turner: A Journal of Poetry and Opinion*.

Laura Quinney is a professor of English at Brandeis University. Her recent book of poems is *New Ghosts*. She is the author as well of *William Blake on Self and Soul, Literary Power and the Criteria of Truth*, and *The Poetics of Disappointment: Wordsworth to Ashbery*.

INDEX

Abrams, M. H., 58
academy, 4–6, 47, 49, 81–82, 85–86, 95, 100, 116, 237, 366, 367
Adorno, Theodor, 59
Ammons, A. R., 190
Anacreon, 195
analysis, categories of: diction, 235, 245, 246, 247, 261, 265; syntax, 31, 36, 42, 49, 166, 244, 245; tone, 113, 356–57; figuration, 49, 198, 200–209, 211–12, 220–21, 227, 249, 331, 331, 332; pacing, 229; phrasing, 76, 119, 123, 128, 130, 131, 135–38, 153, 163, 198, 229, 273, 280, 292; prosody, 49, 114, 176, 178, 180, 189, 302; audience, 114, 165, 217, 220, 222, 226, 233, 366
Arendt, Hannah, 154
Arnold, Matthew, 7, 10, 11, 253
Ashbery, John, 46, 134, 155

Badiou, Alain, 327
Baraka, Amiri, 7, 73, 250
Barthes, Roland, 55
Bates, Milton J., 171
Baudelaire, Charles, 12, 13, 311–12
Bedient, Calvin, 58–59, 70
Benedikt, Michael, 317
Bernstein, Charles, 246
Berry, Wendell, 183
Berryman, John, 365
Bertholf, Robert, 249
Bidart, Frank, 365
Bishop, Elizabeth, 12, 73, 165, 181–83, 287
Blake, William, 7, 12, 287
Bloom, Harold, 366, 367
Blücher, Heinrich, 154
Blumenthal, Walter, 331
Bly, Robert, 8
Bonnefoy, Yves, 346
Brentano, Clemens, 242
Brinton, Ian, 246
Brooks, Cleanth, 51
Brooks, Gwendolyn, 46, 190
Brown, Sterling, 178–79
Bukowski, Charles, 366
Burke, Edmund, 367
Byrd, James Jr., 232

Campion, Thomas, 298
Carson, Anne, 69
Cassity, Turner, 7

Catullus, 195
Celan, Paul, 344
Char, Ren, 308
Chekhov, Anton, 166
Church, Frederick, 345
Clare, John, 165, 247
Clark, Tom, 238
Coleridge, Samuel Taylor, 7, 9, 229
Constable, John, 338
Cox, Kenneth, 262
Crane, Hart, 184, 317
Creeley, Robert, 16, 46, 53, 314, 365
cummings, e. e., 196
Cunningham, J. V., 7, 244

Dante, Alighieri, 10, 12, 107, 242
Davidson, Michael, 236
Davie, Donald, 366
de Kooning, Willem, 329
Deleuze, Gilles, 327, 344
Descartes, René, 55, 188
Dickens, Charles, 299
Dickinson, Emily, 7, 82, 165, 166, 175, 188, 203–4, 233, 287, 343
Donne, John, 135, 195, 346
Donnelly, Timothy, 173
Dorn, Edward, 3, 5–6, 8
Dryden, John, 13, 301
Duncan, Robert, 53, 287, 314, 317, 365
DuPlessis, Rachel Blau, 317
Duran, Eddie, 293
Dylan, Bob, 246, 251

Eliot, T. S., 7, 63, 70, 92, 135, 151, 179–81, 192n12, 236, 268–69, 287, 300
Emerson, Ralph Waldo, 6, 341
Empson, William, 366
evaluative criteria: affirmation, 4, 90, 96, 265; ambition, 22, 47, 239; confidence, 216; contemporaneity, 6–9, 24, 68, 159, 244, 300, 305; contextual, 172; depth, 74, 128, 323, 325; engagement, political, 8–9, 22, 43n1, 60–61, 120, 122, 125, 133, 134, 187, 232, 237, 240, 366; exemplarity, 21–23, 218, 219; formal mastery, 151, 161, 162, 164, 191, 359–60; fun, 227, 229; generality, 25, 39, 57, 209, 219, 221, 270, 289, 290, 293, 338, 339, 351, 356; generosity, 262; identity, 29, 152; impersonality, 23, 26, 279; invention, 227; magnitude, 324, 349; morality, 24–25, 111, 148, 150, 162, 175, 182, 224, 289, 290, 341; philological richness, 301–5; propriety, 2; range, 9, 70, 261, 263, 285; resistance, 48; surprise, 244, 305; truth, 47; universality, 2, 93, 109, 115, 209–11, 226, 289, 344; voice, 310, 356
evaluation, relative, 172

Fichte, Johann, 344
Filkins, Dexter, 68
Ford, Ford Madox, 13, 244
Foucault, Michel, 344
Foxe, John, 167
Frankenthaler, Helen, 326
Fredman, Stephen, 244, 248, 252
Freud, Sigmund, 329, 331
Frost, Robert, 166–67, 189

Gavronsky, Serge, 317
Gelpi, Albert, 104–6, 112
Getz, Stan, 293–94
Geuss, Raymond, 46
Gibbon, Edward, 252
Ginsberg, Allen, 1, 2, 3, 8, 46, 134, 196, 244, 289, 306, 365, 366
Glaser, Michael S., 231, 233
Glück, Louise, 16, 69, 365
Golding, Alan, 242
Gorky, Ashile, 326
Graham, Jorie, 69
Greville, Fulke, 298

Gris, Juan, 335
Grossman, Allen, 3, 6, 12, 16
Guardaldi, Vince, 296

Hass, Robert, 69
Hawkins, Coleman, 293, 295
Hayden, Robert, 365
Hazlitt, William, 343
Hecht, Anthony, 7
Heidegger, Martin, 251
Hejinian, Lyn, 65
Hemingway, Ernest, 156–57
Higgins, Billy, 293
Hill, Geoffrey, 153
Hobgood, Laurence, 296
Hodges, Johnny, 293
Holladay, Hilary, 233
Hollander, John, 147
Homer, 195, 299
Hopkins, Gerard Manley, 7, 16, 287, 340, 341
Horkheimer, Max, 59
Howe, Fanny, 5
Howe, Susan, 6, 16, 46
Hughes, Howard, 248, 250
Hughes, Langston, 7, 181
Hughes, Robert, 167
Hurt, Mississippi John, 135
Huyssen, Andreas, 246

James, Henry, 156
Jeffers, Robinson, 175, 183, 187
Joffé, Roland, 63
Johnson, Samuel, 2, 8, 69, 289–90, 298, 365–66
Johnston, Devin, 115

Keats, John, 174–75, 187–88
Kenner, Hugh, 366
Kerouac, Jack, 288
Kierkegaard, Søren, 361
Killian, Kevin, 243

Klee, Paul, 329
Kleinzahler, August, 3
Kogon, Eugen, 154, 156
Korsgaard, Christine M., 10
Krauss, Karl, 253
Kuenstler, Frank, 308–10, 314, 317

LaFaro, Scott, 293
Latimer, Hugh, 167
Leavis, F. R., 367
Leibniz, Gottfried Wilhelm, 344
Lejeune, Philippe, 65
Leopold, Aldo, 175, 188
Levertov, Denise, 246
Levinas, Emmanuel, 328
Lewis, Wyndham, 247
Lockwood, John, 296
Lowell, Robert, 8, 12, 28, 73, 246, 365
Lucas, John Randolf, 247
Lyotard, Jean-François, 329

McGurl, Mark, 5
McLane, Maureen, 312
McVay, Scott, 187
Ma, Ming-Quian, 84
Mandelstam, Osip, 340
Mariani, Paul, 191n5
Marti, José, 133
Martory, Pierre, 353
Marvell, Andrew, 8
Merrill, James, 7, 21, 147, 151, 155, 287
Merwin, W. S., 183, 187–89, 365
Michaux, Henri, 327
Mill, John Stuart, 3–4
Milosz, Czeslaw, 17, 119, 133–34
Milton, John, 2, 3, 8, 343
Monk, Thelonious, 296
Moore, Marianne, 82, 186, 190
Morrison, Toni, 226, 228
Mortkowicz-Olczakowa, Hanna, 161

Neruda, Pablo, 195

New Criticism, 25–26
Niedecker, Lorine, 190
Nietzsche, Friedrich, 327, 344, 348

O'Hara, Frank, 21, 46, 73, 310
Oppen, George, 16, 53, 190, 308, 314, 317–18
Olson, Charles, 287
Ortiz, Simon, 176, 179
Osman, Jena, 82

Palmer, Michael, 6
Parker, Charlie, 293, 295, 296
Pepper, Art, 292
Perloff, Marjorie, 366
Picasso, Pablo, 329
Pindar, 15
Pinsky, Robert, 3, 130, 237
Plath, Sylvia, 21, 46, 73, 155, 365
Plato, 293
Pollock, Jackson, 326
Pound, Ezra, 7, 80, 82, 253, 287, 300
Poverty, 238, 243, 253
Prynne, Jeremy, 15, 243, 246
Pushkin, Alexander, 295–96

qualities esteemed, or contested: collage, 299, 300, 309; confessional, 156, 158; democratic, 263; didacticism, 16, 175, 182–83, 184, 186, 217, 237; discontinuity, 309; distance, 324, 328; environmentalist, 165; erratic, 361; feeling, 88, 93; generosity, 262, 299; holocaust, 151–55; humor, 127, 216, 218, 225, 233, 245, 246–47, 267, 273, 275, 282, 289, 299, 325, 329, 334, 354, 360; idealism, 366, 367; independence, 95, 366; instability, 310; intelligence, 31, 35, 37–38, 120, 226, 249; juxtaposition, 154, 268, 308, 313; lightness, 273; macabre, 160; mystery, 46–47, 90, 98, 124, 296; novelistic, 132, 134, 139, 155; particularity, 293, 296; personal, 27; plain style, 13, 22, 124, 136, 156, 212, 287, 290–91; power, 333, 341, 343; precision, 120, 135, 136, 141n17, 262, 313; prophetic, 8, 189–90; prosaic, 22–23, 31–32, 37, 42, 84, 86, 291; public, 31; religion, 95, 99–103, 108, 111, 238–42, 283–85, 340, 346; secularity, 46, 59, 86; severity of circumstance, 150; speech, 33, 52, 76, 249, 263, 285, 299; strangeness, 74, 86, 220, 275; understatement, 149; urgency, 326; vitality, 323, 341, 347; vulgarity, 198, 206, 245, 248; wit, 150–51, 156, 159, 279; word-play, 165, 295, 309
Quine, W. V., 51

Rainey, Lawrence, 253
Rankine, Claudia, 1, 3, 17, 22, 366
Ransom, John Crowe, 4, 151
Raworth, Tom, 243, 252
Raz, Joseph, 16
Reiss, James, 171
Rich, Adrienne, 1, 12, 69, 246
Ricks, Christopher, 192n12
Ridley, Nicholas, 167
Riley, Denise, 246
Rilke, Rainer Maria, 201–2
Rimbaud, Arthur, 329
Ruskin, John, 156, 159, 252
Ryle, Gilbert, 51

Said, Edward, 164
Sappho, 195
Saussure, Ferdinand, 66
Sax, Adolphe, 293
Scarry, Elaine, 200
Schiff, Robin, 82
Schönberg, Arnold, 329
Scholl, Hans, 242

Scholl, Sophie, 242
Schumpeter, Joseph, 251
Schuyler, James, 310
Seeger, Pete, 186
Sexton, Anne, 195–96, 204
Shakespeare, William, 10, 11, 15, 107, 148, 159, 291–93, 299, 327
Sleigh, Tom, 299
Snyder, Gary, 1, 173, 183–86
Sophocles, 148
Southern, David, 243
Spahr, Juliana, 22, 173
Spenser, Edmund, 91–92
Spicer, Jack, 308
Stein, Gertrude, 65, 173
Steiner, George, 340
Stevens, Holly, 171
Stevens, Wallace, 1, 166–67, 171, 174–75
Strickland, Stan, 296

Tate, Allen, 151
Thoreau, Henry David, 183, 341
Tieck, Ludwig, 332
Tjader, Cal, 293–94
Traven, B., 242
Trimpi, Wesley, 212n6

Twain, Mark, 247

Unterecker, John, 317

Vaz de Caminha, Pêro, 181–82
Vendler, Helen, 11, 27, 191, 366
Vertov, Dziga, 185

Weil, Simone, 115
Wesling, Donald, 235–36
Whitman, Walt, 184, 234, 262, 287, 290, 312, 340
Wiesel, Elie, 154
Wilbur, Richard, 147–48, 235
Williams, W. C., 187, 215, 227, 263, 265, 276–77, 280, 306, 309, 318, 333
Winters, Yvor, 366
Wittgenstein, Ludwig, 70
Wordsworth, William, 3–4, 13, 58, 77, 227, 229, 290, 352, 354
Wright, C. D., 3, 11–12

Yeats, W. B., 8, 79, 81, 135, 174–75, 228, 247
Young, Kevin, 226–27
Young, Lester, 293

www.ingramcontent.com/pod-product-compliance
Lightning Source LLC
Chambersburg PA
CBHW030517230426
43665CB00010B/659